THE LONG ARM OF LEE

VOLUME I

GENERAL ROBERT EDWARD LEE
COMMANDING THE ARMY OF NORTHERN VIRGINIA

THE

LONG ARM OF LEE

OR

THE HISTORY OF THE ARTILLERY OF THE ARMY OF NORTHERN VIRGINIA

BY

JENNINGS CROPPER WISE

———

ILLUSTRATED

———

TWO VOLUMES

VOLUME 1: BULL RUN TO FREDERICKSBURG

Introduction by Gary W. Gallagher

University of Nebraska Press
Lincoln and London

First Bison Book printing: 1991
Most recent printing indicated by the last digit below:
10   9   8   7   6   5   4   3   2   1

Library of Congress Cataloging-in-Publication Data
Wise, Jennings C. (Jennings Cropper), b. 1881.
The long arm of Lee, or, The history of the artillery of the Army of
Northern Virginia / by Jennings Cropper Wise.
p. cm.
Reprint. Originally published: Lynchburg, Va.: J. P. Bell Co., 1915.
With new introd.
"A Bison book."
Contents: v. 1. Bull Run to Fredericksburg—v. 2. Chancellorsville
to Appomattox.
ISBN 0-8032-9735-1 (pbk.: set).—ISBN 0-8032-9733-5)pbk.: v. 1).—
ISBN 0-8032-9734-3 (pbk.: v. 2)
1. Confederate States of America. Army of Northern Virginia—Ar-
tillery. 2. United States—History—Civil War, 1861–1865—Campaigns. 3. Virginia—History—Civil War, 1861–1865—Campaigns.
4. Confederate States of America. Ordnance Bureau. I. Title.
E470.5.W56 1991
973.7'455—dc20
91-16846 CIP

Reprinted from the 1915 edition published by J. P. Bell Company,
Inc., Lynchburg, Virginia. *Bull Run to Fredericksburg* has been
added as the subtitle for Volume 1 of this Bison Book edition, which
runs through Chapter XXII, instead of Chapter XXV, as in the
original. A map has been included. Volume 2 of the Bison Book edition begins with Chapter XXIII.

Dedicated
To The Memory
of
My Father
John Sergeant Wise

TABLE OF CONTENTS

VOLUME I

PART I

PART II

ILLUSTRATIONS

VOLUME I

INTRODUCTION TO THE BISON BOOK EDITION
By Gary W. Gallagher

Jennings Cropper Wise's *The Long Arm of Lee; or, The History of the Artillery of the Army of Northern Virginia, with a Brief Account of the Confederate Bureau of Ordnance* is a classic work of Confederate military history. First published in 1915, it has stood for more than three-quarters of a century as the best treatment of the subject.[1] An early critic wrote in the *Field Artillery Review* that Wise, "a painstaking historian . . . [and] most skillful word-painter," had produced a book "well calculated to fill the field artilleryman . . . with admiration for the gallant gunners who so admirably supported the infantry of Lee."[2] Echoing this sentiment, another reviewer predicted that "among the almost innumerable books which have been written about the great war" few would "find a more permanent place in the literature describing the great events of that struggle." James Power Smith, who had served on "Stonewall" Jackson's staff, praised Wise's thorough research and attention to the ordnance department. Smith felt certain that *The Long Arm of Lee* would "take its place among the standard works on the Civil War in Virginia."[3] Modern scholars have confirmed the initial high estimates of Wise's book. Douglas Southall Freeman described it as "a most informative study . . . [that] contains many photographs not to be found elsewhere." Richard B. Harwell listed it among two hundred basic Confederate books, while James I. Robertson, Jr., called it "an exhaustive, valuable study, often consulted and widely quoted."[4]

The author of this durable work was born in Richmond, Virginia, on September 10, 1881. A grandson of Henry Alexander Wise (the governor of Virginia between 1856 and 1860 and later a Confederate general), and the fourth son of John Sergeant and Evelyn Beverly Byrd Douglas Wise, Jennings spent his early years in Virginia, where his father and grandfather practiced law together until the latter's death in 1876. John S. Wise moved his family to New York City in 1888, and Jennings lived in the North for ten years and graduated from Phillips Exeter Academy in New Hampshire before returning to his home state in 1898 to enroll at the Virginia Military Institute in Lexington.[5]

The Wise family had profound ties to VMI. John Sergeant Wise had been slightly wounded in the famous cadet charge at New Market on May 15, 1864; his cousin, Henry Alexander Wise, had commanded the students on that memorable day. Three of Jennings's brothers already had graduated from the Institute, and another would follow him five years later. Wise excelled as both an athlete and a scholar at VMI. He played alongside George C. Marshall on the football team, became the second-ranking cadet captain, and developed an abiding love for the school before graduating in 1902 with a B.S. in civil engineering.[6]

Wise spent a decade away from VMI after his graduation. Following four years as a second lieutenant in the U.S. Ninth Infantry and two with the St. Regis Paper Company in Watertown, New York, he entered law school at the University of Virginia in 1907. He opened a practice in Richmond upon graduation in 1909, but moved back to Lexington in 1912 to become professor of economics, political science and international law at VMI.[7]

During three busy years there, Wise served as commandant of cadets, designed an ROTC system, and wrote extensively. Among the works completed during his time in Lexington were a detailed history of VMI from 1839 to

1865, a study of American imperialism and national defense, and *The Long Arm of Lee*.[8] An emotional high point of Wise's stint at the Institute came on May 13, 1913—the fiftieth anniversary of the death of Stonewall Jackson. That day he presided over the retirement of the four cannon of the Cadet Battery, which had gone to war with the Rockbridge Artillery in 1861. William T. Poague, former commander of the battery, was guest of honor among a large crowd of people who listened as Wise delivered a dramatic history of the guns. At the end of his speech, Wise brought the crops of cadets to present arms and then turned to address Poague: "Since you were the first to lead this battery into action, it is fitting that you should cause it to fire its last salute in honor of its first commander, the immortal Jackson." Poague gave the orders, "Battery load, first piece, first platoon fire," and the gun boomed its final report. Veteran cannoneers briskly carried out the firing routine for the other three pieces, which sent swirls of black powder smoke drifting above the spectators.[9] That stirring scene must have been especially evocative for Wise, who was then studying the campaigns of Poague and other famous gunners of the Army of Northern Virginia for *The Long Arm of Lee*.

Wise left the Institute in 1915 to resume the practice of law in Richmond. Alarmed by events in Europe, he urged preparedness and criticized President Woodrow Wilson's cautious approach to involvement in the First World War. Following the American declaration of war on April 6, 1917, Wise accepted a major's commission on May 15 and sailed for Europe to act as an observer with the French and British armies on the Western Front. He subsequently led a battalion in the 318th Infantry of the 80th (Blue Ridge) Division during the St. Mihiel and Meuse-Argonne offensives of 1918. Gassed, twice cited for gallantry under fire, and wounded near Nantillois on October 4, 1918, Wise won the Distinguished Service Cross and promotion to lieutenant colonel.[10]

He resigned his commission with the coming of peace in 1919 and began a long residence in Washington, D.C. There he held various government jobs, renewed his legal career, and devoted considerable energy to seeking justice for American Indians. His call for better treatment of Native Americans had begun early in the century, and through the mid-1920s he rallied support for Indian rights. As counsel for the Yankton Sioux, Wise successfully argued a case before the Supreme Court in 1927 that brought compensation for tribal lands seized in the mid-nineteenth century.[11] He concentrated on a private practice in Washington and New York through the bulk of the 1930s, relocating in 1939 to a farm near Charlottesville, Virginia, where he focused on writing.[12]

Wise returned to his beloved Lexington in 1954. There he pursued a variety of conservative causes, most notably a personal crusade against what he considered communist influences in America. Railing against legislators who allowed the sale of communist newspapers in places where students might purchase them, he distributed at his own expense leaflets and pamphlets advising young people to resist intellectual propaganda, support the armed services, and emulate the examples of R. E. Lee, Stonewall Jackson, and George Washington.[13] He also derived pleasure from prowling the grounds of VMI, attending athletic events, and watching military exercises on the parade ground. As the son of one of the heroes of New Market and a former commandant of the corps, Wise was a link to the martial past of the Institute, and he relished his role as elder statesman. The cadets knew his distinctive figure well—an impressive old man with a gray mustache and Vandyke beard, whose cane, black fedora, and cape made him seem an exotic representative of a vanished South.[14]

Ambition to write a biography of Lee prompted Wise to leave Lexington for Hampton, Virginia, in 1961 because the military library at Fort Monroe could better support his research. The cadets of the Institute bade him farewell in a ceremony on May 30, 1961—nearly sixty-three years after he had entered VMI as a young man. "This is a great honor the Superintendent and the Corps of Cadets have accorded me," Wise told the assembled cadets. "With no model but perfection morally and otherwise," he added, "you must as Cadets soon to pass through the Sallyport of your youth help the Institute press on to the achievement of the possible." Serious strokes in October 1965 and April 1966 left Wise almost helpless and prevented his completing the book on Lee. He died on February 20, 1968, at the age of eighty-six. His remains were interred in the family cemetery at Onancock on the Eastern Shore of Virginia. In Lexington, the Institute honored his memory by lowering its flags to half staff.[15]

Jennings C. Wise crowded far more than ordinary experience and accomplishment into his long life. Fueled by ambition and prodigious energy, he earned success as a lawyer, a soldier, a public servant, and a writer. *The Long Arm of Lee* stands as perhaps his most enduring contribution. It is a rich exploration of the organization, officers, tactics, weaponry, and campaigns of the artillery in the Army of Northern Virginia. As a trained artillerist who also possessed the researching skills of a scholar, Wise brought a unique blend of talents to the study of his subject. His investigation encompassed the available printed sources supplemented by interviews with many former Confederate artillerists. Strict impartiality probably was impossible for one steeped in the history of his state and region, yet Wise managed in most instances to give the Federals their fair measure of credit. His strong feelings about the need for military preparedness colored his discussion of the North and South at the outset of war. The number of errors in the book—such as incorrect middle names for Thomas Henry Carter and Wilfred Emory Cutshaw—is remarkably small for a work of nearly one thousand pages.[16]

The myth of the Lost Cause flourished in the first decades of the twentieth century, and *The Long Arm of Lee* betrayed Wise's acceptance of much of that romantic interpretation of the Confederacy. Promulgators of the myth protected Lee's towering reputation by placing blame for southern defeats on James Longstreet and other lieutenants.[17] Handling Gettysburg in vintage Lost Cause style, Wise argued that "Jeb" Stuart brought on the battle by his absence, Richard S. Ewell and A. P. Hill bungled the fighting on the first day, and Longstreet's sulking and sloth frustrated Lee's plans on July 2. Nowhere did he hint that Lee's orders were far too vague, his staff work deplorably inefficient, and his battle blood dangerously aroused. Wise repeatedly compared Longstreet unfavorably to Stonewall Jackson, a common theme in the literature of the Lost Cause. For example, Wise made the reckless statement that Longstreet was guilty of "willful desertion of his Commander-in-Chief" because he was at Suffolk during the Chancellorsville campaign. In contrast, he dismissed Jackson's abysmal performance during the Seven Days with the comment that "no historian has yet satisfactorily explained the anomaly of Jackson's lethargy on the Peninsula."[18]

The treatment of William Nelson Pendleton and Edward Porter Alexander illuminated the extent of Wise's insistence on Lee's perfection. As one of the principal architects of the movement to canonize Lee in the 1870s, Pendleton did as much as anyone to spread the lie that Lee issued an order for Longstreet to attack "at sunrise" on July 2 at Gettysburg.[19] The young artillerists in Lee's army ridiculed him as hopelessly unequal to his responsibilities. "Pendleton . . . is like the elephant," wrote one young gunner, "we have him & we don't know what on earth to do with him, and it costs a devil of a sight to feed him."[20] But Wise staunchly defended Pendleton as an able and courageous officer of "most intellectual temperament and Christian character." "The retention of

Pendleton as Chief of Artillery by Gen. Lee is but another evidence of the latter's sagacity," wrote Wise with perfect Lost Cause reasoning, "for he realized that he was still free to assign those duties requiring the vigorous qualities of youth to Pendleton's lieutenants . . . and yet retain the many admirable qualities, especially as an administrator, possessed by the senior." Wise went so far as to excuse Pendleton's bumbling loss of the army's reserve artillery at Shepherdstown following the battle of Sharpsburg.[21]

Porter Alexander posed a special problem for Wise. On the one hand, Wise greatly admired the young Georgian as an artillerist: "He was far and away the superior of all others in his arm. . . . Like Gen. Hunt of the Federal Army, he was pre-eminent in the Artillery of his army." The sketch of Alexander in chapter 36 is brilliantly incisive, capturing in relatively few words the essence of Alexander's personality and military gifts.[22] But Alexander was a supreme realist who lacked any hint of devotion to the myth of the Lost Cause. He bluntly said in his classic *Military Memoirs of a Confederate* that Lee committed errors during the Seven Days, at Gettysburg, and elsewhere, and Wise simply could not accept such an attitude. In his discussion of Longstreet at Suffolk, Wise quoted Alexander's assertion that "although Lee at Chancellorsville repulsed Hooker's attack, it was poor policy to take the risk of battle against enormous odds, with one-fourth of his infantry absent." "Truly this is a remarkable criticism!" raged Wise. "Poor policy on the part of whom? The insinuation is at least an involved one. It is clearly directed at Lee. . . ." Elsewhere in his narrative Wise accused Alexander of being hypercritical, by which he usually meant willing to question some of Lee's actions. Predictably, he characterized Alexander's refusal to lay the blame for Gettysburg at Longstreet's feet as "an attempt to defend his old corps commander, beyond the limits of sound reasoning."[23]

Jubal A. Early and other mythmakers of the Lost Cause habitually overstated the importance of superior northern numbers and material in defeating the South. Wise also subscribed to this flawed general view, but when it came to artillery in particular he demonstrated that there *was* a gross discrepancy between Federals and Confederates. Moreover, he persuasively contended that high morale and exceptionally able officers in southern batteries did much to close the gap. Lee's artillerists compiled a record worthy of Wise's conclusion that from late summer 1862 to the end of the war few armies "ever boasted such a brilliant galaxy of gunners, combining as they did the unflinching resolve of maturer manhood with the bravery of youth."[24]

It is a commonplace that the Civil War was an infantryman's fight in which shoulder arms inflicted up to 90 percent of the casualties in most battles. The foot soldier's dismissal of the mounted arm with a smug "Whoever saw a dead cavalryman?" retains vitality today. Similarly, many books convey the impression that artillery made a lot of noise without affecting the outcome on most battlefields. *The Long Arm of Lee* decisively counters the latter impression. "The effectiveness of artillery is not to be measured by the losses it inflicts," observed Wise in an insightful passage. "Any such test is entirely erroneous. Not only do the guns exert a tremendous moral effect in support of their infantry, and adverse to the enemy, . . . They often actually preclude heavy damage from the enemy by preventing him from essaying an assault against the position the guns occupy. . . . Let us hear no more of artillery efficiency as measured by the number of its victims."[25]

The contributions of the artillery in the Army of Northern Virginia shine through the pages of *The Long Arm of Lee*. Confederate gunners played a critical role in defeating John Pope's army at Second Manassas, which Wise considered perhaps the premier artillery engagement of the war. They helped stave off defeat at Sharpsburg, figured prominently in the fighting at Gettysburg, made the difference on more than one occasion during the grueling Overland Campaign of 1864, and matched the determination and persistence of the infantry in the 1864 Valley Campaign and at Petersburg. They achieved their finest hour at Chancellorsville, marching and fighting for a terrible week on a vast field that stretched from the Rappahannock River at Fredericksburg to the gloomy tangle of the Wilderness. Where the artillery was less effective, as at First Winchester and during the Seven Days, Wise searched for the reasons and made no excuses. He clearly preferred writing about the positive side of his subject, however, and derived special satisfaction from the exploits of men from VMI. Unwilling to end his study in the muddy streets of Appomattox Court House, he closed on a romantic note in the fastness of the Blue Ridge Mountains.

Confederate artillerists such as Porter Alexander, Ham Chamberlayne, William T. Poague, John Haskell, Edward A. Moore, and Henry Robinson Berkeley wrote letters, diaries, and reminiscences that reveal much about their branch of the service.[26] But *The Long Arm of Lee* is the indispensible first book to read on the composition, operations, and fighting men of the artillery in the most famous Confederate army. Jennings C. Wise succeeded admirably in his goal of telling "the gunner's part in the great tragedy."

NOTES

1. The J. P. Bell Company, Inc., of Lynchburg, Va., published the first edition in two volumes; Oxford University Press of New York brought out a one-volume reprint in 1959 under the title *The Long Arm of Lee: The History of the Artillery in the Army of Northern Virginia*. The latter edition included a brief foreword by L. Van Loan Naisawald but reproduced none of the original's illustrations. Oxford considered Wise's book a

logical companion to Naisawald's forthcoming *Grape and Canister: The Story of the Field Artillery of the Army of the Potomac* (New York: Oxford University Press, 1960). The Owens Publishing Company of Richmond, Va., issued a complete two-volume reprint under the original title in 1988; the Neale Publishing Company also advertised an edition of the book in 1914, but no copies are known to exist. See Robert K. Krick, *Neale Books: An Annotated Bibliography* (Dayton, Ohio: Press of Morningside Bookshop, 1977), p. 203.

2. Clipping dated May [?] 15, 1916, from *The Cadet*, Jennings C. Wise File, Alumni Files Collection, VMI Archives, Preston Library, Virginia Military Institute, Lexington, Virginia [this file cited hereafter as Wise File VMI]. The reviewer was Captain Marlborough Churchill, who closed with the "hope that some field artilleryman will find in Colonel Wise's story of the Confederate batteries an incentive to give us a similar history of the gunners who opposed them so nobly and so well." Forty-four years elapsed before *Grape and Canister* performed that service, and it was another twenty-four before Larry J. Daniel's *Cannoneers in Gray: The Field Artillery of the Army of Tennessee* (University, Ala.: University of Alabama Press, 1984) examined the western Confederate artillerists. Federal gunners in the West still await coverage of their efforts.

3. George L. Christian in *Confederate Veteran* 25 (November 1917): 526–27 (first quotation); J. William Jones, et al., eds., *Southern Historical Society Papers*, 52 vols. and 2-vol. index (1876–1959; reprint ed., Millwood, N.Y.: Kraus Reprint Company, 1977–80), 41: 150–51 (second quotation).

4. Douglas Southall Freeman, *The South to Posterity: An Introduction to the Writing of Confederate History* (1939; reprint ed., Wendell, N.C.: Broadfoot's Bookmark, 1983), p. 198; Richard Barksdale Harwell, *In Tall Cotton: the 200 Most Important Confederate Books for the Reader, Researcher and Collector* (Austin, Tex.: Jenkins Publishing Company, 1978), p. 69; Allan Nevins, et al., eds., *Civil War Books: A Critical Bibliography*, 2 vols. (Baton Rouge, La.: Louisiana University Press, 1967, 1969), 1: 181.

5. Genealogical table of the Wise family prepared by Colonel William Couper of VMI; obituary for Wise in the Newport News *Daily Press*, February 21, 1968; VMI alumnus card dated De-

cember 31, 1955, and signed by Wise, all in Wise File VMI. For an excellent treatment of Henry A. Wise, see Craig M. Simpson, *A Good Southerner: The Life of Henry A. Wise of Virginia* (Chapel Hill, N.C.: University of North Carolina Press, 1985); on John S. Wise, see Allen Johnson and Dumas Malone, eds., *Dictionary of American Biography*, 20 vols. and index (New York: Charles Scribner's Sons, 1928–37), 20: 429.

6. Obituary in the *Newport News Times-Herald*, February 20, 1968, Wise File VMI. John S. Wise wrote a passionate account of his role at New Market in chapter 19 of *The End of an Era* (Boston: Houghton Mifflin Company, 1899).

7. Obituary in the *Newport News Times-Herald*, February 20, 1968; VMI Headquarters, General Orders Number 24, February 20, 1968 (death notice for Wise); VMI alumnus card dated December 31, 1955; Jennings C. Wise to Mr. Jeffrys, May 30, 1961, all in Wise File, VMI.

8. Jennings C. Wise to Mr. Jeffrys, May 30, 1961, Wise File VMI. Wise was a prolific writer throughout his life, publishing more than two dozen books on historical, literary, and political topics. *Empire and Armament: the Evolution of American Imperialism and the Problem of National Defence* (New York: G. P. Putnam's Sons) and *The Military History of the Virginia Military Institute from 1839 to 1865* (Lynchburg, Va.: J. P. Bell Company, Inc.) both appeared in 1915.

9. Jones, et al., eds., *Southern Historical Society Papers* 39: 144–45. For a photograph of Poague at the head of the procession on May 13, see Monroe F. Cockrell, ed., *Gunner with Stonewall: Reminiscences of William Thomas Poague* (Jackson, Tenn.: McCowat-Mercer Press, 1957), p. xiv.

10. Jennings C. Wise, "The Surest Means of American Defense," *The Service Magazine* (November–December 1925), p. 7; clipping from *Newport News Times-Herald*, February 20, 1968, and copy of citation for Distinguished Service Cross, Wise File VMI.

11. VMI alumnus card dated December 31, 1955, Wise File VMI. Wise recounted his activities on behalf of Native Americans in chapter 32 of *The Red Man in the New World Drama; A Politico-Legal Study, with a Pageantry of American Indian History* (Washington, D.C.: W. F. Roberts Company, 1931). For a brief discussion of Wise by a Native American activist of the

1970s, see the introduction by Vine Deloria, Jr., in the 1971 reprint of *The Red Man in the New World Drama* (New York: The Macmillan Company).

12. "Col. Jennings Wise Is Wed to Mrs. Smith" (clipping dated 1939); "Colonel Wise Buys Farm in Albemarle" (clipping dated August 16, 1939); Quinnan Hodges, "Distinguished Alumnus in Charlottesville Works on Completion of Four Histories," (clipping labeled "U. Va. 'College Topics' " and dated May 27, 1947), all in Wise File VMI.

13. For examples of Wise's anticommunist writings, see *An Appeal to the Patriotic Societies, Veterans, Conservative Organizations, Philanthropies, Educational Foundations, and Conservative Editors of the United States* (flyer), and "A Warning to Lexington Youth" and "Notice to All Patriots!!" (advertisements), Wise File VMI.

14. The flyer cited in the preceding note reproduces a photograph of Wise in this outfit, as does the obituary in the Newport News *Times-Herald*.

15. Jennings C. Wise to H. A. Jacob, May 31, 1961; John Bowen, "Irrepressible Octagenarian Turns Effort to Irrepressible Conflict," *Newport News Daily News*, August 27, 1961; obituaries in the *Lexington News-Gazette*, February 21, 1968, *Newport News Daily Press*, February 21, 1968, *Newport News Times-Herald*, February 20, 1968, and *Roanoke Times*, February 21, 1968; telegram from Superintendent R. E. Shell of VMI to Mr. Henry A. Wise and Family, February 21, 1968, all in Wise File VMI.

16. L. Van Loan Naisawald points out about a dozen errors relating to the Union artillery on pp. 8–10 of his introduction to the 1959 Oxford University Press reprint of *The Long Arm of Lee*.

17. On the development of the myth of the Lost Cause, see Gaines M. Foster, *Ghosts of the Confederacy: Defeat, the Lost Cause, and the Emergence of the new South 1865 to 1913* (New York: Oxford University Press, 1987); on Longstreet as a scapegoat, see William Garrett Piston, *Lee's Tarnished Lieutenant: James Longstreet and His Place in Southern History* (Athens, Ga.: University of Georgia Press, 1987).

18. The quotations are on pages 444 and 246 below.

19. Thomas L. Connelly, *The Marble Man: Robert E. Lee and*

His Image in American Society (New York: Alfred A. Knopf, 1977), pp. 37–40, 44–45, 84–85, and Glenn Tucker, *Lee and Longstreet at Gettysburg* (Indianapolis: The Bobbs-Merrill Company, 1968), pp. 12–13, 17–20, 40–42, discuss Pendleton's role.

20. C. G. Chamberlayne, ed., *Ham Chamberlayne–Virginian: Letters and Papers of an Artillery Officer in the War for Southern Independence 1861–1865* (Richmond: Press of the Dietz Printing Company, 1932), p. 134.

21. The quotations are on pages 342–43 below, the apology for Pendleton at Shepherdstown on page 341. On the latter affair, see Douglas Southall Freeman, *Lee's Lieutenants: A Study in Command*, 3 vols. (New York: Charles Scribner's Sons, 1942–44), 3: 226–35, and Jeffry D. Wert, "The Battle of Shepherdstown," *Civil War Quarterly* 9 (June 1987), pp. 78–81.

22. The quotation is on page 758 below.

23. See Edward Porter Alexander, *Military Memoirs of a Confederate: A Critical Narrative* (New York: Charles Scribner's Sons, 1907). The quotations are on pages 444–45 and 758 below.

24. The quotation is on page 326 below.

25. The quotation is on page 268 below.

26. John Haskell, *The Haskell Memoirs* (ed. by Gilbert E. Govan and James W. Livingood, New York: G. P. Putnam's Sons, 1960); Edward A. Moore, *The Story of a Cannoneer Under Stonewall Jackson, in Which is Told the Part Taken by the Rockbridge Artillery in the Army of Northern Virginia* (New York and Washington: The Neale Publishing Company, 1907); Henry Robinson Berkeley, *Four Years in the Confederate Horse Artillery: The Diary of Private Henry Robinson Berkeley* (ed. by William H. Runge, Chapel Hill, N.C.: University of North Carolina Press [for the Virginia Historical Society]); the works of Alexander, Chamberlayne, and Poague are cited above in notes 23, 20, and 9.

PREFACE

THIS work has been written in my first year as Commandant of the Corps of Cadets of the Virginia Military Institute. Its writing, therefore, has been attended by many interruptions incident to my military and academic duties. Convinced that the Field Artillery of the Army of Northern Virginia has received too little attention on the part of the historian, I have for years projected such a work as this. In fact, writers on the Civil War have almost as if intentionally ignored the subject, referring but casually to the gunner's part in the great tragedy. Their failure to discuss this subject has no doubt been due to a feeling of uncertainty whenever they sought to enter upon what they conceived to be a more or less special domain. Nor was this sentiment uncommon to the participants themselves. The reports of the various commanders engaged in the war are generally vague in matters pertaining to the artillery. Not failing in tribute to the gunners, they have failed to record any definite information concerning the artillery.

The result is that to-day he who enters into an investigation of more than the most casual character finds himself involved in a game of historical dominoes, with many of the pieces lacking. I will illustrate my point by saying that even Maj. H. B. McClellan, Chief of Staff of the Cavalry Corps, in his history of Stuart's campaigns avoids the mention of the horse batteries on certain occasions as if by design. Yet these batteries were as much a part of Stuart's command as the cavalry troops themselves. He does not even include them in the organization of the cavalry, which he gives in an otherwise most valuable work.

More often than not, the corps, division, and brigade returns include the artillery personnel in the strength of the infantry, and rarely are the names of the batteries, or the number of guns engaged, specified. Over such details is merely thrown the cloak of the mysterious word "artillery," as if that should suffice for the curious.

While little in the way of service statistics is to be obtained from the survivors, I have secured many clues from the veteran soldiers of my acquaintance, who have often assisted me to make the mask of time less inscrutable.

Originally, I had intended to treat the subject in three distinct parts,—that is, the Bureau of Ordnance, its resources, operations, and organization; the organization, material and personnel of the Field Artillery, and the tactics of the arm. But almost immediately after beginning the work I concluded that the two last sub-divisions should be combined for the sake of brevity, as well as on account of the difficulty of treating them separately, which would have at least entailed much repetition.

Once, in the literary enthusiasm of youth, I gathered together a number of my speeches and papers, and, having them printed, I distributed copies of the pamphlet among my friends. But, as is usually the case, vanity betrayed me, for some of these pamphlets fell into the hands of able critics, who quite frequently attacked my comparisons between the Confederate and Federal artillerymen, despite my repeated denials that "odious comparisons" were intended to be drawn. My Northern friends simply declared that comparisons were inherently odious, and that I could not make them otherwise. I learned my lesson, and in this work I have endeavored to avoid anything that even savored of a comparison, except in matters of material, organization, equipment, and tangible things in general, believing that history would best be subserved by presenting the facts and allowing each reader to draw his own conclusions.

To me the record of Lee's artillery, or his "long arm," has been one of surpassing interest. Each chapter, as it unfolded itself, seemed more and more in need of a stronger pen than mine. Yet I feel that if I have failed to draw the proper inferences from the tangle of available facts, the proof that I have erred will at least disclose the truth, and I will, therefore, have been indirectly responsible for a better account than my own.

The story of the gunners of Lee's army has always appealed with peculiar force to my imagination, by reason of the lasting repute so many juniors, from the standpoints of both age and rank in the service, acquired. Every Southern child has heard, in terms of praise and tenderest affection, the story of Pegram, the youthful colonel; of the one-armed Haskell; of Latimer, the boy major; of Breathed; of Caskie; of Jimmie Thomson and Preston Chew. And lives there a son of the Southland who has not heard of Pelham, "the Gallant," so named by the lips of Lee himself? It seems almost invidious to mention these few and to omit the names of their peers. *Ab uno disce omnes.*

While the cherished deeds of the Confederate artillery subalterns are in no wise comparable, according to a strict standard of military accomplishment, with the achievements of such soldiers as Longstreet, the Hills, Ewell, Mahone, Gordon, and many others of like mold, yet, in the South at least, of the two, the personal recollection of many of the juniors is the more lastingly tender, and the general interest in them grows greater with each year, by reason of the heroic traditions that cluster about their youthful memories.

Undoubtedly there was something in the spiritual composition of these boyish soldiers, a mixture of dash and conviction, not akin to mere bravado, but more like divine faith, which made them unconquerable. Living, they possessed that quality electric, more spirituelle than physical, which gave temper to their steel and made their thrusts the keener. Dead, there survives in connection with their memory that elusive influence which, lingering, when appealed to, makes brave men of cowards.

It may be suggested that a sympathetic note in the scale of sentiment is struck by the heroes of defeat. But no, the luster of which I write is not the shimmer of pathos. It was while living and victorious that they touched the souls of their people and laid the foundation for that everlasting renown which depends not for its freshness upon the written pages of history,—in which their names are scarcely mentioned.

Amid the cherished traditions and in close association with the companions of Pelham and Pegram and the others of whom I write, I have found an inspiration at least to essay the task of recording some of their heroisms, tarrying now and then to point out the transcendent quality of their valor. And from the pages of the numerous books,—many of them professional works, bearing the autographs of Lee, and Johnston, and Pendleton, and Cocke, and Crozet, and Mercer, and Bomford, and Mordecai, and Gilham, and many others,—to which I have had the privilege of access, I have drawn another inspiration; that is, to be just to the noblest foe an army ever had, to a foe who, after all, whether the equal or the superior, was but the brother of the artilleryman whose history I have sought to record in more collected form than it has hitherto existed.

Should the narrative seem to ignore the part played by the other arms of the service, it must be recalled that this work professes to be but a history of the Field Artillery. In undertaking such a specialized work there is always grave danger that the writer may be charged with undue partiality, that his enthusiasm for his particular subject may be at the expense of others. But, in this case, the author can only deny any intent to laud the Field Artillery by disparaging its sister arms, and he has not failed to point out its faults as well as its virtues. There is glory enough for all, and he recognizes the fact that, in the last analysis, the artillery, however important and valiant its services may have been, was in 1861-65, as it always will be, but the auxiliary arm of the infantry, and that the exploits of the Field Artillery of the Army of Northern Virginia depended upon and were made possible by what was perhaps one of the most superb bodies of foot soldiers war has yet produced.

To Gens. Thomas T. Munford and Scott Shipp, Col. R. Preston Chew, Maj. R. W. Hunter, Capts. William T. Poague, W. Gordon McCabe, William W. Chamberlaine, J. J. Shoemaker, and Judge George L. Christian, all of whom were intimates of and soldiers under "Stonewall" Jackson, and all of whom, except the first, served with his artillery, I am much indebted for aid. And to Capt. James Power Smith,—who was one of Jackson's gunners, and who to-day is the sole surviving member of his staff, and with whom I had the honor to serve on the staff of the First Battalion Field Artillery Virginia Volunteers for several years,—I am also deeply grateful for much information. To Col. R. T. Kerlin, Professor of English, Virginia Military Institute, I desire to express my thanks for his interest and advice.

To Col. J. V. Bidgood, Virginia's efficient Secretary of Military Records, I am also indebted for much assistance. His untiring industry and splendid system has made available for the student a vast amount of historical material which is a priceless asset of the State. There are few who know the real nature and extent of his labor and the results he has attained.

The portraits illustrating this work have been collected with great labor. Many of them have never before been published. Of many of the famous Confederate artillery officers no pictures are to be had.

The author is conscious of the fact that maps showing the topography and positions of the battlefields described in the text would add greatly to the value of the book, but it has been found impracticable to include them. The use of the series of maps published in connection with the Rebellion Records is recommended to military students.

In conclusion, I desire to call particular attention to the part the Virginia Military Institute played in furnishing officers to the Confederacy as a whole, and to the Army of Northern Virginia in particular, and the direct influence it exerted upon the greatness of "Stonewall" Jackson.   JENNINGS C. WISE.

Lexington, Virginia,
   July 1, 1914.

PART I

CONFEDERATE BUREAU OF ORDNANCE

ITS ORGANIZATION, PERSONNEL, MATERIAL, AND RE-
SOURCES, WITH AN ACCOUNT OF THE ORIGINAL
ARMAMENT OF THE ARTILLERY OF
THE ARMY OF NORTHERN
VIRGINIA

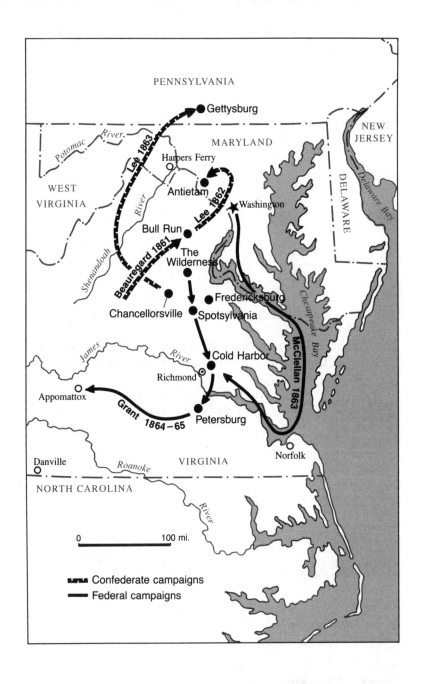

PENNSYLVANIA

Gettysburg

NEW JERSEY

MARYLAND

Potomac River

Harpers Ferry

DELAWARE

WEST VIRGINIA

Antietam

Lee 1863

Shenandoah River

Delaware Bay

Bull Run

Lee 1862

Washington

Beauregard 1861

The Wilderness

Chesapeake Bay

Fredericksburg

Chancellorsville

Spotsylvania

James River

Cold Harbor

McClellan 1863

Richmond

Grant 1864–65

Appomattox

Petersburg

Danville

Roanoke River

VIRGINIA

Norfolk

NORTH CAROLINA

0   100 mi.

⚊⚊ Confederate campaigns

⚊⚊ Federal campaigns

THE LONG ARM OF LEE

CHAPTER I

In the nature of things a study of the artillery of the Army of Northern Virginia involves an investigation of the system under which the material therefor was provided and the resources from which it was drawn. Hence we find ourselves at the very outset face to face with the Ordnance Department, its organization, and its personnel, in addition to the material resources at its command.

Military critics, passing judgment after the event, seldom prosecute their investigations beyond an inquiry into the actual movements of the troops and the battle orders of the commanders. The war chest, the weather conditions, and such things as material and equipment frequently escape their attention entirely. Public opinion, that bogie of military men, is generally totally ignored. The move that would have surely resulted in success, had it been made, is unfalteringly pointed out, and woe to the general who failed to execute it, no matter what the obstacles in his path may have been. There stands the height which, crowned with a hundred guns, could have changed history. The fact that it was on the particular day of the battle beyond human ability to place those guns on that hill, or that, even if they had been there, a sufficient supply of ammunition was lacking, due to some influence beyond the control of the general commanding,—such things as these enter not into the calculations of the critics a century later.

The logicians of war alone appreciate the skill and the labor which others must have brought to the aid of Cæsar. They know that an army moves on its belly, and that its thrusts are no keener than the weapons it wields. And it is well, in studying Lee's artillery, to commence with a proper appreciation of the limitations which circumstances imposed upon its employment. Any layman must know that the artillery is dependent upon the Ordnance Department for material, equipment, and stores, and that however efficient the artillery personnel may be its effectiveness bears a direct relation to the efficiency of that agency which provides it with the machinery of war. Ordinarily, as in the case of Germany in 1866 and 1870, and of the Balkan States in their present struggle with Turkey, material and equipment are manufactured, stored, and issued in advance by a well-organized corps of experts.

Few instances are recorded where a belligerent has actually created the very factories for the fabrication of its arms and munitions of war after the outbreak of hostilities with a powerful adversary. This was true, however, in the case of the Confederate States of America, although it has been frequently charged and very successfully disproved that Mr. Davis and Mr. Floyd used their office while Secretary of War of the United States to transfer arms and military supplies from the North to Southern arsenals where they might be more readily seized in the event of secession.

The condition of his ordnance and ordnance supplies, as well as his Medical, Commissary, and Quartermaster Departments, undoubtedly made impossible Johnston's immediate advance upon Washington after Bull Run.

Had the Confederate Bureau of Ordnance been created *de novo,* we might begin our study with the year 1861, but since it was the offspring of an old system, we must look further back in order to appreciate the character of the foundation upon which it was raised.

At the very outbreak of the War of American Independence Congress appointed a committee to consider ways and means to supply the Colonies with ammunition and military stores, a most important provision, since

Great Britain had prohibited the shipment of such things to America and was in a most advantageous position to enforce the restriction. This, then, was the inception of the American system for the supply of munitions of war, for the mother country had very wisely created no plants for their manufacture in the colonial wilderness.

The recommendations of the committee led to the appointment, in 1776, of a Commissioner of Artillery Stores, in coöperation with whom the business of procuring material and ammunition was conducted by a secret committee of the Board of War. This and various subsequent provisions,—quite inadequate, as shown by experience,—were relied upon until the War of 1812, when, in May of that year, the Ordnance Department was created by Act of Congress. After having passed through various legislative vicissitudes, as an independent bureau of the War Department, it was abolished by Act of March 2, 1821, and merged in the Artillery. The President was authorized to select such artillery officers as might be necessary for ordnance work, and to each regiment of artillery one supernumerary captain was attached for ordnance duty. When assigned to such duty these officers were subject to the direct orders of the War Department only, a provision almost tantamount to preserving the independence of the bureau, yet hampering it in the interest of economy with an organization soon found to be impracticable. As a result of eleven years of bitter experience the Ordnance Department was organized on an independent footing by the Act of April 5, 1832.

Following the reorganization of the system, the War Department, in 1834, during the incumbency of Lewis Cass, sought to define the duties of ordnance officers and regulate their operations. Hitherto the loosely organized system had relied solely upon civilian contractors for the supply of material, but definite regulations were now prescribed for its production, and it was provided that there should be established as many arsenals of construction as the public service might require, not exceeding six in number. It was directed that four of the arsenals should be erected at Washington, Watervliet, Pittsburg, and Fort Monroe, respectively, and upon their completion the fabrication and issue of ordnance stores should commence under the direction of the Colonel or Chief of Ordnance with headquarters at the national capital. In addition to the corps of ordnance officers proper, it was provided that lieutenants of artillery should be detailed to the Ordnance Department, for not more than four years, to engage in the manufacture of gun carriages and artillery equipment.

The regulations published in 1834 were followed in 1841 by a manual prepared by Col. George Bomford, Chief of Ordnance, and again by a similar work in 1850, revised in 1861 under the immediate direction of Maj. Laidley. Meanwhile the regulations for the department were being amplified and enforced, in which work Capt. Alfred Mordecai, of Virginia, and Col. Benjamin Huger, of South Carolina, took an important part as assistants of Col. Talcott, the Chief.

By the year 1852 there had been established twenty-seven ordnance stations in the United States, of which number there were three in Virginia,—one being at Harper's Ferry, one at Old Point Comfort, and the Bellona Arsenal in Chesterfield County, near Richmond.

The labor of Southern officers had largely contributed to the development of the Ordnance Department, and upon the outbreak of the war the Confederacy secured the services of many efficient men, who created much out of little. Under the direction of the Chief of Ordnance, C. S. A., a manual was immediately prepared fully setting forth the material and equipment adopted for use by the Confederacy. Practically no differences existed between that of the two services, except as to the shape of certain pieces of ordnance, more particularly with respect to rifled field guns, columbiads, and the rifled mountain pieces.

The various regulations and manuals published during the period 1834-1860 contain the history of the development of ordnance up to the Civil War and set forth fully the character of the artillery material in use in this country in 1860. These works are also referred to because they are descriptive of the school of training through which many of the Confederate officers had passed. The foregoing paragraphs briefly describe the foundation upon which the Confederate Bureau of Ordnance was based, and in the upbuilding of which a number of former United States officers took important parts. And now, before going further in our investigation, it will be well to examine the stage of development of field ordnance in 1861.

The classification of ordnance shown in the manual of 1861 includes no field pieces except 6- and 12-pounder bronze guns, 12-pounder bronze mountain howitzers, and 12-, 24-, and 32-pounder bronze field howitzers, which were all smooth-bore pieces. The new system of rifling is not referred to in the work and it will be shown later that its status in the United States Army was entirely unofficial until late in 1861. There had been much experimenting going on since 1850, but the fact remains that field ordnance as prescribed in the official manuals at the beginning and end of the decade was identical. With the outbreak of the war, however, iron field ordnance was cast, and in 1862 there were in use 3-inch iron rifled guns, the old bronze pieces, 12-pounder bronze Napoleons, the various old types of bronze howitzers, and 12-pounder iron howitzers, the last-named having been added in 1861. The 32-pounder bronze howitzer had become obsolete for use in the field. Both armies purchased foreign guns of various types, but although they were used they were not prescribed as regulation ordnance for manufacture in this country. The Confederates had developed by 1862 a 2.25-inch bronze mountain rifle which does not appear to have been in use in the Northern Army.

It would be impracticable to discuss here the great variety of ordnance that was used during the war. Officially, at least, a great deal of it was unknown to the Ordnance Department and formed no part, as has been said before, of the regulation material. The development of ordnance in the United States Army, with the exception of a 3-inch rifle, seems to have been left entirely in the hands of private persons, the war giving an impetus to the manufacture of all kinds of artillery material. Some conception of the armament of the time may be had from a report of the field artillery material of Rosecrans' army in 1863, in which it is stated there were thirty-two 6-pounder smooth-bores, twenty-four 12-pounder howitzers, eight 12-pounder light Napoleons, twenty-one James rifles, thirty-four 10-pounder Parrotts, two 12-pounder and two 6-pounder Wiard steel guns, two 16-pounder Parrotts, and four 3-inch rifled ordnance guns. This assortment is typical of the Confederate material of the time.

Rifling as adapted to the use of field ordnance was little known to our ordnance experts at the time and was scarcely more familiar to those of Europe.

William Greener, C. E., in a treatise on Rifles, Cannon, and Sporting Arms, published in London in 1858, points out that gun barrels were grooved first in Vienna about 1498 for the purpose of providing space for the foul residue produced by discharge, thus diminishing friction in reloading. Within twenty years of this time the grooves were given a twist, and some of the bullets had projections to fit the grooves. This was not practicable, however, so the shape of the bullets was changed, and it passed through various stages from being egg-shaped to practically the present form. These rifles were unsuccessful, due to the fact that there was too much of what was then called windage,—gas escaping by the bullet. In 1836 Greener produced the perfect expansive bullet,—that is, a bullet which upon discharge would expand and fill the rifling,—although Capt. Norton, an English officer, had invented an ex-

plosive detonating lead shell in 1822, which incidentally
only partly accomplished the same purpose on account of
its inability to resist the compression due to the explosion. It is interesting to note that the principles of
the invention of Greener were adopted by the English
about 1848 under the name of Miniè rifle, Capt. Miniè
having proposed practically the same things that were
previously rejected when proposed by Greener.

Scoffern, in his New Recourses of Warfare, published
in London, in 1859, discusses rifling of small arms and
cannon. He credits Sir William Armstrong with the
development of the English gun which bore his name,
into a rifled, breech-loading piece, and he gives details
of its construction. He also describes the Swedish or
Wahrendorff breech-loading rifled cannon which was
displayed in the Crystal Palace Exhibition of 1851.
This model was never successful, however, because the
cross section at the breech was not strong enough to
withstand the shock of the explosion. In addition to
these he mentions the fact that Cavalli, of the
Sardinian service, accomplished the act of breech-loading, but he does not give details.

Just as our ordnance officers paid little heed to what
was transpiring in military circles abroad, so the
Europeans ignored our development of the new system
until after the Seven Weeks' War of 1866. Napoleon
and the Prussians had both been experimenting with
rifling as early as 1857, but in the case of the latter the
novelty found much opposition. In England the Lan-
caster gun, with two grooves, was considered by many
decidedly unsatisfactory, if not a failure, and the Armstrong gun was but in the experimental stage at the
time, though its invention had attracted much notice.
The Cavalli breech-loading rifle gun was not well
adapted to use in the field and was considered entirely
too complicated for service.

The views of American experts concerning these guns
are fully set forth in Gibbon's "Artillerist's Manual,"

published August 14, 1859, in which the author, though
stationed at West Point, fails to refer to Parrott.

Napoleon went so far, however, in 1858, as to order
his S. B. guns rifled, under the bastard system known
as the "Lahitte System," which continued in general
use in France until 1870. The French had also developed a rifled 30-pounder, more or less unsuited to
field use, although it was employed in Italy in 1859
with results as to range and accuracy which gave great
impetus to the system on the continent. This seems to
be the first instance of the use of a rifled gun on the
field of battle. Hohenlohe tells us that before the
termination of the War between France and Germany
the Prussian authorities had given orders to construct
three hundred rifled 6-pounders and a number of 4-
pounders. But no convincing results were obtained by
the Prussians with their new field guns in the war with
the Danes in 1864, though some satisfaction was obtained with rifled siege guns at Düppel. The prevailing opinion in Prussia in 1866 as to rifled field pieces is
evidenced by the fact that, despite the American experiences during the preceding five years, one-fourth of
the Prussian guns were smooth-bores, this number being considered necessary on account of their supposed
superiority with case and shrapnel for close fighting.
The satisfaction obtained with their rifled guns in the
Austrian War was by no means universal among the
Prussians. In fact, there was much disappointment, a
result due more to the poor tactical handling of the
artillery than to the material, though this fact had not
then been generally perceived. One soldier at least
there was in Prussia, who, like Jackson, as we shall
see, never faltered in his conviction that rifled field
pieces had come to stay. The sturdy Von Hindersen,
Inspector General of Artillery, made up his mind as to
their superiority and by that persistence for which he
was noted gradually overbore all opposition to a complete armament with the new piece, a condition, how-

ever, which did not obtain until 1870. In the meantime, England had obtained results with a rifled gun in China in 1860.

In America, as early as 1855 experiments were made at Fortress Monroe with a grooved gun, but no satisfactory results had been obtained. This, in brief, was the status of rifled ordnance just prior to the outbreak of the war.

The smooth-bore system which prevailed in this country was of its kind unexcelled elsewhere. The Rodman heavy guns were marvels of their day and the process developed by the inventor for the manipulation of the iron in their casting placed American ordnance experts well to the front in the estimation of the military world. As to field material, the increased use and improvement of the 3-inch rifle sustained the reputation of the American Artillery acquired by reason of its advances in heavy armament, though Europe has been loath to accord to America the credit due the latter for the development of the rifled piece, a development which was eminently practical as opposed to the theoretical or experimental state of the various foreign systems of rifling of the time.

The introduction of rifled field pieces in this country and the events and influences leading up thereto will be considered later at length.

The claims to important inventions and discoveries are generally conflicting, and this is eminently true of revolutionary ones. In a discussion of the artillery material of the Civil War it is proper that the Confederacy should be given credit for its part in the invention of machine guns and breech-loaders. Before entering upon the general treatment of Confederate ordnance operations the subject of these guns will be briefly disposed of.

Attempts to construct multiple firing guns may be traced back to the earlier part of the seventeenth century, and small complicated guns of this character made by the Chinese have been found bearing dates as

early as 1607. It was not until the introduction of fixed
ammunition about 1860, however, that their successful
construction was realized. Dr. Reed of Alabama perfected a shell for rifled guns about this time. During
the Civil War a great variety of breech-loaders and machine guns, generally ineffective, made their appearance, the invention of the first practicable machine gun
being commonly attributed to Dr. R. J. Gatling, of
Hartford County, North Carolina. During the war he
perfected the revolving gun which now bears his name.
The first six which he made were destroyed in his
factory by fire. Afterward he had twelve made which
were first used in actual service by Gen Butler on the
James River. It was not until 1866 that the improved
Gatling gun was adopted by the United States
Ordnance Department. The use of this gun on the
battlefield was antedated by that of a machine gun
manufactured at the Richmond Tredegar Works, the
first year of the war, the inventor being Capt. R. S.
Williams, C. S. A., of Covington, Ky. The gun
was a 1-pounder steel breech-loader with a barrel about
four feet long, and a bore of two inches. It was
mounted on a two-wheeled carriage similar to that of a
boat howitzer and was drawn by one horse in shafts.
It was operated by a lever attached to a revolving cam
shaft which rotated a cylinder, above which was an
ammunition hopper. The cartridges were fired by a
sliding hammer which automatically struck the percussion caps at each revolution of the cylinder. The gun
had a range of about 2,000 yards. Its first test in action
was on May 31, 1862, at the battle of Seven Pines
under the direction of the inventor himself, who accompanied Pickett's Brigade. The results obtained were
so satisfactory that the Confederate Government had
six of the guns made which comprised the material of
Williams', later Schoolfield's Battery, of the Western
Army. A graphic account of their effect in the battle of
Blue Springs, East Tennessee, October 10, 1863, is
given by Capt. T. T. Allen of the 7th Ohio Cavalry.*

*Confederate Veteran, November, 1908, p. 581. Also Ibid., February, 1909,
p. 65.

BRIGADIER-GENERAL JOSIAH GORGAS
CHIEF OF ORDNANCE, C. S. A.

These breech-loading machine guns, probably the first used in war, were discarded according to Capt. T. M. Freeman, of Houston, Tex., Giltner's Brigade, because when firing the breech expanded and failed to relock.

Officers captured by Pickett's Division at Gettysburg asked many questions about the strange rapid-fire gun used by the Confederates at Seven Pines, showing that not only was the use of such a gun novel to them, but that it had made a lasting impression by its noise and the uncanny screech of its spike-like bolts. The subsequent reputation acquired by Williams' Battery in Tennessee and Kentucky undoubtedly attracted the attention of Dr. Gatling, who lived nearby in Cincinnati, Ohio, then a man beyond military age, and already distinguished as the inventor of a steamplow and many other valuable machines. It is not at all impossible that the Gatling gun is the outgrowth of Capt. Williams' revolving gun, which certainly made its appearance on the battlefield before the former did. One of the Williams' guns is now in possession of the United States War Department and has been extensively exhibited.

CHAPTER II

ONE of the most serious problems confronting Mr. Davis upon assuming office as Chief Executive of the Confederate States of America, was the supply of arms and munitions of war, and for this reason it was one of the first to receive his attention. In no branch of the new service were the needs so pressing and the means relatively so inadequate to supply them, as in the matter of ordnance and ordnance stores. Thousands were clammering in vain for arms wherewith to defend their country.

The selection of an officer to organize the Bureau of Ordnance was a wise one, the choice falling upon Capt. Josiah Gorgas, but recently resigned from the Ordnance Department of the United States Army, in response to the call of the South, though he himself was a native of Pennsylvania. The record which this man made as Chief of Ordnance, C. S. A.,* is indeed a remarkable one, and had it not been for such ability and energy as he displayed in the administration of his department, the Confederacy could never have maintained armies in the field as long as it did. It is not too much to say that General Gorgas was himself in large measure the ordnance department, and for this reason a brief sketch of his career is not thought to be inappropriate.†

Born in Dauphin County, Pa., July 1, 1818, he was graduated at West Point sixth in the Class of 1841, and was assigned to the Ordnance Department, in which he served until April, 1861. Soon after entering the Army, he secured leave of absence for the purpose of studying his profession abroad, returning for more

---

*Appointed. Special Orders No. 17, A. G. O., April 8, 1861, Series IV, Vol. I, *Rebellion Records*, p. 211.

†He created the Ordnance Department of nothing.—Joseph E. Johnston.

active service in the Mexican War and distinguishing himself in the siege of Vera Cruz. During the years following, he was assigned to duty at various arsenals throughout the country, among them the Mt. Vernon arsenal in Alabama, where in 1853 he married the daughter of ex-Governor Gayle of Mobile. Promoted captain in 1855, he was transferred to Maine and again to Charleston, S. C., in 1860, but was on duty in Pennsylvania at the time of his resignation. There seems to be little doubt that the Department recognized his great abilities, and sought to retain his services by ordering him from Charleston to his native State at the critical hour, for the influence of his Southern wife and associates had done much to fix his allegiance to the South.

When Col. Gorgas was appointed Chief of the Bureau of Ordnance he at once looked to the several sources of supply for the ordnance material demanded of him from all sides. First the supply in possession of the various States, whether purchased or seized by them, must be husbanded and immediate steps taken in order to prevent its waste and loss, forming as it did the sole reliance of the Confederacy at the outset. Second, while ordnance plants were being created to supply future needs, prompt purchases would have to be made abroad to supplement the present supply of the States. From these sources the troops of the South must secure their armament.

Fully appreciating the material poverty of the country, Col. Gorgas at once sent an efficient officer to Europe, in order to avail himself of that source of supply, having become thoroughly familiar with the foreign markets during a year of travel abroad.

He next set about locating arsenals, powder mills, lead and copper mines, and preparing elaborate and skillful plans for the collection and distribution of the armament of the Confederacy. Not only did he devise and secure the creation of the Bureau of Foreign Supplies, and the Mining and Niter Bureau, but he did much for the establishment of a blockade-running service. His insistent views in regard to the governmental control of the cotton and tobacco crops, if adopted in time, would no doubt have prevented the early dissolution of the Confederate currency system. The power to select officers of ability as assistants was a striking characteristic of this energetic, modest man, so little known to the general public.*

When Gen. Gorgas assumed office in April, 1861, the Confederacy was without a single arsenal, laboratory or powder mill of any capacity, the United States War Department having depleted rather than over-stocked the small depots located in the South. In the entire South, there was but one plant available as a cannon foundry and rolling mill. Fortunately for the Army of Northern Virginia, that one, The Richmond Tredegar Works, was located in Virginia.†

By an act approved March 16, 1861, the Confederate Government appropriated $110,000.00 for the purchase of ordnance and ordnance stores, followed in May by a larger appropriation amounting to $4,440,000.00, directing that out of the latter sum were to be purchased 16 field batteries of 6 pieces each, with harness implements and ammunition. Of the general appropriation of $5,700,000.00 for the public defense made in August, an apportionment of $3,500,000.00 was made to the Bureau of Ordnance, all available funds thereof having

---

*In the spring of 1865, Gen. Gorgas returned to his adopted state, Alabama, and became Superintendent of the Briarfield Iron Works, soon after accepting appointment as Vice-Chancellor University of the South, at Sewanee, Tenn., and becoming President of the University of Alabama in 1877. He died May 15, 1883, having resigned his high office after a brief tenure, on account of ill health, serving until his death as Librarian of the University. Mr. Davis pays no higher tribute to any of his officers than to this unimpeachable man.

It is interesting to know that the son of this distinguished Confederate officer is Col. W. C. Gorgas, U. S. Medical Corps, whose work as Chief Sanitary Officer of the Panama Canal Zone has attracted the attention of the world.

†The Tredegar Works possessed at this time the maximum capacity for the production of rails of 8,000 tons a year.

The noble manner in which the South accepted defeat and set about the up-building of its institutions was in a great measure due to the influence of a very large number of ex-officers, who connected themselves with schools and colleges, and to a host of others who set an example from the pulpit. Nearly every Southern institution of learning was headed by gallant Confederates who commanded the highest respect, and the church was largely in the hands of ex-soldiers, who led their people to accept with humility the outcome of the war as the decree of the Almighty. Lee, Pendleton, Alexander, Maury, Brooke, Randolph, McKim, Gorgas, Mallet, Carter, and McCabe are but a few soldiers who occupied prominent positions in the educational and ecclesiastical walks of life after the war.

been exhausted before the following December. The necessity of a new appropriation of $2,340,000 that month and of $2,660,000.00 the following February, at the instance of Gen. Gorgas, gives some idea of the activity of his department. There were further appropriations on April 3 and 17 of $11,000,000,00 and $200,000.00, respectively.

In September, 1861, the Chief of Ordnance reported that in addition to a small number of 12-pounder iron howitzers in storage, outstanding contracts existed for the supply of one hundred and thirty-five 6-pounder gun carriages and caissons, one hundred and thirty-one 3-inch rifled guns, eighty-one 12-pounder and forty 24-pounder iron howitzers, a number of howitzer carriages, and a few 6-pounder brass guns. There was only one government plant engaged in the manufacture of field gun carriages at this time, and that had a capacity of but one carriage a week, though arrangements for the enlargement of this, the Baton Rouge arsenal, were being completed.

Upon the formation of the Confederate Government, Mr. Davis had placed Caleb Huse as Foreign Purchasing Agent, under the direction of the Chief of Ordnance. Visiting England at once, this agent met the inventors of the Armstrong and Blakely guns, but, failing to secure any material there, repaired to the continent where he purchased in Austria 12 field batteries and 4 batteries of S. B. guns, which he ordered to be converted. This material together with a small quantity of French harness, shell, powder, friction-tubes, and some forge and battery wagons, was shipped from Hamburg, but not until March, 1862.

In April, the Chief of Ordnance reported a total of 35 field pieces of all descriptions, as taken over with the forts which fell into the hands of the Confederacy, stating that only four 6-pounders, two 12-pounder howitzers, and six 6-pounder steel rifled pieces had been ordered in addition to 27,518 rounds of field artillery ammunition.

A report of May, 1861, shows that practically no field artillery material had been seized with the government depots, though ammunition sufficient for 60 field guns was found in the Baton Rouge arsenal.*

From the foregoing facts, we must conclude that such ordnance as was issued to the field artillery up to the fall of 1861 was on hand before the outbreak of the war, with the possible exception of a few small purchases in Mexico immediately thereafter, and it is not conceivable that the armies in Virginia received any great amount from outside of the State until the regular manufacture of ordnance began the following year.

Before examining the resources of Virginia, however, let us see what was done to organize the Bureau of Ordnance of the Confederacy.

The Act of March 6, 1861, providing for the establishment and organization of the Army, charged the Artillery Corps with all ordnance duties, but, in addition, authorized such staff departments to be continued as were already established.

The Act of February 21 created the War Department, as a bureau of which, though attached to the Artillery Corps, the Bureau of Ordnance was formed, it, with the Engineer Bureau, being originally in charge of Gen. Gorgas as Acting Chief, with the rank of Major of Artillery.†

Under this organization of the bureau, in connection with the Artillery, its operations were not satisfactory, since the artillery officers performing ordnance duties were not directly subject to the control of the Chief of Ordnance, leading to the recommendation on the latter's part the following March that a new organization be given the department, to be styled the Bureau of Artillery and Ordnance and to consist of 1 colonel, 1 lieutenant-colonel, 4 majors and 12 captains (to be nominated by the President), and as many lieutenants

---

*The Washington Artillery secured 6 old S. B. guns and a considerable amount of obsolete ordnance equipment from the Baton Rouge arsenal.

†Relieved from duty as Chief of Engineer Bureau, and superseded by Maj. Daniel Leadbetter, S. O., No. 114, A. G. O., August 3, 1861.

detailed from the Army for such time as the service might require.*

The views of the Chief were partially adopted, and definite regulations for the new organization prescribed soon after.†

It was now provided that all officers assigned to ordnance duty with troops in the field should report direct to the head of the Bureau, and in the case where an ordnance officer was not assigned by the Bureau, corps, division and brigade commanders were to designate their own ordnance officers, to be known as Chiefs of Ordnance, Division and Brigade Ordnance Officers, respectively. The Chief of Ordnance of an army, or of a corps, held the rank of major, and the division and brigade officers, the rank of captain of artillery in the regular army. These officers were ordered to be selected by a test for special fitness, were attached to the staffs of their respective commands, and when once appointed, were forbidden to be changed without authority of the Chief of Ordnance. The Division and Brigade Ordnance Officers made monthly returns to the Chief Ordnance Officer of their corps or army, and only in extraordinary cases were they authorized to contract for supplies. Every regimental commander was required to appoint an ordnance sergeant. Full instructions for ordnance officers in the field were issued by the Secretary of War May 20, 1862,‡ the collection of captured arms being dealt with in detail.

The exertions of the Bureau of Ordnance during the first year overcame difficulties thought to be insuperable. "During the harassments of war, while holding our own in the field defiantly and successfully against a powerful enemy; crippled by a depreciated currency; throttled by a blockade that deprived us of nearly all the means of getting material or workmen; obliged to

---

*See letter, Chief of Ordnance, *Rebellion Records,* Series IV, Vol. I, p. 990, March 12, 1862.
†G. O. No. 24, A. G. O., April 16, 1862, Ibid., p. 1065.
‡*Rebellion Records,* Series IV, Vol. I, p. 1124.

send almost every able-bodied man to the field; unable
to use the slave labor, with which we were abundantly
supplied, except in the most unskilled departments of
production; hampered by want of transportation even
of the commonest supplies of food; with no stock on
hand, even of articles such as steel, copper, leather,
iron, which we must have to build up our establishments—against all these obstacles, in spite of all these
deficiencies, we persevered at home as determinedly as
did our troops in the field, against a more tangible opposition; and in that short period created (first two
years of the war), almost literally out of the ground,
foundries and rolling mills at Selma, Richmond, Atlanta, and Macon; smelting works at Petersburg,
chemical works at Charlotte, N. C.; a powder mill far
superior to any in the United States and unsurpassed
by any across the ocean; and a chain of arsenals,
armories, and laboratories equal in their capacity and
their improved appointments to the best of those in
the United States, stretching link by link from Virginia
to Alabama."

The foregoing words of the Chief of Ordnance do
not exaggerate, and give a vivid impression of the conditions in the South at the opening of the war. It is
all but impossible to believe so much could be accomplished in a purely agricultural region, almost wholly
devoid of factories, industrial machinery, manufacturing materials and skilled labor. The fact remains, however, that in the spring of 1862, one year after the fall
of Sumter, the following plants were in operation:

Fayetteville Arsenal and Armory, Fayetteville,
N. C.; Richmond Armory and Richmond Arsenal,
Richmond, Va.; Charleston Arsenal, Charleston, S. C.;
Augusta Arsenal, Augusta, Ga.; Confederate Powder
Mills, Augusta, Ga.; Savannah Depot, Savannah, Ga.;
Montgomery Depot, Montgomery, Ala.; Mount
Vernon Arsenal, Mount Vernon, Ala.; Baton Rouge
Arsenal, Baton Rouge, La.; Texas Arsenal, San An-
tonio, Texas; Little Rock Arsenal, Little Rock, Ark.;

Memphis Depot, Memphis, Tenn.; Nashville Arsenal, Nashville, Tenn.; New Orleans Depot, New Orleans, La. Eight of these were in successful operation before the first summer of the war.

The idea is prevalent that the Confederacy acquired by seizure from the United States Government the machinery and plants with which the manufacture of arms was undertaken, in addition to an enormous supply of ordnance and ordnance stores. This is a most erroneous belief. On the contrary, practically no serviceable artillery material or ammunition was thus acquired, as shown by the reports of the Chief of Ordnance. What little powder was stored in the Southern States before the war was a relic of Mexican days, except about 60,000 pounds of old cannon powder captured at Norfolk and several other points. There were absolutely no batteries of field artillery at the arsenals and forts, only a few old iron guns mounted on Gribeauval carriages fabricated in 1762. The volunteer batteries of the States, however, did possess some serviceable guns, but practically no harness, saddles, bridles, blankets, or other artillery equipment.

The United States arsenals within the limits of the Confederacy had for years been employed as mere depots, the only one possessing machines other than foot lathes being that at Fayetteville, N. C. Not a gun nor a gun carriage, and except during the Mexican war, scarcely a round of ammunition, had for 50 years been manufactured in the South. The only foundry at which a cannon had ever been cast was the Richmond Tredegar Works, and copper, so necessary for field artillery purposes, was just being obtained in East Tennessee. Not a single rolling-mill for bar iron existed south of Richmond, and the few small blast furnaces in operation were located in the border States of Virginia and Tennessee.

The manufacture of field guns was from the first confined almost entirely to the Richmond Tredegar Works, a few pieces only being cast in New Orleans and Nashville, while in Rome, Ga., a very limited number of three-inch iron rifled guns were made.

Gun carriages and field artillery equipment for the army in Virginia were also wholly supplied by the Richmond arsenal, while that at Augusta produced much of the same material for the troops in the South and West.

It has been shown that not only was there no powder for the field artillery on hand in the South before the war, but that no mills of any but the smallest capacity existed in the South for its manufacture, notwithstanding the original plans for the armament of that arm contemplated the placing in the field of 300 guns, with 200 rounds of ammunition for each piece. It became immediately necessary, therefore, to provide not less than 175,000 pounds of powder for the batteries alone. Efforts to satisfy this demand were first made by agents in the North, but only a few orders were filled before the attack on Sumter, when all shipments ceased. It then became necessary to undertake the erection of government powder mills.

Before June 1, 1861, niter had been secured in Northern Alabama, and in Tennessee, and sulphur in Louisiana, into which state a considerable supply had been imported for use in the manufacture of sugar. This supply was supplemented by that furnished under a contract with Doctor Ullmann, of Talapoosa, Ala., who undertook to deliver from 1,000 to 2,000 pounds a day. Efforts were also made to secure the product from the reduction of iron pyrites by private contractors in Alabama and Louisiana, and in the end this was the source from which the necessary sulphur was obtained.

For the third ingredient of powder, viz., charcoal, recourse was had chiefly to cotton-wood from the banks of the Savannah River, in which locality it was abundant and gave an excellent product.

There were 2 small private powder mills in Tennessee, 2 in South Carolina, 1 in North Carolina, and a little stamping-mill in New Orleans. Contracts were immediately made to take over all the powder these plants could produce and they were offered every encouragement to continue and increase their outputs. Messrs. Bowen & Co., of Pendleton, S. C., and J. M. Ostendorff & Co., of Walhalla, S. C., together, accepted contracts for 300 pounds of powder a day. S. D. Morgan, of Nashville, Tenn., also immediately undertook to furnish a considerable supply. An order for 250 tons was accepted by C. D. Yale, of Virginia, the price named being forty cents per pound. Foreign orders were placed for 2,500,000 pounds, and negotiations were opened for the immediate purchase of 650,-000 pounds in Mexico. Gen. Davis, who in the meantime had secured a small supply of sulphur and saltpetre, began the manufacture of powder near Lewisburg, Va., for the immediate use of the troops.* Such was the condition up to August, 1861.

In the meantime, Georgia had imported about 250,-000 pounds of niter, and before the battle of Bull Run the Government had gathered from all sources a supply of about 200,000 pounds of artillery powder. The construction of a great government powder mill at Augusta, Ga., was placed in charge of Gen. G. W. Rains, a North Carolinian, at the time engaged in the manufacture of machinery in New York, in which industry he possessed wide experience.† Only inquiring how he could serve the Confederacy best, this officer immediately repaired to Augusta and undertook the seemingly impossible task assigned him, soon producing a supply of powder of unexcelled quality, due to the skill with which the niter, secured from various sources, was purified.

The immediate demands for saltpetre were satisfied by contracts. In May, Messrs. Leonard and Riddle, of Montgomery, Ala., undertook to furnish 60,000 pounds from local sources. Colonel Hindman, of

---

*Rebellion Records, Series IV, Vol. I, p. 555.
†George Washington Rains, of North Carolina, graduated from the U. S. M. A. in 1838, was first assigned to the Engineers and then transferred to the Artillery. He served with distinguished gallantry in the Mexican War, and received various brevets, resigning from the Army in 1856.

Arkansas, contracted to furnish 100,000 pounds, and
Richard Ross, of Memphis, agreed to secure a like
amount from the caves in East Tennessee. In Northern
Alabama, a section rich in saltpetre, Messrs. Nelson and
Davis, S. D. Bowen & Co., and William Worley, were
the principal contractors, and they controlled an output
of about 1,000 pounds per day, the weekly yield of the
East Tennessee beds being about four tons, a supply
of 8,000 to 10,000 pounds being already on hand for
sale there. The contract price offered by the Bureau
of Ordnance for saltpetre at this time was twenty-five
cents per pound, the market price ranging from twenty-
two to thirty cents.*

Later on, after the supply of saltpetre in the caves
was exhausted, resort was had to tobacco houses, damp
cellars and to artificial beds in which human urine was
largely used for the lixiviation of the earth. The principal beds were established in Columbia, S. C., Charleston, Savannah, Augusta, Mobile, Selma, and Richmond. Thus the inferior imported powder, in the manufacture of which a poor grade of niter was generally
used, the quality depending upon the not too scrupulous
honesty of the foreign shippers, had no longer to be
relied upon as at first.

Upon the recommendation of the Chief of Ordnance,
the Mining and Niter Bureau was created early in
1862. The corps of officers authorized for the Niter
Bureau consisted of one Superintendent of the rank of
a major of artillery, and four assistants and eight subordinates, with the rank of captains and lieutenants
of artillery, respectively.† The officers of the corps
were authorized to impress free negroes to work the
caves.

Some idea of the efficiency of the Niter Bureau may
be derived from the fact that before the close of 1864,
a supply of 2,800,000 feet of nitrous earth was on hand,
of which a large proportion was capable of yielding 1½
pounds of niter per foot. Within a year after the pro-

---

*Rebellion Records, Series IV, Vol. II, p. 556.
†Act approved April 11, 1862. Rebellion Records, Series IV, Vol. I, p. 1054.

duction of the niter was undertaken, the government resources supplied more than half the annual consumption, and at the close of the war, the central laboratory, then about completed at Macon, Ga., in charge of the Superintendent of Laboratories, Col. Jno. W. Mallet, a celebrated chemist and an officer of remarkable energy and ability, coöperating with the Augusta Mills, would have been able to supply the ammunition for an army of 300,000 combatants.* This fact seems almost beyond belief, yet it must be added that the complete mechanical equipment of the powder mills, including the enormous rollers, was made in the South in spite of the almost entire absence of machine shops and factories at the beginning of the war. Due entirely to Generals Gorgas and Rains, Colonels St. John and Mallet, after the fall of 1862, when the powder mills were completed, no requisition of an army in the field was ever dishonored. What higher tribute can be paid these men than the statement of this fact?

So extensive and complete were the Augusta Powder Mills and the Macon Laboratories, that more than mere mention of them should be made. The site selected for the former was a large piece of land on the

---

*As I write these lines, November 8, 1912, the news of Col. Mallet's death yesterday, at the University of Virginia, where he lived in retirement, is received. Born in Dublin, Ireland, in 1832, of English parents, Dr. Mallet obtained his doctorate at the University of Göttingen, and after graduating from the University of Dublin, in 1853, came to this country in the same year, becoming professor of chemistry at the University of Alabama in 1855. There he accomplished, in 1856, the first important work in physical chemistry performed in this country, the determination of the atomic weight of lithium, the lightest metallic element known. This work firmly established his reputation as a chemist of the first rank; and when, during the civil war, the Confederate Government found need for chemists to direct the manufacture of explosives, Dr. Mallet, at that time a member of Gen. Rodes' staff, was transferred to the artillery arm of the service and placed in supervision of the manufacture of ammunition. His distinguished service to the cause led the government to promote him to the rank of lieutenant-colonel.

After the war Dr. Mallet went back to the classroom as professor of chemistry in the medical department of the University of Louisiana. In 1868 he came to the University of Virginia. In 1880 he was chosen by the National Board of Health to consider and report upon the proper analytical methods to be used in the analysis of drinking waters. So well was this work done that it introduced him to a new field of usefulness. He became famous as an expert upon sanitary water supply. Not only was his advice eagerly sought far and wide in the planning of such supplies, but he was very frequently called upon as an expert witness in legal cases involving chemical questions, in all parts of the country. Indeed, his reputation as an expert witness was but little less extensive than his fame as a scientist.

In 1885 Dr. Mallet went to the University of Texas as Chairman of the Faculty, and then to Jefferson Medical College, in Philadelphia, but returned to the University of Virginia in 1885 as head of the School of Chemistry. He was retired on the Carnegie Foundation four years ago.

canal near Augusta, work on the plant commencing in September, 1861. The largest pieces of the machinery, including the heavy incorporating rollers and pans, were made at the Richmond Tredegar Works, while the innumerable small parts were made wherever the necessary equipment for their fabrication could be found.

Powder was actually turned out as early as April, 1862. "The statement may seem startling in view of the difficulties under which this establishment was built up, but it is no exaggeration to say that it was amongst the finest and most efficient powder mills in the world at the time, if not the very best in existence."*

The erection of a central ordnance laboratory for the production of standard ammunition, including that for the field artillery, was decided upon in September, 1862. A tract of about 145 acres, near the city of Macon, was immediately purchased and enclosed, a branch track run out from the Macon and Western Railroad, and the erection of the plant begun by Col. Mallet. The line of the three main buildings, connected with each other, had a frontage of about 1,200 feet, the middle building being about 600 feet long. In addition to this great structure, there were over 40 other buildings. All of the bricks for their construction were made in a great yard near Macon, opened and conducted by the ordnance officers in charge of the work. Orders were sent to England for a large and various assortment of special machinery, including several large steam engines, to furnish the motive power, much of which had reached Bermuda when the blockade service was practically destroyed near the close of the war.

Not only were these plants able to contribute their outputs to the armies in the field, but the ordnance officers conducting them were able, in spite of the greatest difficulties, to make many improvements in the various machines and processes. One of the most notable of these was the method of steaming the mixed

*See article in *University of Virginia Alumni Bulletin*, April, 1910, on "Work of Confederate Bureau of Ordnance," by Col. J. W. Mallet.

materials for gunpowder just before incorporation in the cylinder mills, which was invented and introduced by Col. Rains, not only very largely increasing the capacity of the plants, but greatly improving the quality of the powder. As another example of the skill of the officers of the ammunition laboratories, may be mentioned the casting of shells with polygonal cavities, securing the bursting of the projectile into a determinate number of pieces. It was in these laboratories that the Reed shell with the soft metal base cup for taking the rifling was brought to so practical a state of perfection that it has been little improved upon since, being the very first satisfactory projectile for rifled guns. Many ingenious devices for the ignition of time fuzes for use in rifled guns were also invented in these shops.

From the saltpetre secured as before described, nitric acid could be made, which, with mercury and copper, was necessary in the manufacture of percussion caps and friction primers. The mercury was imported from Mexico, but after the fall of Vicksburg, no adequate supply was available. The ordnance chemists, however, discovered a mixture of chloral potash and sulphuret of antimony which they used in place of fulminate of mercury, the necessary supply of copper being obtained by collecting all the turpentine and apple brandy stills in the country, which were shipped to Richmond, there to be cut up and rolled into strips.

There had been established at Ducktown, Tenn., before the close of the war, a small plant for the smelting and rolling of copper, though on no great scale. A moderate amount of sheet copper was found at Cleveland, Tenn., already manufactured from the Ducktown ores.

Great trouble from the first was experienced in securing the necessary leather for artillery saddles, harness, and equipment. A comparatively small amount could be purchased abroad, and the principal government leather shops at Montgomery were unable to procure a sufficient supply of raw material to fill the tremendous demands of the various armies. The production of this and the Richmond factory was supplemented by means of small contracts placed in the rural districts, especially in the Valley of Virginia, where old men were induced to devote their energies to the fabrication of harness, and other horse equipment. In order to economize the insufficient quantity of leather available, due to the early elimination of the Texas and Mexican supplies, bridle reins and saddle skirts were made of cotton cloth stitched in three or four layers. The tannery industry was encouraged by exemptions from military duty in the field, and a premium was put upon the saving and curing of hides throughout the South.

The friction resulting from the scramble for leather by the Quartermaster Department, and the ordnance agents was, as might have been expected under the circumstances, the cause of frequent War Department orders, endeavoring to regulate the activities of the two interests.

The home resources were supplemented by extensive foreign purchases of leather from time to time. Before the close of the year 1863 harness shops had been established in Clarksville, Va.

In view of the scarcity of leather and the absolute lack of india-rubber, a process was developed for the treatment of the cotton cloth used in the fabrication of blankets, equipments, etc. Linseed oil answered best for making the drying oil, and when the necessary supply could no longer be imported, a fishery was established on the Cape Fear River where it was made.

Country blacksmiths, wheelwrights and carriage builders were perforce generally exempted and subsidized to make horseshoes, gun carriages, transport wagons, etc., The metal for the smiths was precariously obtained, the small individual outputs of these wayside mechanics being gathered by districts. During the year ending September 30, 1863, tremendous efforts were made by the government to supplement the supply of horseshoes procurable through contracts, and of the 266,951 pounds of shoes issued during the foregoing period, nearly half were fabricated in the arsenals.

To provide the metals required in the manufacture of cannon, projectiles, and metallic articles, was a task of tremendous proportions. To supervise and direct this work the Mining Bureau was created, conjointly with the Niter Bureau; Col. St. John, being assigned to the administration of this important organization, assisted the Bureau of Ordnance with distinguished ability.

At the outset, lead had been purchased abroad, much in Mexico, and early in the spring a contract was made for the delivery of 500 tons at Columbia, and a like amount at San Antonio, Tex., the price being seven cents per pound. But this supply was by no means sufficient.

One of the first steps taken by the Chief had been the erection of a small smelting plant in Petersburg, which was in full operation before the summer of 1862.

Every encouragement was now given by government contracts to stimulate the mining and smelting of ores, and much ingenuity and great labor were expended in providing the necessary metals. The Virginia lead mines at Wytheville supplied the bulk of the lead, having an output of from thirty to forty tons a month. There was also a small lead mine operated in Davidson, N. C. To supplement this inadequate supply, the country was literally scoured from end to end, piping, window weights, roofs, cistern linings and utensils of all kinds contributing to meet the demand. Lead and tin in small quantities were also imported from abroad, especially from the West Indies. Under the able direction of Dr. Pigott, formerly of Baltimore, the lead from Wytheville and several other points, as well as the promiscuous supply of scrap, was reduced in the Petersburg plant where some progress in desilverization by the Pattison process was made. The several tons of enriched lead set aside, however, had to be melted up for bullets before cupellation.

Most important of all were the results obtained in the development of the iron ores of the South in 1862, and the following year, especially in Alabama where the foundation for the present vast iron industry was laid. The Mining Bureau both by the labor of its own officers and subsidized contractors opened mines, erected furnaces and rolling-mills, and turned out an immense quantity of iron of superior quality. Scrap was collected from all available sources, and battlefields were carefully gleaned for metals which commanded a price at any of the arsenals.*

This sketch of the Confederate Bureau of Ordnance, however brief, would be utterly incomplete without fuller reference to the Richmond Tredegar Works than has hitherto been made. Prominent in the surrounding landscape of Virginia's Capital City, to-day as in 1861, are the slated roofs and tall chimneys of this plant, rising above the white foam of the rapids. The ominous clouds of smoke by day and the lurid flashes of fire by night, which shoot upward from this island haunt of Vulcan, comport well with the turbulence of the James at this point, the restless waters bounding among the great boulders in the river bed to the very furnace doors. And, as one gazes downward from the height of Gamble's Hill, the site of the great Confederate Hospitals, upon the massive plant, hissing and seething in midstream; the great Dunlop Flour Mills of war-time fame silhouetted against the horizon beyond; Hollywood, the magnificent city of the dead, nearer at hand, an awful consciousness clutches the mind that here indeed life, strife, woe, and death met together, here where the heart of the Confederacy beat the strongest and is now enshrined.

So potent a factor was the firm of Jos. R. Anderson & Co., the proprietors of the Tredegar Works, in the aggressive power of the Southern armies, that it acknowledged no superior among the government plants. When the war began, its foundry was the only

*For early measures to provide supplies of powder, lead, sulphur, saltpetre, etc., see *Rebellion Records*, Series IV, Vol. I, pp. 555, 557.

one capable of casting heavy guns, and its shops continued the only rolling-mill of great capacity, in the South. Initiated into ordnance work as an adjunct of the nearby Bellona Arsenal of the United States Government, its experience was at once turned to account by the Confederate authorities, and even to this day, large projectiles are there manufactured for the united country. Adding to its utility by enlarging its plant, and by importations of costly machinery through the blockade, for which purpose it employed its own ship, in spite of great loss by fire, Jos. R. Anderson & Co. continued operations throughout the war as the strong arm of the Bureau of Ordnance, while the senior partner led his brigade in the field. It was here that the famous 7-inch rifled Brooke gun was first cast, tested and perfected; that most of the heavy guns for coast defense, with their projectiles, were made; that the plates for the first iron clads were rolled and the shells for the first torpedoes were made. Operating mines, mills, and pork packeries, in various sections of the South; obtaining coal and metal at a time when industry was almost at a standstill elsewhere; with a brigade of its own employees, in spite of the closest conscription, organized, armed, and drilled by its own officers, and, on several occasions led against the common enemy to repel raids; no wonder when provisions became scarce the agents of the "Works" proceeded with those of the Government commissary, *pari-passu*.*

---

*An interesting anecdote illustrative of the importance of the Tredegar Works is here borrowed from Mr. T. C. DeLeon, author of "Belles, Beaux, and Brains of the '60's," and "Four Years in Rebel Capitals."

A special train was crossing the bridge *en route* for Petersburg at a time when transportation was rare. A huge negro, blacker than the soot upon his face, sat placidly upon the platform of the rear car.

"What are you doing here?" was asked by the officer in charge.

"Ridin' t' Petersburg," was the placid reply.

"Have you paid your fare?"

"Don' got none to pay, boss. Rides on'r pass, I does !"

"Work for the government?" this rather impatiently.

Ebo rolled his eyes, with an expression of deep disgust, as he responded grandly :

"No—sah ! Fur t'uther consarn !"

CHAPTER III

HAVING familiarized ourselves somewhat with its material development, let us now examine the conditions with respect to the personnel and organization of the Bureau of Ordnance, which continued to be merely a bureau of the War Department instead of possessing the character of a distinct department of the Army. There were, of course, grave disadvantages incident to such an organization; yet, in spite of this defect and a great deficiency in the number of ordnance officers, the work had been efficiently conducted during the early part of the war, far more so with the available resources than could reasonably have been expected.

As soon as Congress was thoroughly awake to the seriousness of the war it became far easier to secure the needed appropriations for ordnance material, and increases in the corps of officers, whose staff duties were no longer viewed in the light of departmental sinecures.

By Act of April 21, 1862, Congress authorized the appointment of 80 officers of artillery in the Provisional Army for ordnance duties, prescribing that from this number there should be one lieutenant-colonel appointed for each command composed of more than one army corps; a major for each army corps composed of more than one division; the others to have the rank of captain and first lieutenant in such proportion as the President might prescribe. This increase proving inadequate the corps was again enlarged by Act of September 16, 1862, authorizing the President to appoint 70 officers of artillery in the Provisional Army for ordnance duties. Having secured this increase the Adjutant-General, in order that capable men only might be detailed to the Corps, announced certain educational requisites to their appointment and created an examining board composed of Col. T. S. Rhett, Col. W. LeRoy Broun,

Maj. S. Stansbury, and Capt. Benj. Sloan, who were directed to visit the various armies in the field, and examine candidates who had made application for appointment to the army commanders through their chiefs of ordnance. Notice of examinations was required to be published in the *Richmond Enquirer*. It was provided that no candidate could be commissioned captain unless proficient in the subjects of algebra, trigonometry, mechanics, and chemistry. Meantime, Brig.-Gen. Benj. Huger, formerly of the United States Ordnance Corps, had been appointed Inspector General of Artillery and Ordnance, and enjoined to enforce the regulations of the branches of the service subject to his inspections. Orders were also published providing for a waiting list of those who might pass the examinations for whom no vacancy existed, the successful candidates to be given rank according to merit when finally appointed, and examination for promotion was also prescribed. Notice of examinations to be held were to be printed in the *Richmond Enquirer,* and applications to stand the same were directed to be made to army commanders through their chiefs of ordnance.* The test applied to candidates proved so exacting that the Corps contained many vacancies as late as January, 1863. The artillery officers authorized to be appointed in the Provisional Army were in addition to those of the Regular Army detailed to ordnance duty by the War Department and those in the Provisional Army and Volunteer Corps so detailed, and those of the Mining and Niter Bureau, appointed by Congress.†

In August, 1863, the officers appointed from the Provisional Army were distributed as follows: 4 lieutenant-colonels, 9 majors, 65 captains, 40 first lieutenants and 32 second lieutenants, there being 150 commissions authorized, two assistants not above the rank of captain being allowed the Chief of Ordnance of

---

*G. O. Nos. 68, 70, 71, A. & I. G. O., September 17, September 23, September 26, 1862. The general educational requirements were a good English education, knowledge of elementary mathematics, and familiarity with the Ordnance Manual published by the Bureau.

†G. O. No. 71, A. & I. G. O., September 26, 1862.

an army, and one not above the rank of first lieutenant the chief of ordnance of a department. Ordnance officers on duty in the field were now assigned, lieutenant-colonels to armies, majors to army corps, captains to departments and divisions, and lieutenants to brigades.*

Shortly after this redistribution, it was held by the Adjutant-General that "Chiefs of Ordnance" of armies and departments were to be assigned by the department only, and that they no longer formed a part of the personal staffs of commanding generals,† subject to appointment by them, when no officer was designated for ordnance duties with their commands as had hitherto been authorized.

The Chief of the Bureau now holding the rank of lieutenant-colonel, recommended to the Secretary of War November 15, 1863, in view of the fact that the officers of the Regular Confederate Army on ordnance duty, with temporary rank dependent upon the duties assigned them from time to time, were entirely distinct from the provisional organization, the rank of the officers of which was fixed by law, that a law creating a permanent ordnance department be enacted. Not only did this long-neglected measure seem necessary to him for the proper administration of ordnance affairs, but it would, he very rightly claimed, give character and recognition to ordnance officers as belonging to a distinct branch of the service, the members of the Corps being promoted in their own branch in accordance with seniority and efficiency.

Becoming curious as to the expenditure of the ordnance appropriations, Congress passed a resolution September 10, 1862, calling upon the President for full information with respect to the disbursements of the War Department for arms, etc. In the report of the Chief of the Bureau, of January 7, 1863, in reply to this resolution, a complete and interesting statement of the number and character of the small arms and equip-

---

*Compare this reassignment with the distribution originally made.
†G. O. No. 84, A. & I. G. O., June 15, 1863.

ments fabricated, issued, and on hand, up to September 1, 1862, showing the cost of production thereof, is given. In this report, however, nothing concerning artillery material appears. Up to this time practically all such material had been purchased abroad, but very little as has been shown, before the summer of 1862.* Major Huse of the Artillery, commissioned in April, 1861, to purchase abroad on account of the Bureau of Ordnance, had been more successful in assisting the Quartermaster Department than the former, and for his trouble became involved in difficulties with the latter. On his own responsibility he had purchased and shipped to the Quartermaster-General large supplies of blankets, clothing, shoes, and cloth, prompted, as he said, by a knowledge of the nakedness of the Confederate soldiers. His strenuous efforts to secure ordnance material were rewarded during the winter of 1862 and 1863, and before February of the latter year he had purchased 129 pieces of ordnance, as follows: fifty-four 6-pounder S. B. bronze guns; 18 S. B. bronze howitzers; carriages and caissons for same; 6 rifled 2.10-inch Blakely guns complete with 18,000 rounds of ammunition therefor; 2,000 fuses; 3 rifled 8-inch Blakely guns with 680 shells for same; twelve 12-pounder rifled steel guns with a large supply of ammunition therefor; 32 bronze rifled Austrian pieces, or 4 batteries complete with 10,000 rounds of shrapnel; 2 bronze rifles with 200 shells therefor; 756 rounds of shrapnel; 9,820 wooden fuses; 4 steel 9-pounder rifles with 1,008 shell and fuses; 220 sets of harness with spare parts, at a total cost of nearly half a million dollars. In addition to the foregoing, he had secured a large quantity of leather, 57,000 pounds of saltpetre, 80,900 friction tubes, 286 ingots of tin, and 931 pigs of lead. Other purchases before November, 1863, brought the number of foreign field pieces issued to date up to 193, the field artillery ordnance having been produced with these exceptions in the arsenals and workshops of the Confederacy.

---

*Letter of Maj. Huse, *Rebellion Records,* Series IV, Vol. II, p. 227.

In a paper written after the war, Gen. Gorgas states that the principal issues of the Richmond Arsenal alone, during the period from July 1, 1861, to January 1, 1865, including the work done for this plant by the Richmond Tredegar Works, embraced the following field artillery material and equipment:*

   1,396 field pieces (including captured guns repaired),
   1,375 gun carriages,
    875 caissons,
    152 forges,
   6,852 sets artillery harness,
  921,441 rounds of field, seige and sea coast ammunition.
 1,456,190 friction primers,
 1,110,966 fuses,
   17,423 port fires,
    3,985 rockets,
   69,418 saddles, artillery and cavalry,
   85,139 bridles,
   75,639 halters,
   56,624 pairs of spurs,
   42,285 horse brushes,
   56,903 curry combs.

The casual reader may weary with such figures as have been here given, but it is the knowledge of such details that gives the serious investigator food for reflection and a true grasp of his subject.

Such importations as were made by the Bureau were transported by its own fleet of four steamers, and a number of smaller vessels subsidized for blockade running. The blockade service, in charge of Maj. T. L. Bayne, assumed great importance at the very beginning of the war. Agencies were established at Bermuda, Nassau, and Havana, and gradually the purchase was made of a number of steamers specially suited to blockade running. The fleet proper, consisting of the *R. E. Lee, Lady Davis, Eugenia,* and *Stag,* all fine

---

*Report Chief of Ordnance, November 15, 1863.

vessels for their day, carried out the cotton apportioned the Bureau of Ordnance, in lieu of drafts or specie, to be sold in foreign markets, the proceeds being applied to the account of purchases from foreign houses. Such was the method enforced by the depreciation of the currency, adding finance on a large scale to the cares and duties of the ordnance officers.

In November, 1863, there were 5,090 persons, of whom two-thirds were non-conscripts, disabled soldiers, boys, women, or slaves, employed in the arsenals and shops of the Bureau of Ordnance, the various establishments, and their superintendents being as follows:

Richmond Arsenal, Lieut.-Col. W. L. Brown;
Richmond Armory, and Clarksville Harness Shops, Supt. W. S. Downer;
Danville Depot, Capt. E. S. Hutter;
Lynchburg Depot, Capt. C. T. Getty;
Fayetteville Arsenal and Armory, Maj. F. L. Childs;
Salisbury Foundry, Capt. A. C. Brenizer;
Charleston Arsenal, Maj. T. J. Trezevant;
Augusta Arsenal, Foundry and Powder Mills, Col. G. W. Rains;
Atlanta Arsenal, Col. M. H. Wright;
Macon Arsenal, Lieut.-Col. R. M. Cuyler;
Macon Laboratory, Col. J. W. Mallet;
Macon Armory, Supt. J. H. Burton;
Montgomery Arsenal, Maj. C. G. Wagner;
Columbus Arsenal, Maj. F. C. Humphreys;
Selma Arsenal, Lieut.-Col. J. L. White.

Their capacity was so augmented that during the year ending September 30, 1863, 677 field pieces, with carriages, caissons, and battery equipment complete, 251 extra carriages, caissons, store and forge wagons, 4,221 sets of harness and 318,197 rounds of field artillery ammunition were issued to the troops in the field.*

*Superintendents of Armories, with pay and allowances of a major of artillery, were authorized by Act of Congress of August 21, 1861. So, also, a number of storekeepers of ordnance, by acts of May 16 and August 21, 1861, the same to have pay and allowance of captain of infantry.

Each of these plants met with peculiar problems demanding ready solution, the labor question being generally foremost. Careful search had to be made for trained mechanics among the troops in the field, details for ordnance service being made only on proper evidence that the applicant was really a mechanic, in order that mere evasion of active duty in the field might not be encouraged. Some attempts were made to import mechanics from Europe, but with practically no success. Every effort was made to convert unskilled into skilled labor by teaching on the part of the few who were already themselves trained. Some of the more competent operators accomplished remarkable results in constructing with but poor appliances special machinery for ordnance purposes. Then there was the grave danger of unfaithful servants who by their treachery might wreck the plants or cause irreparable loss.

To guard the larger mills and arsenals, the operators were generally organized for purposes of defense. The battalion of the Tredegar Works has been mentioned. The powder mills in Augusta were also able to muster a battalion and a field battery as well. At the Macon plants there were two companies of infantry and a section of guns ready at all times, being called out on three occasions to repel attacks. These forces were quite efficient, including among their men many detailed soldiers. Thus, on a number of occasions, they were able to save the plants for which they were the sole guard, and which were naturally a much coveted prize for the raiding parties of the enemy.

Many discouragements in the way of irreparable losses of plants with costly machinery, both by capture and fire were experienced by the Bureau of Ordnance during the period of its phenomenal upbuilding. The arsenals and shops which it had first commanded in Missouri, Arkansas, Texas, Mississippi, Kentucky, Tennessee, Louisiana, and Florida, had not only been gradually cut off by the encroachments of the enemy, but the supplies of raw material from these States had in large measure become unavailable, and in no department of government activity could the slow but steady contraction of Confederate territory have been more forcefully realized. Yet, to the end, the loss of a mammoth plant, erected—created, it might better be said—with so much toil, and in spite of infinite difficulties, only served to inspire the ordnance officers to greater exertions, building, ever rebuilding, as they were, a house of cards upon a foundation of hope. Time and destiny put a period to hope, it is true, but not before the Confederate Bureau of Ordnance had written into history the story of the unexcelled genius of its officers.

The Confederate Bureau of Ordnance, however, did not depend solely upon foreign credits and the creative genius of its own officers, for throughout the war the Federal Ordnance Department proved a prolific source of supply. Seldom has one belligerent so extensively equipped itself, with arms and munitions of war at the expense of its adversary, as did the South in the War of Secession. Nor is this fact in any way discreditable to the Federal Army. It was the outgrowth of that strange inventor, Necessity. Opportunity for the capture of ordnance materials and military stores frequently dictated and controlled campaigns to a degree unknown to pure strategy. Risks, which would have ordinarily appeared foolhardy, were taken because of the possible reward, which success held out in the shape of warm clothing, full haversacks, and new arms. In fact, it is no exaggeration to say that the Confederate military policy was essentially one of material necessity. Of this fact, the unusual frequency of orders concerning, and the completeness of the system for, the collection, preservation and repair of captured arms and munitions, are sufficient evidence. The premium set upon captured property accounts for the large amount of such material thus obtained and reissued to the Confederate troops. Towards the close of the war, the Northern armies practically disarmed the

South, yet the material taken was no better then, and generally not so good as their own; hence there was no reason for its distribution for use among the captors.

To follow the history of the Bureau of Ordnance through the declining days of the Confederacy would be unfruitful. It would be an account of lack of funds, material poverty, absolute bankruptcy in fact, when every possible makeshift was employed to keep arms and ammunition in the hands of the fighting line. Yet, at no time, however pressing the want of food, clothes, forage, harness, and equipment, was there ever a lack of field guns and powder. The roads from Petersburg to Appomattox were blocked with guns, which the available teams could scarcely draw. One thing no carper could well say—"The army surrendered for lack of ordnance."

CHAPTER IV

ORIGINAL ARMAMENT OF THE ARMY OF
NORTHERN VIRGINIA

WERE the account of the Confederate ordnance resources to close here, well might it be said that no light
has been thrown upon the initial armament of the
troops in Virginia. "Whence came the guns at Bull
Run, at Malvern Hill," the reader naturally inquires.
And the answer lies in the preparedness of Virginia,
such as her armament was. To the Old Dominion, the
mother of states and of presidents, who though
struggling to the last to render secession unnecessary,
yet, through the foresight of her statesmen was armed
against a contingency which to many appeared inevitable, is almost entirely due the credit. And, so, when
the flood-tide of circumstances, of political rancor, of
sectional bitterness, or to whatever may be attributed
the fateful plunge, washed Virginia up against the
bulwarks of the Union, she was able to place in the
hands of her sons and those who flocked to her borders,
arms with which to strike for the principles to which,
in the fullness of her conscience, she had finally elected
to adhere.

An examination of the early Codes of Virginia will
show that the militia of the State received constant attention from the Legislature, having a very complete
organization on paper. As early as 1792, the force was
declared to consist of 5 divisions and 26 brigades, the
entire territory being divided into regimental districts.*
While the militia existed merely in the law, volunteer
companies were encouraged by ample provisions as to
arms, equipment, pay, and quarters, being attached to
and forming a part of the district commands existing
on paper. The volunteer artillery companies were assigned to the paper regiments of artillery, there being

---

*The number of brigades was later increased to twenty-eight.

one for each division. Hence the law contemplated the organization of 5 regiments of artillery in the event of the militia being called into actual service. In 1849, the governor was authorized to issue 4 guns to the volunteer artillery companies in Richmond, Norfolk, Petersburg, Fredericksburg, Portsmouth, Wheeling, Alexandria, Lynchburg, and Winchester, these being light batteries; but not more than 2 guns were to be furnished or provided for issue to other companies, presumably heavy batteries, which were liable to service as light artillery under the Act of 1833-34. The organization, discipline, and equipment of the artillery were required to conform to that of the United States. That the volunteers had no effective organization, even as late as 1859, is evidenced by the fact that the State appropriations for its maintenance, including the salary of the Adjutant-General ($1,500.00), aggregated only $5,800.00, a small company known as the public guard and employed as a garrison for the State arsenal and penitentiary being maintained at an additional expense of about $25,000.00. For the rapid and efficient organization of its troops, the State depended upon the Military Institute which it maintained at Lexington, as at present, for the careful and thorough training of its future officers.

While little was done for the armament of the State, the serious aspect of the impending storm in 1859 made its impression upon the Legislature, and, on January 21, an elaborate measure was passed carrying an appropriation of $500,000.00 for the purchase of arms, equipment, etc., and authorizing the appointment of 3 commissioners to secure the same as quickly as possible.

So active was the commission appointed by the Governor, that additional appropriations aggregating $106,-000.00 were made in March, the armory in Richmond having already been put in thorough condition, and steps taken to secure the newest machinery, implements and material for its operation. The commission was furthermore directed to purchase the patent rights of "newly invented arms," wherever the same could be secured, and the armament procured was to be distributed for the immediate use in the more exposed parts of the State. These were drastic measures and clearly show what was in the minds of the people of Virginia, the anticipation having been forced upon them by the country's attitude towards the Harper's Ferry incident.*

The Commission for the Public Defense consisted of Col. Philip St. George Cocke, Capt. George W. Randolph, and Col. Francis H. Smith, the first and third being graduates of West Point, and the second of Annapolis. Col. Cocke, afterwards a Confederate general, was at the time president of the Board of Visitors, and Colonel, afterwards Gen. Smith, was the Superintendent of the Virginia Military Institute. These able men, whose military training qualified them to grasp the true situation, at once determined to visit the various arsenals of the country, and open negotiations with the foremost manufacturers of arms in America and abroad. They were accompanied by the Chief Executive of the State, John Letcher, afterwards famous as the energetic war governor. Their tour embraced visits to Springfield, Harper's Ferry, and the West Point Foundry, at Cold Spring, on the Hudson. While at the last-named place, they were invited by Capt. R. P. Parrott, one of the proprietors, a retired army officer and personal friend of Gen. Smith, to witness a series of experiments he was conducting with his new rifled field piece. The Ordnance Department of the Army had been slow to grasp the importance of Parrott's invention, just as it had declared the percussion cap interesting, but only as a toy, not many years before, and Parrott had, up to this time, failed to secure the adoption of his gun.†

But the Virginians did not hesitate. The effect of the fire of Parrott's ordnance witnessed from behind

---

*See Act passed March 28, 1860, Chap. 29, Acts of Assembly, 1859-60.
†It was not until November 1, 1860, that an experimental board recommended the conversion of fifty per cent of the guns at the forts and arsenals, but even then little attention was paid to rifled field pieces.

epaulments, convinced the commission of its superiority over anything they had seen, and Gen. Smith was instructed to invite the inventor to send 1 gun and 100 shells to the Virginia Military Institute to be tested by Maj. Thomas J. Jackson, Instructor of Artillery.* The suggestion was promptly complied with, the gun was given a fair trial in July by the artillery class, and the results obtained by the cadets, as embodied in Maj. Jackson's report, led to the purchase by the commission of 12 rifled field pieces, with a large supply of shells therefor. These guns were first used, and with great effect, at the Battle of Bethel, and the reputation they there acquired led to the general introduction of the Parrott field piece into the artillery of both armies.†

Jackson had at once grasped the situation. Being an artillery expert, he appreciated the great possibility of rifled field pieces. The results he had obtained with the Parrott gun on the Institute range were startling, to him as well as to all those who had been accustomed to smooth-bore guns, the greatest range of which was from 1,800 to 2,000 paces. Even when firing at 1,000 paces, the results with the old guns had been so doubtful that gunners generally, as Hohenlohe said, acted on the proverb, "The first shot is for the devil, the second for God, and only the third for the King,"—that is to say, that at such a range only one shot in three would hit a target 6 feet high and 50 yards wide.

Jackson could have been little influenced by such rumors concerning rifled ordnance as may have sifted across the Atlantic before his own trial of the Parrott gun. His nature was not one which allowed him to be influenced by less than the most tangible knowledge or experience. That the Americans knew little of European progress with rifling is again borne out by the fact that Gen. Johnston, though frantic in his efforts to secure ordnance for his field artillery, wrote his Chief of Artillery, in Richmond,‡ after the battle of

---

*The famous "Stonewall" Jackson. The gun was received July 5, 1860.
†During the Civil War the West Point foundry furnished the United States Government with 1,200 guns and 3,000,000 projectiles.
‡Col. William N. Pendleton, later Chief of Artillery, A. N. V.

BRIGADIER-GENERAL WILLIAM NELSON PENDLETON
Chief of Artillery, A. N. V.

Bull Run, "Do not fail to urge the making of 12-pounder howitzers. I have faith in them. Let them send guns and equipments and leave us to organize. I enclose a requisition for equipment of a battery of rifles, which cannot be filled here (Manassas). Will you see if the authorities in Richmond can do it? *Do not, however, let them prefer it to the fitting out of field batteries of smooth-bore guns.*" And on the 10th of August, he wrote to President Davis urging an increase of the artillery arm, to be armed and equipped by borrowing material from the States, or by casting guns, especially in Richmond, adding a particular request for 12-pounder howitzers. Though thoroughly aware of the value of artillery, attributing the success of the great Napoleon to its proper use, Gen. Johnston had not yet realized the value of rifled ordnance.

In the light of the present day, it seems strange that so great a soldier, especially distinguished for his ability as an organizer, and for his military learning, should have failed to appreciate the lessons of Bethel, emphasized by current report. *Masked batteries* and *rifled guns* were subjects of common talk among the soldiery, and especially in the press of the time. McDowell's men had heard so much of these terrible things, that they marched into Virginia imagining them to crown every crest. The explanation lies in the fact that Johnston's experience had not so far brought him into personal familiarity with the new invention, already well known to Jackson and Pendleton, both of whom had first-hand knowledge of the new gun through personal experience with it in Lexington the previous year. Having staked his professional reputation, as it were, in his favorable report of the Parrott invention, Jackson was, of course, only confirmed in his views by the events of Bethel, and when Pendleton became Chief of Artillery of Johnston's army, he was soon able to enforce his views as to the new arm and overcome the prejudices of his commanding general.

The United States War Department was not ignorant of the tests made of Parrott's gun in Lexington, and the subsequent report of its own board of ordnance and artillery officers was in its hands. Already it had received exaggerated accounts of the effect of rifled pieces at Bethel. Now came to its ears the story of Hainesville, confirming the sudden reversal of opinion and reassuring the authorities that no mistake had been made in providing McDowell with a large number of rifled pieces for his impending invasion of Virginia.

As to the sudden popularity of the new gun in the Confederate Army, it is only necessary to refer, by way of explanation, to the fact that the influence of Jackson extended throughout the South, hundreds of his pupils holding important offices in the Confederate armies, each one of them, we may be sure, hanging upon the words of their former tutor in arms, by this time become a "martial divinity" in their eyes.

Though not a field gun, the story of the 200-pounder Parrott rifle, known as the "Swamp Angel," used by the Federals during the bombardment of Sumter, had gone the rounds, being eagerly devoured by all, as was every incident connected with this first act of the war.* Then, too, Col. Olmstead in his defense of Fort Pulaski, had used two 4.5-inch Blakely rifles imported from England by the State of Georgia, their employment having attracted much attention.

Before dismissing the subject of rifled guns, one more fact may be cited as evidence that American development of the system was substantially independent of foreign experience. While all powers, whether the fact was known to each other or not, were experiencing the utmost difficulty in securing a satisfactory shell for rifled ordnance, due to the uncertainty of motion of the projectile, and the consequent jamming in the bore, Dr. Reed, of Alabama, invented a projectile which

---

*The "Swamp Angel" is now mounted as a monument in Trenton, N. J. See account of its use, *Battles and Leaders of the Civil War*, Vol. IV, pp. 72, 73, 74. Ibid., Vol. II, pp. 9, 10, 11.

solved the problem. His method was the attachment of a wrought iron band to the base of an elongated projectile, the explosion of the powder forcing the soft metal into the grooves, a device which is still universally employed. The effect of such an invention was far-reaching and led directly to the subsequent improvement in the rifling itself. The Confederate ordnance officers rapidly perfected the Reed projectile, practically unknown until 1860, and soon thereafter followed the making of the first Brooke gun, the invention of Capt. John Mercer Brooke, Chief of Ordnance and Hydrography, C. S. N., this distinguished scientist having resigned his commission in the United States Navy in answer to the call of his native State.*

In a report rendered by the Adjutant-General of Virginia, to the Governor, dated December 15, 1860, it is stated that in addition to the 5 divisional artillery regiments of the militia, there were 26 companies of volunteer artillery fully recruited and organized. Of this number 11 were armed with 6-pounder field guns, there being 24 pieces in all, with full equipment, including artillery sabers, and one with six 12-pounder howitzers, with horse artillery sabers, the 12 field batteries thus armed being fully horsed, the personnel of the artillery aggregating 1,066. In addition to the field material issued to the volunteer batteries, there were the following pieces of ordnance on hand: issued to militia, 44; in depot for immediate issue, 8; at the Virginia Military Institute, 15; in the Richmond Armory, 229; or a total of 296, of which number 77 were bronze, and 219 iron field guns or howitzers. There were 62 gun carriages, 40 caissons, 38 sets of harness, 703 artillery swords, 90 musketoons, and 50,000 pounds of artillery powder on hand in the State depots. The foregoing, with a few

*John M. Brooke, a graduate of Annapolis, had accompanied Perry on his initial visit to Japan. Not only did he invent the gun which to-day retains his name, but he designed and built the iron-clad *Merrimac*. He also had charge of the Confederate experiments, with submarine boats, and contributed much to the development of the torpedo, first employed in war under his direction. He was also noted for many valuable inventions of deep-sea sounding apparatus. He contributed much to science, especially, as a Confederate officer, to the science of war. From 1866 to 1899 he occupied the chair of Physics and Astronomy at the Virginia Military Institute, where he died in 1904, at a very advanced age, as Professor Emeritus.

additional small items, may fairly be taken to represent the resources of the field artillery of Virginia at the outbreak of the war, a large portion of which had been purchased by the commissioners whose expenditures up to June, 1861, had been $1,737,950.49 for the Army, and $100,748.49 for the Naval force of the State.*

We have seen to what extent the Confederacy as a whole enriched itself at the expense of the Federal Government in arms and munitions of war. Now let us inquire what Virginia's record was in this respect.

While the State Convention was in session, debating whether or not Virginia should secede from the Union, it was rumored abroad that the United States Ordnance Department contemplated the immediate removal of a large number of heavy guns from the Bellona Foundry, near Richmond, to Fortress Monroe. The guns were made by Dr. Junius L. Archer, under a contract with the Federal Government, the consideration being $20,-896.47. A joint resolution was passed by the Convention directing the seizure of the guns, and it was ordered that Archer should be paid out of the State Treasury the unpaid balance on his contract of about $8,000.00, and the United States the remaining part of the consideration or about $12,000.00, which had already been paid to the contractor. This action on the part of Virginia could hardly be characterized as other than commendable; if anything, it was overconscientious.

Early in April, the Commandant of the Harper's Ferry Arsenal, in the belief that Virginia troops were approaching to seize it, destroyed the plant with its entire contents. Writing to army headquarters in Washington, Lieut. Jones, who applied the torch, April 18, stated: "The steps I have taken to destroy the arsenal, which contains nearly 15,000 stand of arms, are so complete that I can conceive of nothing that will prevent their entire destruction." Again on the 19th—"In three

---

*Between the date of secession and the following November, the State appropriations for defense aggregated $6,000,000.00. Series IV, Vol. I, p. 938, *Rebellion Records;* also see p. 391.

minutes, or less, both the arsenal buildings containing nearly 15,000 arms, together with the carpenter's shop, which was at the end of a long and connected series of workshops of the Armory proper, were in a complete blaze. There is every reason for believing that the destruction was complete." And on the 22d, he again wrote: "They also report that the fire in the workshops was arrested, but that the arsenal building containing the arms, together with their contents, were [*sic*] completely demolished, and that it is probable not a single gun was saved from them." That the demolition was more or less complete is amply testified to by the congratulatory letter of even date from the Secretary of War to Lieut. Jones, for the success of his work.* Yet, the State troops arrested the conflagration in time to save much of the machinery for the manufacture of small arms, which was later removed to the Fayetteville Arsenal, in North Carolina.†

Coincident with the partial destruction of the Harper's Ferry Arsenal was the evacuation of the Norfolk Navy Yard attended with a similar attempt at destruction, the value of the property lost being estimated at several millions of dollars. From the charred remains of the government plants within her boundaries, Virginia was able to glean little of value. The only Federal property she succeeded in seizing intact, before becoming a belligerent with belligerent rights, she undertook to pay for.

In January, 1861, nearly a million dollars were appropriated by the Legislature for the purchase of arms, in addition to the sums previously placed at the disposal of the commission.

Charles Dimmock, of Massachusetts, a graduate of West Point in the Class of 1817, and a former artillery officer, was appointed Chief of Ordnance of Virginia, with the rank of colonel, and immediately set about the work of securing arms and equipment for the State troops.‡

---

*The total appraised value of arsenal and stores, $1,207,668 to $1,470,513.
†Turned over to the Confederate States Government for use elsewhere.
‡Col. Dimmock died in October, 1863.

Col. Dimmock at once undertook the erection of plants, for the manufacture of ammunition, and by June was able to turn over to the Confederate States a small amount of powder and a laboratory with machines, fixtures, and workmen, of a daily capacity of 75,000 rounds of ammunition. Gen. Lee in command of the Virginia forces, had foreseen from the first that the resources of the State would be called upon for the arming and equipment of the troops sent to Virginia from other quarters, and had done all in his power to assist the Chief of Ordnance in preparing to meet the demand. As early as May, Virginia was called upon by the central government to supply its troops with arms, ammunition, and every variety of equipment. Before the middle of June, over 20 field batteries had been armed, mounted and equipped, and a total of 115 field guns provided for the troops of Virginia and of other States. Field ordnance had even been sent to Missouri. Of heavy ordnance, 40 guns, including 32-pounders, 12- and 6-pounder howitzers, and 8-inch and 9-inch columbiads, had been mounted in permanent batteries for the defense of the James River; 30 similar guns were in position at the mouth of the York; 12 on Aquia Creek; 4 on the Rappahannock; 85 in and about Norfolk; 19 on the Nansemond River; 19 in Hampton Roads, and arrangements had been completed for mounting 60 heavy guns in the lines about Richmond, and a large number in the chains of works extending around Norfolk, across the Peninusula at Yorktown, at Drewry's Bluff, and at Jamestown Island.*

Between June and November of 1861, an immense amount of material was issued to Confederate troops by the State Ordnance Officer, including 15,000 muskets with bayonets, 1,700 sabers, 147 field pieces, including both guns and howitzers, 82 caissons, harness, shells, percussion caps, fuses, miscellaneous supplies, and 97,-450 pounds of powder. In July the Harper's Ferry Arsenal as reconstructed by the State, with all its ma-

*Rebellion Records, Series I, Vol. II, pp. 928, 929.

chinery, was transferred to the Confederate Government, the State forces having been mustered into the Confederate service in June.

About this time, Gov. Brown of Georgia, originally having secured a supply of about 100,000 pounds of powder, was pressing the Confederate Government for the return of the 39,000 pounds previously loaned for use at Savannah and Fort Pulaski, defenses within the borders of his own State.*

Other than the guns brought to Virginia by the gallant battalion of four companies from Louisiana, the Washington Artillery, the most minute investigation fails to disclose that the State was assisted in any respect, in the armament of the artillery with the troops who met the first and second invasions of the common enemy and hurled them back.† Fortunate indeed it was for her sisters that Virginia held the most advanced post.

In the battle of Bull Run, the Army of the Potomac had 8 light batteries available on the field, with a total armament of 27 guns, or an average of about 3 guns to the battery. But 17 of these guns were engaged. The Army of the Shenandoah had 5 batteries, each with 4 guns engaged. Therefore, the Confederates had a total of 47 guns available, most of which were old smooth-bore 6-pounders. Some guns of this pattern had been reamed out to give a larger bore and rifled with three grooves after the manner of Parrott by Col. Dimmock, but the real Parrott rifles which had been purchased by the State were at the time with Magruder at Yorktown. After the battle the Confederate batteries were able to equip with the captured material, which is stated by Gen. Johnston to have consisted of 28 pieces of artillery, with 64 artillery horses and harness. According to an itemized account made at the time by

*Rebellion Records, Series IV, Vol. I, pp. 368, 406.
†The battalion arrived in Virginia with six 6-pounder guns, two 12-pounder howitzers, and one 6-pounder rifled gun, its armament being completed in Richmond. It was superbly appointed as to equipment, but possessed material for only about 2 batteries on its arrival. The battalion had six 6-pounder, four 12-pounder howitzers, and three 6-pounder rifles at Manassas.

Col. Pendleton, Chief of Artillery, he received the following captured material July 23, 1861:

    1 30-pounder Parrott rifled gun,
    9 10-pounder Parrott rifled guns,
    9 12-pounder brass rifled guns,
    3 12-pounder brass howitzers,
    2 12-pounder boat howitzers,
    3 6-pounder brass smooth-bore guns,
   34 caissons, more or less complete with spare parts,
    4 battery wagons,
    6 battery forges,
   24 horses,
   34 sets harness and spare pieces.

In a return of captures made by the ordnance officer of Johnston's Staff, Capt. E. P. Alexander, the field artillery material, etc., captured at Bull Run is itemized as follows:

    1 30-pounder Parrott, with 300 rounds,
    9 10-pounder Parrotts, with 900 rounds,
    3 6-pounder brass guns, with 600 rounds,
    3 12-pounder brass howitzers, with 300 rounds,
    2 12-pounder boat howitzers, with 200 rounds,
    9 James rifles, with 900 rounds,
   37 caissons, 6 forges, 4 battery wagons, splendidly equipped, 64 artillery horses with harness.

McDowell's 11 batteries had a total of 49 guns, a fact which shows an average battery armament of more than 4 pieces. Five Federal batteries, with 25 guns, crossed Bull Run. Most of these guns were rifled pieces, and none escaped, at least 2 additional ones being captured after the battle.

The guns captured at Manassas were promptly refitted by Col. Pendleton, Johnston's Chief of Artillery, and Col. E. P. Alexander, who the day after the battle had been appointed Chief of Ordnance, Army of the Potomac, the armies of the Shenandoah and the Po-

tomac being later consolidated under the name of the
Army of Northern Virginia, in command of Gen.
Jos. E. Johnston.

Col. Alexander was a wise choice for the position
assigned him. A graduate of the United States Military Academy of the Class of 1857, he had served
with distinction in the Corps of Engineers until the
outbreak of the war, when he resigned his commission
as second lieutenant, having served under Albert
Sidney Johnston in the Mormon war, in the Indian
campaigns of Oregon, and at West Point, where he
was on duty for a year as Commandant of the Corps,
and Assistant Instructor of Engineering. In 1859 he
was placed in charge of artillery target practice at the
Academy. While there, he also assisted Capt. Myer
in the development of his wig-wag signal system with
torches and flags. He had also been a member of a
board of officers, who conducted experiments with the
new breech-loading rifles, a number of which were being offered the War Department. He, therefore,
brought to the Army of Northern Virginia a knowledge
of the new ordnance possessed by few others in the
country. Arriving in Richmond, June 1, 1861, after
a long and eventful journey from Washington Territory, where he had been on duty, he was at once appointed Captain of Engineers by President Davis, who
recalled the young officer's appearance before the committee of the Senate, to which he had demonstrated the
Myer system the previous year, and was directed to
start a factory in Richmond for the manufacture of
signal apparatus and to perfect plans for introducing
into the Army the system with which he was so familiar.
While on this duty at the Capital Capt. Alexander was
directed to organize 5 batteries of artillery into a battalion and to prepare them for the field. This work he
undertook with marked ability, being himself responsible for the battalion formation, hitherto unknown to the
service. His whole training and experience had been
along the lines of organization, and as he subsequently

stated, "It would have been a decided step in advance had we inaugurated, so soon, a battalion organization of several batteries. We came to it about a year later, but meanwhile our batteries had been isolated and attached to infantry brigades. So they fought singly, and in such small units artillery can do little."*

While accomplishing great results in the task assigned him, early in July Capt. Alexander was attached to the staff of Gen. Beauregard, and ordered to install the signal system for use in the great battle, then foreseen by all. Capt. Alexander's system of communications during the battle and the days preceding it, was of great value to the generals in command, he himself transmitting the first definite intelligence of McDowell's line of advance.†

The absence of such a staff officer was sorely felt on the Peninsula in the subsequent campaign, where all worked in the dark. What might have been the outcome had the abilities of Alexander been employed by Lee and Jackson in that campaign is interestingly problematical. But this is true of the whole war in which military information was precariously obtained, staff duties being illy defined, and in which no efficient system of gaining intelligence was generally made use of.

The foregoing remarks concerning this officer, somewhat lengthy it may seem, have been indulged in, for the purpose of showing what manner of men had to do with the early equipment and organization of the Confederate artillery. Each one with whom we meet, whether Gorgas, St. John, Mallet, Jackson, Pendleton, or Alexander, possesses character and abilities of high order, a fact which is a tribute to the directing hands. Remarkable results were obtained simply because extraordinary men produced them.

Reverting to the Army of Northern Virginia, it will be recalled that the Chief of Artillery was sent to Rich-

---

*Memoirs of a Confederate, Alexander, p. 14. We shall see later that Gen. Alexander had been the first in the Confederacy to grasp this great fact. True, the Washington Artillery had a battalion organization, but it was employed in battery formation at first.

†Alexander had familiarized himself with the terrain of a large territory in a manner quite unknown to the military service at the time.

mond, after Bull Run, to "rustle" material, as the saying is in the service. The efforts of Johnston, aided by
Pendleton and Alexander, to increase and equip the
artillery were unremitting. In a letter to his wife,
dated July 22, Pendleton wrote from Richmond, "Have
had a great deal to do here pushing up artillery preparations. Will have several batteries at Manassas next
week, and several others the week after, etc. Several
difficulties obstruct the way. Want of tin to make
brass; only one good foundry here, deficiency of hands,
etc.; and not least of all, no suitable head in the War
Department. Still, by hook or by crook, we get along.
And, I trust our force, artillery and all, will be strong
for the work to be done. The Lincoln dynasty will
press the war, I am persuaded, to the bitter end. . . .
My duties about harness, etc., may take me to Staunton
and Lynchburg. . . . I long to be back in the
brigade again. All this equipping work is the plague
of my life, but it must be done, however disagreeable."

Gen. Johnston wrote to him about this time:

"COLONEL—I received duly your note in relation to additional
artillery for this army, and asking if you should continue to attend
to that service or return.

"The duty to which you have been attending is, I think, the most
important to which you can attend. I beg you, therefore, to devote
yourself to it until we have reason to believe another action imminent when, of course, you will be necessary in the field. Do not
fail to urge the making of 12-pounder howitzers, etc. . . ."*

Pendleton's duties at this time were not enviable ones
and it was fortunate for the artillery that a minister of
the gospel, with the patience of his calling, was assigned to the task allotted him. Equipments for the
batteries were almost more difficult to supply than guns.
So many skilled mechanics had gone into active service
that workmen enough to operate the larger establishments were scarcely to be found. These establishments
were, therefore, unable to undertake large contracts for
furnishing the needed artillery supplies.

---

*Remainder of this letter calling for S. B. guns in preference to rifled pieces
has been hereinbefore quoted, p. 65.

To contract for them by the dozen or score wherever blacksmiths, wheelwrights, harness makers, and tinners could be found, was the only solution. This was accordingly done throughout the small towns and villages of the Shenandoah Valley and Piedmont country. From them, with the aid of capable workmen here and there, relieved from active service for the purpose, the necessary equipments were procured. Col. Pendleton, whose influence in the pulpit was very great, even preached sermons arousing the people to redouble their efforts in behalf of the army, stirring the spirit of the people to assist as best they might. Old men and boys wrought at the forge and carpenter's bench, while women made tents, uniforms, knapsacks, blankets, bandages, and similar articles.

To visit the small contractors and encourage them in their work, and, wherever it was possible, enlist the efforts of others, was also part of Col. Pendleton's business. For this purpose, it was necessary to see the cannon founders and other operators in Lynchburg, and the harness makers in Staunton. Passing from one place to another in September, from the pulpit, he persuaded his neighbors in Lexington to make for him harness, canteens, and other small but necessary articles.

The want of ammunition for the artillery was even more pressing than that of larger and better guns. Such, indeed, was the absolute scarcity of it in the army at Manassas, that had McClellan been allowed to advance during the late summer and autumn, no sustained resistance could have been made by Johnston. Referring to his deficiencies in respect to ammunition, the latter has stated that until about the middle of August, he had only half enough for a battle,* and on August 24, the ordnance officer of his army telegraphed Pendleton: "Our cannon ammunition is all exhausted except 6-pounder." Again on August 27, "Most of the very small stock of ammunition on hand when you left has been issued, and, in fact, I may say that the

---

*Johnston's Narrative, pp. 60, 61.

stock is entirely exhausted. . . . If the Army had to take the field just now, the scarcity of ammunition would be alarming." As late as September 14, Pendleton was informed by the ordnance officer with the Army that the necessary shrapnel, shell, and cartridges for the artillery had not been received.* Yet, the failure of Gen. Johnston to advance upon and seize Washington during the summer of 1861 has been frequently charged against him as an inexcusable blunder. All through the summer he had continued with the utmost persistence to urge the forwarding of the necessary artillery material and equipment, the government making strenuous efforts, spurred by Pendleton's presence, to fulfill the ordnance requisitions.

On September 5, Mr. Davis wrote Gen. Johnston: "Every effort shall be made to furnish you the howitzers you want. Col. Pendleton will give you details. . . . My means are short of the wants of each division of the wide frontier I am laboring to protect."†

But, in spite of all efforts, the exigencies continued great and pressing. On October 27, the Acting-Secretary of War,‡ writing to Gov. Letcher of Virginia, mentioned the fact that Gen. Johnston was constantly asking for powder and howitzers, and requested the State to turn over to the Army all of both in its possession.

Pendleton's range of duties constantly increased as his efficiency became more apparent. Before his return to the Army early in October, he had even been called upon to provide men as well as guns for the batteries, and for the cavalry. Confidence in his ability to comply with any demands made upon him seems to have been almost unlimited. At last, however, his trying labors in Richmond came to an end and he returned to Manassas, where he took up the more congenial work of perfecting the organization of his command, assisted and advised by his old friend, Gen.

*See *Memoirs of William Nelson Pendleton,* p. 158.
†*Rebellion Records,* Series I, Vol. V, p. 830.
‡Hon. J. P. Benjamin.

Jackson, whose tent he shared, and preaching to his men while he worked. On October 19, he wrote that his artillery corps consisted of 600 men, 450 horses, and 28 pieces of ordnance, more guns being expected[*]

Some idea of the labor performed by the Chief of Artillery and the ordnance officers with the Army may be had from the results obtained by the end of November. At this time, there were 15 batteries assigned to brigades, in addition to the reserve artillery, of which 8 batteries with about 40 pieces were in command of Maj. Walton, and 9 under the direct command of the Chief of Artillery, with 44 pieces and more batteries on the way to join.[†]

Whence had come the vast amount of material, not less than 150 pieces of ordnance alone, required for this force? The total number of guns in the hands of the army after Bull Run, including those captured, was less than 60. The following statement of material secured by him, made out August 17, by Col. Pendleton, before his return to the Army, answers the question, a statement from which we see again that the Bureau of Ordnance, C. S. A., had not as yet begun to supply the armament.[‡]

"STATEMENT OF GUNS, CARRIAGES, CAISSONS, ETC., ORDERED

CARRIAGES AND CAISSONS

Talbott & Bro., Richmond, Va., thirty 6-pounder carriages; no caissons. Ten will be completed in a few days, and 10 each three months till the order is finished.

Philip Rham, Richmond, Va., fourteen 6-pounder carriages, and caissons. Four of each delivered, 4 will be ready in 10 days, and the remaining 6 in three weeks.

J. R. Cato, three 6-pounder carriages, and caissons.

I. & J. Van Pelt, Petersburg, Va., twenty-five 6-pounder carriages, and caissons.

Tappy & Lumsden, Petersburg, Va., twenty-five 6-pounder carriages, and caissons, and five 24-pounder carriages.

---

[*]Pendleton's son, A. S. Pendleton (Sandie), later one of Jackson's aides, and his nephew, John Page, were on his own personal staff.
    [†]*Rebellion Records*, Series I, Vol. V, pp. 1029, 1032. *Memoirs of W. N. Pendleton*, pp. 165, 168, 169.
    [‡]*Memoirs of W. N. Pendleton*, pp. 168, 169.

Ettenger & Edmond, Richmond Va., sixteen 6-pounder carriages, and caissons. Deliveries of 4 of each will be made every two weeks.

H. M. Smith, Richmond, Va., ten 6-pounder carriages, and caissons.

B. F. Harris, Charlottesville, Va., six 6-pounder carriages, and caissons.

J. R. Anderson & Co., Richmond, Va., twenty-four 12-pounder carriages, and caissons.

Philip Rham, six 12-pounder carriages, and caissons, completed in six weeks.

Rice & Wright, Florence, Ala., forty 24-pounder carriages, and caissons.

J. R. Anderson & Co., sixty 24-pounder carriages, and caissons. No limbers.

GUNS

Anderson & Co., thirty-four 12-pounder howitzers, forty-eight 3-inch iron rifled guns, sixty 6-pounder carriages, and caissons, twenty-four 6-pounder iron guns.

Noble Bros. & Co., Rome, Ga., six 6-pounder brass guns, fifty 3-inch iron rifled guns.

Rice & Wright, Florence, Ala., forty 24-pounder howitzers.

J. L. Archer, Black Heath, Chesterfield County, Va., forty 12-pounder howitzers.

F. B. Deane, Jr., & Son, Lynchburg, Va., forty 12-pounder howitzers.

J. L. Archer, eighty 3-inch iron rifled guns.

RECAPITULATION

6-pounder brass guns	6	
6-pounder iron guns	24	30
3-inch iron rifled guns		178
12-pounder howitzers	104	312
6-pounder carriages		219
6-pounder caissons		189
24-pounder carriages, complete		45
24-pounder carriages, no limbers		40

HARNESS

Messrs. Cottrell & Co., Richmond, unlimited order. Contracted through Maj. Smith, New Orleans, 400 sets of harness."

The foregoing detailed statement is given in full because it illustrates better than anything else could what were the material resources from which the artillery equipment in 1861 was drawn. It also evidences the tremendous energy of Johnston's Chief of Artillery. When it is contemplated that many of the manufacturers had probably never seen a gun before they were called upon to make them, that before undertaking the fabrication of these strange articles it was necessary to install machinery and equipment for their making, that detailed drawings of all the parts had to be carefully prepared and furnished them, the accomplishment seems all the more remarkable. It also serves to call our attention to the changes in material and equipment of recent years. Many of the old firms enumerated above are still in successful operation. Long may they continue so. But the fact remains that they could no more turn out modern quick firing guns with their intricate steel carriages, and caissons, than they could manufacture heavenly bodies.

In November, 1860, we have seen that the United States Board of Ordnance officers recommended the conversion of half the heavy ordnance after the James system into rifled pieces.* But the attempt proved a failure, and was soon abandoned. The United States bought various types of rifled pieces when war became imminent, having unlimited means at its disposal. Less than one year after the receipt of Parrott's trial gun by Jackson at the Virginia Military Institute, we find Pendleton actually manufacturing 178 of them, at three different plants, and these in two different States. Johnston had surely been converted.

This brings us down to the winter of 1861 and 1862, when the organization of the Confederate Ordnance Department had become effective and when artillerymen no longer had to "rustle" for themselves, except for horses and harness. The Artillery, Army of Northern Virginia, has been armed and equipped. Henceforth its requisitions are filled either by the proper department to the best of its ability, or upon the field

---

*Report of this board submitted November 1, 1860, pursuant to S. O. No. 144, A. G. O., 1860.

of battle from the plunder of the enemy. Though it was at all times inferior in the quantity and quality of its material and lighter in metal, yet the brains and the industry of the men behind the guns, whether begrimed with the soot of the foundry or the smoke of the battle-field, enabled it to maintain for four terrible years of almost constant warfare a contest then unparalleled in history.

The weapon we have examined. Now let us pass on to the men who wielded it, first inquiring who they were, and then how they bore themselves.

PART II

THE FIELD ARTILLERY OF THE ARMY OF NORTHERN VIRGINIA

ITS FOUNDATION, ORGANIZATION, PERSONNEL, AND TACTICS

CHAPTER I

THE ARTILLERY OF THE EARLY DAYS

In the first part of this work, an endeavor has been made to give the student of the Civil War a conception of the means which enabled the Confederate Government to place artillery in the field. In the treatment of ordnance operations it was not always easy, nor in many instances possible, for the writer to refrain from infringing upon the present subject. The line of demarkation between ordnance operations and material is at best indefinite, and the patience of the reader is craved when repetition perforce occurs, the excuse being offered that historical continuity will be preserved, even though at times its attainment may entail the tedium incident to a seeming literary defect.

Again, it seems necessary, in order to establish the status of field artillery in the United States and its development prior to the outbreak of the Civil War, to begin with the Revolutionary Period.*

Although American artillery dates from the French and Indian Wars, at which time colonial companies were formed in a number of the large cities, the only artillery organization which seems to have existed in the South, prior to the Revolutionary War, was that of Charleston, S. C. The organization of the early colonial Artillery naturally followed very closely that of the Royal Artillery, with which it was associated.

The first regiment arrayed against the Crown was raised by the Colony of Massachusetts, and adopted by the Continental Congress. It consisted of 10 companies, with a greater number of field officers than was

---

*The facts given in the following brief outline of the Artillery, from 1775 to 1859, were extracted almost entirely from Lieut. William E. Birkhimer's *Historical Sketch of the United States Artillery;* the first four volumes of *United States Ordnance Reports,* kindly presented the writer by the present Ordnance Office, through Capt. Oliver L. Spaulding, U. S. F. A.; *Military Policy of the United States,* Upton; *Historical Register United States Army,* etc.; and *The Late War,* Thompson. Citations will not be given from these, as the sources are available to all.

prescribed by the British regulations, and was commanded by Col. Richard Gridley, a retired British officer, under whose advice it was organized. Passing through various reorganizations, this regiment, together with a Rhode Island battery and two batteries from New York, constituted the entire artillery force of the colonial army until after the disastrous Long Island campaign in the summer of 1776. At this time the Corps of Artillery consisted of about 600 officers and men, of which a large number were with the army in the North, there being 88 authorized battalions of infantry. From the latter, Washington and Gates had each been forced to draft about 600 men for the service of the guns.

When Congress resolved to reorganize the Army, the committee in charge called upon the senior artillery officer, Col. Knox, to submit his recommendations. Laying great stress upon the gross disproportion of artillery to infantry, and the almost utter lack of the former, amongst other things that this able officer urged was the creation of arsenals and cannon-foundries, an ordnance bureau for their conduct, and an *academy on the same plan as that at Woolwich, where the whole theory and practice of fortification and gunnery might be taught;* claiming that to the British school the enemy was indebted for their superiority in artillery to all who had opposed them. Knox, then, we are justified in believing, was the first American artillerist to advocate the scientific study of gunnery, and was in a sense the father of the present excellent system of theoretical and practical instruction, though it has taken over a century to grasp the full meaning of his recommendation.

"There ought to be a respectable body of artillery established which shall be equal to all the services of the war. In proportion to every 1,000 men of the marching regiments, there ought to be one company of 60 men, including officers. This number will be found to be small when the various contingencies of the artillery shall be considered. Supposing, then, the army consist of 80 battalions of 726 men each, making nearly 60,000 men, the number of artillery requisite will be 3,360. These may be thrown into two or three battalions, as may be thought best."

The foregoing words were written by Knox near a century and a half ago! Well might they be pondered to-day by Congress! These recommendations made more impression upon the Government at that time than similar ones do now, and it was at once decided to raise 5 battalions of artillery, and the British—not the French system, as is thought by some—was adhered to by Knox in their organization. Many French officers trained in the school of Gribeauval, it is true, sought service in the American Artillery, but they found at its head a man whose views obtained in preference to their own.*

The artillery force contemplated was intended to supply artillery to all the armies in the field, and the 5 battalions authorized were quickly raised, one of them being converted into an artificer regiment, the forerunner of an ordnance organization.† Pursuant to the resolution of Congress, November 26, 1776, one of the artillery battalions embracing 2 companies or batteries was raised by Gen. Charles Lee, in Virginia, the field officers being Col. Charles Harrison, Lieut.-Col. Edward Carrington, and Maj. Christian Holman.

While the 5 battalions raised by Knox were considered to constitute the regular artillery, the colonies had begun to organize companies, as a rule, however, for State defense only, most of them being heavy or coast artillery. The Provincial Congress of South Carolina, in November, 1775, put on foot an artillery battalion of 3 companies of 100 men each, and this organization, in command of Lieut.-Col. Owen Roberts, was taken into continental pay. And, in 1777, a number of Georgia batteries, in command of a French officer, Maj. Roman de Lisle, were turned over to the

---

*See *Military Policy of United States*, p. 29.
†The terms regiment and battalion were used synonymously.

Federal government.* These southern batteries were not subject to service, however, beyond the limits of their States. They were paid by Congress for the sole reason that the States were unable to maintain them; over them the Chief of Artillery exercised no control.

In November, 1778, another reorganization of the Army followed while Washington lay at Valley Forge. For the first time the organization of the various artillery regiments was placed on a uniform basis, the same number of officers and men being assigned to each. The Virginia regiment, now designated the First, was thus increased to 12 batteries by attaching to it two companies from Maryland.† Due to the reduction in the number of its officers, and to inexperienced hands, the Artillery, in common with the rest of the Army, did not thrive during the next few years. Consequently again in 1780 its reorganization was undertaken. It was finally decided to retain the 4 line regiments but to reduce them to 10 companies of 65 enlisted men and 6 officers each, the regimental field and staff consisting of 7 officers.‡ In accordance with the original plan, the First Regiment was again assigned to Virginia. Soon being placed under Gates, it suffered severely at Camden, and in consequence never rejoined the main army, the fragments of the organization remaining in Georgia and the Carolinas until the end of the war. It was not, therefore, at Yorktown; the Second, or New York regiment, and the Fourth, or Pennsylvania regiment, composed the entire force of artillery at that memorable siege.§

Promotion in the continental Artillery was regimental, the power of appointing officers being retained by the States. During the period after peace had been declared, when Congress was making every effort to re-

---

*The famous Chatham Artillery of Savannah had its origin in one of these batteries.
†Before the reorganization the regiment had already been increased to 10 companies.
‡See *Military Policy of the United States*, p. 48.
§The Fourth Regiment served a short time in the South with the First. Except this and the service at Yorktown, the Second and Third served wholly in the North.

duce the Army to a peace footing, the Artillery as it had existed practically dissolved by reason of the expiration of enlistments, etc. Certain duties, however, connected with the incompleted transfer of property by the British in the Northwest, necessitated the retention in service of a battalion consisting of 138 officers and men drawn entirely from the old Second and Third Regiments. With this exception, the old organizations were disbanded as Federal troops, many of the batteries continuing to exist as State militia. In 1784, even the small battalion which had been continued in the service was discharged, leaving one New York and one Pennsylvania battery as the only artillery force in the Federal Army, it being united with some Maryland infantry of the line to form a mondescript regiment, known as the "First American."

It was not until October 20, 1786, when the Army was increased to 2,040 enlisted men, including those of the "First American," that Knox, then become Secretary of War, was able to organize a separate battalion of artillery under a major in which the present artillery organization as a separate arm of the service originated. The personnel of the new artillery battalion was entirely Northern. After frequent changes in its organization, including one merging it with the Engineer Corps, the Artillery as a separate corps of 3 battalions was increased in 1808 (one being a light regiment of 10 batteries.) Many distinguished Frenchmen had served of late in the Engineer and Artillery Corps, but a distinctly American character was now enforced upon the Artillery. It was some time before the regiment could be properly equipped as light artillery, due to the extremes of the economists, but finally the result was accomplished. Winfield Scott, afterwards commander-in-chief, and a Virginian, stood second on the list of captains of this the first properly-equipped American regiment of light artillery. Among its original officers were other Southern men, afterwards distinguished. The several batteries of the regiment recruited in the

South were soon after their formation concentrated at
New Orleans, pending the settlement of the difficulties
with Great Britain.   But instead of trouble being
averted, war became a fact, and January 11, 1812, two
provisional artillery regiments were authorized by the
measure increasing the Army, each regiment having 10
companies, to be known as the Second and Third Regiments, respectively, the old or regular regiment, being
designated the First.

Capt. George Izard, of South Carolina, formerly of
the older regiment, became Colonel, and Capt. Winfield
Scott, and Francis K. Huger, of South Carolina, Lieutenant-Colonels of the Second Regiment.   Like Scott,
Izard rose to be a general officer.   Educated in the best
military schools of France, he had no superior as an
educated and practical officer in America, being much
relied upon as an organizer by the War Department.
When he was promoted in 1813, he was succeeded by
Lieut.-Col. Scott in command of the Second.   Capt.
George Armistead, of Virginia, had been made a major
in the Third.   In 1814, Scott also became a brigadier-
general.

The status of the Artillery as fixed by the Act of 1814,
was that of a corps of 12 battalions, in the formation of
which Izard had been most influential.   The light
artillery was left as organized in 1808, however, and so
also by the Act of 1815, fixing the military peace establishment.   In the latter year, the territory of the
United States was divided into military departments,
five in the North and four in the South, the line of division being roughly that passing east and west through
the capital.   In the attempt to maintain an artillery
equipoise in the two great divisions, the light artillery
and 4 battalions or half of the Corps of Artillery was assigned to the North, and the other 4 battalions to the
South.   This distribution obtained until the artillery
organization as a corps was abolished in 1821, when 4
regiments of artillery were created, of 9 companies each,
only one company of each being designated to be

equipped as light artillery, the old light regiment being broken up with the Corps. This organization continued until the exigencies of the Seminole War, in 1837, caused an increase of one company in each regiment, and in the company strength from 42 to 58 men. The Mexican War again brought an increase of 2 companies to a regiment, 4 additional companies to be equipped as light batteries, the latter provision resulting from the brilliant service of the field batteries in the Rio Grande campaign, where they astonished not only the country, but the Army itself, by their power and efficiency.

The artillery organization of 1847 was maintained substantially unchanged until the Civil War, in spite of many efforts to alter it. Failing to overcome Gen. Scott's opposition to changes in organization, although such men as Bomford, Talcott, and Mordecai had favored them, it was next sought, and successfully, to establish systematic courses of instruction for the Artillery, among them a School of Fire at Fortress Monroe, which has continued to this day.

Such had been the career of the American Artillery up to the year 1861. To be found in its personnel during the period from the Mexican to the Civil War were an entirely disproportionate number of Southern officers, who had not only received professional training in the service of the Regular Artillery, but many of whom had received extensive experience in the Ordnance Department.*

It must not be thought, however, that the militia had played no part in the education of artillery officers during the wars of the Republic, for the Continental troops during the Revolution and the Regulars subsequent thereto were largely supplemented by the militia on all occasions.† In 1792, Congress, seeking to organize the militia, provided that each State should maintain at least one company of artillery, and a number of South-

---

*Artillery officers of the line were regularly detailed to the Ordnance Department in the old service, as in the Confederate Army. As shown in Part I, Gen. Gorgas, Chief of Ordnance, C. S. A., came from the United States Ordnance Department.

†To what extent, see *Military Policy of United States*, Upton.

ern artillery organizations gained experience in the War of 1812.* Included in the force of 10,000 militia, which assembled on the Virginia coast to defend Norfolk against Cockburn and Warren, in 1814, was the Portsmouth Light Artillery, a previously organized battery.† The Chatham Artillery, of Georgia, also saw service in the War of 1812, in the more Southern quarter, as did the Charleston Battery. In 1828, two other famous militia batteries, the Norfolk Light Artillery Blues, and the Fayette Artillery, of Richmond, were organized in Virginia.‡ Out of their early experiences arose traditions which still permeate the spirit of these corps, while they have ever been valuable military assets to the Commonwealths boasting their allegiance. The *esprit de corps* of these old batteries was not only a military but a social factor during the critical period of our country. The proud records which they had established, and their traditions, generated in many a youthful Southern breast the martial spirit and the love of the service which, in large measure, made the Confederacy possible. Who that has mingled with the men of these gallant commands can put a period to the influence which their *ante-bellum* existence exerted upon the naturally martial spirit of the South?

The popularity of the artillery service in the South from the earliest times is well attested by the fact that of the 25,295 volunteer and militia artillerymen who were called out to supplement the corps of 12 depleted regular battalions of artillery, in the War of 1812, an overwhelming proportion of the officers and men came from that territory which afterwards comprised the Confederate and the border States.§

---

*Of the 49,187 militia called into service at the beginning of this war, Massachusetts furnished 208 men and Connecticut none, these States declining to assist in the general defense. Maryland, Virginia, Delaware, and North Carolina furnished 66,376 militia in 1813.

†In 1861 this was the oldest artillery company in the South, and took the field under command of Capt. Cary F. Grimes, winning great distinction.

‡The Norfolk Blues Battery was known as Vickery's or Grandy's Battery in the Civil War. From it was organized Huger's Battery.

§*Military Policy of United States*, Upton, p. 138; and *Historical Register United States Army*, Heitman.

While the volunteers and militia which served in the Mexican War were largely drawn from southern territory, the only artillery organizations from that quarter which served as such, were the "Native American Artillery," and a French battery of New Orleans, known as the "Orleans Artillery." Organized in 1838, the "Native American Artillery" was commanded by Capt., afterwards Gen., E. L. Tracy, being attached to the Washington regiment of New Orleans in 1841. This regiment was a mixed command modeled after the "First American," being composed of infantry, cavalry, and artillery. In command of Col. Persifer F. Smith, the Washington Regiment became the crack corps of the State. The army of occupation dispatched to Corpus Christi, July 26, 1845, was entirely lacking in artillery, the regular mounted batteries not having yet arrived from the North. Gen. Taylor, therefore, called upon Gen. Gaines, commanding the Department of the South, for a force of "skilled volunteer artillerists." All the volunteer batteries in the South responded with alacrity, but two were deemed sufficient, and the "Native American," with its six 6-pounder bronze guns. and Capt. Bercier's Orleans (French) Battery, were selected. These two batteries were placed under command of Maj. Golly of the "Orleans Artillery," and embarked at Jackson Barracks, New Orleans, August 22, 1845, for the front. At the expiration of three months' service on the Texas frontier, the regular mounted batteries having arrived in the meantime, the Louisiana batteries were ordered home. When on May 9, 1846, Gen. Gaines made another call upon the State for volunteer infantry, Capt. Henry Forno, having become Lieutenant-Colonel of the Washington Regiment, the Native American again responded under its new Captain, Isaac F. Stockton, serving as Company A (infantry). The regiment, now in command of Col. J. B. Walton, was the first of the six Louisiana infantry regiments to volunteer, all of which were discharged from the United States service July 21, 1846, their services having been accepted only for six months.

Reorganized in 1852, the "Native American" Battery became theWashington Artillery, Col. J. B. Walton becoming its Captain in 1857.*   At the outbreak of the Civil War there was not a finer organization of citizen soldiery in America. So great was its prestige and influence in the South that, immediately expanding to a battalion of 4 companies, one equipped as a battery, it was ordered to Richmond in time to be fully armed and to participate in the first great encounter of the Civil War.†

So much for the status of artillery in the South at the outbreak of the war. The outlook, while not bright, was, as has been shown, comparatively satisfactory. It would have been quite impossible to begin the study of the Confederate Artillery without at least the foregoing knowledge of its resources of personnel, of the school of experience in which many of its officers had been trained, and of the model after which it was organized.

---

*In Camp and Battle with the Washington Artillery, Owen. Also see historical sketch in the Washington Artillery Souvenir, p. 30.
†Much of the equipment of the battery, including six 6-pounder guns, with ammunition for same, was obtained by the command when it seized the Baton Rouge Arsenal, April 11, 1861.

CHAPTER II

EVEN before officers of the Old Army were invited by the various States to resign and enter their service, and before the Confederate States government offered them offices in the new military establishment, resignations had begun to pour in upon the War Department in Washington. Exactly how many of these officers entered the Southern Artillery it is difficult to determine. Of the 821 graduates of West Point in the United States Army at the close of 1860, 184 resigned and entered the armies of the South, and of the 313 graduates in civil life at the time 99 did the same. The Confederacy thus obtained a total of 283 trained officers, 8 of whom attained the rank of general, 15 that of lieutenant-general, 48 that of major-general, and 11 that of brigadier-general in the Confederacy, leaving but 101 who were given lower rank, and it is fair to assume that most of these became field or staff officers. We know that there were but 4 officers with rank above that of colonel in Lee's Artillery—Pendleton, Alexander, Walker, and Long—three of whom were West Pointers, but few of his artillery field officers and battery commanders were graduates of the United States Military Academy. All the more, then, since the Artillery was not largely officered by former United States officers, are we astounded at the comparative efficiency of its personnel, and constrained to inquire whence came that gallant corps which handled the guns.

The answer is plain, though no historian as yet has ever sought it. The results obtained by Lee's Artillery were not accidental, nor did they flow from the inherent quality of Southerners as artillerymen. Artillery is a science, as pointed out by Gen. Knox during the Revolution, as understood by the founders of Woolwich, and as perceived by the "Grand Monarch" centuries ago.

War may produce, now and then, a great natural soldier. Such men as Forrest are exceptions, however. They become noted, not because they have had no military training, but for the very reason that they are born with qualities for the development of which in others study and experience are required. Too often we hear the Southern orator refer in eloquent words to the leaders of that division which recoiled only after reaching the fire-wreathed muzzles of Cemetery Ridge, as typifying the inherent martial character of Virginia's sons. At heart, it is true, they were soldiers, but by no means adventitiously so. They were trained soldiers, educated in advance for the service of their country, in a school of arms second to none in this country, that which stood upon the Hudson not excepted. Nearly every field officer who participated in Pickett's charge was an *élève* of the Virginia Military Institute, and a former pupil of the distinguished soldier William Gilham, and of the immortal Jackson himself. In order to grasp the full meaning of this assertion, it is necessary to examine the character of that school.

In 1836, J. T. L. Preston, Esq., conceived the idea of substituting for the company maintained by the State for garrisoning the western arsenal in Lexington, a corps of cadets, who in addition to the duties of an armed guard should pursue a course of scientific and military instruction. Pursuant to this proposal, the Virginia Military Institute, since generally styled "The West Point of the Confederacy," was established by Act of the General Assembly, March, 1839, the first corps being mustered into the State service the following November. The President of the first Board of Visitors, one who had much to do with the original organization of the school, was Col. Claudius Crozet, a Frenchman by birth, a graduate of the great Polytechnic School of Paris, and a distinguished veteran of Napoleon's Grand Army. Before accepting the appointment as Chief Engineer of Virginia, in which office he designed, and put into effect the scheme of her

BRIGADIER-GENERAL ARMISTEAD LINDSAY LONG
CHIEF OF ARTILLERY, SECOND CORPS

physical development, he had for some years occupied the chair of Engineering at the Unites States Military Academy. With scientific attainments of the highest order, and an intimate knowledge of the distinctive organization of West Point, to the upbuilding of which in company with Bernard he had contributed much, he was well fitted to assist in the organization of a school of arms in Virginia. Other members of the Board with military experience were Capt. John F. Wiley, a maimed veteran of the Canadian campaign of 1812, Gen. Bernard Peyton, Gen. Peter C. Johnston, Gen. Thomas H. Botts, and James McDowell, afterwards Governor of Virginia. To these must be added Col. John T. L. Preston, who had originated the enterprise, and who for thirty years was one of the professors of the school. Soon followed the appointment of Gen. W. H. Richardson, Adjutant-General of Virginia at the outbreak of the Civil War, and the veteran soldier William Ligon, vice Peyton and Wiley.

At the outset, it was provided that a certain number of cadets should be appointed by State authority, and the number has since been increased to about 60. Frequent visits were paid the school in its early days by such distinguished scholars as Professors Bartlett, Church, Mahan, and Hardie, of the United States Military Academy. Thus it was moulded closely after the national school. Some idea of its character from the first may be had from a knowledge of the careers of the sixteen cadets who composed the first class to graduate.* Of these, John B. Strange, after a distinguished career as Principal of the Norfolk Academy, was killed at Boonsboro, Md., while in command of a Virginia regiment. William Forbes, a professor in a college in Texas, was killed at Second Manassas while commanding a Tennessee regiment. J. H. Jameson died with the rank of Captain C. S. A., while a prisoner of war. Col. Edmund Pendleton was wounded while in command of a Louisiana regiment; Gen. Wyatt

---

*July 4, 1842.

Elliott commanded a Virginia regiment in the War, served in the State Legislature, and became Rector of the University of Virginia; C. P. Dyerle died before the war while an Assistant Surgeon, U. S. A.; O. M. Knight held the rank of Surgeon in the Confederate Army; William D. Fair became a member of the Senate of California; and Capt. James Marshall commanded a cavalry troop in the Confederate Army.

The military instruction of the school during the first few years of its existence had been solely in the hands of its Superintendent, Col. Francis H. Smith, a distinguished graduate of West Point. With the advice and assistance of the brilliant Crozet, his was the master mind which laid the foundation upon which all its success was based, and by him the school in its formative period was given its character as a real school of arms. Its educational aims were never lost sight of by this illustrious man, nor were the distinctive purposes to which it owed its origin. First, last, and all the time, a cadet must be a soldier, which in the Superintendent's mind was not a requisite in conflict with the education of useful citizens.

We hear much of Jackson as the military genius of the school. Undoubtedly he did much in the preparation of a corps of officers for the Confederacy, but he was not appointed Professor of Natural and Experimental Philosophy until March 21, 1851, and his military duties were restricted to artillery instruction. Long before this great soldier took up his work in Lexington, Lieut. William Gilham, a distinguished graduate of West Point, who had gained distinction in the army of Gen. Taylor, in the battles of Palo Alto, and Resaca de la Palma, had been appointed Commandant.*

As a military instructor and drillmaster, Maj. Gilham had no superior. Quick, accurate, and self-possessed, he had a magnetic power of command, which in the opinion of many made the drill of his battalion of cadets superior even to that of the West Point corps.

---

*Appointed in 1846 as Major and Commandant, and head of the Department of Physical Science.

He also excelled as a teacher, having been three years assistant to Prof. Bartlett at the National Academy. So celebrated had Gilham become as an organizer and tactician that his manual of instruction for the volunteers and militia, including the three arms, was adopted by the Confederate Government in preference to all other works of the kind.

Before 1861, the Corps numbered over 200 cadets, and in April of that year it was ordered to Richmond in command of Maj. Jackson, its members to be assigned to duty as drillmasters for the volunteers then assembling at Camp Lee. Soon the Corps dissolved by the appointment of the cadets as officers throughout the Army. But their work had been well done and their drill squads formed the army which overthrew McDowell at Bull Run. The cadets not only drilled the green companies of volunteers, but they were largely responsible for the equipment and organization of the troops, including the batteries, furnishing a large proportion of the staff officers for the Army, a number of them taking part in the battle of Bull Run before they were commissioned.* Though their work has not attracted due notice from the historian, it was well appreciated by Lincoln, who, when asked by a United States Senator in the early part of the war, why he had not put an end to the rebellion, is said to have answered that there was a certain military school in Virginia which made it impossible. Certainly no one can estimate the value of the service which the school rendered the Confederacy at this time in welding the raw levies into shape, and furnishing to the Army as a whole a nucleus of trained and educated young officers.

But so apparent to the Confederacy was the need of the institution as a training school for its officers that immediate steps were taken by the State to reopen it after the first crisis had passed, and in 1862 its regular work was resumed. Upon its parade ground were marshalled the scions of nearly every distinguished family

---

*Three were killed in this battle: Moore, Moffett, and Norris.

of the South, from Texas to Maryland, from Missouri to Florida, then as to-day; nor were these youths content to bide the time of graduation. The wounded officers ordered back to the Institute to drill and instruct the Corps filled their boyish breasts with such ardor, and such a longing for active service, that the problem arose how to keep them in hand. Many deserted to face the enemy. Hundreds who never graduated flocked to the combatant forces in the field. Nor were those who remained deprived of all chance of seeing active service, the Corps being repeatedly called upon for duty in the Valley of Virginia, and on the various defensive lines of the State. Already, in 1859, the Corps had been ordered by Gov. Wise to Harper's Ferry, as a part of the State force present at the execution of John Brown.* After the reorganization of the Corps in 1862, it was sent to the support of Jackson at McDowell, and took part in the pursuit of Fremont's Army as far as Franklin. Then came in 1864 the battle of New Market, in which the cadets saved the day for Breckinridge by a superb charge, unsurpassed for gallantry in the annals of war, losing 57 of their number, including 9 killed, a loss of 20 per cent of those engaged.†

The Institute was completely demolished by Gen. D. H. Hunter, the following month, June, 1864, when the Corps was assigned to duty with the cavalry command of Gen. John McCausland, who fell back before the invader upon Lynchburg, at which point the Federal force was checked and driven off. Ordered to Richmond, the Corps soon found itself on the Richmond lines before Grant, being dispersed only when the Capital of the Confederacy was evacuated, not to be assembled until the fall of 1865. The Corps organization had been throughout that of a battalion of infantry of 4 companies, and a battery of artillery.‡

---

*For a graphic description of the event, by Col. Preston, see *History of the Virginia Military Institute*, Wise.
†In addition to the 5 cadets killed on the field of battle, 4 died within a month from wounds received.
‡Only 1 section of cadet artillery took part in the Battle of New Market.

Besides the most thorough instruction in the art of war, embracing all arms, practical artillery instruction under Jackson had been given for nearly a decade, not less than 600 cadets having been instructed in this time in the theory and practice of gunnery.

At the outbreak of the war, every inducement was offered graduates of West Point to enter the Confederate Army, 182 attaining the rank of general officer during the first year of their service. Up to June, 1861, there had been 554 graduates of the Institute, and 1,210 matriculates who had served one year or more as cadets. Of this number, there were not more than 1,100 available for military service, and three-fourths of these were under 30 and half under 25 years of age, for the school had been in existence but 22 years.* West Pointers were naturally preferred to Institute men by the authorities in order to reward them for resigning from the United States Army. But at the time of the reorganization of the Army, Institute men won the recognition due them, the efficient military organization of the school with its distinctive scientific courses of instruction being then fully appreciated.

We have seen that West Point sent a total of but 283 officers to the Southern armies. Statistics are instructive, if dry at times, but in this case they will enable us to estimate the comparative influence of the two schools upon the military career of the Confederacy. While the records of the Institute are not complete as to the matriculates up to 1861, they show that the school produced 3 major-generals, 17 brigadier-generals, 92 colonels, 64 lieutenant-colonels, 107 majors, and over 300 captains, besides a host of junior officers. This list, incomplete as it is, comprises a total of 20 general officers, and 263 field officers, an overwhelming proportion of whom served in the Army of Northern Virginia. Among the generals were such men as Mahone, Rodes, Wharton, Echols, R. L. Walker, Colston, J. R. Jones, Garland, Lane, McCausland, and Munford,

*The number of graduates during the decade 1851-1861 was double that of the preceding 10 years; the proportion of matriculates much larger.

most of whom were mere youths.*   Among the field-
officers were Col. Walter H. Taylor, Gen. Lee's Ad-
jutant-General, Col. Edwin J. Harvie, Gen. Johnston's
Inspector-General, Col. Briscoe G. Baldwin, who suc-
ceeded Gen. Alexander as Chief of Ordnance, A. N. V.,
Cols. Thomas H. Carter, Stapleton Crutchfield, and
R. Preston Chew, Chiefs of Artillery of Jackson's,
Early's, and Stuart's commands, respectively, and
Col. A. R. H. Ranson, Assistant Chief of Ordnance,
C. S. A. Gen. R. Lindsay Walker, of the Class of 1845,
was Chief of Artillery of Hill's Corps.

The Institute furnished 1 brigadier-general, Carrington, 1 colonel, 2 lieutenant-colonels, 3 majors, and 2
lieutenants to the Northern Army, all save one of the
officers being from the western part of the State, now
West Virginia.

In the Mexican War, an incomplete list shows that
one of her graduates was a major, 2 were captains, and
15 or more were lieutenants, 3 of whom were killed in
action. The school had then been in existence but seven
years.

Since 1865, the school has furnished nearly 200
officers to the United States Army, Navy, and Marine
Corps, there being in 1912 over 100 holding commissions
in the Army alone. The average number commissioned
each year since 1898 is 12.

In the Spanish-American War, the Southern volunteers included many Institute men, a very incomplete
list showing 6 colonels, 2 lieutenant-colonels, 9 majors,
and more than 100 officers of junior rank.

In the National Guard of the country, imperfect
records show that there have been 2 major-generals, 7
brigadier-generals, 20 colonels, 10 lieutenant-colonels,
12 majors, more than 100 captains, 12 State adjutant-
generals, 2 inspector-generals, 1 surgeon-general, and
1 judge-advocate-general. These figures are up to

---

*Among the other generals were Payne, Terry, Terrill, J. A. Walker,
Slaughter, Rives, Fry, Elliott, Bass, Vaughan, Penn, and A. C. Jones.

1909. An immense number have since joined the organized militia, due to the increasing interest of the country therein.

From the foregoing we see that whether the remark attributed to Lincoln is authentic or not, well might it have been founded upon fact. We are also able to see the gross fallacy of the current belief that West Pointers and untrained civilians, with a few exceptions, led the men of Lee's Army. While the enlisted men were citizen soldiers, the Confederacy owed more than can ever be determined to the Virginia Military Institute, and the pupils of Smith, Crozet, Gilham, and Jackson.* Particularly was this true of the artillery of that army in which Carter, Crutchfield, Latimer, Chew, Nelson, Barton, Shields, Rouse, Baldwin, Ranson, Thomson, Carpenter, Ford, Harman, Keiter, Ker, Macon, Otey, Rogers, Selden, Porter, Truehart, Thornton, Waddey, Stanard, Moorman, Flowerree, Hutter, Lynch, Oliver, Cutshaw, Paris, Cunningham, Reverley, the Browns, Smiths, and Johnstons were a few of the field officers and battery commanders among the graduates of the school, who attained distinction in the service of the guns.

Before dismissing the subject of the influence of the Virginia Military Institute upon the success of the Confederate arms, it would seem proper here to mention what, to the writer, has always explained, in great measure at least, the wonderful performances of Jackson's troops. One frequently finds the historian alluding to the ability of Jackson to exact greater sacrifices from his officers and men than is customary, and endeavoring to analyze the character of the man in order to arrive at the reason for this exceptional power on his part. That he possessed a remarkable character and unusual ability to command is unquestioned. Indirectly these traits explain his success, but there is a more direct ex-

---

*In the Superintendent's Report of 1863, an incomplete list of losses in service among the Alumni of the Institute appears as follows: Officers killed, 86; wounded 85; total, 171, including 4 general officers, 36 colonels, 22 lieutenant-colonels, 41 majors, and 94 officers of lesser rank. Can West Point show such a record up to this time?

planation. Stonewall Jackson, besides being inherently
great, had the good fortune to exercise command over,
and to be associated with armies the very backbone of
which consisted of young men who had but recently
borne the relation to him of the pupil to a beloved tutor.
The full import of this fact becomes more apparent
when it is recalled that nearly 300 field officers alone in
the Army of Northern Virginia, distributed among the
three arms, besides not less than an equal number of
junior officers, had for varying periods been closely associated with him, and subjected to the influence of his
personality before they were called upon to follow or
coöperate with him upon the field of war. They were
his children, his wards, and knew each and every whim
of the leader, for whom only the highest respect was
entertained. In him they reposed that sublime confidence which knows not reservation, content to rely upon
the judgment of one who in the closest relations of life
had never failed them in the past. Unconsciously, perhaps, but if so, then all the more thoroughly, they had
absorbed his teachings, and become able to follow the
habit of his mind. When his first successes crowned
him with a halo of military glory they, who had already
accorded him the fullest measure of confidence, en-
throned him as the special object of their pride. From
the very first Jackson's success was redolent of glory
for a host of followers who held him up to the admiring
world as their own tutelary genius. So far as they were
concerned it was not an unfamiliar general whose
orders bade them follow and suffer and die upon the
field of battle. Their leader was Maj. Jackson, and
they were cadets as of yesterday, each vying with the
others to merit the favor of his approving eye. The
stern, and occasionally harsh, drillmaster of former days
had become a leader of acknowledged ability, and they
had become the company, the battery, the battalion, the
regimental, yea, the brigade leaders in such numbers as
to leaven the entire army, and to transmit to the whole,
receptive as it was, their own spirit of pride and de-

votion. Not only was this true, but to no one was it so well known as to Jackson himself. Conscious of the sincerity of his own purpose, confident of the power he held, and that no demand he might make would fail to elicit the fullest possible response from his men, in this spirit it was that at Chancellorsville, the supreme hour of his life, having given his commands, he viewed with pride the army which swept before him to execute his bidding, and, in the joy of a commander who felt the responsive throb of his army's pulse, exclaimed, "The Virginia Military Institute will be heard from to-day." The remark is capable of but one reasonable interpretation. Other constructions may be placed upon it, but the true one is that Jackson, surrounded by Rodes, Colston, Crutchfield, and Munford, all of whom had been his associates at the Institute, and closely scrutinizing the countenances of his men as they filed past him, saw in the faces of his youthful but seasoned field-officers something portentous of more than the usual *élan* of his troops; yes, from the eyes of the regimental, battalion, and company leaders, a host of whom he had guided to manhood's estate, bearing as they were the burden of his fame, flashed a mute assurance that nothing save death would deter them in executing his behest. And so, when smitten by fate at the hour of his greatest glory, it was not his officers alone who lamented his loss, but a multitude of his children, whose hearts were wrung with anguish as they gazed upon his fallen form. No mere loss of an heroic leader was this to an army, but a wound which tore the very heart strings of its men, many of them regarding the blow as prescient of the future.

Without desiring in any respect to detract from the fame of the man who, deprecating the advent of fratricidal strife, yet could throw away his scabbard, let us ask where in all the history of war was there another so fortunately circumstanced as was Jackson?*

---

*The following incident, illustrating the character of Jackson, is related on the authority of Gen. Henry T. Douglas: "After Lincoln's election, the papers were filled with discussions as to the probable outcome and the possibility of

It has been reiterated by such military philosophers as Bulow, Jomini, Willisen, Clausewitz, Moltke, Von der Goltz, Henderson, and Balck, that the moral force, is the preponderant one in war. The moral force which gives men the will-power to overcome all obstacles, to shrink from no danger, and to strive for victory at any cost, emanates in those sentiments which inspirit men to become courageous soldiers. "In a general way, these sentiments are, religious fanaticism, patriotism, enthusiasm for a commander, discipline, and, most of all, confidence resulting from experience."* The prestige of Jackson gave him complete moral ascendancy over his men, and that prestige was decidedly the outgrowth of an experience which many of his subordinates had gained with him, his officers comprising the psychological or suggestive medium by which the spirit of confidence in and enthusiasm for the commander was generated in his army. "The best obeyed commanders are neither the best instructed, the most intelligent, the most paternal, nor the most severe, but are those who have innate or acquired prestige. . . . It is because of it that his suggestions take on an irresistible power, that he is able to throw his soldiers against the enemy in an enthusiastic assault. and that he can stop with a gesture the first fugitives, transforming them into heroes."† The suggestions contained in the foregoing remarks about the personal power of Jackson as a soldier may be followed up with benefit by the military student. His circumstances as a leader were in a psychological sense fortuitous.

war between the sections, and the *New York Herald* was read with great interest. Ned Cunningham was an assistant professor to Maj. Jackson at the Institute, and he told me that one night he and Maj. Jackson were sitting in his section room absorbed in reading the papers. Neither had spoken for some time, when Ned put to Maj. Jackson this question: 'Major, would you like to see war?' He said Jackson stopped reading the paper and for five minutes hung down his head before replying. He then looked up, and, in a low and deliberate tone, said: 'Capt. Cunningham, as a Christian I wouldn't like to see war,' and then raising his voice until it rang out like a bugle call, with eye flashing and every fiber of his body filled with excitement, added, 'but as a soldier, sir, I would like to see war.' "

*Psychology of War, Eltinge, p. 64.
†Ibid., p. 70. For *Psychology of War* see *Études sur le Combat*, Dupicq; *Psychology du Combat de l'Infantere*, Louque; *Les Realites du Combat*, Daudignac; *Actual Experiences in Warfare*, Solaviev.

CHAPTER III

HAVING examined the experience which the South
had had in the service of artillery, and what material
there was for its officers, it is time to consider the steps
taken by the Confederate authorities for the organization of the artillery of the army in Virginia.

On December 28, 1860, the State of South Carolina
seceded from the United States of America, followed
in January, 1861, by Mississippi, Florida, Alabama,
Georgia, and Louisiana. The Congress of these States
assembled in Montgomery, Ala., February 4, 1861, and
ratified the Constitution of the Confederate States of
America four days later.

The only material of war possessed by this new
government was that held by the various States of the
Confederacy, and immediate military measures were
taken to provide for the public defense. On February
20 and 21 acts were passed providing for munitions of
war and establishing a War Department, respectively,
and on the 28th, one creating the Provisional Army,
C. S. A. This last Act authorized the President to take
charge of all military operations in the various States, to
provide for their common defense, to receive from the
States the arms and munitions, the forts, arsenals, etc.,
which they had seized from the United States, and such
other arms and munitions as they might desire to turn
over and make chargeable to the central government,
and to muster into the Confederate service such State
forces as might be tendered, or which might volunteer,
with the consent of their States, for a period of not less
than a year, unless sooner discharged. State forces accepted by the President were to be received with their
own officers, vacancies occurring thereafter to be filled by
appointment of the President, and the pay and allow-

ances of all were to be as prescribed for the Army of
the Confederacy. March 6, another Act for the establishment and organization of the Confederate States of
America was passed, declaring the military establishment to consist of a corps of artillery, 6 regiments
of infantry, 1 regiment of cavalry and the staff departments already established by law.

The Corps of Artillery which, as in the old service, was
charged with ordnance duties, was to consist of 1
colonel, 1 lieutenant-colonel, 10 majors, and 40 companies of artillery.* The company organization was
1 captain, 2 first lieutenants, 1 second lieutenant, 4
sergeants, 4 corporals, 2 musicians, and 70 privates, or
a total personnel of 3,072 for the Corps. Such portion
of the force as the President deemed expedient was
authorized to be equipped as light artillery with 6 pieces
to a battery.

The monthly pay of the Artillery was fixed as follows: colonel, $210.00; lieutenant-colonel, $185.00;
major, $150.00; captain, $130.00; first lieutenant,
$90.00; second lieutenant, $80.00; adjutant (detailed
from among first lieutenants), $10.00 in addition to pay
of his grade. Officers of artillery serving in the light
artillery, or performing ordnance duties, were to receive the pay of cavalry officers, which was the same
as that of the Artillery for field-officers, but for captains,
$140.00; first lieutenants, $100.00; and second lieutenants, $90.00. The monthly pay of enlisted men in
the light artillery was declared to be the same as that
for the cavalry, namely: sergeant-majors, $21.00; first
sergeants, $20.00; sergeants, $17.00; corporals, musicians, farriers, artificers, blacksmiths, $13.00; privates,
$12.00. The President was authorized to enlist as
many master armorers, master carriage makers, master
blacksmiths, artificers, and laborers for ordnance service as he might deem necessary, not exceeding 100 men
in number, all of whom were to be attached to the Corps
of Artillery. The master workmen were to receive

---

*Some of these were to be artificer companies.

$34.00 and the others $20.00, except artificers and ordinary laborers whose pay was fixed at $17.00 and $13.00 per month, respectively.

The Articles of War and Regulations for the Army of the United States were adopted *in toto,* with the exception that two slight changes were made in the former.

The following August an Act was passed increasing the Corps of Artillery to the extent of 1 lieutenant-colonel and 2 majors. But even this increase proved inadequate, for the limitations which had been imposed by law upon the number of field-officers in the Artillery rendered it impossible to reward conspicuous service by promotion or to take advantage of the abilities of certain artillery officers by placing them in positions of important command. While the act creating the Corps did not contemplate the organization of field batteries into battalions and regiments, which had not up to that time been united to form such large units, the regular practice being to assign individual batteries to brigades, yet, the President was empowered to so unite light batteries when tendered in separate companies, should he deem it advisable. This power on the part of the Commander-in-Chief was appealed to by the Secretary of War, in November, 1861,* and in order to remedy the defect arising out of the lack of authority for the appointment of officers to command the larger units, it was recommended that Congress should immediately pass an act providing for additional artillery officers in the Provisional Army, and the volunteer corps, not to exceed in number 1 brigadier-general for every 20 batteries, 1 colonel for every 10 batteries, 1 lieutenant-colonel for every 6 batteries, and 1 major for every 4 batteries, without reference to the number of batteries under the actual command of the officers so appointed. This wise recommendation was carefully considered, and soon the increase was authorized.† Again, the following spring, the Artillery Corps was increased by

---

*J. P. Benjamin to the President, November 30, 1861, *Rebellion Records,* Series IV, Vol. I, p. 761.
  †Act approved January 22, 1862. *Rebellion Records,* Series IV, Vol. I, p. 867.

an act authorizing the appointment of 80 captains and first lieutenants in the Provisional Army for ordnance duties, a measure, which had great effect upon the line by relieving it of a burden of details.* But so extensive were the operations of the Bureau of Ordnance in its various branches of activity, that even this increase did not relieve the line of the onus of ordnance work, and the following fall the appointment of 70 additional artillery officers in the Provisional Army for ordnance duty was authorized.†

The fact that the appointment of brigadier-generals and additional field-officers in the Artillery Corps was authorized in January, 1862, does not mean that the field artillery was organized at that time into battalions, regiments, and brigades. This was not to come until after the disastrous lesson yet to be learned at Malvern Hill. Until that time batteries acted more or less independently with their brigades.

In 1861, a battery of light artillery of 6 guns consisted of 1 captain, 2 first lieutenants, 2 second lieutenants, 1 sergeant-major, or first sergeant, 1 quartermaster-sergeant, 6 sergeants, 12 corporals, 2 buglers, 1 guidon, 2 artificers, and from 64 to 125 privates. The organization of a battery of 4 guns was the same except that but 1 first lieutenant, 4 sergeants, and 8 corporals were prescribed therefor.‡ From the foregoing, it will be seen that the personnel of a light battery in 1862 was not dissimilar to that of the present day.

In the early part of the war, the material of a battery consisted of as many as 8 pieces, the company being divided into as many platoons as there were guns. Six pieces were considered to constitute the most desirable armament, four of which were ordinarily 6-pounder S. B. guns, and two of which were 12-pounder howitzers. As the 3-inch iron rifle made its appearance it was generally substituted for the 6-pounder guns. The regu-

---

*Act approved April 21, 1862. *Rebellion Records*, Series IV, Vol. I, p. 1080.
†Act approved September 16, 1862. *Rebellion Records*, Series IV, Vol. II, p. 198.
‡G. O. No. 81, A. & I. G. O., November 1, 1862, *Rebellion Records*, Series IV, Vol. II, p. 153.

lations as to the material of a battery, however, were perforce departed from and batteries possessing from 2 to 8 pieces were employed.* Each piece of a battery had its own caisson, which together constituted a platoon, and 2 platoons formed a section, the reverse of the present organization. To fully mount a light battery of 6 pieces with six-horse teams, 84 animals were required. The cannoneers being mounted, 149 horses were required to mount a horse artillery battery. These figures do not include the teams for forges and battery wagons.

It should be said here that the regulation complement of horses was seldom possessed by a battery, especially towards the close of the war when draught animals were no longer to be found on the farms. There was, of course, no adequate remount system in effect, and horses and mules for the mounted and transport services had to be impressed wherever found. Nothing became so tempting a prize to the Confederate artillerymen as the sleek teams of the enemy. With their capture in view, and in order to prevent their withdrawal from the field in the event of a successful issue of the fight, certain teams of a Confederate battery were so disposed in advance as to be available for the purpose of dashing with their riders in among the hostile teams, and securing them during the excitement.† This method was often successful, and caused the drivers of a battery to become as active in a combat as their gunners.

---

*In 1861 Carter's Battery was equipped with 2 S. B. bronze 6-pounders, one 12-pounder bronze howitzer, and one 3-inch iron rifle. The Washington Artillery when it arrived in Virginia, composed of 4 companies, was armed with 6 bronze 6-pounders, 2 bronze 12-pounder howitzers, and 1 iron 8-pounder rifle. The Letcher Artillery, a battery, fought until after Antietam with 2 bronze 6-pounder guns.
†G. O. No. 90, A. & I. G. O., November 11, 1862, *Rebellion Records,* Series IV, Vol. II, p. 194.

CHAPTER IV

THE VIRGINIA VOLUNTEERS

WE have examined the organization contemplated by the Confederate States Government. In the meantime the State of Virginia had not been idle in the organization of her field artillery.

Until April 21, 1861, the personnel of the volunteer artillery of Virginia which had been armed consisted of but 780 men, a large portion of whom comprised heavy batteries without guns.* The personnel of the militia regiments prescribed by law had not been mustered into the service. The organizations existed merely on paper, except as to the few volunteer companies which under the militia acts automatically attached to one of the five territorial or divisional artillery regiments. In the Fourth Regiment, for instance, the Fayette Artillery, of Richmond, was the only battery actually armed and equipped.†

In the First Regiment were two batteries, not however fully equipped as light batteries, the Portsmouth Light Artillery and the Norfolk Light Artillery Blues. These two batteries, the former with 4 S. B. iron 6-pounders, and the latter with 4 brass 12-pounder howitzers, were ordered out by the Governor April 19, 1861, and were therefore the first batteries in the field. The Portsmouth Battery, in command of Capt. Cary F. Grimes, was stationed at the Naval Hospital during the evacuation and burning of the Gosport Navy Yard by the Federal authorities, being sent to Hoffler's Creek in May as part of the Confederate force guarding the line from Craney Island to the mouth of the Nansemond River. The Norfolk Battery, in command of Capt.

---

*Rebellion Records, Series I, Vol. II, p. 940. There were also at this time but 3,350 cavalry and 7,920 infantry troops armed in the State, making a total armed force of 12,050.

†Letter of Col. T. H. Ellis to Gov. Letcher, Rebellion Records, Series IV, Vol. I, pp. 300, 301.

Jacob Vickery, was sent down the harbor to Craney Island on the morning of the 20th, to apprehend the Baltimore boat supposed to have on board a number of Federal marines for the Navy Yard. From this battery were created Huger's Battery, and Company H 16th Virginia Infantry, the latter being reorganized as a light battery March 26, 1862. In May of that year, when Norfolk was evacuated, these batteries were ordered to Petersburg, where they were rearmed, and then joined the Army of Northern Virginia, having had a number of experiences with Federal gunboats while on duty about Norfolk.*

On April 23, Robert E. Lee was appointed Major-General, Virginia Volunteers, and in *General Orders No. 1* of that date, assumed command of the military and naval forces of Virginia. On April 26, Maj.-Gen. Jos. E. Johnston, Virginia Volunteers, was assigned to the command of the forces gathering about Richmond, Maj.-Gen. Walter Gwynn, to the command of those about Norfolk, and on the 28th, Col. Thomas J. Jackson relieved Maj.-Gen. Kenton Harper, in command of the mobilization camp at Harper's Ferry.† These officers were directed to receive, and to muster into the service such organizations as might volunteer. Lieut.-Col. John McCausland was also sent to the Kanawha Valley, and specially directed to organize a light battery, for which the guns would be forthcoming.

At this time there was but one light battery, mounted and equipped as such, in the field, the Governor having ordered the newly raised Purcell Battery of Richmond, in command of Capt. Reuben Lindsay Walker, with its four 3-inch Parrott rifles, to Aquia Creek, early in the month. This battery was named after Mr. Purcell of Richmond who, when hostilities became imminent, had out of his own pocket equipped the battery. Its first

---

*Grimes' Battery was given 2 iron rifles, making 6 pieces in all, and the Norfolk Blues, now become Grandy's Battery, was given 2 3-inch iron rifles, 2 12-pounder brass howitzers, and 2 Napoleons.
   For facts about Norfolk Light Artillery Blues, and Portsmouth Light Artillery, see *History of Norfolk County, Virginia, 1861-65*, Porter, pp. 38-247.
   †See G. O. No. 3, S. O. Nos. 2 and 7, *Rebellion Records*, Series I, Vol. II, pp. 783, 787. Ibid., p. 788.

captain afterwards became Chief of Artillery, Hill's Corps, with rank of brigadier-general. Not having been formally mustered into the service of the State, it was now ordered back to Richmond to refit and recruit, its total personnel numbering but 40 men.

There were at this time three other light batteries being drilled and equipped in Richmond. The old Fayette Artillery of Richmond, with its 4 pieces, (it was named in honor of LaFayette, having had its origin about the time of his visit to America), was fully recruited by its Capt. H. C. Cabell.* The Richmond Howitzers, commanded by Capt. Geo. W. Randolph, a battery which had been raised and sent to Harper's Ferry just after the John Brown raid in 1859, had on its rolls 225 men, and Latham's Lynchburg Battery, with 4 pieces, had also reported for duty at the instruction grounds at Richmond.

Upon the suggestion of Capt. Alexander, Capt. Randolph took steps to organize a battalion with his surplus men, and on April 21, the First, Second, and Third Companies of Richmond Howitzers were mustered into the service of the State as a battalion, Randolph being appointed its major. The batteries were commanded by Capts. J. C. Shields, J. Thompson Brown, and R. C. Stanard, respectively.

There were now in the State 6 light batteries, in addition to the Cadet Battery, which had arrived in Richmond with the Corps from Lexington; the organization and instruction of these was assigned to Col. J. B. Magruder, but recently resigned from the old service. This officer had commanded the regular battery at the battle of Chapultapec, in which Jackson had served with such gallantry as a lieutenant. He was an accomplished artilleryman in every sense of the word, and well qualified to perform the duty assigned him. Immediate steps were taken by him to secure the 356 horses necessary to complete the complement of the light batteries, and the saddles, bridles, halters, picket ropes,

---

*He subsequently became colonel, and commanded a battalion of artillery in Longstreet's Corps.

girths, blankets, horseshoes, and forage, which the exigencies of the moment demanded. He also urged that 10 cadets be detailed to drill and instruct the batteries, and that as many former artillery officers of the service as could be spared should be ordered to report to him.* In response to the latter request, Capt. E. P. Alexander, of Georgia, who had been in the United States Engineer corps, was assigned to him for duty, and assisted by a large detail of cadets took charge of the drilling of the batteries.

Early in May, the Second and Third Companies of Richmond Howitzers, under Maj. Randolph, and Cabell's Battery, were ordered off to Yorktown with Magruder, leaving the entire work of organization to Alexander and the cadets.

There were at this time enough field pieces in the State, including thirteen 3-inch Parrott rifles, one of which was in possession of the cadet battery, to provide material for 20 batteries, though the necessary harness, caissons, and equipment were entirely lacking. A minimum of 1,000 horses was therefore needed in addition to those already provided in order to put the available guns in the field.

The Ordinance of Secession was passed April 17, 1861. Before May 1, not only had the Convention authorized a Provisional Army of 10,000 men, but arrangements were made to call out 50,000 volunteers if necessary, and on May 3 the call was made by proclamation of the Governor.†

That the Commander-in-Chief intended to take full advantage of the available field artillery material is evidenced by the fact that on the day this proclamation was issued he directed Gen. P. St. George Cocke, in command of the district comprised of the eighteen Piedmont counties, to raise 8 light batteries, urging Gen. Ruggles, in command of the Northern Neck section, to raise two.‡

---

*Magruder to Adjutant-General, April 29, 1861, *Rebellion Records,* Series I, Vol. II, pp. 789, 790.

†*Rebellion Records,* Series I, Vol. II, p. 797.

‡Letter of Gen. Lee to Gen. P. St. George Cocke, May 3, 1861, *Rebellion Records,* Series I, Vol. II, p. 797, and letter to Gen. Ruggles, May 4, 1861, Ibid., p. 803.

Col. Jackson, at Harper's Ferry, had already mustered into the service the Rockbridge Artillery, a battery armed with the four 6-pounder bronze cadet guns, from Lexington, but possessing no regular caissons or equipment.* He had also raised 2 companies of artillery for which he urged that horses, material, and equipment be sent, as well as 2 extra 12-pounder howitzers and caissons for the Rockbridge battery.† Occupying the heights along the Potomac, opposite the Point of Rocks, Berlin, and Shepherdstown, he was energetically endeavoring to secure heavy ordnance to defend his line, convinced that the enemy would be well provided therewith in addition to their field guns, some of which he thought would be long range rifled pieces.‡ Jackson's frequent references to rifled guns and his constant endeavor to secure them show plainly what his estimate of their value was even at this time.§

On May 7, the Inspector-General, Col. J. B. Baldwin, was authorized and directed to raise 6 batteries of light artillery, of 4 guns each, from among the Southside and James River Valley counties. Thus, at the very outset, provision was made for the raising and equipping of 25 or more light batteries.

Such ability had Gen. Lee shown in the organization and arming of the Virginia troops, and so confused had the Confederate War Department become with its various commanders, that on May 10, Gen. Lee was authorized to assume control of all Confederate States troops in Virginia.¶ Up to this time the contingents from the South, arriving in the State, had been under the sole command of their own individual leaders. Some of these troops had to be partly armed by the State of Virginia. This was true of the Washington Artillery, the gallant battalion of 4 companies from New Orleans, which arrived in Richmond June 4, with but six 6-

*These had not been taken to Richmond by the Cadet Battery, which now had iron pieces.
†*Rebellion Records,* Series I, Vol. II, pp. 793-809.
‡Ibid., pp. 823, 836.
§See references in Part I.
¶*Rebellion Records,* Series I, Vol. II, p. 827.

pounder bronze guns, two 12-pounder howitzers, and one 8-pounder rifled piece, and with a personnel of nearly 300 men in command of Maj. J. B. Walton, a veteran of the Mexican War.

The Act of May 10, 1861, authorized the President to muster into the service of the Confederate States any companies of light artillery, with such complement of officers as he might see fit, and encouragement of every kind was given the raising of batteries, for up to this time little had been accomplished in the organization of the light artillery.* There were but 6 light batteries actually mounted and on duty in the field, the two batteries of the Howitzer Battalion and Cabell's Battery, which had been sent to Yorktown; Walker's; Pendleton's, and Imboden's batteries which were with Jackson at Harper's Ferry. Most of the batteries which had been raised were yet without material, horses, and equipment.† Yet, the men were being well drilled and disciplined. Within the next 30 days, however, the army of 40,000 men which Virginia had placed in the field included 20 light batteries fully equipped and mounted, with 4 guns each, and a total personnel of near 2,500 men.‡ Up to this time, including a number sent to Missouri, and issued to troops from other States, Virginia had provided 115 pieces of field ordnance.

We are now prepared to understand to some extent what Virginia actually turned over to the Confederacy in the way of artillery material, equipment and personnel on June 8, 1861, when, by proclamation of the Governor, her entire force was legally transferred.

---

*Report of Inspector General, May 23, 1861, *Rebellion Records,* Series I, Vol. II, p. 868.
†Even the Richmond Howitzers were much disorganized by the necessity of using their horses for videttes, there being little cavalry with Magruder.
‡Ibid., pp. 885, 893.

CHAPTER V

ALREADY, on the 14th of May, at Gloucester Point, a section of Brown's Battery of the Howitzer Battalion, in an affair with the Federal gunboat "Yankee," had fired the first shot of the field artillery in Virginia. And, now, on the very day on which the Virginia troops were transferred to the Confederacy, it was to engage in a brush with the enemy on land. Being informed that a marauding party was operating along Back River, Magruder ordered a small detachment of infantry and one gun of Maj. Randolph's Battalion from the lines to drive the raiders off, a single howitzer shell sufficing to disperse the plunderers. Two days later, June 10, occurred the battle of Big Bethel, in which the artillery, armed with a 3-inch Parrott rifle and a number of 12-pounder howitzers, received its real baptism.

The Union force, consisting of between 2,500 and 3,500 men actually engaged, included a section of a regular battery with two 6-pounder S. B. guns, commanded by Lieut. John T. Greble.* The Confederate force engaged numbered about 1,200 men with 5 guns. Advancing boldly against the position which Maj. Randolph had prepared for his guns, the enemy were fired upon at 9:15 A. M., the fight opening with the discharge of a Parrott rifle. Greble promptly replied with his guns, but his fire was wild and ineffective, and was soon silenced by the more accurate rifles of the Confederates. About 11 o'clock a fresh Federal regiment arrived on the field, having dragged another gun with great labor from Hampton. With this piece Lieut. Greble heroically sought to stem the pursuit, but had fired not more than a dozen shots when he was killed and

---

*Battles and Leaders, Vol. II, p. 148, and Report of Gen. D. H. Hill, in "The Confederate Soldier in the Civil War," p. 36.

the gun abandoned, both it and the body of the young officer being gallantly rescued by Capt. Wilson and his company of the Second New York.

In this affair the effect of Randolph's guns was more startling, perhaps, than destructive, the Federal loss being only 18 killed and 53 wounded. But greatly exaggerated reports were at once circulated about the accuracy and power of the new Parrott rifle, which led to its more general introduction in the two armies. The fact remains, however, that Randolph's guns were well served, and whether by superiority in number or in other respects, had completely overwhelmed the regular battery opposed to them. This fact brought great prestige to the Confederate field artillery, and did much to arouse enthusiasm for, and create interest in, the "long arm."

The report of Maj. Randolph of the part played by his command in this engagement is so intensely interesting, and so full of information as to the defects of his artillery material, and so conclusive of the manner of handling the guns, as well as of the real effect of the fire of the new rifled field pieces, employed for the first time at Bethel, that it is given almost in full, especially as it was written almost immediately after the affair and before the facts could be unconsciously perverted by the trickery of time. To an artilleryman, nothing could be more interesting.

"YORKTOWN, June 12, 1861.

"COLONEL—I have the honor to report that in the action of the 10th instant, the Howitzer battalion under my command fired 18 solid shot and 80 shells, spherical, case, and canister, and was injured in the following particulars: A lieutenant and 2 privates were wounded, one severely and 2 slightly; 5 horses and 3 mules were killed or disabled; the Parrott gun (iron rifled) had its linstock splintered, and a musket ball passed through the felloe of the left wheel; a musket ball pierced the corner plate and the partition of the limber chest of one of the howitzers, and lodged against a shell; two poles of caissons, one set of swinglebars, one large pointing ring, a chain for a rammer, and several priming wires were broken, and one of the howitzers was spiked by the breaking of a priming wire in its vent.

"As the position of the pieces was under your own observation, it is only necessary to state that the Parrott gun and one howitzer were posted in the battery immediately on the right of the road leading to Hampton; that a howitzer was placed in the battery erected on the right beyond the ravine, through which a passway was made for the purpose of withdrawing the piece if necessary; a howitzer was posted near the bridge; the rifled howitzer was placed on the left of the road behind the right of a redoubt erected by the North Carolina Regiment, and a howitzer was posted in the rear of the road leading from Halfway House, a howitzer having been previously sent to the Halfway House under the command of Lieut. Moseley.

"Early in the action, the howitzer in the battery on the right, having been spiked by the breaking of the priming wire, was withdrawn from the position, and the infantry supporting it fell back upon the church; but it was subsequently replaced by the howitzer of Lieut. Moseley, which arrived at a later period of the action.

"The ford on the left being threatened, the howitzer at the bridge was withdrawn and sent to that point, and the rifled howitzer was withdrawn from the left of the road and sent to assist in the protection of the rear. The same disposition was subsequently made of the howitzer at the main battery, situated immediately on the right of the road.

"The enemy came in sight on the road leading from Hampton a few minutes before 9 o'clock A. M., and their advance guard halted at a house on the roadside about 600 yards in front of our main battery. Fire, however, was not opened upon them for 10 or 15 minutes, when, from the number of bayonets visible in the road, we judged that a heavy column was within range. The action then commenced by a shot from the Parrott gun, aimed by myself, which struck the center of the road a short distance in front of their column, and probably did good execution in its ricochet. At no time could we see the bodies of the men in the column, and our fire was directed at their bayonets, their position being obscured by the shade of the woods on their right, and two small houses on their left and somewhat in advance of them. Our fire was immediately returned by a battery near the head of their column, but concealed by the woods and the houses so effectually that we only ascertained its position by the flash of the pieces. The fire was maintained on our side for some time by the 5 pieces posted in front of our position; but, as already stated, one of them being spiked and another withdrawn to protect the ford early in the action, the fire was continued with the 3 pieces, and at no time did we afterwards have more than 3 pieces playing upon the enemy. The fire on our part was deliberate, and was suspended whenever masses of the enemy were not within range, and the execution was good, as I afterwards ascertained by a personal inspection of the principal position of the enemy. The cannonade lasted with intervals of suspension from a few minutes before 9 o'clock A. M., until 1:30 o'clock P. M., and the fact that during this time but 98 shot were fired by us tends to show that the firing was not too rapid. The earthworks thrown up by the battalion were struck several times by the cannon shot of the enemy, but no injury was sustained. They fired upon us with shot, shell, spherical case, canister, and grape from 6- to 12-pounders, at a distance of about 600 yards, but the only injury received from their artillery was the loss of one mule.

"We found in front of our main battery, in and near the yard of the small house already mentioned, 5 killed and one mortally wounded by the fire of our artillery. We heard of 2 others killed at Crandall's, about a mile from us, and have reason to believe there were many others. The injury done to our artillery was from the fire of musketry on our left flank, the ground on that side between us and the enemy sinking down so as to expose us over the top of the breastwork erected by the North Carolina Regiment.

"After some intermission of the assault in front, apparently a reënforcement or reserve made its appearance on the Hampton road, and pressed forward towards the bridge carrying the United States flag near the head of the column. As the road had been clear for some time, and our flanks and rear had been threatened, the howitzer in the main battery had been sent to the rear, and our fire did not at first check them. I hurried a howitzer forward from the rear, loaded it with canister, and prepared to sweep the approach to the bridge, but the fire of the Parrott gun again drove them back. The howitzer brought from the Halfway House by Lieut. Moseley arriving most opportunely, I carried it to the battery on the right to replace the disabled piece. On getting there, I learned from the infantry that a small house in front was occupied by sharpshooters, and saw the body of a Carolinian lying 30 yards in front of the battery, who had been killed in a most gallant attempt to burn the house.

"I opened upon the house with shell for the purpose of burning it, and the battery of the enemy in the Hampton road, being on the line with it, and supposing probably that the fire was at them, immediately returned it with solid shot. This disclosed their position and enabled me to fire at the house and at their battery at the same time. After an exchange of 5 or 6 shots, a shell entered a window of the house, increased the fire already kindled until it soon broke out into a light blaze, and, as I have reason to believe, disabled one of the enemy's pieces. This was the last shot fired. They soon afterward retreated, and we saw no more of them.

"The action disclosed some serious defects in our ammunition and equipment, for which I earnestly recommend an immediate remedy. The shell of the Parrott gun have a fixed wooden fuse which cannot be extricated, the shortest being cut for four seconds. The consequence was that the shells burst far in the rear of the enemy and served merely as solid shot. Had they been plugged and uncut fuses furnished, I think that our fire would have been much more effective. The power and precision of the piece, demonstrated by the 30 rounds fired from it, render it very desirable that all of its advantages should be made available. I, therefore, respectfully suggest that the shell be hereafter furnished plugged and the fuses left uncut.

"It is reported to me that the Borman fuses used by one of the howitzers were defective, the shells cut for 5 seconds exploding as soon as those cut for 2.

"The caissons of the Navy howitzers were made by placing ammunition chests upon the running gear of common wagons, and the play of the front axles is so limited that the caisson cannot be turned in the ordinary roads of this part of the country, and wherever the road is ditched, or the woods impassable, it cannot be reversed. There is also great danger of breaking the poles in turning the caisson quickly, as was shown in the action of the 10th inst. I am aware that the expedient of using wagon bodies was resorted to in order to save time, but, as it might lead to great disaster, I recommend that their places be supplied as speedily as possible with those made in the usual way.

"The small size of the limber of the howitzer (Navy) renders it impossible to mount the men, and the pieces cannot move faster than the cannoneers can walk. In a recent skirmish with the enemy, in which we pursued them rapidly, we could only carry 2 men, and having gotten far ahead of the others we had to un-limber and fire with only 2 cannoneers at the piece. The piece having only 2 horses, and the carriages being very light, it is hazardous to mount any person on the limber. I, therefore, recommend that 4 horses be furnished to each Navy howitzer, one for the chief and the other three for the men usually mounted on the limber.

"We have succeeded since the action in unspiking the howitzer disabled by the breaking of the priming wire, but, from the inferior metal used in making our priming wires, we shall have to lay them aside altogether, and I must request that better ones be furnished. At present I can say nothing more of the conduct of the officers and men of the battalion than to express the high grati-fication afforded me by their courage, coolness, and precision, and to ask permission at a future time to call your attention to individual instances of gallantry and good conduct. I have re-quested the commandants of companies to furnish me with the names of such non-commissioned officers and privates as they think especially worthy of notice.

"I am happy at having an opportunity to render my acknowl-edgment to Col. Hill, the commandant of the North Carolina

Regiment, for the useful suggestions which his experience as an artillery officer enabled him to make to me during the action, and to bear testimony to the gallantry and discipline of that portion of his command with which I was associated The untiring industry of his regiment in intrenching our position enabled us to defeat the enemy, with a nominal loss on our side."*

In his report of the engagement, Gen. Magruder wrote: "Whilst it might appear invidious to speak particularly of any regiment or corps where all behaved so well, I am compelled to express my great appreciation of the skill and gallantry of Maj. Randolph and his Howitzer batteries," and D. H. Hill wrote: "I cannot close this too elaborate report without speaking in the highest terms of admiration of the Howitzer batteries, and their most accomplished commander, Maj. Randolph. He has no superior as an artillerist in any country, and his men displayed the utmost skill and coolness."† Neither Magruder nor Hill were ordinarily given to such expressions, both being officers of experience in the old service.

Before the first of July, the various forces assembled at Norfolk, Yorktown, Richmond, Harper's Ferry, and other points, had begun to show the results of the strenuous efforts which had been made to organize, arm and equip them, and some of the commands were attaining to a degree of mobility approaching effectiveness.

May 23, Col. Jackson was superseded in command at Harper's Ferry by Brig.-Gen. Joseph E. Johnston. The force there gathered, consisting of troops from many sections of the South, was promptly reorganized into brigades, as nearly as possible according to States, the whole assuming the name of the Army of the Shenandoah.‡ Col. Jackson, who was soon promoted to brigadier-general, was assigned November 4 to the command of the Virginia Brigade. To this brigade was

---

*Rebellion Records, Series I, Vol. II, pp. 98-101.
†Major George W. Randolph was a graduate of Annapolis, and had served in the U. S. Navy. He was soon appointed Colonel and Chief of Artillery on Magruder's staff; and later became Secretary of War, C. S. A.
‡The Army of the Shenandoah was really the Second Corps of the Army of the Potomac.

very naturally attached the Rockbridge Artillery from Lexington, in command of Capt. Pendleton, a graduate of West Point, who had for years been the Episcopal minister of his town, and an intimate friend of Jackson while the latter was a professor at the Virginia Military Institute.

About the time the Cadet Corps was ordered to Richmond to drill the troops gathering there, the Rockbridge Battery was raised and soon ordered to Harper's Ferry, being given the old bronze 6-pounder guns of the cadet battery, the Corps having taken with it other pieces, including the 3-inch Parrott rifle, with which Jackson had obtained such surprising results in Lexington the year before.* For caissons, the Rockbridge Battery constructed large chests on the running parts of hay wagons, the cadets having taken all the material of their battery except the guns.

The history of the cadet battery which had afforded instruction to so many artillery officers of the Confederate Army, and the guns which were now to be used in battle, is so full of interest that it should be given here.

In 1850, the Adjutant-General of the State ordered the Corps of Cadets to Richmond as the personal escort of President Taylor on the occasion of the laying of the corner-stone of the Washington Monument. So impressed was the old soldier with the bearing of the cadets, that he ordered a field battery of four 6-pounder guns and two 12-pounder howitzers to be cast of bronze, somewhat lighter than ordinary service pieces, with the arms of the State of Virginia thereon, and to be presented to the Cadet Corps. This beautiful battery, known as the "Cadet Battery," is still used for artillery instruction at the Institute. With it a large number of the Confederate artillery officers of note were trained between 1851 and 1861.

After Bull Run, the Rockbridge Artillery was issued rifled pieces captured in the battle, and the cadet guns were returned to Lexington. In the meantime, how-

*See Part I.

ever, the two 12-pounder howitzers of the battery had been issued to Milledge's Battery, one of which was later lost in the Potomac* on the retreat from Antietam. The remaining 5 pieces were captured by Gen. D. H. Hunter in June, 1864, when he destroyed the Institute, and were carried off by him as trophies of war, but were returned to the Corps completely remounted and refitted by Secretary Stanton, in 1865, upon the ardent solicitation of Gen. Smith, the Superintendent. This battery is now undoubtedly the oldest in actual use in the United States.

When on June 15, Johnston withdrew from Harper's Ferry to Winchester, he left Jackson at the front along the Baltimore & Ohio Railroad to observe Patterson's preparations. It was not long before the opposing forces came into contact near Martinsburg, and at Hainesville, a fight occurred on July 2. So well did Capt. Pendleton handle one of the old cadet guns that the reputation which had been acquired by the field batteries at Bethel, at once attached to the Rockbridge Artillery. In a letter to a home paper describing the affair, Pendleton wrote:

"Col. Jackson, with his staff, rode back to the point in the road occupied by my gun, and directed me to withdraw it further back to the rear, to a point better situated. Meantime, the enemy began to ply their artillery with vigor, firing around our little force a number of balls and shells. We, however, quietly took our position and awaited the best moment for opening fire with our single gun (the only one present). That moment arrived when I saw a body of horse, which seemed to be a squadron of cavalry about to charge on the turnpike about a half mile in front of our position. At that body I instantly had the gun directed, with careful instructions how it should be aimed. In another instant the messenger of death was speeding on its way. The effect was obvious and decided. Not a man or a horse remained standing in the road, nor did we see them again. . . . Our next shot was aimed with equal care at one of their cannon, in a field on the left of the road. The effect was scarcely less. The gunners scattered, and I am sure that gun fired no more. David Moore, of Lexington, fired our first gun, and J. L. Massie loaded it. The order from Richmond

---

*Its mate has been used as the evening gun at the Institute since 1865. For loss of the howitzer see Gen. Pendleton's report to Gen. Lee, September 24, 1862, *Memoirs of W. N. Pendleton*, p. 223. Also *Rebellion Records*.

promoting Col. Jackson to a brigadiership has just arrived. He richly deserves it. His part the day of the fight, as heretofore, was admirably performed. The enemy speak admiringly of our artillery firing of that morning; they ascribe it all to 4 rifled cannon, although we fired 8 shot from a common (smooth-bore) 6-pounder."

Thus it is seen that one of the cadet guns fired the first shot in the Valley, and, that the Federal troops were looking for the terrible rifled guns, of which they had recently heard so much, as well as for masked batteries, on every hillside, the press of the country echoing with terrifying accounts of these objects of the popular imagination.

CHAPTER VI

IN the meantime the troops which had been assembled and drilled at Richmond were ordered to Manassas Junction. At this point they were organized, June 20, into a corps of 6 brigades, and placed under Beauregard as commander of the 1st Corps or Army of the Potomac, independent of the 2d Corps or Army of the Shenandoah, in the Valley.

July 13 Capt. Pendleton was appointed Chief of Artillery of the Army of the Shenandoah, with rank of colonel, under authority of the original act creating the Artillery Corps of the Confederacy. He was thus from this time the senior artillery officer of the Army. His abilities as an organizer were well known to Gens. Johnston and Lee, and Mr. Davis, with all of whom he had been a cadet for several years at West Point.* His appointment, however, since he had held only the rank of captain, was not made without misgivings, for the gallant Maj. J. B. Walton, of Louisiana, had been mustered into the service with his battalion with the rank given him by his State, and it was feared lest this officer and his command might consider the elevation of Pendleton as a slight upon them† As stated before, this led to the recommendation on the part of the Secretary of War that additional field-officers in the Corps of Artillery be authorized by Congress, which was done the following January.

Upon being made Chief of Artillery, Col. Pendleton at once assigned the batteries of his corps to brigades as follows:

Pendleton's, or the Rockbridge Battery, 4 pieces, remained with the 1st or Jackson's Brigade; Alburtis'

---

*Memoirs of W. N. Pendleton, Lee, pp. 146, 147.
†See letter of Secretary of War to the President, November 30, 1861, Rebellion Records, Series IV, Vol. I, p. 761.

Wise Battery, 4 pieces, to the 2d or Bartow's Brigade; Imboden's Staunton Battery, 4 pieces, to the 3d or Bee's Brigade; and Groves' Culpeper Battery, 4 pieces, commanded by Lieut. Beckham, to the 4th or Elzey's Brigade. Later Stanard's Thomas Battery joined the 2d Corps.

The Artillery was not to wait long for a chance to test its metal, for on the 18th of July the Federal force resumed its slow advance, reaching Blackburn's Ford, where 2 guns of the Washington Artillery were brought into action against the enemy's cavalry, which promptly withdrew. In the meantime, Richardson's Brigade had gained close contact with Longstreet, who occupied the opposite bank of the stream. Both brigades withdrew in more or less disorder, and were rallied and led back with some difficulty, a few of Longstreet's men, after much wavering, finally crossing the stream and gaining a slight advantage over the enemy, who endeavored to withdraw. At this point a sharp artillery duel, lasting about forty-five minutes, occurred. The Federals engaged 8 guns, two 20-pounder and two 10-pounder Parrott rifles, two 6-pounder guns and two 12-pounder howitzers, which fired 415 rounds. Longstreet brought up 7 guns, four 6-pounders, and three of the converted rifles, which fired 310 rounds of the new Burton and Archer projectiles, all these pieces being from the Washington Artillery.* One of the brass 6-pounders soon became useless on account of an enlarged vent, and the new ammunition used by the rifles was entirely ineffective, although most favorable reports were made about it at the time by the inexperienced officers who conducted the fire.† During the first part of the duel both sides fired wildly, almost at random, neither being able to see much of the other on account of the screens of trees which the opposing guns had sought. But, after a pause, the Federal guns reopened

---

*In Camp and Battle with the Washington Artillery, Owen, pp. 27-28. Military Memoirs of a Confederate, Alexander, p. 24.

†The first competent test of these projectiles a few weeks later showed them to be worthless, and their manufacture was discontinued. They would not fly point foremost, but tumbled and had no range.

BRIGADIER-GENERAL EDWARD PORTER ALEXANDER
CHIEF OF ARTILLERY, FIRST CORPS

with better effect, having taken advantage of the lull to better determine the position and range of Longstreet's guns, and soon practically silenced them. Capt. Eshleman, commanding one of the batteries, was wounded along with 4 enlisted men, another being killed, whereupon Capt. Squires, calling for reënforcements, was ordered by Longstreet, who had no more artillery, to withdraw the guns gradually, one at a time, covering the movement by the fire of the pieces remaining in position.

The Confederate Artillery was undoubtedly overmatched in this affair, yet, at the very moment of its withdrawal, the Federal batteries, which had suffered a loss of but 2 killed and 2 wounded, ceased firing, allowing Capt. Squires the honor of the last shot. It was this fact, perhaps, which gave credence to the report that Longstreet's guns had prevailed and upon such a belief Beauregard wrote in his official account of the affair:

"Our artillery was manned and officered by those who, but yesterday, were called from the civil avocations of a busy city. They were matched with the picked artillery of the Federal regular army,—Company E, Third Artillery, under Capt. Ayres, with an armament, as their own chief of artillery admits, of two 10-pounder rifled Parrott guns, two 12-pounder Parrott rifled guns, two 12-pounder howitzers, and two 6-pounder pieces, aided by two 20-pounder Parrott rifled guns of Company G, Fifth Artillery, under Lieut. Benjamin. Thus matched, they drove their veteran adversaries from the field, giving confidence in and promise of the coming efficiency of this brilliant arm of the service."

From Beauregard's account one would hardly derive a proper understanding of the comparative effect of the fire of the batteries engaged in this opening duel, and it is no disparagement to the Washington Artillery to say that the report is an exaggeration, conscientious though it may have been. Against such an armament as the enemy possessed, the actual result was to be expected. But Beauregard was quite correct in saying, "The skill, the conduct and soldierly qualities of the Washington Artillery engaged were all that could be desired.

The officers and men attached to the 7 pieces already specified won for their battalion a distinction which, I feel assured, will never be tarnished, and which will ever serve to urge them and their corps to high endeavor."

In the 1st Corps, Maj. Walton, Acting Chief of Artillery, assigned his batteries on July 21 as follows, in which order they served at Bull Run:

First, or Bonham's Brigade, Shields' 1st Co. Richmond Howitzers, and Kemper's Alexandria Battery, of 4 and 2 pieces, respectively; 2d, or Ewell's Brigade, 1 battery of Washington Artillery, 4 pieces; 3d, or Jones' Brigade, 1 section Washington Artillery, 2 pieces; 4th, or Longstreet's Brigade, 1 section of Washington Artillery, 2 pieces; 5th, or Cocke's Brigade, Latham's Lynchburg Battery, 4 pieces; 6th, or Early's Brigade, 1 battery Washington Artillery, 3 pieces; 7th, or Evans' demi-brigade, Rogers' Loudoun Battery, 4 pieces; 1 battery of Washington Artillery held in reserve, a total of 27 pieces.*

In order to describe the part of the Confederate Artillery in the battle of Bull Run, it is not necessary to discuss the movements of the two armies leading up to the affair, but only to show in what manner the guns were employed. About 6 A. M., July 21, Tyler's Federal Division approached Evans' force holding the Stone Bridge, and opened fire with a 30-pounder Parrott rifle, soon followed by that of several other pieces from the hills about a half-mile north of the run, to which Evans made no reply. It not appearing that Tyler intended to advance immediately, Gens. Johnston and Beauregard, with their staffs, made a reconnaissance to the right in the direction of Mitchell's Ford about 8 A. M. About 8:45 A. M. Capt. Alexander, the signal officer, discovered by the reflection of the sun from a brass field gun the advance of a heavy flanking column on the left, at Sudley, 8 miles from his station, on the right of the Confederate line near McLean's Ford, and immediately informed Evans that his left was being turned about two miles from the bridge, and sent a prompt warning to Beauregard.* Leaving 4 companies in front of Tyler's Division behind the bridge, Evans immediately dispatched his remaining 6 companies to his left to oppose the flanking column of the enemy, and check it until reënforcements could be brought up, informing Gen. Cocke on his right of the movement. Bee's four regiments, Hampton's one, Jackson's five, with an average distance of three miles to go, were ordered from near the center of the line to proceed rapidly to the left in support of Evans. For the next half-hour while the turning column was resting at Sudley, Tyler merely endeavored to occupy the attention of Evans' pitifully weak force with a desultory cannonade. By 10 A. M. the column had entirely crossed the stream at Sudley, and soon its batteries opened a heavy fire on Evans' men, who, extending to their left, had come in contact with the Federal advance. The Federal batteries were briskly replied to by two guns of Rogers' Loudoun Battery, which Evans had sent forward, and with them the six companies of infantry succeeded in delaying the enemy for over an hour, whose first attack was made by a single regiment, thus giving the reënforcements time to cover the larger portion of the three miles. Had McDowell rushed forward even one of his brigades, and several of his fine regular batteries, his movement would undoubtedly have succeeded, for just at this junction the right of Evans' line which he had pushed out to the left to meet the column from Sudley, formed almost at right angles to the stream, was taken in flank by Sherman's and Keyes' brigades of Tyler's Division, assisted by their batteries. When this movement became apparent Holmes' and Early's brigades, with two regiments of Bonham's Brigade, and Walker's and Kemper's batter-

*See Beauregard's and Johnston's reports. Also see reference to Alexander's signal and ordnance work in Part I.

ies were at once put in motion towards the left.* The
fire of Tyler's batteries upon Evans and Bee increased,
and after a gallant stand the small force under their
command fell back upon the Warrenton Pike, parallel
to and about a mile in rear of their advanced line, where
it was partly rallied about Hampton's Regiment which
had reached that point. Here the remnants of Evans'
command, thus reënforced by the Hampton Legion,
with Kemper's two guns and Imboden's Battery, maintained the position along the Warrenton Pike, against
great odds, for two hours, finally being driven back to
the Henry House Hill, a short distance to the rear,
where another rally was made upon Jackson's Brigade,
which had just arrived and taken an excellent position
on the protected inner edge of the ridge, which had a
plateau-like top. Jackson had with ready perception
seen the advantage of such a position. In the meantime the remainder of Johnston's Army was arriving
from Winchester, and the two batteries brought upon
the field at this instant after tremendous exertion by Col.
Pendleton, Alburtis' and his own, were thrown into
position by Jackson on the line established by his
infantry to oppose the five regular batteries and the four
brigades of the enemy, which were rapidly advancing.
Thus, Jackson, with eight old 6-pounders, was face to
face with three regular and two finely equipped volunteer batteries, with 24 pieces, mostly heavy rifled guns.†
Imboden's Staunton Battery, the first of Pendleton's
Artillery to arrive upon the scene, having made an heroic
march from Winchester, and previously having gone
forward to the support of Evans and Bee, had been
terribly punished by the Federal Infantry, as well as
by the hostile batteries, and, rallying for a time on Jackson's line, had been ordered to the rear when its remaining few rounds were expended.‡

---

*Holmes' Brigade with Walker's Battery had joined the 1st Corps from
their previous positions east of Manassas Junction.
†Ricketts', Griffin's, Arnold's, R. I. Battery, and 71st New York Regiment
Battery. See Pendleton's reports to Johnston and Jackson, *Rebellion Records*,
Series I, Vol. II, Part I, pp. 35, 36, 37.
‡*Battles and Leaders,* Imboden's account, Vol. I, p. 233.

While McDowell continued to bump his head against Jackson's stone-wall, on the Henry House Ridge, sending regiment after regiment to the assault, supported by the fire of Griffin's and Ricketts' batteries, the Confederate reënforcements were arriving in ever-increasing numbers, going into action always on the left of those which had preceded them, thus extending Jackson's original line. Failing to make a lodgment on the plateau with his infantry, McDowell now sent Griffin's and Ricketts' batteries in closer to take up the task of battering a way through at a decisive range. Nothing in war was ever more gallant than the efforts of these magnificent batteries, which, fearlessly advancing to within canister range of the Confederate lines, poured round after round into the enemy. Their infantry supports having been driven off by the freshly arrived regiments of Johnston's Army, the Federal batteries even then continued their fight.

This particular artillery fight, commencing about 3 P. M., had lasted for perhaps half an hour, when the 33d Virginia Regiment, commanded by Col. A. C. Cummings, boldly advanced from Jackson's left to take the guns. Griffin, in the act of opening upon it with a blizzard of canister at short range, was persuaded by Maj. Barry, Chief of McDowell's artillery, that the advancing men were Federal troops. Cummings' Regiment deliberately halted, and from a distance of but seventy yards fired a volley into Griffin's Battery, killing and wounding 40 of his men and 75 of his horses. Ricketts, whose battery was next to that of Griffin, was also wounded and captured, and one of his officers killed. Griffin managed to drag off three of his guns, but the other nine of the two batteries were left isolated between the two infantry lines. A terrific struggle now ensued, finally resulting in favor of the Confederates who turned a number of the captured guns against the retreating Federals.*

---

*Barry's Report, *Rebellion Records,* Series I, Vol. II, p. 345.

Meanwhile, Stanard's and Beckham's batteries had been coming up on the left of the guns with Pendleton, and assisted in hurling back the enemy. Upon the arrival of Kirby Smith's Brigade on the extreme Confederate left, the Federal lines began to waver, and when Beckham's Battery changed position, and opened a most demoralizing enfilade fire upon their flank from a well-chosen position, the resistance of the Federal Infantry, with which there were no longer any guns on their right to reply to Beckham, dissolved into a rout. Thus not only did Jackson and Pendleton exercise a great influence upon the battle at a most critical juncture, by the skillful disposition of the latter's batteries, in a position which nature herself could hardly have improved upon, but whether accidentally so or not, the fire of Beckham's guns, in the most effective manner possible—that is, from the immediate flank—was delivered upon the enemy at the psychological instant of the uncertainty incident to a check. Again evidence was given of a proper appreciation of field artillery when Kemper's and Walker's batteries, the latter just arrived with six 3-inch rifles, were ordered forward after the flight of the enemy set in to open upon the disordered masses retreating across Cub Run. The fire of Kemper's guns almost immediately wrecked a team on the bridge, causing an inextricable jam of guns, caissons, wagons, and ambulances, from which the panic-stricken drivers cut many of the teams. No guns could ever have been employed in a pursuit to better advantage, for at this point alone, 17 guns, including the immense 30-pounder Parrott rifle, with over 20 caissons, were captured and brought in by the Confederate Cavalry. Had the batteries on the Confederate right, which had not been engaged, been pushed forward to Centreville with proper infantry supports when the retreat commenced, and followed Kemper's example, there would be little indeed to criticise in the manner in which the Artillery as a whole was handled. Yet, this was not to be. Batteries in those days were tied to the apron strings of brigade commanders, and possessed little or no independence until after they had been set in motion. If Walton with his guns scattered to the four quarters, and for the most part idle, behind Ball's, Mitchell's, Blackburn's, and McLean's Fords, had but been a Hohenlohe with the organization and independence permitted the latter on such occasions, Centreville would have been the scene of glorious achievements for the Artillery, since rarely has a retreat presented such a helpless mass of humanity to the tender mercies of the pursuers, as blocked the roads at Centreville the evening of July 21, 1861. A Hohenlohe might have known of the true condition. It is quite certain, however, that the brigade commanders to whom Walton's guns were assigned did not know until too late to send their guns forward. Writing after the event, it is quite easy to point out how Walton should have assembled his fresh batteries, and galloped along one of the two available roads leading from the Confederate right to intercept the Federal retreat at Centreville. But a study of the conditions which actually existed the evening of July 21 will disclose the fact that not only was it impossible for him to do so because of the wide dispersion of his guns, but that far away from the actual scene of the conflict, he was even more ignorant of the opportunity than Johnston and Beauregard were.

The total personnel of the Artillery of the 2d Corps numbered 350, an average of 70 officers and men for each of the 5 batteries, and of Beauregard's army 533, or an average for each of his 8 batteries of about 67 officers and men. All of Johnston's batteries were engaged in the battle of Bull Run, but in the Army of the Potomac, or the 1st Corps, part of Rogers' Loudoun Battery, and some of the guns of the Washington Artillery, 10 in all, were not engaged; thus, there were engaged a total of 638 officers and men of the Artillery, with a total of 47 guns. With Beauregard's army were several companies of Pickens' heavy artillery, numbering 293 officers and men, who were also not engaged. The losses in Beauregard's artillery were: killed 2, wounded 8, total 10, and probably about the same for Johnston's batteries, or a grand total of losses for the Confederate Artillery of not more than 20.

The Federal batteries which crossed Bull Run were Ricketts', Griffin's, and Arnold's regular batteries, a Rhode Island and a New York Battery, with ten 10-pounder and eight 13-pounder rifled guns, four 12-pounder howitzers, and two 6-pounder smooth-bore guns, or a total of 24 pieces. In addition to these, McDowell had Hunt's, Carlisle's, Tidball's, Greene's, Ayres', and Edwards' regular batteries, or a grand total of 49 pieces, most of which were heavy rifled guns.* Of the Union guns, 27 in all were captured, with 37 caissons, 6 forges, 4 battery wagons, 64 artillery horses, with much harness, and nearly 5,000 rounds of field artillery ammunition.†

In his account of the battle Gen. E. P. Alexander states, with some degree of sarcasm, that McDowell should have had at least 100 guns, for, says he, "Artillery is the best arm against raw troops." But, if with 49 pieces only 24 could be brought up into effective range, it is not clear what Gen. Alexander's meaning is unless he was not satisfied with the number of guns captured. By such an increased train McDowell's road to Washington could have only been more effectually blocked, for he certainly could not have gotten so many guns on the field.

Most of the Confederate guns were 6-pounder S. B. pieces, or 12-pounder howitzers. There were a few old 6-pounders, which had been reamed out and rifled with three grooves after the Parrott system.‡

Thus, although the number of available guns in the two armies were about the same, Federal, 49; Con-

---

*Battles and Leaders, Vol. I, p. 195, Rebellion Records, Series I, Vol. II, p. 345.
†Rebellion Records, Series I, Vol. II, p. 571. Report of Capt. E. P. Alexander, Acting Ordnance Officer.
‡The 3-inch Parrott rifled guns, which had been purchased by the State of Virginia, were at Yorktown, with Magruder.

federate, 47; and although 37 of the latter were engaged at close range, as opposed to 24 of the former, the Federal Artillery had the advantage in weight of metal in the proportion of at least three to one, besides a great superiority in range. Yet, it was the general belief in the Army that the Confederate Artillery had again more than proved a match for the regular batteries of the United States.

"The efficiency of our infantry and cavalry might have been expected from a patriotic people accustomed, like ours, to the management of arms and horses, but that of the artillery was little less than wonderful. They were opposed to batteries far superior in the number, range, and equipment of their guns, with educated officers and thoroughly instructed soldiers. We had but one educated artillerist, Col. Pendleton,—that model of a Christian soldier,—yet they exhibited as much superiority to the enemy in skill as in courage. Their fire was superior both in rapidity and precision." Thus wrote Gen. Johnston in his report of the battle, and Gen. Beauregard wrote that all the batteries displayed "that marvellous capacity of our people as artillerists which has made them, it would appear, at once the terror and the admiration of the enemy."* In his report of the battle Jackson wrote: "Nobly did the artillery maintain its position for hours against the enemy's admiring thousands. Great praise is due Col. Pendleton and the officers and men."† Longstreet, in writing of that portion of the Washington Artillery under his command, said: "I am pleased to say that our young artillerists proved themselves equal, if not superior, to the boasted artillerists of the enemy."‡ Capt. Arnold of McDowell's army stated in his report, in regard to the part played by his battery: "During all this time the battery was exposed to a severe and most accurate artillery fire."§ And this officer's testimony with re-

*_Rebellion Records_, Series I, Vol. II, p. 494.
†Jackson's Report, Ibid., p. 481.
‡Longstreet's Report, Ibid., p. 462.
§See his report, Ibid., p. 416.

gard to the effectiveness of the fire of the Confederate guns is supported by all the Federal officers who participated in the fight.* But the Federal accounts of the artillery fire of the enemy are not over-trustworthy, for McDowell had himself instilled in them, as if by premeditation, a fear of the "long arm," altogether unwarranted by its actual power. Yet one of the greatest effects exerted by artillery in any battle is, after all, its moral effect, and in this particular manner it exercised a tremendous influence upon the Northern troops in the battle of Bull Run. McDowell's order of march was excellent with respect to the disposition of his troops but, as frequently pointed out, he spoiled the high morale he had created in his army by unwise caution which only sufficed to fill the minds of his men with fears. It "would not be pardonable in any commander to come upon a battery or breastwork without a knowledge of its position," cautioned the misled McDowell. These words were sufficient, and the mischief was done. His officers as well as his men advanced slowly, step by step, peering at each distant crest, and poking in every wayside thicket to locate the awful bugbear of the Press and of their own leader—"masked batteries." This direful term had originated in the Sumter episode—a battery having been constructed on the mainland behind a house which was demolished when the fire was ordered to be opened.† After that a masked battery figured in every affair even though but a skirmish. According to the pestilential swarm of press agents, which infested the safer places near the front, it was a masked battery which caused Butler's reverse at Big Bethel; and it was masked batteries which brought misfortune upon the Federal troops in various other instances.

The psychological effect upon his army resulting from McDowell's words was at best most adverse.

---

*Particularly interesting is Franklin's account, *Rebellion Records,* Series I, Vol. II., p. 406.
†*Memoirs of a Confederate,* Alexander, p. 21.

It has frequently been averred by military critics, and even by officers of professional repute who took part in the Bull Run campaign, both Confederate and Federal, that Johnston should have at once advanced and seized Washington after the overthrow of McDowell. The writer does not propose to discuss the general merits of this contention, but in so far as the Artillery is concerned, it seems necessary only to refer those supporting such a view to the records and correspondence of the hour.* Nor do I refer to the reports and statements of the generals in command, but to those of the ordnance officers occupying subordinate positions, and without responsibility for the movements of the Army as a whole. It would seem that if Johnston's guns were practically without ammunition as late as the middle of September he was hardly in position the night of July 21 to order an advance upon Washington, with a view to forcing his way through the outlying defenses, and laying siege to the National Capital.

---

*See Part I, as to armament and condition of artillery at this time.

CHAPTER VII

DURING the weeks immediately succeeding the victory at Manassas, Col Pendleton, who as Chief of Artillery of Johnston's army had displayed great ability as an artillerist, was temporarily appointed Chief of Ordnance to distribute the captured material and refit his batteries. But so destitute of ammunition and equipment was the Artillery found to be that it became necessary for him to repair to Richmond to beg, borrow, or secure in any way possible, the barest necessities for the batteries.* During his enforced absence Capt. E. P. Alexander, a most efficient officer, who had resigned from the Engineer Corps of the Old Army, and who had rendered splendid service as signal officer in the battle of Bull Run, was assigned to duty as acting Chief of Artillery.† Thus, while Pendleton with all but superhuman energy urged on the manufacture of material, ammunition, equipment and artillery stores of every kind in Richmond, and throughout the State, Alexander devoted his efforts to the better organization and discipline of the batteries already in the field, and to those which arrived from day to day.‡ The task assigned Pendleton was neither a simple nor a pleasant one, but before the end of October he was able to rejoin his command with the satisfaction of having accomplished the seemingly impossible.§

When Pendleton rejoined the Army of the Potomac, the artillery personnel consisted of 129 officers and 2,416 men, and with Loring in the Army of the Northwest, operating along the western frontier of Virginia, were 12 officers and 302 men besides a smaller number

---

*For the success of his efforts and the absolute lack of ammunition after the battle, see Part I.
†For sketch of Alexander, see Part I.
‡*Memoirs of W. N. Pendleton*, Lee, p. 154.
§For an intimate account of his labors in Richmond and elsewhere at this time, see *Memoirs of W. N. Pendleton*, Lee, pp. 154-167, and also Part I.

with Holmes in the Aquia District.* The personnel
of the main army was distributed as follows: 1st, or
Beauregard's Corps, 63 officers and 1,273 men; 2d, or
G. W. Smith's Corps, 27 officers and 480 men; artillery
reserve, 39 officers and 663 men.†

Before being assigned to duty as signal officer with
the Army in the field, Capt. Alexander had been engaged in the organization and drilling of the batteries in
Richmond in April, and had persistently advocated the
formation of battalions of light artillery of three or more
batteries, a suggestion entirely novel at the time. Had
he been allowed to remain on this duty longer, it is quite
probable his views would have obtained, but as it was,
he did succeed in inducing Magruder and Randolph to
create the Richmond Howitzer Battalion, of three companies. His influence being withdrawn, however, even
that battalion was divided, two of its batteries being assigned to the force at Yorktown, and one, Shields', to
Beauregard's Army. Thus, it was never employed as a
unit in accordance with Alexander's views. The Washington Artillery had arrived in Virginia with a battalion
formation of 4 batteries but it was at the very outset, as
has been shown, persistently split up into small, and
comparatively ineffective, detachments, conformable
with the prevailing custom of the time. The success
which had attended Pendleton in handling the Rockbridge, Alburtis', Imboden's, and Stanard's batteries,
in the movement from Winchester to Bull Run, and the
ability he had displayed to direct and control the massed
fire of at least three of these batteries in action, only
sufficed to call attention to the practicability of Alexander's ideas, and convinced Johnston that an artillery
reserve should be formed, though it was not for some
time that the true value of artillery masses was perceived.

When the winter of 1861-62 set in, Johnston withdrew his army to Centreville, and before January had

---

*Abstracts from Field Returns, *Rebellion Records,* Series I, Vol. V, pp.
932-933.
    †For return dated December 1, see Series I, Vol. V, p. 974. There had been
little change.

reorganized his increased force into 4 divisions, two of 4 brigades each, and two of 5 each. These 18 brigades averaged about 4 regiments of 500 men each. Besides the main army, Jackson had a force in the Valley, and Holmes lay in observation behind Aquia Creek. The total effective strength of the Confederate forces, February 28, 1862, was 47,617, with 175 guns. The distribution of the batteries was, approximately, as follows:

FIRST DIVISION (Van Dorn)

Kemper's Alexandria (Va.) Battery, 1st or Bonham's Brigade.
Bondurant's Jeff Davis (Ala.) Battery, 2d or Early's Brigade.
Carter's King William (Va.) Battery, 3d or Rodes' Brigade.

SECOND DIVISON (G. W. Smith)

Alburtis' Wise (Va.) Battery, 1st or S. Jones' Brigade.
Thomas (Va.) Battery, 2d or Wilcox's Brigade.
Blodget's (Ga.) Battery, 3d or Toombs' Brigade.

THIRD DIVISION (Longstreet)

Rogers' Loudoun (Va.) Battery, 1st or Ewell's Brigade.
Stribling's Fauquier (Va.) Battery, 2d or D. R. Jones' Brigade.
Latham's Lynchburg (Va.) Battery, 3d or Cocke's Brigade.

FOURTH DIVISION (E. Kirby Smith)

Baltimore Light Artillery (Md.) Battery, 1st or Elzey's Brigade.
Courtney's Henrico (Va.) Battery, 2d or Trimble's Brigade.
Bowyer's Bedford (Va.) Battery, 3d or Taylor's Brigade.

WHITING'S DIVISION AT DUMFRIES

Imboden's Staunton (Va.) Battery, 1st or ———— Brigade.
Reilly's (N. C.) Detachment, 2d or Wigfall's Brigade.
Rives' (S. C.) Battery, 2d or Wigfall's Brigade.

HILL'S FORCE AT LEESBURG

Shields' Richmond Howitzer (Va.) Detachment, Griffin's Brigade.

HOLMES' FORCE AT AQUIA

Braxton's Fredericksburg (Va.) Battery, 1st or French's Brigade.
Cooke's Stafford (Va.) Battery, 2d or J. G. Walker's Brigade.
Walker's Purcell (Va.) Battery, 2d or J. G. Walker's Brigade.

JACKSON'S FORCE IN THE VALLEY

McLaughlin's Rockbridge (Va.) Battery, 1st or Garnett's Brigade.
Carpenter's Alleghany (Va.) Battery, 2d or Crittenden's Brigade.
Chew's Horse Artillery (Va.) Battery, Ashby's Cavalry.

RESERVE ARTILLERY WITH MAIN ARMY

(Col. Pendleton, Commanding)

Woolfolk's Ashland (Va.) Battery.
Cocke's Fluvanna (Va.) Battery.
Coleman's Morris Louisa (Va.) Battery.
Cutts' Sumter (Ga.) Battery.
Dance's Powhatan (Va.) Battery.
Hamilton's (Ga.) Battery.
Holman's Fluvanna (Va.) Battery.
Kirkpatrick's Amherst (Va.) Battery.
Lane's (Ga.) Battery.

(Maj. Walton, Commanding)

Squires' (La.) Battery, 1st Company, Washington Artillery.
Rosser's (La.) Battery, 2d Company, Washington Artillery.
Miller's (La.) Battery, 3d Company, Washington Artillery.
Eshleman's (La.) Battery, 4th Company, Washington Artillery.

From the foregoing schedule of assignments it will be seen that there were, before the close of 1861, not fewer than 35 batteries with the troops along the Potomac alone, 24 of which were raised in Virginia, and that 13 of these had been assigned to a reserve in two sections, commanded by Pendleton and Walton, respectively.*

About the first of March the aggregate present for duty of the field artillery personnel, was 2,967, including 146 officers, which gives an average strength for the 35 batteries present of about 85 men.

Just at this time the Federal Army had been reorganized by McClellan, his 5 corps together aggregating 185,420 men, with 465 field guns. Thus it is seen that the Federal Army had available nearly 3 guns for each one with Johnston's force, the disparity in per-

---

*Rebellion Records, Series I, Vol. V, p. 1086.

sonnel, horses, character of armament, ammunition and
equipment being even greater. Indeed the odds in the
latter respects were overwhelming, particularly as to
ammunition, the Confederate Ordnance Department
lacking throughout the war the material and skilled
labor with which to make really reliable fuses and projectiles.

Before the close of 1861 Gen. Johnston had been
much annoyed by the interference of the Secretary of
War with matters affecting the organization of the
Army. Mr. Benjamin had granted indiscriminately to
officers, private soldiers, and even to civilians, authority
to raise troops of cavalry and batteries of artillery.*
Many of the batteries thus raised were recruited from
amongst the men of the infantry regiments, and while
Johnston's objection on the ground that the field artillery arm already exceeded the European proportion
was perhaps ill founded, yet, the creation of heavy batteries for local service away from the actual field of
campaign, and to the detriment of the infantry, was
a most injurious practice. "Fortunately," says Johnston, "the Ordnance Department was unable to arm
and equip them; otherwise the Army would have been
deprived of several regiments of excellent infantry, and
encumbered with artillery that could not have been
taken into battle without danger of capture, for want
of infantry to protect it." The interference of the
Secretary, so bitterly resented and complained of by
Gen. Johnston, led to the organization of many light
batteries which it would have been necessary to create
later, if not at the time they actually were created. Yet,
Gen. Johnston was much perplexed over the condition
of the batteries already in the field, many of which still
had four-horse teams, and, realizing their immobility, it
is not strange that he desired the addition of no more to
his army, in spite of the preponderance of the Federal
guns.

*Johnston's Narrative, pp. 90, 91.

By special order the strength of the light artillery companies of Virginia militia was fixed in March at 150 men, rank and file, those containing over 120 men being entitled to an extra second lieutenant.*

We have seen that the Act of January 22, 1862, authorized the appointment of brigadier-generals, and additional field-officers in the field artillery arm. On the 27th the Secretary of War addressed the following letter to Gen. Johnston at Centreville:

"SIR—Congress has provided by law for the appointment of field officers of artillery in the provisional army in proportion to the number of guns in each command. You are respectfully requested to report as early as convenient the number of guns in each of the three armies under your command, and a list of the artillery officers in each army, in the order of their merit, so as to assist the President in doing justice to your meritorious subordinates by proper promotion. It would be agreeable to us to have a like list prepared separately by the commanders of each of the three armies in relation to the officers under his command, so as to compare the estimate made of their respective merits, and thus increase the probability of doing justice to all."

This communication evidences a worthy desire on the part of the appointing authority to increase the officers of the Artillery by judicious appointments in such numbers as to give the arm not only those needed, but officers of approved ability. Immediate steps were taken to make the appointments contemplated by Congress.

Early in March, it became certain that McClellan was preparing for a forward movement either by Fredericksburg or the Peninsula, and Johnston withdrew his army behind the Rappahannock, along which a line had been fortified.

The Artillery had been in cantonments about Culpeper during the winter, and the horses had been given a long rest, the men being drilled and instructed whenever the weather permitted. For the

*S. O. No. 2, A. G. O., Virginia, March 21, 1862, *Rebellion Records,* Series IV, Vol. I, p. 1011.

better mobilizing of the Army, Col. Pendleton's reserve corps was now ordered to abandon its cabins, and moved with the division of G. W. Smith to Warrenton, leaving the winter quarters March 8. The Artillery was in fine spirits when it reached Warrenton four days later where it lay for about a month, at the end of which time it was called upon to make various changes of position in the worst imaginable weather, finally arriving at Louisa Courthouse with Longstreet's Division. Here it was a serious problem to secure provender for the 750 animals of the Reserve Artillery.

April 10, Col. Pendleton received his well-earned promotion, his commission of brigadier-general of artillery bearing date of March 26. The news of this appointment was received with great favor throughout the Army, but there was undoubtedly jealously in some quarters.* Pendleton had entertained serious misgivings about his promotion over the gallant Maj. Walton who, himself, was too high and patriotic a soldier to be piqued by the advancement of the Virginian. Yet, a feeling existed among the men of the far South that favoritism had been too generally shown Virginians, though their resentment was in no sense directed against Pendleton.

To guard against the possibility of friction, it will be observed that the portion of the Reserve Artillery placed under Pendleton as Chief of Artillery, when he had previously been promoted from a captain to the rank of colonel, did not include the battalion of Maj. Walton.

The Reserve Artillery was now ordered to Richmond, where it arrived April 14, whence it was ordered to proceed two days later to Yorktown, Gen. Pendleton being sent on in advance by Gen. Johnston to confer with Gen. D. H. Hill in command, and to inspect the defences of the place. He reported at once that the

---

*Memoirs of W. N. Pendleton, p. 173. Also see Benjamin's letter to the President, November 30, 1861, Rebellion Records, Series IV, Vol. I, p. 761.

country was entirely unsuited for the use of field artillery, or large masses of men, and that with its armament it was impossible to hold Yorktown against the heavy rifled ordnance of the enemy.* On April 30, he wrote that Johnston's army would have to fall back to the neighborhood of Richmond before a land battle could be thought of. Pendleton, at the time, must have contemplated with misgivings the tremendous superiority of McClellan's artillery in numbers, material and general efficiency, yet his energies, in common with those of all his subordinates, were bent to the task of preparing his arm to meet its antagonist upon the best footing possible. New batteries continued to be added to the Army of Northern Virginia, to the equipment of which the Confederate Bureau of Ordnance was now contributing, and there were other conditions in favor of the Confederate Artillery. Not only was Jackson so playing upon the fears of Lincoln and Stanton that McClellan was continually being crippled, but the country through which the invader must pass was such that it would surely reduce the immense force of his artillery in large measure to the status of a train, which, blocking every road, would only add to the difficulties of his maneuvers. Pendleton at once perceived that for these reasons the numbers of the enemy, in so far as his artillery was concerned, would by the very nature of the field of operations be largely discounted.

To Lincoln and his cabinet, McClellan's movement to the Peninsula, in view of Jackson's activity in the Valley, seemed to uncover Washington. They feared an irruption of the Confederates, just as Lee's defensive strategy contemplated they would, which might expose the Federal Capital to capture. McClellan was, therefore, commanded to leave a force so disposed as to cover Washington and to protect it in any emergency. This he thought he had done when he left 63,000 men and 85 pieces of artillery distributed between the Valley, Warrenton, Manassas, and the lines about Washington. In

*Memoirs of W. N. Pendleton, Lee, p. 181.

addition to this force he had detached Blenker's Division of 10,000 men and 24 guns to join Fremont. But with fears greatly aroused by Jackson's attack at Kernstown, augmented by lack of confidence in McClellan, 75,000 men and 109 guns were not deemed sufficient to guard the Capital against the Army of the Valley, and McDowell's Corps of between 30,000 and 40,000 men was taken from McClellan and held between Washington and Richmond.* Thus McClellan was deprived of about 200 of his 465 guns.

---

*Jackson's Valley Campaign, Allan, pp. 84-85.

CHAPTER VIII

Up to this time little has been said about the tactics of the Confederate Artillery, except to refer to Alexander's early conception of the organization of battalions. But the organization of the artillery reserve of the Army of Northern Virginia marks an event in its career which requires notice. Up to that point, there had been little attention bestowed upon the tactics of the arm, other than upon the mere drill of the battery and the evolutions of several when maneuvering together. Such was the scope of the treatise prepared by Capt. Stevens in 1792, the author having been an artillery officer in Lamb's continental regiment. Then appeared in 1809 a work called "The American Artillerist's Companion, or Elements of Artillery," by Col. Louis de Tousard, formerly of the British service, and later Colonel of the Second Continental Regiment of Artillery, and inspector of the Artillery of the United States. In 1800, Alexander Hamilton, Inspector-General, and Gen. Pinckney, had endeavored to formulate drill regulations for the Artillery, followed by Gen. James Wilkinson, in 1808, but nothing of permanent character had resulted from their efforts, so that other than a simple drill manual for horse, or flying artillery, as it was then called, written by Gen. Kosciusko, in Paris in 1800, and Tousard's work, there were no definite regulations for the arm when the War of 1812 was declared.

France at this time was generally recognized to be the school of highest artillery development, and in 1809, Capt. Winfield Scott had sought authority to repair thither for a study of its system upon which to base a comprehensive work, but his application was refused and no manual of instruction was adopted in the United States, until 1821, at which time a work by H. Lallemand, formerly a general in Napoleon's Imperial

Guard, known as a "Treatise on Artillery," was adopted. As the spirit of both Tousard's and Lallemand's works was essentially French, it will be well to gain some knowledge of the status of artillery and artillery tactics of the time in France.

The soldiers of the French Revolution had initiated many improvements in ordnance and artillery generally. The casting and boring of guns, the cleaning of saltpetre, and the preparation of powder, were much improved by the clever chemists and men of science of the Republic. The campaigns in the Alps led to the introduction of mountain guns, portable enough to be of real use in rough country, and Gribeauval's heavy gun carriages, and ammunition wagons were much simplified and improved for ordinary field use. On the whole, light and horse artillery material was brought up to a stage of perfection proportionate to that of the other arms of the service in which radical advances had been made since the days of Frederick the Great. Regimental guns were taken from the battalions and collected in batteries, and particular attention was paid to the artillery as a separate and not as a mere auxiliary arm. Prior to 1789, the French Artillery consisted of 7 regiments of foot artillery, with 6 companies of miners and artificers, but although Austria, Prussia and some other nations had introduced the horse batteries so dear to Frederick, the French had not done so.* The material of the field batteries consisted of 6-, 8-, and 12-pounder guns, and 6- and 8-pounder siege pieces. The whole field artillery arm was divided into regiments and companies. The guns of the foot regiments were mostly 4-pounders, and of these there were 1,200, which with the battery artillery made a disproportionate number of guns. But the object in this was to back up the courage of the ill-drilled and inexperienced conscripts by means

---

*The creation of horse artillery is generally attributed to Frederick the Great, a claim asserted by many countries; but, in an interesting article which appeared in the *Voyennui Sbornik*, translated for the *Journal of the Royal Artillery*, by Lieut. H. D. Ashby, R. F. A., and reprinted in the *Journal of the Military Service Institution* (American), July-August, 1912, p. 120, much evidence is adduced to prove that it was the conception of Peter the Great, of Russia.

of a heavy artillery fire. The creation of a large body of light infantry led to the production of lighter batteries, which might keep pace with the men; and in 1791, there were already two companies of this light artillery, each with two 8-pounder guns and two 6-inch howitzers, the men serving with them being carried along in wagons of peculiar construction. But soon the gunners were mounted, and thus the arm grew into horse artillery, an arm so well suited to the quick-acting French temperament that it at once assumed undue proportions.

When in 1793-94, the Army was reorganized, each half-brigade was given a battery of 6 guns, that is, the same number of two pieces to each battalion was retained. As, however, it was soon discovered that too much artillery on account of its comparative immobility retarded the movements of the Army without actual corresponding gain, the allowance was cut down to one gun for each brigade—a better proportion. The battalions were no longer hampered by each dragging its own gun, as had been largely done by the American troops in the War of Independence, since the guns were now consolidated into batteries capable of following the maneuvers of their respective brigades. Thus regimental guns gradually disappeared and batteries came into use, consisting of foot and horse artillery. In 1794, the French field artillery comprised 8 regiments of foot, and 8 regiments of horse artillery, 12 companies of artificers, and a battalion of pontoniers. The regiment of foot artillery had a staff and 20 companies; each company with a battery of 6 guns with 8 men per gun, having, also, supernumeraries for general service, a company thus aggregating 93 men. The mounted artillery regiment had a staff and 6 companies; each company was a battery of 6 guns, with 10 men per gun; a total of 60. This made 960 guns and 15,000 artillerymen in the foot, 280 guns and 3,000 artillerymen in the mounted artillery; a total of 1,248 guns and 18,000 men. In charge of the corps artillery were 228 general, staff, and superior officers, including those assigned to duty as inspectors.

The artillery had its own regulations and tactics, and in maneuver the field batteries possessed great mobility. Gunnery was scientifically studied and the schools, for which the foundation had been laid by Louis XIV, were greatly improved. With its many polytechnic schools, its military school at Chalons, and its regimental schools at La Fere, Besancon, Grenoble, Metz, Strasburg, Douay, Auxonne and Toulouse, where the several artillery regiments were stationed, the French system of instruction was advanced and thorough, ahead of that of any other country at the time.

But, it remained for the great master to teach the world the meaning of artillery, and how to employ it in battle. "A good infantry," said Napoleon, "is without doubt the backbone of the army, but if it had to fight long against superior artillery, it would be discouraged and disorganized."* And, so, possessing an unequalled ability to direct and control masses of men, he applied his principles to the tactical employment of his artillery, perceiving the great power of field guns, when the fire of a large number were used in combination. He had also learned that with the short range of the smooth-bore guns, it was practically impossible to change their position when once they had become engaged under fire, because of the vulnerability of a mounted battery, and the large target it presented while in motion.

He therefore created divisional artillery, thus securing his masses, and a reserve artillery which he was able to withhold until it could be thrown into action at the crisis to decide the issue. Writing to Eugene, he declared that "the artillery, like the other arms, must be collected in mass, if one wishes to attain a decisive result."†

Addressing Clarke in 1809 concerning the latter's green troops, he gave expression to his great belief in the artillery arm when he wrote: "Troops such as you have are just the kind which need most entrenchments,

---

*Dixhuit Notes, etc., XXXI, p. 395.
†C. N. to Eugene, Schönbrunn, 16 June, 1809, 5 P. M.

earthworks and artillery. The more inferior the quality of a body of troops, the more artillery it requires. There are some army corps with which I should require only one-third of the artillery which I need for other corps."*

After Lützen and Bautzen, he wrote, "It is the artillery of my guard which generally decides my battles, for as I have it always at hand, I can bring it to bear, whenever it becomes necessary.†

And, after the end of the campaign, he wrote, "Great battles are won by artillery."‡

Previous to the time of Gustavus, and his great artillery general, Torstenson, the number of guns per thousand men had varied from 1 to 5. Gustavus generally had 3, but at one time 6. In the Seven Years War, the average number was 4, though Frederick once increased it to 10 per thousand, endeavoring to compensate with additional guns for his losses in infantry. Napoleon rarely got more than 5 or 6 per thousand, though he possessed at one time the enormous total of 1,300 guns.

At Friedland, the French general, Senarmont, advanced his great line of guns to within 300 yards of the Russian Infantry and broke its front with a murderous storm of canister, and at Austerlitz, Wagram, and Gross-Görshen, the issue had been decided by Napoleon's masses of guns. Yet, it took the allies many years to perceive the cause of Napoleon's successes, employing as they did, against his great masses of artillery, individual batteries or small groups. It was not until 1813 that Blücher gave voice to the need of more guns with which to combat him. But while it took the allies time to learn the game, finally Napoleon was forced to exclaim angrily, when he saw their great masses on the field of Leipzig open fire upon him, "At last they have learned something."§

But, just as in the course of years the Napoleonic art had been learned by the world, so in a short time was

---

*C. N., Schönbrunn, 18 August.
†C. N. to Clarke, New Markt, 2 June.
‡C. N. to Eugene, St. Cloud, 20 November, 1813.
§Jomini's *Napoleon's Campaigns.*

it forgotten, and other than a knowledge of the minor tactics contained in the "Manual for the Artillery of the Garde Royale," little information as to the employment of field guns was possessed in America. This work had in 1826 been recommended to the Secretary of War by a board of officers of which Gen. Scott was president, being subsequently published under the title of "A System of Exercise and Instruction of Field Artillery, including Maneuvers of Light or Horse Artillery." By Act of Congress 5,000 copies of this work were authorized to be purchased and distributed for the use of the militia, the regular batteries retaining Lallemand's treatise as their manual. The next step was to send Lieut. Tyler of the regular service to Metz, in 1828, to translate the existing French manuals, but the old Gribeauval system becoming obsolete, Capt. Robert Anderson's translation of the French "Instruction for Field Artillery, Horse and Foot" appeared in 1839, and superseded all previously adopted works.* The manual of instruction employed during the Mexican War was that contained in Anderson's translation as revised by Maj. Ringold, in 1843, and adopted in 1845. These instructions, although excellent so far as they went, embraced little more than the manual of the piece and the maneuvers of a battery. The proper organization of artillery for, and its management in the field were merely touched upon. A new set of instructions going somewhat into the tactical employment of the arm, and also another translation from the French by Maj. Robert Anderson, entitled the "Evolutions of Field Batteries," and comprehending the school of a battalion of 3 or 4 batteries, appeared in 1860. This book was adopted by the Army and adhered to by the Federals during the entire Civil War. The Confederate States to a certain extent adhered to the same work, but a treatise entitled, "Manual of Instruction for the Volunteers and Militia of the Confederate States," by Col. William Gilham, Instructor of Tactics and Com-

*Major Anderson of Fort Sumter fame.

mandant of Cadets at the Virginia Military Institute, was given precedence over all others in so far as the school of the battery was concerned. This work was a most comprehensive manual of drill for the three arms, containing also the Articles of War of the Confederacy, and the regulations for military courts.*

But, as has been said before, in 1861 artillery was an arm consisting of so many individual batteries. The conception of field artillery at this time embraced nothing more than the evolutions of several battery units maneuvering together. Its tactical employment in accordance with Napoleonic principles was entirely forgotten, and indeed artillery tactics had reverted to the pre-Napoleonic stage of batteries, distributed throughout the army to brigades and even sections to regiments, simply by reason of the fact that there had never been enough artillery in this country at one time to attract the attention of our officers to the Napoleonic methods of employing large masses. This was not strange, but most natural. Indeed, the Prussians evidenced the same neglect in 1864, during their war with Denmark, and had to relearn the great principles of artillery masses from Austria, in 1866, Austria having been reminded of them in the French War of 1859. The Prussian lapse is far more inexplicable than that of the Americans in their civil conflict, for Prussia had maintained a large artillery arm for years.

We are now in position to grasp the true meaning of the formation of reserve artillery under Pendleton and Walton, and to appreciate the stand which Capt. Alexander had made early in 1861 for the organization of field artillery battalions to act as combat units. It was yet to be some time before the knowledge of "the way it should be done" was to enable the Confederate generals "to do it," and many hard knocks were to be received by the loosely organized and poorly handled Confederate field artillery until experience prevailed and added its dearly bought lessons.

---

*It had appeared in 1861 before the outbreak of the war as a semi-official publication of the United States Army.

CHAPTER IX

It will be well now to look more minutely at the artillery of McClellan's Army, so vastly superior in numbers, material and organization, in order that the inequality of the two armies in respect to this arm may be appreciated from the first.

Many of the Federal regiments which took the field in the spring of 1861 had batteries attached to them, true to the system of Gustavus and Frederick. As was to be expected, these batteries were found to be useless. When the Union Army marched to Manassas, the batteries not belonging to regiments, most of which were regular batteries, were assigned to brigades in accordance with the custom of the day. But, when McClellan undertook the reorganization of the defeated army in July, he inaugurated numerous imperative changes, many of which were innovations. Among the latter was his organization of the artillery. Perceiving the utter lack of artillery reserves, and that brigade commanders were not capable of supervising and directing artillery, of which they were generally quite ignorant, he set about the task before him of bringing order out of chaos. The force turned over to him July 27, 1861, consisted of 50,000 infantry, 1,000 cavalry, and 650 artillerymen manning 9 incomplete batteries, with an aggregate of but 30 guns. These figures should be borne in mind by all who are prone to question the ability of "Little Mac" as an organizer. Upon the foundation which he laid, single-handed, was erected the whole structure of Grant's success in Virginia. He gave the Army of the Potomac in its formative period the character, the cohesion, and indirectly, therefore, the stamina, which enabled it to withstand the severest punishments ever administered to an army ultimately victorious.

In the reorganization of the artillery the following radical and comprehensive regulations were promulgated by McClellan, largely proposed by Wm. F. Barry, his Chief of Artillery.

"1st.   The proportion of artillery should be in the ratio of at least 2½ pieces to 1,000 men, to be expanded, if possible, to 3 pieces.

"2d.   The field guns should be restricted to the systems of the United States Ordnance Department and of Parrott, the smoothbores (with the exception of a few howitzers for special service), to be exclusively the 12-pounder guns, model 1857, variously called the gun howitzer, light 12-pounder, or the Napoleon.

"3d.   Each field battery to be composed, if practicable, of 6, and none to have less than 4, guns, those of each battery to be of uniform caliber.

4th.   The field batteries to be assigned to divisions, and not to brigades, in the proportion of 4 to each division, one of which should be a regular battery, the rest volunteers; the captain of the regulars to command the artillery of the division.   In the event of several divisions being united into an army corps, at least one-half of the divisional artillery to be withdrawn from the divisions and formed into a corps reserve.*

"5th.   The reserve artillery of the whole army to consist of 100 guns, comprising besides a sufficient number of light mounted batteries, all the guns of position, and, until the cavalry be massed, all the horse artillery.

"6th.   The amount of ammunition to accompany the field batteries to be not less than 400 rounds per gun.

"7th.   A siege train of 50 pieces to be provided.†

"8th.   Instruction in the theory and practice of gunnery, as well as the tactics of that arm, to be given to the officers and non-commissioned officers of the volunteer batteries, by the study of suitable books and by actual recitations in each division, under the direction of the regular officer commanding the divisional artillery.

"9th.   Personal inspections, as frequent as circumstances will permit, to be made by the Chief of Artillery of the Army, to see to a strict observance of the established organization and drill, of the special regulations and orders issued from time to time, under authority of the commanding general, to note the improvement of officers and men of the volunteer batteries, and the actual fitness for field service of the whole, both regulars and volunteers."

---

*This contingency arose on the Peninsula in June, 1862. See subsequent mention.

†Subsequently expanded to 100 pieces at Yorktown, including 13-inch seacoast mortars and 100-pounder and 200-pounder Parrotts.

As early as August 21, Gen. Barry had urged Mc-Clellan to reorganize and increase the field artillery arm in the following words:

"To insure success, it is of vital importance that the army should have an overwhelming force of field artillery. To render this the more effective, the field batteries should, as far as possible, consist of regular troops."

While McClellan was not prepared to enlarge the regular establishment, he lost no time in increasing the general efficiency of the Army, by encouraging and directing his artillery officers. In his report, he wrote: "The creation of an adequate artillery establishment was a formidable undertaking, and had it not been that the country possessed in the regular service a body of accomplished and energetic artillery officers, the task would almost have been hopeless."

Assembling all the regular batteries he could secure for his army, when the 3 corps, or his 8 divisions embarked for the Peninsula, they were accompanied by 49 batteries aggregating 299 guns, of which 100, comprised of 18 batteries, were in the reserve. Of the 49 batteries, 20 were of the regular service and 14 of these were in the reserve. These figures do not include the guns of McDowell's 1st Corps, of which McClellan was soon deprived.*

The batteries of McClellan's Army were organized, equipped, and instructed in as exact accordance with the regulations he had prescribed, as a number of active and efficient officers, directed by a most capable chief, could cause them to be.

When the divisions were organized into corps for service on the Peninsula, corps commanders were ordered to create out of a half-part of their divisional batteries a corps reserve, in charge of a chief. This was done the first week of June.

The contemplated employment of field guns in masses as provided for by the organization of divisional,

---

*Historical Sketch of the Artillery of the United States Army, Birkhimer, p. 82.

corps, and reserve artillery in the Army of the Potomac, while a radical advance in tactics in one sense,
was yet but a reversion to Napoleonic principles. It
has been stated that the reason for the reserve was to
withhold from committing to action all the guns, since
once under fire they might not be shifted. By retaining in hand a large group, its massed fire might be suddenly hurled against any point, thereby bringing about
a decision. The introduction of horse artillery made
the very rapid concentration of guns at any point all
the more possible.

Du Teil was the original exponent of increased mobility in field artillery, and the concentration of its
fire.* "One must concentrate the bulk of the troops
and a superior artillery on that point where one wishes
to defeat the enemy, while one must deceive him in the
other points. The artillery will gain superiority over
the hostile artillery if it invariably concentrates its fire
on the decisive points. The artillery must be increased
against those points which decide the victory; thus it
gives decisive results. When attacking a position, it is
only a question of concentrating one's fire and efforts
upon some of its weak points, in order to force the
enemy to evacuate it. The moment when troops are to
act is determined by the havoc which the artillery will
have caused. If the redoubts are breached, the hostile
troops demoralized and beaten, the victory which the
artillery has prepared only depends then on the valour
of the assailant, etc." The representative of these views
had left the regiment la Fere shortly before young
Bonaparte joined it, and du Teil's elder brother, in
thorough accord with such views, was the Commandant
of the Military School at Auxonne, where the young
officer received his professional training.† Bonaparte,
Senarmont, and Drouot, were therefore early impressed
with the offensive possibilities of field artillery, and
Napoleon, as Von Caemmerer says, thought of his guns
when he exclaimed, "Le feu est tout, le reste n'est rien."

---

*The Development of Strategical Science, Von Caemmerer, p. 17.
†Von Caemmerer. See also L'Education Militaire de Napoleon, Colin.

Napoleon, then, was not so much the originator of artillery masses as the military executor of du Teil, as well as of Guibert and Bourcet. In his day the increased mobility of field guns over those of Frederick the Great, and the terrible power of case-shot preparation, together with the more judicious use of reserves, made it possible for him to shatter the resistance of the enemy.* But a vast change in conditions had come about with the introduction of the rifled gun.† Ranges so increased that no longer were field pieces finally committed when they first became engaged and the old reserve constantly tended to keep out of action guns which might better have been employed from the first. Superior ranges over the small arm not only enabled the guns to be retained in hand when pushed into action, but the increased range gave them a wider zone of efficiency, for without changing position rifled pieces were able to coöperate with others at distant points, in concentrating their fire on any given position of the enemy. Thus the effect of concentrated fire could be secured from dispersed groups as well as from great masses of guns.‡ Such conditions, rendering it unnecessary to hold back a great reserve group of guns, led to the change of name for the component groups of the reserve which now became known as corps, or divisional reserves.

"Many philosophers have said," wrote Prince Kraft, "What's in a name? But, you think with me on this subject, that the Army is not composed of philosophers. On the contrary, they are men, and thus human, and in the stress of battle, pay little attention to abstract principles. Names, gaudy uniforms, orders and an empty stomach, all things which a philosopher treats with contempt, play a decisive part in war. Thus the change of name by regulation was an act of far-reaching results. When the reserve artillery had been renamed corps artillery, every leader of troops and every

*Evolution of Infantry Tactics, Maude, pp. 118-120.
†Field Artillery with the Other Arms, May, pp. 60, 61, 62.
‡Letters on Field Artillery, Hohenlohe, p. 140.

BRIGADIER-GENERAL REUBEN LINDSAY WALKER
CHIEF OF ARTILLERY, THIRD CORPS

staff officer was at once compelled to recognize that they were no longer to be held in reserve, but had become a part of the line of battle."

What the learned Prussian has written concerning the change in the tactical employment of field artillery in Germany, after the war of 1866, applies with great directness to conditions in America in 1862, but an admission cannot be found in his work that American experience had contributed to the Prussian knowledge. There are indications that Von Hindersin, the Inspector-General of Artillery, did take notice of our development of, and experience with, the new rifled piece in the Civil War. But the lessons of this war were not heeded by the Prussians until after they had received many reverses with their artillery in their struggle with Austria. The faulty employment of their guns through a continued adherence to the reserve formation led the Prussians into many snares in 1866, their antagonists having profited by their own experiences in 1859. But in their disregard of what had transpired in Virginia we find a striking admonition not to ignore what our neighbors may be able to teach us. That America had sounded the practical note of divisional artillery many years before it reverberated through the continent there can be little question, although the Austrians and Prussians had both in theory provided for divisional artillery. That Johnston totally ignored the tactical principles of Napoleon and the French, as displayed at Solferino, in 1859, with respect to artillery masses, is also beyond dispute.

It may be argued that the Americans were merely groping in the dark; that realizing that something was wrong somewhere, a change was necessary; that the fact that a reserve was maintained in addition to divisional groups indicates the imperfection of tactical ideas. Yet, the fact remains that new conditions which could only be thrown into relief by experience were promptly met and that nowhere do we find a practical guide for the radical changes effected by McClellan and Lee.

CHAPTER X

THE principle event in the field artillery arm of the Army during the fall of 1861, outside of the arrival of new batteries, including a number from Maryland, North and South Carolina, and Georgia, and the general activity in refitting and drilling, was the organization under special authority of the Secretary of War, November 11, 1861, of a horse battery. This battery was created at the suggestion of Col. Ashby, commanding the cavalry with Jackson's Army in the Valley, who perceived the great value of guns possessing sufficient mobility to accompany his troopers, and its organization was the first step toward the formation of that wonderful horse artillery corps which, for the next four years under Pelham, Chew, Beckham, Breathed, Thomson, and others, astounded the world with its daring and deeds of valor.

Organized with an enlisted personnel of 33 men, its first officers were: Robert Preston Chew, Captain; Milton Rouse, First Lieutenant; James Thomson, Second Lieutenant; all young graduates of the Virginia Military Institute and former pupils of Jackson, to the fame of whose army they were now to contribute many laurels. Chew's Battery soon earned for itself a name and reputation second only to that of Ashby himself, and second to no other battery in the Confederate armies. The clatter of its horses' feet, the rumble of its guns upon the turnpike, the shriek of its shells, were sounds familiar to every resident of the Valley from the Potomac to Staunton, and it probably took part in more engagements than any other battery in the war, North or South. The membership of this celebrated command increased rapidly after its organization, up to April 9, 1865, when it surrendered 197 men. After the death

of Ashby and Jackson, Chew's Battery became a part
of Stuart's horse artillery battalion, of which in 1864
the gallant Chew became commander. The history of
the first horse battery is so inseparably interwoven with
that of Ashby, Jackson, and Stuart, that it cannot be
written apart from that of those famous soldiers and
their cavalry. In the minds of the men of the Army it
and Ashby's Cavalry "belonged to each other as by
natural affinity."

The armament of the battery from first to last consisted of 3 pieces; a Blakely imported British rifled
piece, which fired a percussion shell; a smooth-bore 12-
pounder howitzer; and a 3-inch iron rifle.

When Chew and his officers, mere beardless youths,
called upon Gen. Jackson, their former instructor, to
report for duty, the face of the stern soldier wore a
quizzical, though amused, expression,* as he said,
"Young men, now that you have your company, what
are you going to do with it?" The deeds of the battery
from then on were to be the answer, a reply which appealed far more to Jackson than words could have done.
Nothing in the history of artillery ever surpassed in
skill and courage the service of Ashby's horse battery
in the Valley campaign. Unlimbering on every hill, it
held the pursuers in check, and dashing to the front with
the foremost troopers it opened every fight; in pursuit
it was always on hand working havoc among the fleeing
foe. The remarks of Henderson regarding the unsurpassed character of Jackson's light horse under Ashby
apply to that portion of the latter's command known as
Chew's Battery.

Horse artillery had also been early recognized in the
Union Army as the associate of properly organized
cavalry, and about the time Chew's Battery was formed,
Company A, Second Regiment, Field Artillery, United
States Army, was equipped for that service at Wash-
ington. This and Chew's Battery were the first horse

---

*Chew was 19, Rouse 17, and Thomson 18 years old in November, 1861.
See Chew's address at the unveiling of Ezekiel's statue of Jackson, at the
Virginia Military Institute, June 19, 1912.

artillery in America since Bragg's company was dismounted at Sante Fé after the Mexican War.*

The force which was given Jackson in November 1861, with which to play upon the fears of the Washington Administration by threatening the Capital from the Valley, was indeed a small one, but by the first of the following year it had been largely increased. On January 10, he had with him McLaughlin's (Rockbridge) Battery, 6 guns; Waters' Battery, 4 guns; Carpenter's Alleghany Battery, 4 guns; Marye's Battery, 4 guns; Chew's Battery, 3 guns; or a total of 25 pieces, having lost Cutshaw's 2 guns at Romney on January 7.† Jackson's Chief of Artillery was at this time Maj. Daniel Truehart, an old cadet, with Lieut. Ed. Willis as his assistant, and his ordnance officer was Lieut. J. M. Garnett, who was succeeded by Lieut. H. H. Lee and the latter by Lieut. R. H. Meade.

When in February, 1862, Banks began his advance to seize Winchester, arriving at Martinsburg March 3, Jackson was instructed "to endeavor to employ the invaders in the Valley, but without exposing himself to the danger of defeat, by keeping so near the enemy as to prevent him from making any considerable detachment to reënforce McClellan, but not so near that he might be compelled to fight."‡ Jackson's force now consisted of 3,600 infantry, 600 cavalry, and the 6 batteries, with their 27 guns before mentioned, the artillery with a total personnel of 369.§

Banks had with him when he crossed the Potomac 38,000 men, including 2,000 cavalry, and 80 pieces of artillery, a large proportion of which were the most modern rifled guns, fully horsed and equipped.¶

In the great campaign which followed, the artillery, far inferior in equipment to that of the Federals in every respect, except as to personnel, was able by the daring

*Birkhimer, p. 70.
†Chew was with Ashby at the time.
‡Johnston's Narrative, p. 106.
§Henderson's Stonewall Jackson, p. 270; Jackson's Valley Campaign, Allan, p. 39.
¶Henderson's Jackson, p. 265.

and skill of its men successfully to oppose the enemy on almost every battlefield. The marching ability of the batteries, more often provided with four-horse teams than otherwise, was on a par with that of the wonderful infantry. "Whilst it is absolutely true that no soldiers ever marched with less to encumber them than the Confederates, it is no empty boast that none ever marched faster, or held out longer." "Fine feathers, though they may have their use, are hardly essential to efficiency in the field."*

In the Valley campaign there is little of a tactical nature to be considered concerning the light artillery. The batteries, though poorly armed, horsed, and equipped, were officered by bold, gallant, intelligent men, who did all which under the prevailing system could have been expected of them. The enlisted personnel, consisting largely of highly educated and socially superior volunteers, while not possessing the discipline of the men in the Northern batteries, surpassed the latter in individual efficiency. Of this, there can be little doubt, and to this fact must be largely attributed the ability of the Confederate gunners so successfully to oppose the highly efficient batteries of the Federal Army. The batteries of Jackson's army displayed the same endurance, tenacity, ability to stand punishment, and *élan* common to the rest of his troops. They were fought with few exceptions as batteries; massed fire when employed resulting from the accident of position, rather than from a preconceived plan. Jackson, an artilleryman himself, did much to scout the old idea that artillery was incapable of facing the fire of infantry. The practice of withdrawing the guns when infantry fire was opened upon them, so common in the armies of his opponents, received no sanction from him, and soon his gunners learned the fallacy of such tactics and took their punishment unflinchingly.

But, if no new principle of light artillery tactics developed, or no old forgotten ones were revived, in this

*Thus wrote Henderson of Jackson's troops, p. 273. In 48 marching days they covered 676 miles, an average of 14 miles per diem.

campaign, the same cannot be said of the horse artillery which introduced and adopted a maneuver in battle hitherto known to have been executed in but insolated cases, one of which was when Ramsey's horse battery at Fuentes de Onoro, finding itself cut off by French cavalry, limbered up, charged the enemy, and cut its way out. But this action, nor the charges of the mounted Prussian detachments of the horse artillery, which the gunners were trained to make to save their guns from capture, can be said to have constituted shock tactics for artillery. This new development in the Confederate artillery was the natural outgrowth of Ashby's reckless daring, and the courage of Capt. Chew. Born of an accident, as it were, when the practicability of the maneuver was perceived, the practice became more or less general in the Confederate horse artillery and was frequently repeated during the war as will be shown. The facts concerning the first instance of guns charging with the cavalry are given in the words of Col. R. Preston Chew himself, whose recollection of the incident is borne out by numerous authorities.*

"Gen. Jackson had assembled his army at Cedarville, on the road from Front Royal to Winchester, on the night of the 23d of May, 1862. On the 24th Gen. Ashby was ordered, with his cavalry, supported by a part of Taylor's Bridgade, to take Chew's Battery and two guns from the Rockbridge Artillery, and assail the enemy at Middletown on the Valley turnpike. His advance was stubbornly opposed by the Federal Infantry, but he succeeded in driving them back, and emerged into the open field near Middletown. Telling me to move with the cavalry, he charged the enemy's cavalry, from 2,000 to 2,500 strong, in the road at Middletown. Our guns charged with the cavalry, and when within a short distance, probably 100 yards from the turnpike, we unlimbered and opened on the Federals. There was a stone fence on either side of the road, and we caught them at a great disadvantage. . . . The enemy fled in every direction, and Ashby pursued them along the turnpike toward Newtown. When we came to a point called Crisman's, he reformed his cavalry, and telling me again to charge

*Col. Chew's statement is contained in a letter to the author, dated November 9, 1912. See also the *Laurel Brigade*, McDonald, pp. 60, 61; *Ashby and His Compeers*, Avirett; *Ashby and His Men*, Thomas.

with his troops, he assailed the enemy, who were drawn up upon the crest of a hill. We went at them with the same maneuver adopted at Middletown, and drove the enemy back in great confusion."*

In referring to the first charge of Ashby's cavalry, with Chew's guns, Jackson, in his official report, wrote: "In a few moments the turnpike, which just before had teemed with life, presented a most appalling spectacle of carnage and destruction. The road was literally obstructed with the mingled and confused mass of struggling and dying horses and riders. Amongst the survivors, the wildest confusion ensued, and they scattered in disorder in various directions, leaving some 200 prisoners in the hands of the Confederates."

Col. Chew recently gave the author a verbal and a more detailed account of the affair, stating that he was utterly amazed when Ashby told him to charge with the guns and that he hardly had time to consider the order before it was to be executed, the command and the time of execution being almost simultaneous. Forming behind a thin line of cavalry, the guns moved off at a gallop, the troopers passing to the flanks as the guns unlimbered and went into action. The enemy, unable to discern the guns at first, and seeing but a few troopers, were dumfounded when they perceived their peril and became panic stricken upon the first discharge of the "Blakely," and the bursting of a shell.

Writing of subsequent charges of the Horse Artillery, Col. Chew says:

"In 1864, when I commanded the Horse Artillery, we joined Rosser on the Cartharpin Road. He was engaged with Wilson's Division, cavalry, and, immediately after we joined him, we charged the enemy with his brigade. I carried Thomson's Battery into the charge with the cavalry, and, after Rosser had struck the head of their column, we threw the guns into position, and did fine execution. The next day at Rose's farm, when Stuart was in command, we went into the fight with the cavalry again. This was often done by the Horse Artillery in subsequent fights."†

---

*The incident as narrated is also declared to be correct by Col. W. T. Poague, who commanded the Rockbridge Battery at the time, and who is now an officer of the Virginia Military Institute with the author.
†Same personal letter hereinbefore referred to.

Such action on the part of horse artillery was as novel as it was effective, but it must be admitted its proper execution required extraordinary qualities. True, the chief duties of horse artillery, then as it now is and always has been, was to stay with the cavalry at all costs, and coöperate with it by preparing the road for its advance and retarding pursuers, but having prepared the road, it was never before contemplated that the gunners should accompany the troopers to the assault. The feats of Chew with his battery excelled even those of the horse gunner, Kostenetski, at Austerlitz, and more than fulfilled the maxim of Napoleon, that "Horse Artillery and Cavalry must be the complements, the one of the other"; and of Leer, that "Horse Artillery must be Cavalry with guns."

The Prussian Horse Artillery, of 1866, was considered by the greatest artillery authority on the continent to have done its full duty when it moved into position, perhaps the last 500 yards at a gallop, and silenced the enemy's guns in the artillery duel preceding the charge of its cavalry.* And, later, when rifled pieces were generally introduced into the horse batteries, it was not deemed necessary for them to approach as close to the enemy as before. In comparison with the Prussian ideas, Ashby's innovation was, to say the least, a radical one.

The limited scope of such a work as this is designed to be precludes the possibility of following in detail the performances of Jackson's gunners, which, while in innumerable instances quite remarkable, displayed few departures from the tactical principles of the time. For an intimate knowledge of officers, men, and conditions of the Artillery of the Army of the Valley, one must consult the numerous delightful works to be had, dealing with the minutia of the service.†

---

*Letters on Artillery, Hohenlohe, p. 144.
†Three Years in the Confederate Horse Artillery, Neese; The Story of a Cannoneer Under Stonewall Jackson, Moore; The Laurel Brigade, McDonald; Ashby and His Compeers, Avirett; Ashby and His Men, Thomas. For full and accurate accounts of Jackson's campaigns, see Jackson's Valley Campaign, Allan; and Stonewall Jackson, Henderson.

It is interesting, however, to note the comparative strength in personnel and guns of the artillery of Jackson and his various opponents.

At Kernstown, Jackson had with him 27 pieces of artillery, 18 of which only were engaged, while Shields had in command of Lieut.-Col. Philip Daum, Jenks' and Davis' brigade batteries, and Clark's regular battery, with a total of 24 guns. In this engagement, Carpenter's, McLaughlin's, and Waters' batteries, silenced the main body of the Federal guns and were withdrawn only as a result of Garnett's untimely retreat. The Confederate batteries on this occasion were divided between the two flanks of the infantry line, and the Federal batteries, 5 in number, occupied 5 quite distinct positions, and of course with the available lines of communication, were capable of little concert of action.

The massed fire of batteries contemplates more than proximity of position of guns. At Kernstown there was neither concentration of fire nor proximity of position, a number of the batteries on both sides merely having the same target. There is nothing to lead us to believe that the fire of the three batteries which Jackson placed on his right was even expected to be directed with any definite purpose, except to do the most harm possible to the enemy.

When Garnett fell back from his position near Jackson's main group of artillery on the right, a swarm of Federal skirmishers in the thickets fired upon the batteries, severely punishing them before they withdrew. In limbering up one of the 6-pounders was overturned, and as some of the enemy's infantry was already within 50 paces, the sergeant in charge cut loose the remaining three horses, the gun being abandoned to the enemy. Jackson had, therefore, lost three pieces of artillery, including the two guns captured from Cutshaw at Romney.

In the battle of Kernstown, the artillery personnel engaged was, Federal 608, and Confederate about 200.* The latter suffered a loss of 17 wounded and 1 missing, the former, killed 4, wounded 2.†

*For Federal strength, see *Rebellion Records*, Vol. XII, Part III, p. 4.
†*Stonewall Jackson*, Henderson, p. 262. *Battles and Leaders*, Vol. II, p. 299.

Soon after the battle of McDowell, in which there was no good opportunity to employ artillery, Gen. Jackson applied to have Lieut.-Col. Stapleton Crutchfield, of the 58th Virginia Infantry, assigned to him as Chief of Artillery. This officer had the previous Spring been assigned to duty as a major of the 9th Virginia Artillery, stationed at Craney Island near Norfolk, but not liking the monotony of coast defense duty, he had transferred to a more active branch. Crutchfield was just twenty-six years of age when he became Jackson's Chief of Artillery, but their relations were born of mutual confidence in one another. Not only had the young officer been a pupil of Jackson's at the Virginia Military Institute, graduating first in the Class of 1855, but he had served as an assistant professor of mathematics in the faculty of the school for six years with the man who was now to be his commander.

May 21, Jackson's force was largely increased by the union of his own division with that of Gen. Ewell, to which was attached Courtney's and Brockenbrough's batteries, the Army of the Valley now numbering about 1,600, including an artillery personnel of from 300 to 400.* The artillery with the Army at the time of the battle of Winchester was composed of the following batteries:

Poague's Battery, 6 guns; Carpenter's Battery, 4 guns; Cutshaw's Battery, 4 guns; Wooding's Battery, 4 guns; Caskie's Battery, 4 guns; Raine's Battery, 4 guns; Rice's Battery, 4 guns; Lusk's Battery, 4 guns; Courtney's Battery, 6 guns; Brockenbrough's Battery, 4 guns; Chew's Battery, 3 guns; total pieces of artillery, 47 guns.†

The Federal force at Strasburg, under Banks at this time, numbered between 6,000 and 7,000 men, including 3 batteries with a personnel of about 280 and an armament of ten 3-inch Parrott rifles, and six S. B. 6-

---

*Jackson's Valley Campaign, Allan, p. 93.
†Jackson's Valley Campaign, Allan, pp. 91, 92, 93, 108, 109, 111. Chew's Battery did not have four pieces as stated by Col. Allan. Poague's (Rockbridge) Battery, formerly commanded by Pendleton, then McLaughlin, had had 8 guns for some time, but 6 in May.

pounders. Jackson had captured the two 10-pounder Parrott rifles of Knapp's Battery at Front Royal, on the 22d of May, thus collecting the debt which the enemy owed him for the 3 guns he had lost.*

In the battle of Winchester, while the Confederates were greatly superior to Banks in artillery, as well as in infantry, 2 well-placed Federal batteries with rifled pieces, and a loss of but 2 killed, 14 wounded, and 12 missing, severely punished 3 batteries, Poague's, Carpenter's, and Cutshaw's, with which Jackson engaged them in a duel, the first alone losing 2 officers, 16 men, and 9 horses; the second, 1 officer, and 5 men. The Federal batteries were assisted to some extent by their skirmishers, who effectually harassed the Confederate gunners, but the great damage sustained by Poague's Battery was due to the fact that one of the Federal batteries skillfully changed position, supported by an infantry regiment, and enfiladed it. Yet, the fact remains that acting more or less together in their duel with Banks' guns, the three Confederate batteries almost entirely diverted the artillery fire of the enemy from the infantry, thus enabling Taylor's and Winder's men to charge home and win the day.

But the question naturally arises, if Banks had but 3 batteries and Jackson had 8, besides the two on the right with Ewell, and the horse battery off with Ashby, where were the five disengaged batteries? Surely they were not all being engaged by the remaining Federal battery of 6 pieces. It is quite plain now to see that with such a superiority in the number of guns, Jackson should not have allowed a few of his batteries to do all the work, but should have smothered the enemy's fire early in the day with the combined, or we should say, the simultaneous fire of every available gun, not only saving his batteries, but his infantry as well. The error committed by Jackson in this respect was one repeatedly committed by the Prussians in 1866, who did not under-

*Jackson's Valley Campaign, Allan, pp. 94, 109. These were Best's Battery, 6 guns; Cothran's Battery, 6 guns; and Hampton's Battery, 4 guns. Ibid., pp. 96, 98.

stand how to bring up their guns to the front, a lesson
which the Austrians had learned in 1859, and applied
throughout the war with disastrous results to their
enemy. But, if the manner of the employment of his
artillery was faulty in the engagement itself, the manner in which he caused two of his batteries to hang upon
the heels of the retreating enemy is especially worthy
of praise, the Potomac alone stopping the batteries
which had suffered the most. Indeed, one is constantly
surprised at the remarkable mobility and pertinacity of
Poague's and Carpenter's batteries, which had won for
themselves the name of the Stonewall Artillery, fitting
companions of the Stonewall Brigade, acting on more
than one occasion with Ashby's horse artillery.

The main difference between the artillery fire at
Kernstown and Winchester, was in the range at which
the guns fought in the two battles. At Kernstown, the
opposing batteries certainly did not approach each other
at any stage of the battle, nearer than one mile and
much of their fire was delivered at a range of over 2,500
yards. On the other hand, at Winchester, the artillery
duel between Poague's, Cutshaw's, and Carpenter's batteries, and the two Federal batteries, was conducted at a
short range even for that period, not exceeding 800
yards in the main, and for some of the batteries as close
as 500 yards. This sudden drawing together of the
two artilleries was undoubtedly due more to the con-
figuration of the terrain, than to any desire to develop
the fire of the guns at a decisive range. Then, too, ar-
tilery positions were determined to a large extent by
considerations for the supporting infantry, as well as
for the guns, a feature which has become less important
as the range of the latter has increased, since batteries
with long range guns can secure great effect at distances
which forbid the idea of a serious fire fight between infantry. In 1862, before infantry received its support
from the guns, it had first to support them. Improved
material, however, enabled the artillery to give the
infantry effective support, more or less independently

of the position of the latter, and the batteries now are expected to enter the zone of effective infantry fire only after the opposing artillery has been silenced and their own infantry has advanced to the assault, masking to a large extent the fire of the guns which have helped them forward. During this phase of the combat it is assumed that either the infantry will divert the musketry fire of the enemy from its guns, enabling the latter to move up to a decisive range, or that if the defenders neglect the assaulting infantry, the guns by receiving the fire will make it all the easier for the assaulting infantry to reach the position of the enemy. In either case, the artillery will do its part, but the former will be the general result of the modern method of attack, when the guns of the offense have obtained a superiority over those of the defense.

In the battles of Port Republic and Cross Keys, Crutchfield's artillery consisted of 6 batteries, Carpenter's, Caskie's, Cutshaw's, Wooding's, Poague's, and Carrington's, with a total personnel of about 300 men, the last having joined since the battle of Winchester. Only 5 batteries were actually engaged.* Ewell's Division had in addition to Brockenbrough's Baltimore Battery, attached to the Maryland line under Steuart, 4 batteries, Latimer's Courtney, Lusk's, Raine's, and Rice's. Thus, exclusive of Chew's Battery (under Munford since Ashby's death), Jackson had 11 batteries with a total personnel of about 600 men, and 48 guns.

In the two engagements the losses of the Confederate Artillery were 8 killed, 29 wounded, and 9 missing, a total of but 46.

Shields' Division at Port Republic had 16 guns, the batteries being the same as at Winchester under Daum. These batteries fought with great gallantry, losing 31 men, and 7 of their guns in hand-to-hand encounters with the Confederate Infantry after having all but routed the attackers before the latter were reënforced. But if anything, they had by far the worst of the artillery

---

*Stonewall Jackson, Henderson, p. 474; Battles and Leaders, Vol. II, p. 301; Jackson's Valley Campaign, Allan, p. 145, et seq.

fight proper, though they were most skillfully disposed, about half being placed on a wooded mountain side.

Fremont's artillery consisted of 10 batteries which, arriving with their supine leader, were overwhelmed by the Confederate guns, occupying as they did a most favorable position.

At Cross Keys, the batteries of Courtney, Lusk, Brockenbrough, and Raines, were massed in the center of Ewell's line and acted more in concert than artillery had hitherto done in the campaign. Their fire was well conducted, with all the advantages of position to which artillery is entitled by a prior selection for the defense of a given point.

At Port Republic, Wooding's, Poague's, and Carpenter's batteries, in position on the north bluff of the river, safe from infantry attack, the brigade being defended by Carrington's guns, exerted by a well-directed fire great influence upon the issue, raking the Federal Infantry with deadly effect, and playing upon Daum's guns whenever an opportunity to shift from the infantry was allowed them. The employment of the artillery at Port Republic and Cross Keys evidences a growing tendency on the part of Jackson to use his batteries, to a certain extent, in concert, instead of distributing them here and there on the battlefield with his brigades, and thereby dissipating the effect of their fire.

Early in the war, the Confederate Bureau of Ordnance had developed a 2.25-inch mountain rifle, which was transported in parts on the backs of mules, much after the present system of mountain artillery. There was also a 12-pounder mountain howitzer, of the model of 1841, in use in the service, though but few pieces of ordnance of this character were ever placed in the field. For occasional draught, when the roads permitted, the gun carriage was provided with a thill, which was attached to the same saddle that carried the pack.* A mule battery of 12-pounder mountain

---

*See pp. 9, 49, *Ordnance Manual*, C. S. A., 1863, and plate 6.

howitzers, in command of Maj. Imboden, reported to Jackson just before the action of Port Republic, but did not accomplish much in the way of results by reason of the conduct of the mules under fire. Their loads weighing about 300 pounds were so securely attached to them, that they resorted to the tactics of rolling on the ground to free themselves, and the gunners were principally occupied in holding down the recalcitrant mules, rather than delivering a fire upon the enemy.* But while the battery did not accomplish much from a military standpoint, it afforded rare amusement to the men of the Infantry. With the air of men seeking technical information, they would seriously inquire whether the mules or the guns were intended to go off first, and whether the gun was to fire the mule, or the mule the gun.† In the estimate of Jackson's artillery at Port Republic, Imboden's Battery was not included, for under the circumstances its guns could not be properly classed as effective ordnance.

In the Valley campaign the Confederate Artillery as a whole demonstrated its mobility beyond a question. It had been constantly engaged in fighting and marching for many days, pitted always against superior material. Yet, it had lost but 3 pieces, while the enemy lost 9. An unusual proportion of its officers subsequently attained higher rank, the experience they had gained in the Valley proving of great service to the Army as a whole.

*A 3-inch rifled Parrott gun which Imboden had brought with him was turned over to Poague's Battery at Port Republic.
†*Battles and Leaders,* Vol. II, p. 291, *et seq.; Stonewall Jackson,* Henderson, Vol. V., p. 465.

CHAPTER XI

THE PENINSULA CAMPAIGN

THE details of the movement of the Artillery down the Peninsula to Yorktown are simply those of monotonous marches day after day, through sand and mud, till men and beasts were exhausted. But, on this long and arduous march, the light batteries were well seasoned to work the character of which always tends to the elimination of surplus train, and the weaker element of the personnel. It was the first duty of this kind which the Field Artillery, except that in the Valley, had been called upon to perform.

In front of Yorktown McClellan had established siege batteries, mounting 71 guns, including two 200-pounder, and five 100-pounder rifles, and a number of 13-inch mortars, with which to overwhelm Magruder's weak lines. On May 1, his batteries opened fire. To oppose the Federal land force, Magruder had mounted in his works about 15 nondescript pieces of ordnance, including a number of field guns, for which there were from 30 to 60 rounds of ammunition, according to the caliber of the pieces.* Desperate efforts were now made to transfer some of the heavier ordnance from the water batteries to the land side of the defenses.

The Army of the Peninsula, or the right wing of the Army of Northern Virginia, numbering 22,740 men of all arms, on April 23, 1862, included a field artillery personnel of 646, with 49 pieces, and a heavy artillery brigade of 697 men.† With such a deficiency of artillery, both as to men and material, Johnston never once contemplated risking siege operations at Yorktown, although on the 18th he had brought up the left wing and had reorganized his army, placing it in position behind the lines already established. The right of

---

*Rebellion Records, Series I, Vol. XI, Part III, pp. 438, 439, 447.
†Ibid., p. 460.

the position commencing at Dam No. 1, and extending to the Warwick River, was assigned to Magruder; Yorktown proper to D. H. Hill; the center to Longstreet; and the reserve to G. W. Smith. With the last was the reserve artillery.*

May 2, the artillery, except the heavy guns, was ordered to be quietly withdrawn from the lines after sunset, and put in motion for Williamsburg,† and on May 3, the entire Army began to retire before the enemy up the Peninsula.

The artillery at this time was quite dependent upon infantry supports, even on the march. Magruder's battle orders, he himself having been an artilleryman, prescribed that commanding officers should always designate a sufficient force of infantry to protect the guns in action, and that in all marches, whether to the front or rear, the artillery should be placed at intervals in the infantry columns. In marching on narrow roads, brigade batteries were to be split up into sections, one moving near the rear of the brigade to which its battery belonged. If a column were attacked in retreat, the practice was for the cavalry and infantry to leave the road in order to allow the rear guns a clear field of fire, and in the event the enemy's cavalry undertook to charge the guns, the infantry formed a square, or circle, about them at charge bayonets, firing when necessary.‡ Such dispositions were induced mainly by the closeness of the country in which the Army of the Peninsula was operating and were generally adhered to in that section.

The retrograde movement of the Artillery from Yorktown was attended with the utmost difficulty and hardship. Execrable weather had rendered the roads all but bottomless, and without the constant assistance of the infantry commands, the gunners would have been utterly unable to save their pieces from the mires and later from the enemy. No march of artillery was ever,

---

*Rebellion Records, Series I, Vol. XI, Part III, p. 448, G. O. No. 1.
†Ibid., p. 489, General Order.
‡Ibid., p. 410, G. O. No. 168.

perhaps, made under more adverse conditions, for the route of the Army lay over roads which were delusions as highways. Horses for the additional guns taken from the Yorktown defenses were sadly lacking, and not even those of the cavalry, the personal property of the men themselves, were available for purposes of draught. Thus, the worn-out teams of the light batteries, already much reduced by the march of the preceding week, were called upon for the most unreasonable exertions. Sunday night, the 4th, the Reserve Artillery had reached Hickory Neck Church, and by the most tremendous efforts succeeded in reaching Barhamsville on the 5th. On that day occurred the fight at Williamsburg, in which nothing of special import concerning the artillery of either army took place, except that Hooker and Smith lost 12 pieces of artillery and young Capt. John Pelham of Stuart's horse battery greatly distinguished himself for daring. In this affair, a detaining engagement on the part of the Confederates for the purpose of saving their trains, the Confederate Artillery played a minor rôle and only the brigade batteries were present.

During the retreat, Gen. Rains, commanding the rear guard of Johnston's Army, had placed in the path of the pursuers an explosive shell which caused consternation among the enemy, and violent protests on the part of the Federal authorities. The actual result had been slight, however, yet, the practice led to an almost immediate investigation by Gen. Johnston.* In a communication, he took occasion to say: "It is the desire of the Major-General commanding that you put no shells or torpedoes behind you, as he does not recognize it as proper or effective method of war." On this communication were endorsed the following remarks:

"A shell which can be prepared and unprepared in a moment, and a sentinel to keep our own people off, are all that is wanted for our protection.

*Rebellion Records, Series I, Vol. XI, Part II, pp. 509, 510, 516.

"Our volunteers cannot be restrained from firing their guns when they ought not, and so frequent is this fault that the small report of a gun of a sentinel, as a rifle, for instance, is not heeded, and our troops liable to surprise and destruction, of which we have had three notable cases. A shell prepared would remedy this, for the advancing enemy would explode it, and that would lessen their force, demoralize their troops, and give us time with loud warning to prepare for the conflict. As it is, I am compelled to approximate to the same results—to send forward a picket of artillery, supported by infantry, which is liable to be cut off, and have our men killed or captured by such rigid philanthropy for the enemy, which I have myself possessed until lately.

"These shells give us decided advantage over the foe invading our soil, especially in frustrating night surprises, requiring but little powder for great results in checking advancing columns at all times.

"For their being proper for war, they are as much so as ambuscades, masked batteries, and mines. The enemy, I learn, intended to mine and blow up Redoubt No. 4, known as Ft. Magruder, at Yorktown; and if such means of killing by wholesale be proper, why should not smaller mines be used? Can we accord to them alone the privilege of using against us those vast supplies of gunpowder for which they have raked the world, by advantages derived from a navy much of which properly belongs to us? For their effectiveness, I refer to the enemy.

"Believing as I do the vast advantages to our country to be gained from this invention, I am unwilling to forego it, and beg leave to appeal direct to the War Department.

"I have the honor to be very respectfully, etc.,

"C. J. RAINS,
"*Brigadier-General, Commanding Brigade
in the Field, near Richmond.*"

"Respectfully forwarded.

"In my opinion all means of destroying our brutal enemies are lawful and proper.

"D. H. HILL,
"*Major-General.*"

"HEADQUARTERS, DEPARTMENT OF NORTHERN VA.,

"NEAR CROSS ROADS, May 12, 1862.

"MAJ.-GEN. D. H. HILL.

"GENERAL—Gen. Johnston desires that you inquire into the enclosed report, taken from the *New York Herald*, to ascertain if there is any truth in the statement, to find out if there were any torpedoes placed, and, if so, when, where, and by whom.

"Most respectfully,

"Your obedient servant,

"A. P. MASON,
"*Asst. Adjutant-General.*

"P. S.—The works where the enemy say the torpedoes were placed were those at Yorktown."

(INCLOSURE)
"Torpedoes."

(Extract from Gen. McClellan's report):

"The rebels have been guilty of the most murderous and barbarous conduct in placing torpedoes within the abandoned works, near wells, and springs, and near flag staffs, magazines, and telegraph offices, in carpet-bags, barrels of flour, etc.

"We have not lost many men in this manner—some four or five killed and perhaps a dozen wounded. I shall make the prisoners move them at their own peril."

This letter was referred by Gen. Hill to Gen. Rains in much the same manner as in his indorsement before set forth, the latter being referred to the Secretary of War,* who returned the same with the following remarks:

INDORSEMENT

"Whether shells planted in roads or parapets, are contrary to usages of war depends upon the purpose with which they are used.

"It is not admissible in civilized warfare to take life with no other object than the destruction of life. Hence it is inadmissible to shoot sentinels and pickets, because nothing is attained but the destruction of life. It would be admissible, however, to shoot a general, because you not only take a life but deprive an army of its head.

*Major G. W. Randolph, formerly in command of the Richmond Howitzer Battalion.

"It is admissible to plant shells in a parapet to repel an assault, or in a road to check a pursuit, because the object is to save the work in one case, and the army in the other.

"It is not admissible to plant shells merely to destroy life and without other design than that of depriving your enemy of a few men, without materially injuring him.

"It is admissible to plant torpedoes in a river or harbor, because they drive off blockading or attacking fleets.

"As Gens. Rains and Longstreet differ in this matter, the inferior in rank should give way, or, if he prefers it, he may be assigned river defenses, where such things are clearly admissible.

"G. W. RANDOLPH."

In answer to the communication of May 12, referred to him by Gen. Hill, Gen. Rains wrote as follows:

"CAMP, REAR GUARD, May 14, 1862.

"MAJ.-GEN. HILL,
    "Commanding Third Division.

"GENERAL—Yours of yesterday is acknowledged, and in answer I beg leave to recall to your mind that my command was the first to leave Yorktown by your order, and consequently I know nothing of the location of torpedoes at the places mentioned, nor do I believe it, as wells, or springs of water, barrels of flour, carpet-bags, etc., are places incompatible with the invention.

"That invention is strictly mine, as well as the essential parts of Colt's weapons, for the use of which I have never been called to account.

"If it be required to know what use I have made of the invention, I answer I commanded at Yorktown for the last seven months, and when Gen. McClellan approached with his army of 100,000 men and opened his cannon upon us, I had but 2,500 in garrison, and our whole Army on the Peninsula under Maj.-Gen. Magruder amounted to but 9,800 effective men; then, at a salient angle, an accessible point of our works, as part of the defenses thereof, I had the land mined with the weapons alluded to, to destroy assailants and prevent escalade. Subsequently, with a similar view, they were placed at spots I never saw.

"And, again, when at Williamsburg we were ordered to turn upon our assailants and combat them, which we did successfully, most of us without food for forty-eight hours, having stood all night in the rain without fire or light, the second of our vigils, cold and drenched to the skin, we took up our line of march to the rear by order, and when physical endurance had been taxed to the utmost, at a place of mud slushes, where it was impossible for us to fight or bring a single cannon to bear, some six or seven miles this side of Williamsburg, my command forming the rear guard of the army, and the enemy advancing upon our wearied and scattered troops, firing his cannon along the road, some four small shells found abandoned by our artillery were hastily prepared by my efforts and put in the road near a tree felled across, mainly to have a moral effect in checking the advance of the enemy (for they were too small to do more), to save our sick, wounded, and enfeebled, who straggled in our rear.

"Finally, I conclude by stating that the enemy's vessels approached Yorktown April 6, 1862, and without a word of warning to innocent women and children, as at New Berne, N. C., my native place, they commenced to pitch into the town, at a distance of four miles, entirely beyond the range of our guns, massive beams of iron 18 feet long, and enormous shells (which they continued for a month), both by day and even at the hour of midnight, bursting with awful noise and scattering their death-dealing fragments among the innocent and unoffending; fiendish acts unknown among civilized nations, reversing the scriptural text that it is better for ninety-nine guilty persons to escape than for one innocent to suffer.

"Very respectfully, your obedient servant,

"C. J. RAINS,
"Brigadier-General, Commanding Brigade, Rear Guard."

The merits of Rains' argument cannot be discussed here. The facts have been set forth in full merely to controvert the exaggerations emanating from McClellan, and it is suggested that the enforced removal of the torpedoes, mines, shells,—whatever they were—by prisoners of war as described by him in such merry vain was, perhaps, as great a breach of the rules of civilized warfare as the use of the objectionable explosives by the Confederates. The equitable principle that "he who comes into court must do so with clean hands" applies to military as well as to civil cases. The foregoing correspondence should forever acquit the Confederate authorities from the charge that they resorted to foul practice on this occasion, or failed to take immediate steps to discontinue a questionable practice, which to the minds of many was admissible in war.

May 7, the artillery train reached New Kent Court House, after resting the 6th while waiting for the Army to catch up. Meantime, Pendleton had heard of the movement of the enemy along the York River. On the

9th, the Army had reached the north bank of the Chickahominy and had escaped the Peninsula trap, as it was thought by all to be.* Thus we see that the Confederate Army had actually returned in the course of a few days to the locality which Pendleton had hitherto declared the only suitable point for successful resistance.

The *morale* of the Federal Army had been maintained at a high pitch in spite of the weather conditions by reason of the almost uninterrupted advance upon Richmond, while that of Johnston's Army had most certainly been depressed by the retrograde movement and the exertions incident to the retreat. But the news of Jackson's exploits at Cross Keys and Port Republic now arrived to cheer the drooping spirits of the Confederates and counteract the influences mentioned, as well as to increase McClellan's uncertainty due to the constant interference with his movements by the timid Administration in Washington. It is impossible even to estimate the importance of such moral factors in the game of war. To trace a campaign, without according them much weight, is, as Clausewitz constantly points out, but to mislead one's self. Indeed they supply the reason for the delays as well as the motive for the various moves, on the part of the opposing commanders. They sharpen the edge of the weapon of the one, while they dull that of the other adversary. It was under the influence of just such conditions that McClellan and Johnston were feeling for their openings in the impenetrable fastness of the Chickahominy Valley, the former now in the mire, the latter with his feet on firmer ground.

When the Army was reorganized at Yorktown, the light batteries were disposed as follows:†

RIGHT OF POSITION (Magruder)

FIRST DIVISION (McLaws)

McLaws' Brigade—

Garrett's Williamsburg Battery----------------	50 men
Young's Norfolk Battery ---------------------	57 men

Memoirs of W. N. Pendleton, Lee, p. 183.
†*Rebellion Records*, Series I. Vol. XI, Part III, pp. 479, 485, April 30, 1862.

Griffith's Brigade—
Cosnahan's Peninsula Battery_____ 51 men
McCarthy's Richmond Howitzer Battery_____ 103 men
Manly's North Carolina Battery_____ 37 men
Read's Georgia Battery_____ 72 men
Sands' Henrico Battery_____ 80 men

Kershaw's Brigade—
Kemper's Alexandria Battery_____ 77 men

Cobb's Brigade—
Page's Morris Louisa Battery_____ 48 men

SECOND DIVISION (Toombs)

Toombs' and Semnes' Brigades, no batteries

FORCE AT WILLIAMSBURG (B. S. Ewell)

No light batteries, but 621 heavy artillerymen

CENTER OF POSITION (Longstreet)

A. P. Hill's Brigade—
Rogers' Loudoun Battery_____ 62 men

R. H. Anderson's Brigade—
Stribling's Fauquier Battery_____ 68 men

Colston's Brigade—
No batteries _____ 00 men

Pickett's Brigade—
Dearing's Lynchburg Battery_____ 60 men

Wilcox's Brigade—
Stanard's Richmond Howitzer Battery_____ 60 men

Pryor's Brigade—
Macon's Richmond Fayette Battery_____ 60 men

LEFT OF POSITION (D. H. Hill)

EARLY'S DIVISION

Early's Brigade—
Jeff Davis Alabama Battery_____ 80 men

Rodes' Brigade—
Carter's King William Battery_____ 80 men

RAINS' DIVISION

Rains' Brigade—
 Nineteen Heavy Batteries----------------------- 1,151 men

Featherston's Brigade—
 No batteries ---------------------------------- 00 men

Crump's Force at Gloucester Point—
 Armistead's Mathews Battery------------------ 46 men
 Battalion Heavy Artillery--------------------- 332 men

RESERVE (G. W. Smith)

WHITING'S DIVISION

Whiting's Brigade—
 Imboden's Staunton Battery------------------- 111 men
 Reilly's North Carolina Battery--------------- 132 men

Hood's Brigade—
 No batteries ---------------------------------- 00 men

Hampton's Brigade—
 Moody's Louisiana Battery--------------------- 72 men

S. R. Anderson's Brigade—
 Braxton's Fredericksburg Battery------------- 50 men

Pettigrew's Brigade—
 Andrews' 1st Maryland Battery---------------- 130 men

Cavalry Brigade—
 Stuart Horse Artillery (1 battery, Capt. John
  Pelham) ------------------------------------- 141 men

RESERVE ARTILLERY (Pendleton)

Pendleton's Corps (10 batteries), 36 pieces ⎫
Walton's Corps (Washington Artillery Battalion, ⎬ 1,050 men
 4 batteries), 20 pieces ⎭

The foregoing figures are instructive. With the brigades were 23 light batteries, with a total personnel of 1,727, or with an average strength of 75 men. With the Reserve Artillery were 14 batteries.* Allowing each battery 75 men, the personnel of the Reserve Ar-

---

*Memoirs of W. N. Pendleton, Lee, pp. 184-5.

tillery numbered 1,050. The total field artillery personnel of the Army then numbered at this time 2,777, very unequally distributed among 37 batteries, with an average of 4 pieces each, or a total of 152 guns. There was absolutely no equality of distribution of guns, with respect to divisions and brigades. In Magruder's command consisting of 16,106 men, exclusive of heavy and light artillery personnel, there were 9 light batteries, or about 36 guns, a proportion of slightly over 2 guns per 1,000 men of the other arms, the field artillery personnel numbering 575. To the center, or Longstreet's command, numbering 13,506 men exclusive of a field artillery personnel of 310, were assigned 5 light batteries with about 20 guns, a proportion of less than 1.5 guns per 1,000 men. The left, or Hill's command, exclusive of 1,483 heavy, and 206 field, artillerymen numbered 10,945 men. With this portion of the Army were but 3 light batteries, or 12 guns, a proportion of about 1 gun per 1,000 men.* With the reserve division under G. W. Smith, were 5 field batteries with a total personnel of 520 and 20 guns. Smith's command, exclusive of his artillerymen, numbered 10,072 men. The proportion of guns was therefore about 2 per 1,000 men. Stuart's cavalry brigade numbered 1,148 men, and with it he had Capt. John Pelham's horse battery of 141 men and 8 pieces.† The proportion of horse guns to cavalry was, therefore, about 8 per 1,000 men. This battery was the second horse battery to be organized in the Army of Northern Virginia, and had been assigned to Stuart with his original brigade in December, 1861. It was always spoken of as the "Stuart Horse Artillery," a name given it at first to distinguish it from Ashby's or Chew's Battery in the Valley with Jackson. It was commanded after Pelham's death by the gallant Breathed.

Johnston's return of April 30, 1862, shows a total strength for his army, exclusive of the Reserve Artillery,

---

*Naturally a small proportion by reason of the fact that the command was largely assigned to fortifications, in which were mounted the heavy guns.
†See Pelham's Report of Battle of Williamsburg, *Rebellion Records*.

of 55,633 men. If from that number, 2,104 heavy artillerymen, 1,727 field artillerymen, and 1,289 men of the cavalry brigade, including Pelham's Battery, be deducted, or a total of 5,120, it appears that the infantry force must have been 50,513. Since the total number of his field guns, exclusive of those of the horse battery, was 144, the general proportion of guns to infantry was less than 3 per 1,000 men.

It is not so much for the strength of his field artillery as for its loose distribution that fault is to be found with Johnston, a condition which extended to the other arms of his command, and which very justly led to constant demands on the part of Mr. Davis, that the Army be reorganized into divisions and brigades of some degree of equality as to strength. Johnston, like McClellan, is often referred to in handsome terms as a soldier of marked ability for organization. This is undoubtedly true of them both, and it is not the only point of similarity between the two. But, the fact remains, that the Army of Northern Virginia in April and May, 1862, was very poorly hung together, a defect which became sorely apparent in the jungle of the Peninsula, where cohesion, of all things, was most to be desired. It must be said, however, that its organization had been given it at Yorktown for the specific work of defending the lines at that point, the topography of which enforced a distribution entirely unsuited to the subsequent retrograde movement. The conditions to be met in the one case were entirely in opposition to those of the other. But, if Johnston intended from the first to fall back, as he invariably claimed, he should have foreseen the needs of the future and organized with the certain contingency of retreat before him. He had been advised from the first by Pendleton, if by no one else, that a battle, if it were to be fought, must be undertaken near Richmond, and the character of the terrain in that quarter was well known to him. It was not until he reached the Chickahominy that Johnston reorganized his army into 4 divisions, giving it a somewhat more cohesive character. The artillery is now found distributed as follows:*

FIRST DIVISION (G. W. Smith)

Whiting's Brigade—
Imboden's Staunton Battery.

Hampton's Brigade—
Moody's Louisiana Battery.

Hood's Brigade—
No artillery.

Hatton's Brigade—
Braxton's Fredericksburg Battery.

Pettigrew's Brigade—
Andrews' 1st Maryland Battery.

Strength of division, 10,592. Number of guns, 16.

SECOND DIVISION (Longstreet)

A. P. Hill's Brigade—
Rogers' Loudoun Battery.

Pickett's Brigade—
Dearing's Lynchburg Battery.

R. H. Anderson's Brigade—
Stribling's Fauquier Battery.

Colston's Brigade—
No artillery.

Wilcox's Brigade—
Stanard's Richmond Howitzer Battery.

Pryor's Brigade—
Macon's Richmond Fayette Artillery.

Strength of division, 13,816. Number of guns, 20.

THIRD DIVISION (Magruder)

McLaws' Brigade—
Garrett's Williamsburg Battery.

Rebellion Records, Ibid., pp. 530, 533, May 21, 1862.

Cobb's Brigade—
  Page's Morris Louisa Battery.

Kershaw's Brigade—
  Kemper's Alexandria Battery.

Toombs' Brigade—
  No artillery.

Griffith's Brigade—
  McCarthy's Richmond Howitzer Battery.

D. R. Jones' Brigade—
  No artillery.

Strength of division, 15,920. Number of guns, 16.

FOURTH DIVISION (D. H. Hill)

Early's Brigade—
  Jeff Davis Alabama Battery.

Rodes' Brigade—
  Carter's King William Battery.

Rains' Brigade—
  No artillery.

Crump's Brigade—
  Armistead's Mathews Battery.

Featherston's Brigade—
  No artillery.

Ward's Command—
  No artillery.

Strength of division, 11,151. Number of guns, 12.

CAVALRY BRIGADE (Stuart)

  Pelham's Horse Battery.

Strength of brigade, 1,289. Number of guns, 8.

RESERVE ARTILLERY (Pendleton)

  Pendleton's Corps, 19 batteries, about 56 guns.
  Walton's Battalion, Washington Artillery, 20 guns.
  Cabell's Corps (attached to 3d Division).
  Cosnahan's Peninsula Battery
  Manly's North Carolina Battery } 16 guns.
  Read's Georgia Battery
  Sands' Henrico Battery

The foregoing assignment shows a total of 160 guns, bearing a proportion to the entire army strength of 53,688, of about 3 guns per 1,000 men. With the brigades were 64 guns, or a proportion of slightly over 1 gun per 1,000 men, supported by a reserve in 3 sections of 92 guns, and one battery of horse artillery.

Having become familiar with the relative strength of the artillery, it will prove interesting to examine the condition of other armies in this respect.

It has ever been impossible to establish dogmatically the proper proportion of field guns to the other arms, and strictly adhere thereto, for the question depends upon many considerations, such as the theater of operations, the composition of the enemy's forces, the special adaptability of the people of the country to one arm or another, and even upon the casualties in campaign. A comparison of the field armies of the past century will show that the number of guns has generally varied from 2 to 5 to 1,000 infantry, limits which have not been infrequently exceeded. It would appear that the common desire has been to provide from 3 to 4 guns for every 1,000 men of the other arms of the service, but in mountainous or heavy-wooded countries, where operations could only be conducted over a few poor roads, this proportion has quite generally been reduced. For instance, in Lombardy, in 1859, the French found it impossible, owing to the narrow roads and marshy fields, to get all their guns into action, although they had only 3 guns to 1,000 men.* Referring to conditions in the Wilderness Campaign, Gen. Grant wrote: "Artillery is very useful when it can be brought into action, but it is a very burdensome luxury where it cannot be used. Before leaving Spotsylvania, therefore, I sent back to the defenses of Washington over 100 pieces of artillery, with the horses and caissons. This relieved the road over which we were to march of more than 200 six-horse teams, and still left us more artillery than could be advantageously used."†

---

*Organization and Tactics, Wagner, p. 12.
†Memoirs, U. S. Grant, Vol. II, p. 241.

In Sherman's march to the sea, and in his subsequent campaign in the Carolinas, his artillery was reduced to 1 gun to every 1,000 men of the other arms, the reduction being induced by the character of the country, but made possible by the deficiency in the enemy's artillery. The broad and hard chaussées of France enabled the Germans in 1870 to maintain a proportion of 4 guns to 1,000 men, their artillery being always on hand when needed and rendering splendid service.

Due to the fact that losses are generally heavier in the infantry, no matter how efficient the service of the guns may be, the tendency is for the proportion of the latter to increase towards the end of a campaign. The personnel of the artillery may diminish in numbers, but the loss of guns is ordinarily slight. In the Franco-German War, notwithstanding the admirable recruiting methods of the Germans, their army corps were at times reduced to 15,000, or even as low as 7,000 men, while the number of guns remained unchanged. The increased proportion due to depletion is more desirable than otherwise, for an infantry weak in numbers, or in *morale* due to depressing losses, more than ever needs the support of a large and efficient artillery.

While, therefore, it is impossible definitely to fix the proportion of artillery to the other troops, it may be safely prescribed that guns with an army should be as many as there is prospect of being effectively employed on the field of battle.* Malvern Hill and Sedan bear witness that, under favorable circumstances, the fire of artillery may, almost alone, crush the enemy. But the fact should not be lost sight of that the terrible "circle of fire" was made possible by a gallant infantry.

In view of the dense character of the Peninsula country, and the entire absence of any but primitive roads, the available ones being few in number, we are forced to the conclusion that in point of numbers Johnston's, as well as McClellan's, artillery was more than adequate to the work at hand.

---

*Organization and Tactics, Wagner, p. 14. The same is said by Hohenlohe.

Anticipating a great struggle about Richmond, Pendleton had been ordered to place the redoubts and batteries of the lines in condition for effective defense, in addition to his regular work with the field batteries. Much material had been lost during the month of May, and the deficit in the number of horses for the light batteries was appalling. There was little to be expected of field artillery maneuvers about the Chickahominy. All that could be done was to dispose such guns as the terrain permitted in earthworks, near the various crossings, or on the more commanding eminences of the swamps, in support of the infantry lines. The nature of the country was such as to permit McClellan slowly to move his heavy guns up into position, but yet to prevent their successful resistance by the lighter field pieces of his enemy. On one occasion, May 12, the Reserve Artillery had been brought upon the field several miles below Chickahominy bridge to support the infantry in a pending action, but its services were not called for.

On May 30, the battle of the next day, known as Seven Pines, or Fair Oaks, was planned. D. H. Hill had made a reconnaissance which disclosed McClellan's awkward position astride the Chickahominy. On that day the following note was addressed to Gen. Johnston by his Chief of Artillery:

"I venture to offer a suggestion based upon some information respecting the Chickahominy River. It is said to rise immediately after a rain like this, and to continue in flood some twenty-four hours. Would not this seem a providence to place all the Yankee force this side that stream, almost centainly in your power? Might not an active, sudden, and adequate movement of troops to-night and at dawn in the morning so overwhelm the divisions confronting Gen. Hill as to crush and capture them with next to certainty? I submit it with great deference. Your judgment will, I know, determine sagaciously on the subject."*

When this note was written, 7:30 P. M., Pendleton was at Oakwood Cemetery, in the northern environs of Richmond. Shortly after noon that day, Johnston in-

*Rebellion Records, Series I, Vol. XI, Part III, p. 685.

COLONEL JAMES B. WALTON
CHIEF OF ARTILLERY, LONGSTREET'S CORPS

formed D. H. Hill that he would lead an attack upon the enemy next morning.* But at that time the details of the attack had not been worked out. This was done by Johnston in conference with Longstreet some time later in the day. Gen. Alexander states that the conference was prolonged by a violent storm, in which probably over three inches of rain fell. Pendleton could not have penned his note until after the rain commenced, for he refers to the fact of its violent character. The suggestion was undoubtedly received by Johnston within two hours after it was written, that is before 10 P. M., and the influence it exerted upon the deliberations of Johnston and Longstreet, coming as it did from one of Pendleton's character, must be estimated by the reader. It is possible, of course, that McClellan's situation at once suggested a similar plan to Johnston and Longstreet. At any rate, the idea was clearly as original with Pendleton as with them, a fact which testifies to the ready and accurate military perception of the Chief of Artillery, who was destined to see the failure of the plan, which appeared so simple to him. Before dismissing this point, let us inquire if it is possible that, receiving Pendleton's suggestion after Longstreet was dismissed from the conference, Johnston sought to act upon it, and that Longstreet's failure the next day to co-operate as expected was due to the late alteration of the plan being imperfectly comprehended by him? This suggestion is fruitful of many explanations.

The Reserve Artillery took no part in the battle of Seven Pines, nor were the Confederate brigade batteries employed with any degree of effect or intelligence. It must be borne in mind, however, that the artillery had no organization competent to rapid movements in such a country, no field officers to direct its batteries, hither and thither in groups as needed, and that the staff of the Chief of Artillery was entirely deficient in numbers as well as in experience with large bodies of artillery. In the light of the time, there is

---

*Military Memoirs of a Confederate, Alexander, p. 74.

more to commend than to censure, for not only had the
idea of a reserve taken firm root, but this reserve was
being steadily increased from time to time, already containing half again as many guns as the total number
with the brigades, a fact which to the unprejudiced
mind was a presage of the future. Again, let the plea
be advanced for a judgment based on conditions as they
existed in 1862. Criticism after the event, and in the
light of modern days, is of no value whatever, and only
serves to muddle history. In his memoirs, a work of
great military value, Gen. Alexander is given to this
fault.* Writing of the battle of Seven Pines, he says:
"Perhaps our greatest deficiency at this period was in
the artillery service. None of our batteries were combined into battalions, but each infantry brigade had a
battery attached to it. There were no field officers of
artillery, charged with combining batteries and massing them to concentrate heavy fire upon important
points. There was never greater need or better opportunity for this than in Johnston's battle of the 31st.
The enemy had but two batteries, Kirby's and Brady's,
and no more were available. They did not receive a
single hostile cannon shot, and were able to devote their
whole fire to our infantry lines, which in every instance
seemed to be finally repulsed, only by heavy canister at
close quarters.

"We had no lack of batteries. The roads were full
of them, but there was no organization to make them
effective. Both roads and open fields were in very miry
condition, and all movements would have been slow, but
a competent officer by doubling teams could have
brought up the guns with little delay."

This last sentence contains rather a caustic criticism.
It certainly reacts more on Johnston than on Pendleton,
who held his reserve batteries at all times ready for use
when called upon. But it is in no small measure a self-
accusation, for who better than the Chief of Ordnance
of an Army, and in this instance one of the acknow-

*Military Memoirs of a Confederate, E. P. Alexander, p. 90.

ledged authorities of the commanding officer's staff on all matters pertaining to artillery, was better able to employ the guns as they should have been employed? Magruder, equally as able an artilleryman as Alexander had shown himself to be, was in command of a division. Certainly it was not his office to advise Johnston about the employment of the auxiliary arm. Had Alexander really seen such opportunities at the time for the tactical employment of artillery masses, which we now know existed, then he himself as much as any other was to blame for the omissions he complains of. The guns were at hand. He should have urged their being ordered forward at the proper time. Certainly Johnston and Pendleton would not have opposed anything which when explained would so materially have contributed to the success of the Army and the credit of the Artillery. In his usual full and fair account of the Confederate military operations, Col. William Allan, makes no such criticism as does Alexander.*

After the disjointed affair of Seven Pines, every one began to seek for a scapegoat, and one was at last found in Huger. But earnest investigation and search disclosed many facts hitherto disregarded, among them the tactical neglect of the artillery.

Before closing this chapter an anecdote may well be included which throws an interesting light on the conditions of the time. On the retreat from Yorktown to Williamsburg Johnston ordered his cavalry to bring up the rear and help the cannoneers with their guns when necessary. A single piece of a certain battery had become stalled and the Gloucester troop undertook to assist in saving it. Meantime the Federals were streaming over a hill about half a mile distant and already hurrying to seize the gun. In the troop was a young Britisher who wore a monocle and who afforded his

---

*Lieut.-Col. William Allan, Chief Ordnance Officer, Second Corps A. N. V., author of *Chancellorsville, Stonewall Jackson's Valley Campaign,* and *The Army of Northern Virginia in 1862,* has contributed three of the most trustworthy military narratives yet written concerning the Civil War. He is invariably followed by Henderson in preference to all others, and much of Col. Henderson's greatest work is based on Col. Allan's writings.

comrades much amusement with his broad accent. Riding up to his troop commander he said:

"I beg pahdon, Capting, but may I enquire why we are staying here so long?"

"To save this gun," the Captain replied.

"What, that d—n thing," the Englishman enquired in a most puzzled manner.

"Certainly. We can't afford to leave it," said the officer.

"Pahdon me again," rejoined the gentleman with the monocle, "If I ask how much it is worth."

"I suppose about a thousand dollars," answered the Captain.

The Englishman readjusted his monocle in the most deliberate way, looked once more at the approaching enemy who were now popping at the troop, and turning to his officer, said in the most off-hand way:

"Well, Capting, let's move on, I'll give you my check for it at once."

Such were the conceptions of military service which were held by some of the gentry who served in the Confederate ranks at the beginning of the war. But it was not long before these pampered volunteers learned better and became as fine soldiers as ever bore a musket, strode a horse, or swabbed a gun.

CHAPTER XII

JUNE 1, 1862, Robert E. Lee assumed command of
the Army of Northern Virginia, Gen. Johnston having
been wounded that day. He immediately directed his
Chief of Engineers to make a thorough examination of
the country in the vicinity of the lines occupied by his
army, with a view to ascertaining the best position in
which a battle might be brought on, or the advance of
the enemy resisted. The commanding points on the
line selected were to be promptly prepared for occupation by the field batteries. This order was given June
3. "My object," explained Gen. Lee, "is to make use
of every means in our power to strengthen ourselves
and to enable us to fight the enemy to the best advantage."* June 5, Gen. Lee suggested the construction of a railroad battery consisting of plated cars and
a heavy gun for the purpose of resisting the transportation by the enemy of heavy ordnance over the York
River railway. And on the same date he urged that
an imported Armstrong breech-loading piece be
mounted on wheels and sent forward with a supply of
projectiles.† There were at this time in the opinion of
Gen. Lee a sufficient number of Parrott rifles with the
Army. His main effort was to perfect the batteries
already in the field, and the organization of the artillery
as a whole, rather than to increase its numbers. Thus,
on the 8th, he wrote the Secretary of War discouraging
the organization of light batteries in Richmond, and
suggesting that the horses and men available there be
transferred to other branches of the service, since
Beauregard was in no more need of field artillery than
he himself was.‡

---

*Rebellion Records, Series I, Vol. XI, Part III, pp. 572, 573.
†Ibid., pp. 574, 575.
‡Ibid., p. 583, Lee states that Beauregard had already sent 150 surplus field
pieces to the rear.

The point has now been reached when not only the numbers but the material of the field artillery seemed adequate to the commanding general. More than the necessary number of light batteries were available, and the Bureau of Ordnance was at last prepared to supply more guns than were actually needed in the field. But, as has been said, the artillery organization was most defective, and to the increase of its efficiency, Gen. Lee's attention was at once directed.

June 2, the day after taking command, he sent for Gen. Pendleton, with whom he had been a cadet at West Point, and requested him to continue as Chief of Artillery, and to make every effort to bring that arm of the service up to the fullest possible efficiency. The directions Gen. Lee gave his engineers the following day were significant of his determination to make more use of the guns.

Encouraged by his conference with his new commander, for whom he possessed profound admiration, Gen. Pendleton now set about the task of reorganization. One of the first measures was to complete his staff. His nephew, Dudley D. Pendleton, was appointed his adjutant-general, and George Peterkin, a son of a clerical brother, Bishop Peterkin, was assigned to duty on his staff as aide-de-camp. Edward P. Dandridge was appointed inspector of artillery, with Charles Hatcher, of Richmond, and Thomas N. Randolph, of Clarke County, Virginia, as volunteer aides. His original quartermasters, Maj. John Page, and Capt. William Meade; commissary, Maj. B. L. Wolffe; ordnance officer, Major John C. Barnwell; and medical officer, Dr. Isham Randolph Page, were retained.

With the assistance of a more complete staff, the Chief of Artillery at once undertook the reconnaissance of the Chickahominy lines, to determine upon suitable positions for his guns, in accordance with Gen. Lee's views.

Before the first week of June was over, Gen. Pendleton's reserve corps had been divided into 3 battalions under Col. Cutts, Maj. Richardson, and Maj. Nelson, respectively. With Walton's and Cabell's commands, the Reserve Artillery now consisted of 5 battalions. These battalions were, in the main, camped in different places in rear of the lines, but daily there was some popping away between these and the enemy's guns, a random practice, which resulted only in disclosing the position of the artillery, without accomplishing any material results.

The promptness with which Gen. Pendleton carried out Gen. Lee's instructions to render the artillery as effective as possible was most commendable. With increased independence of action and support, the Chief displayed marked abilities as an organizer, and at once put into effect reforms which his experience and general grasp of the situation enabled him to inaugurate. His letter book shows that as early as June 5 he drafted regulations for the more systematic administration of the artillery, which, being submitted to Gen. Lee, were approved.* Some of Pendleton's more radical ideas, in his own phrasing, were incorporated in *G. O. No. 71,* June 22, 1862, an order by which the new commander sought to overcome many defects in the Army. Those paragraphs relating to the artillery are here quoted:†

"4. The artillery of the army is necessarily so extensively diffused that it becomes essential for its due efficiency there should be in its administration rigid system.

"5. The Chief of Artillery in each division will have charge of all the batteries thereto attached, whether acting with brigades, or held in reserve. A battery duly assigned to a brigade will, until properly relieved, report to and be controlled by the brigade commander. It must also, however, report to and be inspected by the division Chief of Artillery, as he may require. When a brigade battery needs relief it will, when practicable, be made to change place with the division reserve. Should this be impracticable, application, authorized by the division commander, must be made to the army Chief of Artillery for temporary relief from the general reserve.

---

*This book is on file at Washington.
†*Rebellion Records,* Series I, Vol. XI, Part III, p. 612.

6.   The army Chief of Artillery will have general charge of that branch of service and special direction of the general reserve.   He will, under instructions from the commanding general, see that the batteries are kept in as efficient condition as practicable, and so distributed as to promise the best results.   To this end, he will require from the several chiefs of artillery weekly returns exhibiting the condition of each battery, and where it is serving.   He will, also, make to the commanding general a tri-monthly report of his entire charge."

These provisions, secured by the initiative of Pendleton alone, establish the claim that his tactical conceptions were well abreast of his time.   Not only did he preserve the general army reserve, also possessed by the enemy, but he went further and provided for divisional reserves for the more immediate support of the brigade batteries, and even before the promulgation of Gen. Lee's order, he had organized his general reserve into battalion groups.   The creation of this general reserve was a distinct tactical advance for the Confederates, who were by no means slow in profiting by the reforms of McClellan and Barry.

During the reorganization of the Artillery in June, 1862, it was found that many superfluous and quite inefficient heavy artillery companies were stationed in the various redoubts of the Richmond lines.   To Pendleton was assigned the task of mustering them out, reducing their officers, and distributing the better men among the troops of the mobile army.   A number of new light batteries were also broken up, and their men used to fill the ranks of the seasoned batteries.   In the meantime, the divisional reserves had been assigned to position near the lines for use as prescribed in the order regulating the better employment of the Artillery. Anticipating the assault on McClellan's right, the reserve corps was so disposed as to aid in the operations on the north bank of the Chickahominy and to resist any approach of the enemy towards Richmond, also to provide support wherever it might be required.*

---

*General Lee's Report, *Rebellion Records,* Series I, Vol. XI, Part III.   See also letter to Pendleton, Ibid., Part III, p. 686.

There was now a distinct effort on the part of the various division commanders to employ with better advantage the batteries assigned them and the conception of divisional groups for the support of the brigade batteries had taken firm root. On the 17th, Magruder had appointed Lieut.-Col. Stephen D. Lee, Acting Chief of Artillery, of the Right Wing, and had provided for his reserve.

At the beginning of the Seven Days fighting, the field pieces with the various brigades had been generally placed in entrenched positions along the infantry lines, the redoubts for the guns of the reserve battalions, being placed in their immediate rear, and further back the army reserve. It was hoped that with such a disposition of the guns any threatened point might be supported by a heavy fire of artillery, and that any advance of the lines which became expedient might be accompanied with the requisite artillery force.

The efficiency of the field artillery was yet far from satisfactory, as will appear from an analysis of the 14 batteries of Magruder's command.*

Yet, all of the batteries were rated as good by Col. Lee, except 3, which he urged should be sent to the reserve for repairs and refitting. The personnel of the batteries varied in strength from 26 to 121 men, the average personnel being 65 men and 3 officers. Thirteen of the batteries were armed with two 24-pounder and twelve 12-pounder Howitzers, two 24-pounder guns, three 1-pounder guns, six 6-pounder guns, two 6-pounder Parrotts and six 3-inch rifles, or 34 pieces in all, an average armament of less than 3 pieces. One battery had but 1 piece, others had 2, some 3, 4, 5, and 6 pieces. The number of horses varied from 93 to 15 per battery, with an average number of 53.†

Magruder's artillery, at this time, was composed of Carlton's Troup, Jordan's Bedford, Read's Pulaski (Ga.), Brown's Wise, Cosnahan's Peninsula, Lane's

*Ibid., p. 688.
†It will be recalled that 84 horses were prescribed for a battery of 6 pieces. Regulation strength, 150 men and 5 officers.

Georgia, Kemper's Alexandria, Page's Magruder, Richardson's James City, Ritter's Henrico, Woolfolk's Ashland, Young's Norfolk, Manly's North Carolina, and Moody's Louisiana batteries.

Longstreet's artillery with a total personnel of 1,600 men, of which number 395 were absent, consisted June 23, of Carter's King William, Nelson's Hanover, Hardaway's Jeff Davis, Clarke's, Peyton's Orange, Huger's Norfolk, Grimes' Portsmouth, Moseley's Richmond Howitzer, Turner's Goochland, Rogers' Loudoun, Stribling's Fauquier, Dearing's Lynchburg, Macon's Richmond Fayette, Anderson's Thomas, Coke's Williamsburg, Watson's, and Chapman's Dixie batteries, 17 in all, the average strength being 94 men.*

With Holmes there were, about this same time, 6 light batteries. According to the report of Col. Deshler, Chief of Artillery of Holmes' Division, French's Battery with 98 men, three 12-pounder howitzers, one Parrott rifle and two 3-inch iron rifles, was excellent in point of efficiency, but the other five, namely, Branch's, Brem's, E. Graham's, Grandy's, and Lloyd's, needed much drilling.† Of a personnel of 636 with an average strength of 106 men, but 440 were reported effective for the 6 batteries, the armament of which consisted of eight 6-pounders, thirteen 12-pounder howitzers, one Parrott rifle and nine 3-inch rifles, or a total of 31 pieces.

The foregoing figures give some idea of the armament and strength of the field batteries of the Army at the beginning of the Seven Days campaign, and will enable a fairly accurate estimate to be made of the total strength of the Artillery at that time.

Before this campaign commenced many changes were made in the disposition of the batteries, their assignments during that period being, approximately, as follows:

---

*Rebellion Records, Ibid., p. 615.
†The last two joined after July 1. See Rebellion Records, Series I, Vol. XI, Part II, p. 912.

JACKSON'S COMMAND

Col. Stapleton Crutchfield, Chief of Artillery

WHITING'S DIVISION

Balthis' Staunton Battery,	Capt. W. L. Balthis.
Reilly's Rowan (N. C.) Battery,	Capt. James Reilly.

JACKSON'S DIVISION

Poague's 1st Rockbridge Battery,	Capt. William T. Poague.
Carpenter's Alleghany Battery,	Lieut. John C. Carpenter.
Caskie's Richmond Hampden Battery,	Capt. William H. Caskie.
Wooding's Danville Battery,	Capt. George W. Wooding.

EWELL'S DIVISION

Courtney's Henrico Battery,	Capt. A. R. Courtney.
Carrington's Charlottesville Battery,	Capt. J. McD. Carrington.
Brockenbrough's Baltimore Battery,	Capt. J. B. Brockenbrough.

D. H. HILL'S DIVISION

Maj. S. P. Pierson, Chief of Artillery

Carter's King William Battery,	Capt. Thomas H. Carter.
Hardaway's Alabama Battery,	Capt. R. A. Hardaway.
Jeff Davis Alabama Battery,	Capt. J. W. Bondurant.
Nelson's Hanover Battery,	Capt. George W. Nelson.

HILL'S RESERVE BATTALION (Temporarily attached)

Maj. Hilary P. Jones

Clarke's Long Island Battery,	Capt. P. H. Clarke.
Richmond Orange Battery,	Lieut. C. W. Fry.
Rhett's South Carolina Battery,	Capt. A. Burnett Rhett.

MAGRUDER'S COMMAND

JONES' DIVISION

Brown's Wise Battery,	Capt. James S. Brown.
Washington (S. C.) Battery,	Capt. James F. Hart.
Madison (La.) Battery,	Capt. George F. Moody.
Dabney's Richmond Battery,	Capt. W. J. Dabney.

McLAWS' DIVISION

Manly's North Carolina Battery,	Capt. Basil C. Manly.
Kemper's Alexandria Battery,	Capt. Del Kemper.

Magruder's Division

Carlton's Troup (Ga.) Battery,	Capt. Henry H. Carlton.
1st Co. Richmond Howitzers,	Capt. E. S. McCarthy.

Magruder's Reserve Battalion

Lieut.-Col. Stephen D. Lee, Chief of Artillery

Pulaski George Battery,	Capt. J. P. W. Read.
James City Battery,	Capt. L. W. Richardson.
Magruder Battery,	Capt. T. Jeff Page, Jr.

Longstreet's Division

Rogers' Loudoun Battery,	Capt. Arthur L. Rogers.
Anderson's Thomas Battery,	Capt. Edwin J. Anderson.
Donaldsonville (La.) Battery,	Capt. Victor Maurin.
3d Co. Richmond Howitzers,	Capt. Benj. H. Smith, Jr.

Longstreet's Reserve Battalion

Col. J. B. Walton, Chief of Artillery

1st Co. Washington Artillery,	Capt. Chas. W. Squires.
2d Co. Washington Artillery,	Capt. John B. Richardson.
3d Co. Washington Artillery,	Capt. M. B. Miller.
4th Co. Washington Artillery,	Capt. Joseph Norcom.
Dearing's Lynchburg Battery,	Capt. James Dearing.
Chapman's Dixie Battery,	Capt. W. H. Chapman.

Huger's Division

Lieut.-Col. J. A. de Lagnel, Chief of Artillery

Grimes' Portsmouth Battery,	Capt. Carey F. Grimes.
Lynchburg Beauregard Battery,	Capt. M. N. Moorman.
Huger's Norfolk Battery,	Capt. Frank Huger.
Stribling's Fauquier Battery,	Capt. Robert M. Stribling.
Goochland Battery,	Capt. William H. Turner.

A. P. Hill's (Light Division)

Maj. R. Lindsay Walker, Chief of Artillery
Maj. Lewis M. Coleman, Assistant Chief of Artillery

Andrews' 1st Maryland Battery,	Capt. R. Snowden Andrews.
Charleston (S. C.) German Battery,	Capt. Wm. K. Bachman.
Braxton's Fredericksburg Battery,	Capt. Carter M. Braxton.
Crenshaw's Richmond Battery,	Capt. William G. Crenshaw.
Davidson's Letcher Battery,	Capt. Greenlee Davidson.
Richmond Battery,	Capt. Marmaduke Johnson.
Masters' Battery (improvised siege),	Capt. L. Masters.
Pee Dee (S. C.) Battery,	Capt. D. G. McIntosh.
Pegram's Purcell Battery,	Capt. W. J. Pegram.

HOLMES' DIVISION

Col. James Deshler, Chief of Artillery

Branch's Petersburg Battery,	Capt. James R. Branch.
Brem's North Carolina Battery,	Capt. T. H. Brem.
French's Stafford Battery,	Capt. David A. French.
Graham's North Carolina Battery,	Capt. Edward Graham.

WISE'S LEGION

Andrews' Henry Battery,	Capt. W. C. Andrews.
Rives' Nelson Battery,	Capt. J. H. Rives.

RESERVE ARTILLERY, ARMY OF NORTHERN VIRGINIA

Brig.-Gen. Wm. N. Pendleton, Chief of Artillery

First Virginia Artillery,	Col. J. Thompson Brown.
Williamsburg Battery,	Capt. John A. Coke.
Richmond Fayette Battery,	Lieut. William I. Clopton.
2d Co. Richmond Howitzers,	Capt. David Watson.
Jones' Battalion (temporarily attached to D. H. Hill's Division)	Maj. H. P. Jones.
Long Island Virginia Battery,	Capt. P. H. Clarke.
Orange Richmond Battery,	Lieut. C. W. Fry.
Rhett's South Carolina Battery,	Capt. A. Burnett Rhett.

FIRST BATTALION ARTILLERY

Lieut.-Col. A. S. Cutts

"D" Bat'ry, Sumter (Ga.) Battalion,	Capt. James A. Blackshear.
"E" Bat'ry, Sumter (Ga.) Battalion,	Capt. John Lane.
"B" Bat'ry, Sumter (Ga.) Battalion,	Capt. John V. Price.
"A" Bat'ry, Sumter (Ga.) Battalion,	Capt. H. M. Ross.
Georgia Regular Battery,	Capt. S. P. Hamilton.

SECOND BATTALION ARTILLERY

Maj. Chas. Richardson

Ancell's 2d Fluvanna Battery,	Capt. John J. Ancell.
Milledge's Georgia Battery,	Capt. John Milledge, Jr.
Woolfolk's Ashland Battery,	Capt. Pichegru Woolfolk.

THIRD BATTALION ARTILLERY

Maj. William Nelson

Huckstep's 1st Fluvanna Battery,	Capt. Charles T. Huckstep.
Kirkpatrick's Amherst Battery,	Capt. Thomas J. Kirkpatrick.
Morris Louisa Virginia Battery,	Capt. R. C. M. Page.

CAVALRY BRIGADE

Stuart Horse Artillery Battery,   Capt. John Pelham.
Chew's Battery,   Capt. R. Preston Chew.

An analysis of the foregoing organization of the Artillery shows a total of 45 batteries assigned to the brigades exclusive of the 6 batteries of Walton's Battalion attached to Longstreet's Division, and Lee's Battalion of 3 batteries attached to Magruder's command, both of which were organized as a reserve force. In the general reserve, we now find 5 battalions, four of 3, and one of 5 batteries, or a total of 17 batteries. With the Army then, there were not less than 71 batteries, including the horse artillery. Taking 75 men as the average effective strength of a battery, the total personnel must have numbered in the neighborhood of 5,500 men.

Between June 11 and 15, Stuart, with about 1,200 men, including a section of Pelham's horse battery with 2 guns, had performed a most remarkable exploit. Perhaps nothing that occurred during the early days of the war so awakened the Army to the possibilities of the more mobile guns as did this raid around McClellan, in which Pelham took part. But, while it was a brilliant feat, its results were adverse to Lee and far-reaching. It warned McClellan of a fatal opening on his right, through which other troops with more guns would soon endeavor to pass, and his change of base to Harrison's Landing was but the consequence of the cavalry exploit. Soon Jackson approached this very exposed point, accompanied by Col. Crutchfield and his artillery, as yet not organized in the new manner.

According to the general order of battle, *No. 75,* June 24, Jackson was to march from Ashland on the 25th, in the direction of Slash Church, encamping for the night west of the Central, or the present Chesapeake & Ohio Railroad, and to advance at 3 A. M. on the 26th, and turn Beaver Dam. A. P. Hill was to cross the river at Meadow Bridge when Jackson's advance beyond that point should be known and move directly upon Mechanicsville. As soon as the bridge at that point should be uncovered, Longstreet and D. H. Hill were to cross, the latter to proceed to the support of Jackson, and the former to that of A. P. Hill. The four commands were then to sweep down the north side of the Chickahominy River toward the York River Railroad, Jackson on the left in advance, Longstreet nearest the river and in the rear. Huger and Magruder were to hold their positions on the south side of the river, and on the right of the line, to observe the enemy and pursue in the event of his retreat. Stuart, with the cavalry and Pelham's horse battery, was to cover Jackson's left. A part of the Reserve Artillery under Pendleton himself was to support the movement on the north side, the remainder to be held in readiness for use whenever required.*

In the execution of this excellent plan, Jackson's arrival at the contemplated point on the 26th was delayed, but A. P. Hill crossed the river at Mechanicsville and attempted to turn the left of the enemy's position, being severely punished by musketry and artillery fire; yet, he drove the enemy from his intrenchments and forced him back about a mile to his works on the left bank of Beaver Dam, the strong character of the position preventing an assault that night. Hill had taken with him but 6 field batteries of 4 guns each.†

Before daylight on the 27th, the Federal batteries along Beaver Dam opened, and under cover of a brisk cannonade Porter's troops gradually withdrew to his lines at Gaines' Mill and Cold Harbor. On the Confederate side, A. P. Hill and Longstreet replied to the enemy's fire, and advanced their skirmishers to the borders of the stream. D. H. Hill was ordered to advance on the road from Mechanicsville to Bethesda Church, and turn the Federal right flank, while Jackson, having left his bivouac of the night before at Hundley's early in the morning, was moving south to gain their rear.‡ By the time Jackson was fairly across Beaver Dam, and D. H. Hill had gained the flank of Porter's former line, the bird had flown.

---

*Rebellion Records, Series I, Vol. XI, Part III, pp. 490, 498.
†From Manassas to Appomattox, Longstreet, p. 123.
‡The Army of Northern Virginia in 1862, Allan, p. 84.

In this affair not over 8 Confederate brigade batteries were engaged. Of any employment of masses
or of the new divisional reserve battalions as such, of
any effort to prepare the way for the infantry attack
in accordance with a previously well-defined schedule,
there is no evidence. Coöperation, or "the need to do
it," might have been understood; "how to do it" was
still not known. Porter met the purely frontal attack
of Pender's and Ripley's brigades, and 5 batteries, with
a withering fire from his guns; he suffered little from
those opposing him. Jackson's guns, so tardy in their
arrival, did succeed in delivering their fire upon the
head of Hill's column before the identity of the latter
was discovered.

Porter had employed 6 of his 20 batteries, massed,
losing but one, though forced to retire by Jackson's
enveloping movement. Had the Confederate Artillery
been properly handled, no such wholesale retirement of
the Federal guns could have occurred in the face of not
less than 19 hostile batteries. In fact, many of the 80
guns which Porter undoubtedly had should have been
unable to retire had the Confederate Artillery, even
without the support of Jackson's batteries, been
properly employed. But, again, let us not blame the
gunners. The pernicious brigade distribution destroyed
their power at the outset to cope with Porter's masses.
They were but victims of a system. The reserve battalions, just organized, were not brought into action
for pure lack of experience in handling such large
masses of artillery, not only on the part of the artillerymen, but on the part of Hill as well, whose attack was
too headlong even to have permitted an artillery
preparation, had the guns been on hand. The general
who hurls his infantry columns upon the enemy's
position at sight, simply chooses the precipitate assault
in preference to the more deliberate attack with the artillery support which he might have elected, and if he
neglects his guns, the artillery is not to blame.

The time had not yet come, nor ever will, when an
artillery column can patrol the battlefield, undirected

by the will of the commanding-general, or by the lieutenants to whom particular sections of the field have been assigned, and push its guns into action at the points which subsequent investigation will show to have been necessary and proper. Artillery officers must be conversant with the general design, and particular duties must be assigned them. The more definitely its mission is outlined in advance, the more definite will be the results which the artillery will attain. While an efficient artillery is the bone of an army, it is not like the cavalry, an arm of sudden movements, of rapidity of action, of improvisation, and especially is this so when it is in masses.

In the study of the earlier battles of the Civil War, the student must be deeply impressed by the nerve of the attacking infantry, which advanced to the assault practically without the support of artillery, the latter primarily designed to give the attack that solidity so characteristic of the arm. In the infantry, the human element dominates everything. "Its essential is solid character, unity of action, and mutual confidence. The man and the man alone makes the measure of these elements. All the power of the arm resides in the man himself."* To supplement the individualistic qualities of the foot-soldier a sufficient proportion of the "long arm" is essential. In the artillery, the part of the men is a secondary one. The reason for their being is the material about which the men are united, and they fight only by serving the guns. Within certain limits, losses in its personnel do not affect the fighting efficiency of a battery, the fire of which can continue undimished until a percentage of the gunners is lost, which occurring in the infantry would render the force of its blow harmless. Hence, the artillery is the "supporting arm par excellence." Its very nature makes it so. All the more remarkable then does the early power of the Confederate Infantry seem when it is recalled that not only did it fail to receive the moral support of artillery, but that it faced an enemy abundantly provided with such aid.

*Psychology of War, Eltinge, p. 92.

CHAPTER XIII

WHEN the morning of the 27th was half gone, the four Confederate divisions were at last united about 3 miles from the new line of the enemy. That line was an arc of a circle about 2 miles in extent, behind Powhite Creek, covering the approaches to the bridge which connected the Federal right wing with the troops on the south side of the Chickahominy, to hold which Porter now had not less than 27,000 men and 20 batteries or 80 guns, 12 batteries being held in reserve. Naturally strong, it was rapidly strengthened with abattis and rifle pits, and before noon an excellent disposition of the defending force had been made, the guns having been adroitly placed along the commanding ground in groups between the divisions and brigades. Besides the division batteries, there were Robertson's and Tidball's excellent horse batteries from Hunt's reserve. One of these batteries was posted on the right of Sykes' Division, and the other on the extreme left of the line where it rested in the Valley against the river. The left flank in the bottom was heavily supported by pieces of position as well as field guns placed in batteries on the south side of the stream. The approach to the Federal position was generally over an open plain, about a quarter of a mile wide, affording a splendid field of fire for the defender's guns.

As soon as it had become evident that Porter was retiring from his position of the night before, Gen. Lee ordered A. P. Hill to follow and attack, while D. H. Hill was directed to unite with Jackson in operating against the flank and rear of the new line. The Confederate commanders on the south side were meantime ordered to keep up a vigorous demonstration with a view to preventing the reënforcing of Porter. Pressing on toward the York River Railroad, A. P. Hill encountered the enemy near New Cold Harbor about 2 P. M. and soon became hotly engaged. The arrival of Jackson upon the field was now momentarily expected. Longstreet, unexpectedly delayed, in order to repair a bridge over Beaver Dam for the crossing of his artillery, had been expected to arrive as the effect of Jackson's threat became apparent. But again the plan miscarried. Jackson and Longstreet were both late in coming up, and A. P. Hill, counting on their support, launched his division against the centre and left of the enemy's position, with little effective support from his artillery, except on the part of Braxton's Battery, which accompanied Archer's Brigade, maintaining a desperate struggle for nearly 2 hours. Though it succeeded in reaching and piercing Porter's lines at a number of points, as was to be expected under such conditions this gallant division was finally repulsed, though not, however, until heavy reënforcements including 2 batteries had reached Porter's lines, nor until it had been decimated by the almost undisturbed fire of the batteries on the crest as well as on the south side of the river.

Again we must pause to marvel at the prowess of this infantry. Few of the men of this particular division had been under fire before June 26.* Yet, on two consecutive days, it had made the most desperate frontal assaults upon exceptionally strong artillery positions, without the slightest preparation by its own guns. In fact, such batteries as had attempted to deliver their fire upon the enemy acted the rôle of infantry rather than that of supporting guns. At Beaver Dam, Pegram's, Andrews', McIntosh's, Johnson's, and Braxton's batteries had forced their way to as close quarters as possible, and at Gaines' Mill, Braxton's, Pegram's, Johnson's, Crenshaw's, Pelham's, Brockenbrough's, Carrington's, Courtney's, Bondurant's, and perhaps a few other batteries had been engaged, but their fire

---

*General Lee's Report, *Rebellion Records*, Series I, Vol. XI, Part II, p. 492.

action had been entirely independent of each other, and entirely without unison with the infantry.

But, to resume. A number of Hill's brigades were broken and his division as a whole was forced to recoil from sheer lack of the necessary weight. Realizing the unsupported character of Hill's attack, Gen. Lee had ordered Longstreet, who had now come up, to make a diversion on Hill's right. In spite of the strength of the enemy's position in this quarter, as previously described, Longstreet determined at once to carry the heights by assault, and while his columns were deploying Whiting's Division of Jackson' force, which had lost its way, arrived on the field and formed on Longstreet's left. At the same time, D. H. Hill with the sole aid of Bondurant's Battery, soon overwhelmed and forced to retire, pushed his way to the front, Ewell coming up on his right. Jackson's other two brigades now filled the gap between Ewell and A. P. Hill. The position on the left was defended by Sykes' Division of regulars, supported by 18 guns, afterwards increased to 24. This portion of Porter's line was in some respects stronger than his right, for the field of fire for the guns widened towards the east of the position, to 1,000 yards or more of cornfields sloping from the opposing ridges to a thick swamp, in the bottom of which it was impossible to advance a battery. Crutchfield had to move to the extreme left with his artillery, 6 batteries of which forced their way through the dense thickets in the direction of Old Cold Harbor, and were able later to cover McGehee's Hill, raking Sykes' right, with a storm of shell.

Between 4 and 5 o'clock a general assault commenced which lasted about two hours in the face of a tremendous artillery fire. So rapidly were Porter's guns discharged, that his gunners had difficulty in loading the foul pieces, accomplished in some instances only by jamming the rammers against the trees.* Finally, after terrific losses, the Federal lines were carried, in-

---

*Letter from Porter to Longstreet.

cluding the artillery position, and 22 guns were taken
on the field. Night put an end to pursuit and daybreak
the 28th found the north bank clear of the enemy.

Why, is it asked, was the Confederate Artillery
totally neglected in this engagement as at Mechanicsville, especially when Porter had given such evidence
the day before of his ability to prepare his position for
defense? The same answer may be made. There was
no reconnaissance of the new position, no staff to discover its outlines in advance of an attack. A. P. Hill
before leaving one field of battle was ordered to follow
up the enemy and attack. Without hesitation, and with
undiminished ardor, he complied. As Longstreet and
Jackson came upon the field to the support of Hill, their
onrushing columns alone located the position of the enemy. The Artillery could not have preceded these columns upon the field. There was not time allowed it for
a duel nor was there time in which it might prepare for
the attack. Go forward with the attacking lines it must
or not at all, for once those lines were launched in their
headlong assaults the leaders had but one thought and
that to reach the position of their adversary. Thus in
large measure, the guns were masked from the first, and
at no time was their rôle more than a secondary one.

The better employment of his guns by Porter in these
two engagements in no wise argues a superior skill with
respect to artillery on his part. The effective use of his
artillery was due to his defensive attitude more than to
his skill as an artilleryman. Had the Confederates been
on the defensive, their artillery would no doubt have occupied the first line. Under such conditions, there is
nothing to do with the guns but mass them. It is on
the offensive that the massing of artillery requires
knowledge, coupled with skill and experience.

The errors of A. P. Hill with respect to his artillery
are attributable to A. P. Hill. When preparing for
operations on the north side of the Chickahominy, he
issued orders that but one battery would accompany each
of his 6 brigades, and that the rest of his batteries in-

cluding those of his reserve battalion would remain in the position previously prepared for them on the south side.* He did take the precaution of carrying with him 6 teams of spare horses for each of his batteries, but drew them, nevertheless, from his remaining batteries, thus crippling the latter for effective use.

---

*Rebellion Records. Series I, Vol. XI, Part III, p. 616, G. O. No. ——, June 24, 1862.

CHAPTER XIV

SAVAGE'S STATION AND FRAZIER'S FARM*

FROM the field of Gaines' Mill, long columns of dust rising above the forest to the south were descried by the Confederates on the morning of the 28th of June, and it soon became apparent that McClellan had abandoned his base on York River. That evening, after a reconnaissance of the cavalry, Lee rightly concluded that McClellan was falling back upon the James instead of retreating down the Peninsula.

While McClellan was much embarrassed by the necessity of moving his enormous trains and over 50 field batteries across the White Oak Swamp, and then past the front of Magruder's and Huger's lines, Lee was equally hindered by the dense character of the country, the lack of roads, and the destruction of the bridges across the river, by means of which Jackson, Longstreet, and A. P. Hill could pursue the enemy, their columns by necessity being widely separated.

The Federal movement was completed the night of the 28th, and the following morning saw the corps of Sumner and Heintzleman, and the division of Smith of Franklin's Corps, occupying a strong position covering Savage's Station, with Slocum's Division in reserve. In the meantime, Keyes was instructed to retire to the James and occupy a defensive position near Malvern Hill, the extreme left of the Federal line. Late in the afternoon Magruder gained contact with the enemy in position at Savage's Station, but was heavily repulsed without receiving support from Huger. Jackson, Longstreet, and Hill also failed to come up as contemplated.

During this disjointed attack, 3 Federal batteries, Hazzard's, Pettit's, and Osborn's, severely punished Magruder's Infantry. Later, Kershaw's Brigade with Kemper's Alexandria and Hart's South Carolina bat-

---

*Frazier's Farm also called Glendale.

teries came upon the field and pierced the enemy's center, creating some confusion until reënforcements reestablished the line.   Kershaw also made excellent use of a 32-pounder rifled gun under Lieut. Barry, which had been mounted on a railway car, protected with a sloping roof of iron plates. Magruder utterly failed to bring the remainder of his artillery into action, and succeeded in employing only a small portion of his infantry.   Thus, McClellan was able by means of this rear guard action to withdraw the last of his trains from Savage's Station, and cover the retreat of his army during the night, though he had lost many prisoners and several batteries.

At nightfall, Jackson was still on the north side of the Chickahominy, Ewell's Division near Bottom's Bridge, and the others at Grape Vine, or Alexander's Bridge; Magruder lay in front of the Federal position at Savage's Station; Huger was at Brightwell's on the Charles City Road.   Holmes had crossed to Drewry's Bluff on the north of the James; and Longstreet and A. P. Hill were on the Darbytown Road at Atlee's. Again Gen. Lee ordered his lieutenants to press forward from their positions in order to deliver to the enemy a decisive blow on the morrow.

The morning of the 30th, Longstreet, with Hill in support, moved forward and found a Federal division in position near Glendale.   Bringing his artillery into action with most creditable decision, instead of rushing headlong upon the first position against which his column happened to bump, Longstreet now held his men in hand until Huger should come up on his left, and Jackson's guns should be heard at White Oak Swamp which he did not reach until about noon.   But when Jackson's guns did open Longstreet was ordered to attack.   The Federals holding their position until nightfall, made good their escape again, losing many prisoners, and 10 pieces of artillery including Randolph's Battery, but having inflicted heavy losses upon Longstreet in the sanguinary conflict.   Huger failed

utterly to support Longstreet and hardly a man of
Jackson's Infantry pulled a trigger, Hill alone being
employed to assist Longstreet in repelling a determined
counter attack.   Holmes accomplished little in his
quarter.

While Longstreet employed his guns at Glendale, in
a manner approximating an artillery preparation, it
would seem that the opportunity given them was more
due to the necessity of his delay in the attack than to
any intention of sending his infantry forward after the
enemy had been shaken by the fire of artillery.

On the left the artillery performed with credit the
task assigned it, though the end for which it was used
and the delay incident thereto may be subject to
criticism.   Reaching the swamp about noon, Jackson
met with a determined effort on the part of the enemy
to prevent his junction with Longstreet.   The bridge
at the only crossing was destroyed, and the point was
commanded by two batteries of artillery with heavy
infantry supports.

The ground on the north bank of the swamp by no
means favored the action of guns.   To the right of the
road the slopes opposite the position of the enemy were
entirely open, but the crest was covered with a dense
forest, while on the left both the ridge and valley lay
beneath a heavy growth of pine.   The artillery of the
enemy occupied an excellent position on a crest opposite
Jackson's right, and below the guns which commanded
the crossing a thick growth on the south bank of the
stream was occupied by a swarm of sharpshooters.
Finding no ground for the deployment of his infantry,
Jackson determined to force a crossing with his guns.
Much time was consumed in cutting a road through the
woods on the right of the road by means of which his
batteries could gain the crest, but finally when Crutchfield's 28 guns, moving forward simultaneously, ready
shotted, opened fire on the enemy, the surprise was complete.   One of the Federal batteries which had already
driven the cavalry back, dispersed at once in confusion,

and the other soon disappeared. Whereupon Jackson ordered up 2 guns of Wooding's Battery to shell the belt of trees occupied by the skirmishers, who were also driven off. While he was engaged in repairing the bridge, 3 Federal batteries with infantry supports came up and drove off the working parties, and an artillery duel in which neither side could see the other continued throughout the afternoon, but Crutchfield's guns, mostly smooth-bore pieces, were quite unable to silence the Federal artillery of superior range and caliber.

Gen. Alexander is most critical of Jackson's failure to effect a crossing, claiming that even had the enemy been able to prevent it at the main bridge, a nearby ford was available. That that ford too was defended by artillery, there can be little doubt.* He asserts that Jackson's failure on this occasion to coöperate effectively with Longstreet was due to the same reluctance to bring his infantry into action which he had displayed ever since his arrival on the Peninsula.† "Here infantry alone could accomplish anything, but only cavalry and artillery were called upon. He could have crossed a brigade of infantry as well as Munford's Cavalry, and that brigade could have been the entering wedge which would split apart the Federal defense, and let in 13 brigades which followed. The bridge, whose destruction is mentioned, was not necessary to a crossing. It was only a high water bridge with a ford by it, which was preferably used except in freshets. Now the floor of the bridge, made of poles, had been thrown into the ford, but Munford's Cavalry got through without trouble, and the infantry could have swarmed across." This is a severe arraignment of Jackson. The feat which appears so simple to the critic certainly must have been attended with some elements of difficulty not mentioned. It is not in reason that so simple an undertaking would have been foregone by Jackson. Of the artillery, Gen. Alexander writes: "The cannonade, which was kept up during all the rest of the day, was

*Stonewall Jackson, Henderson, Vol. II, pp. 68, 69.
†Military Memoirs of a Confederate, Alexander, p. 147.

not only a delusion, but useless burning both of daylight and ammunition, for it was all random fire. The Federal and Confederate artillery could not see each other at all. They could scarcely see the high-floating smoke clouds of each other's guns. They fired by sound, at a distance of three-quarters of a mile, across a tall dense wood, until they exhausted their ammunition. One Federal battery reported the expenditure of 1,600 rounds. The noise was terrific, and some firing was kept up till 9 o'clock at night, but the casualties on each side were naturally trifling. Only one Confederate battery, Rhett's, mentions any, and it reported but 2 killed and 5 wounded."*

But, however correct the criticism may be as to the faulty delays of Jackson, it is to be observed that his guns were properly employed in the execution of the work assigned them. Jackson encountered artillery in position. Whether he should have maneuvered around them or not is a consideration without the scope of this work. When he did decide to silence them with his own artillery, the attempt was made by the employment of all his guns and here again we find evidence of his growing tendency to make use of massed fire. The very fact that he delayed, however unnecessary his action may have been, in order to bring his entire artillery to the front, is significant in our investigation of a better conception on his part of the use of artillery, and in its employment we are alone concerned. One thing is certain, Jackson sought to prepare a passage for his infantry by the massed fire of his guns, even at the cost of the time required for bringing his batteries into position. A. P. Hill might have essayed a crossing without such aid. Had he succeeded, his batteries would have been blocking the roads far to the rear. Jackson failed to cross in the proper way. On the other hand, Hill might have crossed, but certainly not without tremendous loss to his command. On this point, Henderson says: "It is quite true, as a tactical principle, that

*Military Memoirs of a Confederate, Alexander, p. 148.

demonstrations, such as Jackson made with his artillery, are seldom to be relied upon to hold an enemy in position. When the first alarm has passed off, and the defending general becomes aware that nothing more than a fight is intended, he will act as did the Federals, and employ his reserves elsewhere. A vigorous attack is, almost invariably, the only means of keeping him to his ground. But, an attack which is certain to be repulsed, and to be repulsed in quick time, is even less effective than a demonstration. It may be the precursor of a decisive defeat."*

In conclusion, it may be remarked, that not only was the closest student of Jackson's campaigns who has yet contributed to military history thus convinced that Jackson could not have effected a crossing, his conviction being based upon an actual inspection of the terrain, but that Jackson's action on the 30th was in no wise a feint. It was a serious effort on the part of Jackson to attain that superiority of fire over the enemy which would permit his choked columns to pass through what amounted to a tactical defile. In the topographical features of the position, Jackson undoubtedly recognized many elements of danger for his command and sought in vain to overcome them.

*Stonewall Jackson, Vol. II, pp. 69, 70.

CHAPTER XV

In connection with the history of warfare, one involuntarily thinks of Austerlitz, of Friedland, of Wagram, of Malvern Hill, of Gettysburg, of Königgratz, of Sedan, of Plevna, of Mukden, each in its own time, as typifying the great power of concentrated artillery fire. It is one of these, the great battle of Malvern Hill, now about to be considered, which Maj. May, R. H. A., states is as worthy to be remembered by gunners as is Friedland and Wagram.

About 10 P. M., June 30, Franklin, followed by Slocum, Heintzleman, and Sumner, fell back from the positions they had so stoutly maintained against Jackson and Longstreet, and by daylight had reached Malvern Hill overlooking the James River, at Turkey Bend, where Porter had been placed the day before, and where McClellan determined to make another stand.

The battlefield selected by McClellan is an elevated plateau rising to the height of 150 feet above the surrounding forests and embraced by the two branches of Western Run, and possessing nearly every requirement of a strong defensive position. The main branch of the stream gathers near the battlefield of the day before, and flows with a marshy course until it expands into the long milldam that supplies Carter's Mill. After passing this mill, it turn with a sinuous course at a sharp angle to the northwest, along the base of the bluff that constitutes the south end of Malvern Hill, and enters the James at Turkey Bend. Before entering the river, it receives a branch, which, rising about a mile further west, pursues a southeast course, parallel to the main branch and, skirting the western base of the hill, joins the main stream. Small tributaries drain the country to the north of the plateau between the two branches.

The open ground on the top of the hill is about 1½ miles in length by half a mile in breadth. Sloping gradually to the north, northwest and northeast, the hillsides were covered with wheat standing or in shock, to the edge of a wood some 800 yards or more from the commanding crest. The base of the hill, except to the east and southeast, was covered with a dense growth of trees, in the edge of which lay the marshy bed of a stream. Towards the southwest, and south, the plateau terminates in abrupt bluff-like hills, overlooking the river. To the southeast, it slopes away to the milldam bounding it on that side. On the left, or more open side of the upland, was an excellent artillery position, commanding a broad stretch of meadows, drained by a narrow stream and numerous ditches, capable of being flanked by fire from gunboats on the river. To Malvern Hill there were but three practicable approaches by land —the Quaker Road, from the north, the River Road from the west, and a track joining the Quaker Road from the northwest and connecting that road with the Long Bridge Road something over a mile from the summit.

Reconnaissance early on July 1 disclosed the fact that the Federal Army was drawn up in an arc on the summit of Malvern Hill, the center convex towards the north; the left wing extending southward to the bluffs above the river and facing west, the right wing curved back along the eastern side of the plateau, and facing east. A powerful artillery, posted just in rear of the crest, swept the wheat fields on the slopes, the guns capable of ranging well into the woods beyond. Behind the guns were stationed heavy masses of infantry, well under cover, with a strong line of skirmishers pushed down the hillside below the batteries.

Col. H. J. Hunt, McClellan's Chief of Artillery, had for some time been familiar with the striking features of the position, which once seen would not soon be forgotten by an artilleryman. Anticipating the battle, he had undertaken the posting of a number of his batteries on June 30, rearranging the artillery lines the following

morning. On the west side of the hill overlooking Warren, to whom had been assigned Martin's Battery of 12-
pounders, he had placed about 36 guns, some of long
range, to sweep the Low Meadow Valley. To these,
later in the day, were added the siege guns of the 1st
Connecticut Artillery under Col. Robert O. Tyler.
These guns were supported by Sykes' Division, the line
of which was extended in a northerly direction to the
Quaker Road by Morell's Division, with which were 7
batteries under Weeden and Griffin, the latter our gallant friend of Bull Run. Couch's Division extended the
line to the right almost as far as Western Run, and to
his right and rear were the troops of Heintzleman and
Sumner. Hunt's reserve artillery of 100 guns, complete in itself, and only a reserve in name, was held
closely in hand and from it batteries were sent to the
front line to replace those whose ammunition was exhausted, others being used to strengthen the line.*
Thus, we see that there was no question as to a sufficiency of guns, but simply one as to space for their
effective employment.

The setting was complete for a tremendous disaster,
the certainty of which to an attacking force unsupported
by a preponderance of artillery fire would have been pat-
ent to a novice who had become familiar with Porter's
position. But the same *élan* which had borne A. P.
Hill on at Beaver Dam and Gaines' Mill, now swept
forward the Confederate Army. But one man there
was in Lee's Army who forecasted the result. D. H.
Hill was familiar with the character of the new Federal
position, for a resident had described it to him, his in-
formant stating that "its commanding height, the difficulties of approach, its amphitheatrical form and ample
area, would enable McClellan to arrange his 350 field
guns, tier above tier, and sweep the plain in every
direction."† Meeting Gen. Lee early on the 1st, Hill
promptly apprised him of the substance of this report,

---

*Battles and Leaders, Vol. II, pp. 410, 411.
†Ibid., p. 391.

and remarked that "if Gen. McClellan is there in force, we had better let him alone," but Longstreet who was present, jocularly scoffed at the suggestion.

On rushed the Confederates and orders were immediately issued for an attack, Jackson having crossed White Oak Swamp early in the morning. Preparatory to the launching of his troops against the formidable Federal position, Gen. Lee, who was by no means well, directed Longstreet to reconnoiter the enemy's left. Jackson upon coming up had opposed a frontal attack, and advised an enveloping movement about the enemy's right. But Longstreet again took the lead, reporting that there was a good position for batteries opposite the Federal left from which the guns could sweep the field over to their right, and suggested that 60 pieces be stationed there for the purpose.* The open space along Jackson's front, also appeared to him to offer a field of fire for a hundred or more guns, and it was his opinion that Porter's batteries, under a cross fire from the two great Confederate groups, posted as he suggested, would be overwhelmed and the infantry thus enabled to make a successful assault.†

While Longstreet's conception was good, its execution for many reasons proved impossible. Lee ordered the attempt to be made.

The line of battle was formed about 4 o'clock with Jackson on the left, Whiting's Division extending beyond the Quaker Road, and D. H. Hill to its right. Ewell's and Jackson's own divisions were in reserve. About half a mile to the right of Hill's 5 brigades, came 2 of Huger's, 6 of Magruder's, and then 2 more of Huger's, including Ranson's detached from Holmes' Division, the latter occupying the extreme right near the River Road. Longstreet and A. P. Hill were in reserve on the Long Bridge Road, a mile or more to the rear of Magruder.

At the outset, warning was given by the enemy of what was to be expected, for heavy losses were inflicted

---

*Battles and Leaders, Vol. II, p. 403.
†From Manassas to Appomattox, p. 13.

COLONEL STAPLETON CRUTCHFIELD
CHIEF OF ARTILLERY, JACKSON'S CORPS
Killed at Sailor's Creek, 1865

by Hunt's guns upon D. H. Hill's Division while deploying in the woods.

The battle order sent about noon to Magruder, Huger, and D. H. Hill, with their 14 brigades, was remarkable. It consisted of the following words:

"July 1, 1862.

"Batteries have been established to rake the enemy's line. If it is broken, as is probable, Armistead, who can witness the effect of the fire, has been ordered to charge with a yell. Do the same. By order of Gen. Lee.

"R. H. CHILTON, *A. A. C.*"

Of one thing we are sure. When this order was penned, no batteries had been established to rake the enemy's line, nor was it possible to do so at any time during the day, in spite of the fact that the pioneers had made an unsuccessful effort to open a road by means of which guns could be brought up, and the evidence is that Gen. Pendleton did all in his power to overcome the insurmountable difficulties presented by the terrain. Holding well in hand his four reserve battalions in which were to be found the best material of the artillery, he sought in vain for an opening for their employment. His official report is as follows:

"Tuesday, July 1, was spent by me in seeking, for some time, the commanding general, that I might get orders, and, by reason of the intricacy of routes, failing in this, in examining positions near the two armies toward ascertaining what could be best done with a large artillery force, and especially whether any position could be reached whence our large guns could be used to good purpose. These endeavors had, of course, to be made again and again under the enemy's shells, yet no site was found from which the large guns could play upon the enemy without endangering our own troops, and no occasion was presented for bringing up the reserve artillery. Indeed, it seemed that not one-half of the division batteries were brought into action either Monday or Tuesday. To remain nearby, therefore, and await events and orders in readiness for whatever service might be called for, was all I could do."*

Rebellion Records, Series I, Vol. XI, Part II, p. 536.

Again we may feel sure of one thing, and that is, that Pendleton had not seen the Commanding-General the morning of the battle of Malvern Hill. In other words, Gen. Lee and Gen. Longstreet had decided to attack, the latter making the artillery reconnaissance, without the slightest consultation with the Chief of Artillery of the Army and the immediate commander of the reserve, from which, presumably, the large groups to be employed for the purposes of artillery preparation were to be drawn. And this in spite of the fact that upon the success of that preparation the entire action was to hinge. It could not have been that Pendleton was lost. His 5 battalions of not less than 17 batteries were literally blocking the few roads that existed in rear of the Army, not a brigade of which but had stumbled across them in winding its way from the direction of Glendale and White Oak Swamp. If there was one officer in the Army easy to find it was certainly the Chief of Artillery with his immense column of guns and trains. It is quite clear that Pendleton had no part in the conference before the battle, and we find the remarkable situation of a contemplated artillery duel, in which over 100 guns were to participate, unknown to the Chief of Artillery and the commander of those guns.

Referring to Gen. Pendleton, Alexander has this to say: "Pendleton graduated from West Point in 1830, one year after Lee. He resigned in 1833, and entered the ministry in 1837. In 1861, he returned to military life, and was appointed Chief of Artillery of the Army October, 1861, under Gen Johnston. His command did little during the Seven Days, and Col. Brown, commanding his largest battalion, in his report mentions the great superabundance of artillery, and the scanty use that was made of it."* Couched in these words is a direct accusation of his old chief. There is in them an intentional insinuation of incompetence, a practice to which many participants in the great Civil War have been too freely given. As a rule, such remarks only re-

---

*Military Memoirs of a Confederate, Alexander, pp. 158, 159.

act upon the author as they certainly do in this case, in a way to be shown later.

Again referring to that portion of Pendleton's report which has been cited, Alexander writes: "Between the lines one can but read a disappointing story. Pendleton did not find Lee all day long, nor did any orders from Lee find him. He implies that his reserve artillery was not expected to go in until all the division batteries were first engaged. The division batteries were not organized as battalions, and, acting separately, were easily overpowered when brought out one by one, in face of many guns, already in position. Pendleton's battalions, of from 3 to 6 batteries each, would have stood much better chances; and while there were not many places, there were two extensive ones, in either of which all of these battalions could have been used—Poindexter's field, and the position on Magruder's right, to which Lee made the pioneers open a road. As matters were, our whole reserve artillery stood idle all day."*

If General, then Col. Alexander, Chief of Ordnance, on Lee's staff at the battle of Malvern Hill, knew of such positions as those to which he refers a half century later; knew that a road had been cut to one of them, and then failed to find the Chief of Artillery with his 5 battalions, may the good God have mercy on his soul, for he knew what the majority of the generals did not know at the time, and yet let thousands of their men be sacrificed while he remained silent. With such information, it was his duty as a staff officer and one so closely affiliated with the artillery, to find the guns and guide them to the positions so obvious to him over the routes already blazed! The reserve battalions, the superabundance of artillery to which he alludes, could certainly have been found. A verbal order from Gen. Lee, transmitted by the initiative of Col. Alexander, for which initiative he was justly noted throughout his military career, would have brought them all galloping to the front, even had Gen. Pendleton been absent from his post as Alexander naïvely insinuates he was.

---

*Military Memoirs of a Confederate, Alexander, pp. 158.

That there is any inplication in the words of Pendleton, already quoted, that the reserve artillery was not expected to become engaged until the divisional batteries had gone into action, is denied. Gen. Alexander's conclusion is unwarranted. The obvious meaning of the words referred to is that there was not space, due to the dense character of the terrain and the lack of roads, in which the divisional batteries, even acting individually, could maneuver, and that since this was so, all the more impossible was it for large masses of artillery to act. Nor is there anything novel in Gen. Alexander's criticism of the artillery in the Seven Days campaign. Referring to Pendleton's report, dated July 26, 1862, penned not less than fifty years before Alexander wrote his book, we find the following remarks: "In conclusion, while gratefully recognizing that Divine favor which crowned us with victory, I would commend to the consideration of the commanding general what seems to me to have been a serious error, with regard to the use of artillery in these several fights—too little was thrown into action at once; too much was left in the rear unused. One or two batteries brought into position at a time to oppose a much larger artillery force well posted must greatly suffer, if not ultimately yield, under the concentrated fire. This was in several instances our experience.* We needed more guns taking part, alike for our own protection and for crippling the enemy. With a powerful array opposed to his own, we divide his attention, shake his nerves, make him shoot at random, and more readily drive him from the field worsted and alarmed. A main cause of this error in the present case was no doubt a peculiar intricacy in the country, from the prevalence of woods and swamps. We could form little idea of positions, and were very generally ignorant of those chosen by the enemy and of the best modes of approaching them; nor were good maps readily accessible by which in some measure to supply this deficiency; hence a considerable degree of

---

*Beaver Dam, Gaines' Mill, Glendale, Malvern Hill.

perplexity, which nothing but careful reconnaissance, by skillful officers, experienced in such service, could have obviated, but being obviated, attack had been more coöperative, concentrated and effectual, the enemy's condition more crippled, and our success more triumphant, with less mourning in the land."

The man, who three weeks after Malvern Hill wrote this accurate, thorough, and terse resumé of the Confederate operations on the Peninsula, and of the erroneous tactical employment of field artillery in the campaign just over, is more entitled to credit than his critics of a half century later, for they show beyond dispute that the Chief of Artillery appreciated at the time the errors which had been committed. If the causes had not been beyond his control, in a measure at least, the Chief of Artillery would never have so placed himself on record.

The order for the attack was distributed, we have seen, about noon. Not only did it contain false information, in that it declared as a matter of fact supporting batteries to have been established, but it left the decision as to the proper time for the assault entirely in the hands of a brigade commander. Armistead commanded but one of the 14 brigades ordered to attack. Those brigades extended over a mile or more of shell-swept field, many of them entirely hidden from view in the dense thickets. In such circumstances it is difficult to conceive how any but a disjointed effort could result, even were Armistead competent to determine when the enemy had been effectively shaken. Not only was Armistead unable to decide upon the time at which the assault should be made, but he would have been equally unable to observe from his position the effect of the Confederate batteries, had they come into action as contemplated. But this fatal order, which should have been used by Buddecke and Von Kiesling in their works on Battle Orders to illustrate how not to write one, stood, with what results we shall see.

The difficult advance of Magruder's, Huger's, and D. H. Hill's brigades to the positions in line assigned them, at once disclosed the impossibility of executing the proposed plan, for it became apparent that the batteries not only could not be massed as contemplated, but that they could hardly force their way to the front through the swampy thickets. Yet, instead of abandoning so hopeless a plan, every prospect of its success, and every reason for its adoption, depending upon the massed fire of artillery, upon the unison of action of large groups of guns, which had never been attained by the Confederates, even in favorable country, the few batteries which could press through the thickets were ordered forward singly to their fate. Gallantly they essayed the task assigned them, and quickly they reaped the fruits of the error which committed them to so hopeless an undertaking, for as they unlimbered at the edge of the thicket they were swept from their positions by the concentrated fire of the Federal guns. From battery to battery, Hunt shifted the enormous sheaf of fire of more than 50 superior pieces, disabling four of Huger's and several of Jackson's batteries almost the instant they came into action. Those with Jackson which did manage to hold on in spite of the most terrible punishment not only acted without concert, but were entirely too few to make an impression, much less subdue the opposing batteries.

The manner in which, on this occasion, Hunt handled his superb battery of 60 pieces, together with a very similar performance at Gettysburg, the next year, show that he at any rate recalled the secret of Napoleon's success with artillery, and no doubt justifies the high encomium bestowed upon him by Col. Wagner, who declares that his "ability as an organizer and commander of artillery places him in the same rank with Lichtenstein, Senarmont, and Drouot.*"

On the Confederate side the batteries of Poague, Carpenter, Pegram, Davidson, Grimes, Balthis, Moor-

---

*Organization and Tactics, Wagner, p. 347.

man, and the few others which singly from time to time took up the fight, while so ineffective against the artillery of the enemy that Gen. D. H. Hill described their efforts as almost farcical, succeeded in driving Sumner's infantry to the cover of the bluffs above the river, Porter being ordered to follow, which he refused to do. "How eloquent," writes Gen. Alexander, "is this episode of what might have been the effect of bold and energetic use, early in the day, not only of our large artillery reserve, but of all our brigade and division batteries, brought in under their protection, as might have been done under efficient management." Again, we say, Col. Alexander of Gen. Lee's own staff, should have contributed something besides a half century of criticism. It was clearly, as has been shown, within his power to do it at the battle of Malvern Hill. According to his own words, the occasion was rife with opportunities for an artilleryman. The commanding general would have gladly permitted him to suggest the way to accomplish that which the original plan had contemplated.

Realizing the inequality of the contest which the few batteries that had succeeded in gaining position were waging, and the ineffectiveness of their fire, Gen. Lee himself, about 3 o'clock, abandoned his intention of assaulting with the infantry and so notified Longstreet, who was in direct charge of the battle. Shortly before this Gen. Lee, accompanied by Longstreet, had reconnoitered the enemy's right, passing along the entire left of the Confederate position. Strange to say, even before directing Longstreet to break off the fight, neither he nor the latter, the originator of the contemplated artillery duel, now detected a practical position for the massing of the reserve batteries. Had the developments of the Confederate position not been contrary to their original expectations, it seems reasonable to suppose some concerted effort to bring up the reserve artillery would have been made by them, for neither Lee nor Longstreet was given to vacillation or indecision on the field of battle, especially when once engaged.

While the generals were making their reconnaissance, the infantry became heavily engaged, and from then on, the various commands advancing by detachments, continued a spasmodic though desperate effort to carry the crest, all in vain. The field of Malvern Hill was the scene of unsurpassed heroism on the part of the Confederate troops, destined as they were by the attending circumstances to defeat. Let Porter describe the assault.

"The spasmodic, though sometimes formidable, attack of our antagonists, at different points along our whole front up to about 4 o'clock, were, presumably, demonstrations or feelers preparatory to their engaging in more serious work. An ominous silence, similar to that which had preceded the attack in force at Gaines' Mill, now intervened, until, at about 5:30 o'clock, the enemy opened upon both Morell and Couch with artillery from nearly the whole of his front, and soon after pressed forward his columns of infantry, first on one, then on the other, or on both.

"As if moved by a reckless disregard of life equal to that displayed at Gaines' Mill, with a determination to capture our army, or destroy it by driving us into the river, brigade after brigade rushed at our batteries, but the artillery of both Morell and Couch mowed them down with shrapnel, grape, and canister, while our infantry, withholding their fire until the enemy were in short range, scattered the remnants of their columns, sometimes following them up and capturing prisoners and colors."*

Every account of this battle, whether upon Northern or Southern authority, has for its main feature the overwhelming and irresistible artillery fire of Hunt's 50 field pieces, and 10 siege guns, which, continuing their fire until after 9 P. M., always concentrating on the most threatening points, completely overthrew in detail the 3 of Lee's 9 divisions, which were engaged, inflicting upon them a loss of not less than 5,000 men.† But in spite of their losses and the succession of mistakes, there seems to be little doubt that the Confederates came very

---

*Battles and Leaders, Vol. II, pp. 416, 417.
†Alexander says 5,965; Allan says a little over 5,000, so also does Henderson.

near winning the day. The most positive indications of this fact are to be found in Porter's account as well as in Hunt's report. The latter stating that 3 horse batteries and eight 32-pounder howitzers, were "brought up to the decisive point at the close of the day, thus bringing every gun of this large artillery force (artillery reserve of 100 pieces) into the most active and decisive use. Not a gun remained unemployed; not one could have been safely spared."*

Before 10 P. M. the great battle had become a matter of history, the Federal force was in full retreat to Harrison's Landing, the haven of which it reached before morning, and one-third of Lee's Army lay bleeding and exhausted before Malvern Hill, the awful sepulchre of victory, which for 6 of the past 7 days had attended the Confederate arms.

One episode of the pursuit the next morning alone concerns the artillery. At 9 A. M., Stuart's Cavalry had occupied Evelington Heights, overlooking and commanding the Federal position and camp at Harrison's Landing. These heights were peculiarly the position for the immediate occupation by Lee's artillery, a fact which the slightest forethought should have grasped. Dominating as they did the upper part of the peninsula which McClellan had occupied, thereby placing himself in a position in which the alternatives were further retreat down the river, or a frontal attack upon the heights, crowned with artillery they would have been impregnable. But, on the morning of the 3d, unable to resist the temptation, Stuart ordered Pelham, with one of his howitzers, for which little ammunition remained, to fire upon the enemy's camp below. "Judging from the great commotion and excitement below, it must have had considerable effect," wrote Stuart. Thus, by Stuart's horse-play, McClellan was at once apprised of his peril, and by causing the Federal general to immediately reoccupy Evelington Heights, Lee's last opportunity to force him to the offensive was sacrificed by Stuart.

---

*Rebellion Records, Series I, Vol. XI. Part II, p. 239.

One more incident in which the rôle of the Artillery was a leading one in connection with the Peninsula campaign remains to be mentioned. McClellan, as well as a number of his more ardent admirers, had, fortunately for the peace of their own minds, been able to find solace in the belief that in reaching Harrison's Landing, *via* the Seven Pines and Seven Days route, beset as it had been by so many dangers and the loss of some 20,-000 men, the Army of the Potomac was at last in a most advantageous position to threaten Richmond from the south side of the James. The contemplated route in that quarter was no doubt less circuitous than the one pursued from Hampton Roads to Westover. Whatever the proposed course may have been, preparatory thereto McClellan had for several weeks neglected to secure his army, confident in the ability of the gunboats to keep the opposite bank free of the enemy.

Late in the month of July, it was decided by Gen. Lee to bombard McClellan's camp and shipping by night from Coggin's Point, to which task an expeditionary force of artillery in command of Gen. Pendleton was assigned. The force of artillery designated for the work consisted of parts of Brown's Regiment and the battalions of Cutts and Nelson. Leaving Richmond with 32 field pieces, and 2 heavy rifles on siege carriages drawn by the teams of Milledge's Battery, Pendleton reached Petersburg the night of July 29, where he was joined by Gen. D. H. Hill with an infantry force and several batteries. After spending the next day and night in reconnoitering the south shore in the neighborhood of Coggin's Point, Hood's Point, and Claremont, Gen. Hill returned to Petersburg, leaving the expedition in charge of Gens. French and Pendleton. Having successfully kept the guns concealed from the observers in the Federal balloons, they were ordered on the night of the 31st into the positions which had been selected with great care for the various detachments. At 12:30, 41 of the 43 pieces which had been brought up opened fire simultaneously, firing from 20 to 30 rounds apiece, the total expenditure being about 1,000 rounds, whereupon the guns were limbered and quietly moved to the rear as previously directed, and proceeded to Petersburg after a slight rest.

The result of the enterprise was principally a great excitement in the Federal camp, and 40 or 50 casualties among the sleeping troops. A number of vessels were also slightly injured. The Confederate casualties were 1 killed and 7 wounded.* The results obtained were in no wise commensurate with the labor and risk incident to the undertaking and well illustrate the unfruitful character of such enterprises, however deliberately planned and carefully executed. The range to the shipping was some 600 to 800 yards; to the camp on the opposite shore much greater, and owing to these facts no great results should have been expected. The whole affair was farcical, but while it served the purpose of causing McClellan to grasp the strategic advantages of a position astride the river, it also necessitated the construction of intrenchments about Petersburg, which in 1864 enabled Beauregard with a small force to ward off Grant for three whole days until reënforcements came to his support. The result, then, of Pendleton's expedition, was solely one which was not anticipated.† This incident practically ended the Peninsula campaign.

The battles of the Seven Days cost the Confederates 20,000 men. The Federal loss was not more than 16,-000, of which 10,000, about half wounded, were prisoners. In addition to their loss in men, was that of 52 guns, 35,000 rifles, and vast quantities of stores, captured and destroyed. The loss of the Confederate Artillery in material was slight, and in personnel, the strength of which just after the battle of Malvern Hill was 186 officers and 3,778, did not exceed 500.‡ In the Reserve Artillery, the loss, as stated by Alexander, was 2 men, a figure at variance with the casualty return

---

*Rebellion Records, Series I, Vol. XI, Part II, pp. 944-6, Pendleton's Report.
†Gen. Alexander is much confused as to the character of the ordnance used on this occasion as well as to dates. See his book, p. 171, and compare with Official Records.
‡Rebellion Records, Series I, Vol. XI, Part II, p. 506, and Ibid., Part III, pp. 645, 976.

which shows a loss of 8 killed and 30 wounded.* The heaviest individual loss of any battery was that of Pegram's. Engaged in every battle of the Seven Days campaign, the gallant Purcell Battery had suffered a loss of 59 out of 80 men, and was able to man but a single gun at the close of the battle of July 1. Johnson's, Davidson's, and Rhett's batteries were next in order, with a loss of 19 men each. The loss in horses suffered by the Artillery was especially great, many of the batteries being almost dismounted.† But the damage done in this respect was soon remedied and was more than compensated for by the fine rifled pieces captured from the enemy, among which were listed 3 repeating guns.‡

It would be tedious and unfruitful to discuss in detail the individual movements of the various Confederate batteries engaged in the Seven Days campaign. Enough facts have been given to show that the brigade batteries merely acted as best they could with the commands to which they were attached, being called upon to inflict such damage upon the enemy as they might without any special time or assistance being given them for the purpose. It was simply a case of blaze away for the brigade batteries. Of the Reserve, Jones' Battalion had alone accompanied a division in the various egagements, eliciting from Gen. D. H. Hill, to whom it was assigned, high praise. The other battalions of the Reserve and Brown's Regiment had endeavored with only slight success to render service, but due more to a total ignorance of the tactical employment of such masses on the part of the division commanders than to anything else no opportunity was afforded them to coöperate with the infantry and brigade batteries. On several occasions, however, while hovering about the flanks or rear of the lines of battle, in an entirely independent way, these battalions had

*Military Memoirs of a Confederate, Alexander, p. 174; and Official Casualty Return, Rebellion Records, Series I, Vol. XI, Part II, p. 505, and also p. 973.
†Rebellion Records, Series I, Vol. XI, Part III, pp. 689-690.
‡Ibid., Part II, pp. 510-513. Also see a reference to revolving gun on p. 938, no doubt one of those referred to in Part I of this work.

found openings, as in the case of Richardson's and Nelson's battalions at Gaines' Mill, and Golding's Farm.* The absence of the Reserve Artillery on the various battlefields of the Peninsula was as conspicuous as the presence of the splendid Federal batteries on all occasions, a result due in some degree to the artillery organization and experience of the two armies, but principally due to the fact that McClellan invariably defended selected and prepared positions, while Lee assailed them, as a rule, without previous reconnaissance and in the most headlong manner. The element of time requisite to the proper employment of field artillery in so difficult a country was lacking in every instance. The one case in which an artillery duel was attempted, that of Jackson at White Oak Bridge, incurring almost universal adverse criticism.

If the topography of the theater of operations during the Peninsula campaign be considered, with its dense covering of forest, its lack of all but the crudest highways, these facts alone, as Pendleton pointed out, would seem to account for the neglect of artillery masses on the part of the Confederates. But to repeat what has been said before, coupled with the adverse conditions of the terrain were even stronger influences which militated against the effective employment of the artillery, especially in masses. Lack of training and experience on the part of the division commanders, and the entire absence of trained staff officers, both in the infantry and artillery, from which resulted accidental contact with the enemy, precluded the deliberate use of artillery masses.

It is not so easy to overcome the enormous friction which must occur in war as it is to propound new theories. The novelty of reserve battalions of artillery, while readily accepted, was not, and could not have been expected to be, immediately adopted in practice. This will always be the case with tactical innovations, in all armies, at all times. Nothing is more natural in

*Pendleton's Report, *Rebellion Records*, Series I, Vol. XI, Part II, pp. 533-537.

green armies entirely lacking in anything approximating a tactical doctrine. It was true even in the Prussian Army of 1866, the leaders and staff of which were the carefully trained products of a school of thought, founded by Scharnhorst, tested by Napoleon, codified by Clausewitz, and put into more practical form by Gneisenau. But, in spite of their past experience, an experience which the Confederates had not had, in spite of all their training, the Prussians utterly failed in 1866 at Munchengratz, and Gitschin to bring up their reserve artillery, and at Nachod, Trautenau, and Sor, only succeeded in getting it into position very late in the day, not indeed until nightfall. In Austria, just as on the Peninsula, the long columns of reserve artillery with their ammunition trains were allowed to march in rear, the foremost gun following the hindmost combatant of the other arms. Thus it was that even a division marching alone when it gained contact with the enemy, more often than not unexpectedly, found its artillery reserve many miles to the rear. During the advance of the infantry the sight of the artillery columns filled the infantry officers with alarm, lest the roads might be blocked and the batteries were invariably side-tracked to make way for the foot columns. In both campaigns, orders were given from time to time tending to the more timely arrival of the artillery, but such orders when given suddenly, and when opposed to all previously existing principles, were very naturally rendered inoperative by that friction ever present with the movement of troops in the field.

It is not sufficient merely to wish and to order that masses of artillery be brought into action on time; it is necessary also to have learned and practiced the manner of doing it. The Prussians had partly learned the lesson before Königgrätz, and profited by it in 1870; the Confederates did not learn and practice it during the seven days terminating in the catastrophe of Malvern Hill. In his noted work on artillery, Prince Kraft devotes an entire chapter to the subject of "How it was

that the artillery always came up at the right time," in
the Franco-German War, and yet another, "How the
Artillery saved itself," during that war. These chapters
are merely complements of an unnamed one, "How the
Artillery rarely came up at the right time," in the war
of 1866. Most of Hohenlohe's deductions apply with
peculiar force to the artillery operations on the Peninsula.

Before summing up the campaign, it should be said
that Gen. Lee undoubtedly appreciated the many glar-
ing defects of his army, yet was of great enough mind
to recognize them as natural ones and not merely due to
inefficiency on the part of his lieutenants. With respect
to the Artillery, he knew that conditions and inexperience with the arm on the part of all was at the root
of the trouble, and did not cast the blame upon the
shoulders of its chief as Gen. Alexander has sought to
do, for in his report he stated that Gen. Pendleton,
Chief of Artillery, attended unceasingly to his duty.*

Finally, it may be said that the following conclusions,
concerning the Peninsula campaign, seem to be justified by the facts:

1. The Confederate Army, especially with respect
to the artillery, was poorly organized, and possessed but
little cohesion among the divisional units; though
slightly improved in this respect by Gen. Lee, who, in
immediate contact with the enemy from the day he was
assigned to command until the end of the campaign,
had no opportunity to reorganize his forces.

2. The success of the Confederate arms was entirely
due to the almost irresistible force of the infantry, the
morale of which, in spite of the severest punishment,
never waned.

3. In no general action during the campaign was
anything approaching coöperation between the divisional units attained, a result due to the lack of a trained
staff, sufficient cavalry, and the ignorance and almost
entire neglect of reconnaissance duty.

Rebellion Records, Series I, Vol. XI, Part II, p. 498.

4. The artillery failed to perform the rôle of that arm by reason of inexperience on the part of divisional leaders, the impetuosity of their attacks, defective organization, the topographical features of the terrain, and comparatively inferior material and equipment.

5. Lee overthrew McClellan, not by superior tactical dispositions, which on the part of the Confederates were in the main inferior to, though of an entirely different character from those of the Federals, but by the sheer *élan* of his lion-hearted infantry, which, though unsupported by artillery, and poorly led from a tactical point of view, simply could not be stopped.

6. The superior tactical employment of artillery on the part of the Federals was due, not merely to a better organization, material, equipment, and ammunition, but in far greater measure to the defensive attitude it was invariably called upon to assume, thus minimizing those elements which kept the opposing artillery from the field.

7. The final situation of the two armies arose from the fact that without consideration of the tactical results which had been, or were to be attained, Lee, morally the stronger, always ordered his lieutenants forward to assail the enemy, while McClellan uniformly ordered his to retire to defensive positions, each in adherence to a strategic plan from which there was no departure after Lee took command.

CHAPTER XVI

CEDAR MOUNTAIN

WITH the close of the Peninsula campaign the Artillery of the Army of Northern Virginia may be said to have passed its formative period in which the great crisis of its youth had been Malvern Hill. The Army which had been united and fused in the fiery furnace of experience was now prepared to prosecute a greater career.

The salvation of the Artillery lay in the fact that in all matters connected with it, save in the undaunted courage of its officers and men, and the native talent they had displayed for the arm, grave defects were recognized to exist. A great effort was now made to increase its efficiency and to provide for its more adequate employment in battle. For its tactical neglect, the general consensus of opinion rested the blame on conditions. No one was particularly blamed at the time, though frequent harsh criticisms of individuals have since been made by those possessing belated sagacity.

Before the end of July a redistribution of the field batteries had been made and a number of new batteries had reported for duty in the field, among them Girardey's, and Crawford's or "C" Battery of the Sumter Battalion from Georgia, Joseph Graham's from North Carolina, Coit's from South Carolina, and Parker's Richmond, Fleet's Middlesex, Ruffin's Surry, Wyatt's Albemarle, Hupp's Salem, and Dance's Powhatan batteries of Virginia.

The Reserve Artillery was now organized as follows:

FIRST VIRGINIA LIGHT ARTILLERY REGIMENT

Col. J. Thompson Brown

1. Williamsburg Battery,   Capt. J. A. Coke.
2. Powhatan Battery,   Capt. Willis J. Dance.
3. Salem Battery,   Capt. A. Hupp.
4. Fayette Battery,   Capt. M. C. Macon.
5. James City Battery,   Capt. L. W. Richardson.
6. Henrico Battery,   Capt. W. B. Ritter.
7. 3d Richmond Howitzers,   Capt. B. H. Smith.
8. 2d Richmond Howitzers,   Capt. D. Watson.
9. Albemarle Battery,   Capt. J. W. Wyatt.
10. Fairfax Battery,   Capt. E. R. Young.

FIRST BATTALION RESERVE ARTILLERY

Lieut.-Col. A. S. Cutts

1. "A" Battery, Sumter Battalion,   Capt. H. M. Ross.
2. "B" Battery, Sumter Battalion,   Capt. J. V. Price.
3. "C" Battery, Sumter Battalion,   Capt. C. P. Crawford.
4. "D" Battery, Sumter Battalion,   Capt. J. A. Blackshear.
5. "E" Battery, Sumter Battalion,   Capt. J. Lane.

SECOND BATTALION RESERVE ARTILLERY

Maj. Charles Richardson

1. 2d Fluvanna Battery,   Capt. J. J. Ancell.
2. Georgia Battery,   Capt. John Milledge.
3. Ashland Battery,   Capt. Pichegru Woolfolk.

THIRD BATTALION RESERVE ARTILLERY

Maj. William Nelson

1. Charlottesville Battery,   Capt. Jas. McD. Carrington.
2. 1st Fluvanna Battery,   Capt. C. T. Huckstep.
3. Amherst Battery,   Capt. Thomas J. Kirkpatrick.
4. Morris Virginia Battery,   Capt. R. C. M. Page.

FOURTH BATTALION RESERVE ARTILLERY

Maj. Hilary P. Jones

1. Long Island Battery,   Capt. P. H. Clarke.
2. Richmond Orange Battery,   Capt. T. Jefferson Peyton.
3. South Carolina Battery,   Capt. A. B. Rhett.
4. Goochland Battery,   Capt. W. H. Turner.

This, indeed, was a powerful array which Gen. Pendleton had collected. With the 26 batteries of the reserve were not fewer than 100 guns, including much of the best material in the service. Among the guns captured from McClellan were many fine, serviceable pieces. In point of ordnance, the Confederate reserve now approached that of Hunt, but in discipline, mounts, and equipment, the artillery always fell far behind the Federal standard. The deficiencies in harness and equipment were now beginning to be made up to some extent by the Bureau of Ordnance, its manufacturing activities being in full swing by this time, thanks to the unremitting efforts of Col. Gorgas. Foreign importations of ordnance material and stores were also now being received and distributed to the Army by this energetic officer. Among the ordnance of the Army at this time was to be found a small number of Hotchkiss, Whitworth, Armstrong, and Blakely guns, purchased abroad by foreign agents, and brought in by the fleet of blockade runners operated by the Bureau of Ordnance. The Blakely field pieces were especially favored by the horse batteries.

In the lull succeeding the activities of June and July, strenuous efforts were also made by Pendleton to recruit the depleted batteries of the Army to full strength and to overcome the existing deficiencies with respect to their horses. It is probable, therefore, that the personnel of the reserve numbered 3,000 men or more by the middle of August, and that most of the batteries were well horsed, that is, with a sufficient number of four-horse teams, for the stringency in the South in the supply of remounts had not yet begun to pinch.

Another great stride forward occurred about this time in the enlargement and reorganization of the reserve ordnance train by Col. Alexander, Chief of Ordnance. While the service of ammunition supply on the Peninsula had been remarkably efficient, yet, for the contemplated increase in the activity of the artillery it did not appear adequate to its chief.

The batteries with the divisions were neither as strong in personnel, nor as well equipped and mounted as were those of the reserve at this time. For instance, on July 21, the 4 batteries with Early's and Trimble's brigades of Ewell's Division, namely, Johnson's Bedford (W. Va.), Brown's Chesapeake, the Manchester, and Latimer's Courtney batteries, possessed a personnel of but 222 men, present and absent, increased to 12 officers and 384 men by July 31. But of the latter number only 236 were present for duty, or an average of 3 officers and 56 effective men, and up to August 10, there had been no additions even to make up for the losses sustained, though the tri-monthly return for August 20 shows 14 officers and 276 men present, with an aggregate present and absent of 419. On paper, therefore, the individual battery strength was about 105 men, while in the field it was but 72. Since Ewell's Division had been ordered to take the field July 13 for active work, it is fair to assume that the figures of these batteries, if not typical, were rather above than below the average.*

G. O. No. 150, A. N. V., July 13, 1862, directed Jackson, with his own and Ewell's Division, to proceed to Louisa Court House and if possible to Gordonsville, to check the advance of Pope from the direction of Orange Court House. The same day Crutchfield assigned to Ewell Latimer's (Courtney's), Lusk's 2d Rockbridge, the 2d Baltimore or Brockenbrough's, and Rice's Star, batteries. On the 14th, in addition to Poague's 1st Rockbridge, Carpenter's Alleghany, and Caskie's Hampden batteries already with Jackson's Division, Balthis' Staunton, Brown's 4th Baltimore or Chesapeake, and J. R. Johnson's Bedford, batteries were attached to it. Maj. R. Snowden Andrews, and Maj. A. R. Courtney, former battery commanders, were promoted and assigned to the command of the artillery of Jackson's and Ewell's divisions, respectively. Carrington's Albemarle Battery was detached from

---

Rebellion Records, Series I, Vol. XII, Part III, pp. 964, 965, 966. Ibid., p. 915.

Ewell's Division and ordered to report for duty with the reserve. All of Jackson's batteries were to move with the infantry by train.*

Upon arriving at Gordonsville, July 19, Jackson at once perceived that his force of 12,000 was inadequate as opposed to Pope's 47,000 and called for reënforcements. A. P. Hill was consequently ordered to join him July 27, with 12,000 men, and Pegram's Purcell, Fleet's Middlesex, Braxton's Fredericksburg, and Latham's North Carolina or Branch, batteries. Lieut.-Col. Reuben Lindsay Walker commanded the artillery of the division.

Before the battle of Cedar Mountain, August 9, a number of changes were made in the assignment of the artillery. With the three divisions under Jackson which were present with him in that action were the following batteries:

First Division (Winder (K) Taliaferro)

Maj. R. Snowden Andrews, Chief of Artillery

1st Rockbridge Battery,	Capt. W. T. Poague.
Alleghany Battery,	Capt. Joseph Carpenter.
Hampden Battery,	Capt. W. H. Caskie.

Second (Light) Division (A. P. Hill)

Lieut.-Col. Reuben Lindsay Walker, Chief of Artillery

Purcell Battery,	Capt. W. J. Pegram.
Middlesex Battery,	Lieut. W. B. Hardy.
Fredericksburg Battery,	Capt. Carter M. Braxton.
Branch (N. C.) Battery,	Capt. A. C. Latham.

Third Division (Ewell)

Maj. A. R. Courtney, Chief of Artillery

1st Md. or Andrews' Battery,	Capt. Wm. F. Dement.
4th Md. or Chesapeake Battery,	Capt. Wm. D. Brown.
La. Guard (Girardey's) Battery,	Capt. Louis E. D'Aquin.
Courtney's Henrico Battery,	Capt. J. W. Latimer.
Bedford Battery,	Capt. J. R. Johnson.

*Rebellion Records, Series I, Vol. XII, Part III, p. 915, and Vol. XI, Part III, p. 652. But compare with batteries enumerated in Vol. XII, Part III, p. 964.

Thus, with 23,750 men, Jackson had about 47 guns, or a proportion of 2 per 1,000 men of all arms. But, though small in numbers, his artillery was better organized than it had ever been before, that is in divisional masses, each commanded by an efficient officer, and all under the able Crutchfield, between whom and Jackson a perfect mutual confidence existed.

Jackson was now in his element. The sight of the Blue Ridge was to his soul like a tonic. Independence again roused him to emulate himself. No longer were his actions circumscribed by superior authority at which, whether intentionally or not, he ever chafed.

Released from the monotonous swamp-land of the Peninsula, the eagle had returned to his native hills where from familiar eyrie he might swoop upon the prey, or freely wheel from craggy peak to peak. No historian has yet satisfactorily explained the anomaly of Jackson's lethargy on the Peninsula. The very variance of the proffered solutions only serves to dissatisfy the student. Given this or that set of facts it can be explained. Taking them all together, again we become mystified. With his battery in Mexico, the young Jackson had in the independence of such a command won fame. As a professor in a subordinate position at the Virginia Military Institute, his initiative waned, and over his whole career in Lexington there hung a moody gloom, with only occasional flashes of his fiery soul, as when in his section room he expressed a soulful longing for war, and declared that if war must come, the South should throw away its scabbard. From the moment Jackson joined Lee near Richmond he was no longer the "Eagle of the Valley," but became a falcon, and, perched upon the wrist of a master, it seemed as if his wings were clipped. No longer did he swoop hither and thither glorying in his power. But, the hood removed, once more we discern the eagle-like character of his old self, for Jackson had become Jackson again. Some men are great when their efforts are directed by a guiding hand; the souls of others perish from dependence like wild animals in captivity.

On the 2d of August, while Jackson's command lay about Gordonsville, a brisk cavalry skirmish near Orange Courthouse gave warning that Pope's force must be struck promptly, if it were to be encountered in detail. August 7, therefore, the three divisions moved forward to gain contact with Banks, who had become separated from and was in advance of McDowell. The Federal Cavalry being driven back to Culpeper Courthouse, the Army crossed the Rapidan, Ewell's Division leading, early on the 8th. Continuing to press forward in spite of the many delays and misunderstandings which interefered with his plans, Jackson at last reached the vicinity of Cedar Run, where he gained contact with the Federal Infantry, disposed for the purpose of disputing his advance.

The Federal position lay behind a tributary stream running southward and joining Cedar Run near the eastern end of Slaughter Mountain, a range of hills running from northeast to southwest and overlooking the battlefield. The road from Orange, or the Culpeper Road, over which Banks and Jackson approached each other, crossed the tributary stream at right angles, the Federal position lying in an elevated wood to the west side of the latter. In front of the Federals lay an open and broken country, with a large wheatfield on the north side of the road, surrounded by woods, except along the highway. Farther to the north lay heavily-wooded high ground, but on the south side of the road was an open plateau of cornfields and pastures, gently ascending to the mountain. Ewell with Trimble's and Hays' brigades, Latimer's Courtney Battery, and a section of Johnson's Bedford Battery, under Lieut. Nathaniel Terry, was ordered forward about 1 o'clock, and occupied a commanding position on the northeast point of the mountain, completely overlooking the Federal left wing. Early's Brigade moved forward along the Culpeper Road and pressing back the enemy's cavalry, took up a position on the crest opposite the Federal center, perpendicular to the road and a little south of it, posting one 3-inch rifle from Brown's Chesapeake and 2 from Dement's 1st Maryland Battery on his right, near a clump of cedars just in advance of, and 2 of Dement's and 3 of D'Aquin's in rear of, Mrs. Crittenden's house. In Early's front was open pasture ground sloping gently downward, beyond which was a cornfield sloping upward to the Federal position; thus the ground at this point afforded an excellent field of fire for the guns on both sides. North of the Culpeper Road the wheatfield mentioned was just opposite the cornfield on the south side, but the country on the north side was much less open than to the south. To Early's immediate left was timber, which everywhere on the north side of the road extended up to the wheatfield. Winder, whose division had followed Ewell's, was directed to support Early. Advancing along the main road he placed Garnett's Brigade in the woods to the north facing the wheatfield with his right facing the road, near which 5 guns from Poague's, Carpenter's, and Caskie's batteries were posted, supported by Taliaferro's Brigade. Winder's own brigade was held in reserve. From left to right of the Confederate line the distance was probably 2 miles, a considerable gap intervening between Early and Ewell's other brigades. The 26 guns of Jackson's artillery which had been brought up were disposed in a crescent, the horns of which were to the rear, in 3 small groups; that of Maj. Andrews on the left with 5, that of Early in the center with 8, and that of Ewell on the right with 6 pieces, the range of the center group being perhaps 500, and the ranges of the others as much as 2,500 yards from the enemy's batteries.

In Banks' Corps, were 9 batteries well grouped about opposite Early. As soon as the latter took up his position, the Federal guns opened upon him, to which Dement and Brown at once replied, soon supported by Maj. Andrews' guns on the left and Latimer's on the right. The ensuing artillery duel continued with great vigor for about 2 hours. Gen. Winder was mortally

wounded while directing the fire of his batteries. About
3 P. M. from Hill's divisional artillery, then in park in
rear, Col. Walker was able to bring forward Pegram's
Purcell, and Hardy's Middlesex batteries, to the support of those already in action, but found it impossible
to bring up more guns before the action was over, due to
the blocked condition of the roads in rear of the field.
Thus the number of pieces engaged in this duel was
finally about equal on the two sides.

Between 5 and 6 P. M. Banks, who, with his superior
ordnance, had gotten somewhat the best of the artillery
duel, advanced to the attack. His right, overlapping
the Confederate left, threw the latter into confusion,
routing Garnett's Brigade. Maj. Andrews ordering
his batteries with those of A. P. Hill, which Walker
had brought up, to change front, maintained a terrific
fire from his guns upon the Federal Infantry, which
had approached to within 300 yards before A. P. Hill's
Division began to arrive upon the scene, and enabled the
Confederates to repulse the assault and drive the Federals across Cedar Creek. By this time it was dark,
but favored by a moon, almost full, two fresh brigades
with Pegram's Purcell Battery undertook the pursuit,
but were checked by Ricketts' Division, 3 of the batteries of which inflicted a loss of 2 killed and 14
wounded on Pegram's Battery alone. Pegram's action
on this occasion was characteristically cool and gallant.*

In the whole affair, the loss of the Confederate Artillery was 2 killed and 28 wounded; that of the enemy
was 7 killed, and 29 wounded, and 6 missing. In material, the Federal loss was the greater, involving, however, but one 12-pounder Napoleon.

Some idea of the severity of the artillery duel may
be derived from the fact that Knapp's Pennsylvania
Battery of six 10-pounder Parrotts reported an expenditure of 980 rounds during the day.

In this exceptionally bloody action on the part of the
infantry, much less so, however, than it would have been

---

*Rebellion Records, Series I, Vol. XII, Part II, p. 171, Report of Major Davis
Tillson, Chief of Artillery, 3d Army Corps.

had Jackson made the usual headlong assault on the Federal position, we again find him delaying until his better guns could be brought into action. While not all of his artillery was brought up, yet that employed was grouped in masses, small though they were, in order to secure from them the benefits of a cross fire on the Federal artillery. Jackson had undoubtedly learned the lesson that with long range guns concentrated fire did not necessarily require massed guns. Though Banks anticipated him in the infantry attack, yet the disposition of his guns had enabled Jackson, both on the right, between Early and Ewell, and on the extreme left, to assist his infantry with the canister of his batteries. In the battle of Cedar Mountain, in which the batteries were directed by divisional chiefs, is to be found by far the best tactical employment of field artillery up to that time exhibited by the Confederates, and in point of individual battery action in pursuit, nothing could have excelled the skill and dash displayed by Pegram, who, though severely punished, adroitly followed up the retreating infantry, working havoc in its ranks with his guns until they were silenced by the concentrated fire of 4 fresh batteries.

To Pegram belongs the credit of having been first to make Pope, with his entire staff, turn his back on the Army of Northern Virginia, a practice which he had boastingly declared was the great fault with his predecessor.*

We shall frequently meet with the name of William Johnston Pegram in this narrative from now on. As no officer of the Artillery of Lee's Army was more noted than he, some account of his career up to the time of which we write should here be given.†

"In October, 1860, he matriculated as a student in the University of Virginia, entering the School of Law.

---

*The disappearance of Pope, when a salvo from Pegram's Battery suddenly burst upon him as he arrived on the field, is an amusing incident in the career of that general.

†For complete sketch of his life see "The University Memorial," by the Rev. John L. Johnson. The sketch of Pegram is by W. Gordon McCabe, his brilliant adjutant and inseparable comrade.

He was then nineteen years old, reserved almost to shyness, grave and gracious in his manner, in which there was little of primness and much of the charm of an old-fashioned politeness. His apparent shyness was owing partly to his extreme near-sightedness, partly to the modesty of his nature. To those students who were not his intimates, but happened to meet him occasionally in the rooms of common friends, it was often a matter of wonder and remark how keen a sense of humor there was in this quiet, sober-looking lad, who assuredly yielded to no one in his thorough appreciation of the most delicate criticism.

"In the autumn of this year the students determined to organize two companies of infantry, and Pegram at once became an active promoter of the enterprise. He entered the first company formed, known as the 'Southern Guard,' and was appointed 1st Sergeant. He was then a capital infantry soldier, having been for two years a member of the famous 'Company F' of Richmond, and proved untiring in drilling his men. In 1861 came Lincoln's proclamation calling for 50,000 volunteers. From that moment books were little thought of in the University. All were eager to exchange gown for sword. Pegram at once left college and reported for duty with his old company, which had been ordered to Aquia Creek. With this company he remained but a short time. Sent as drillmaster to exercise the artillerymen of Walker in the infantry tactics, he was elected Lieutenant of the 'Purcell Battery.' It was as commander of this battery that he was destined to achieve his hard-won fame—a battery which was with him from the first battle of Manassas, through every general action in Virginia, to the trenches of Petersburg—which, always skillfully handled in the presence of the enemy, yet lost during its four years of service more than 200 men killed and wounded; and which he declared repeatedly when colonel that 'the Purcell men were the coolest and the most desperate men he ever saw in a tight place.' Lindsay Walker, afterwards

Brigadier-General and Chief of Artillery of Hill's
Corps, was then captain of the battery, and was not
slow to discover what a thorough soldier he possessed in
his young subaltern. Long afterwards Walker gener-
ously said that Pegram spared him all trouble, and that
commanding a battery, the most troublesome thing in
the world, became a pleasure with such an executive
officer. In the campaign of '61 the battery was engaged
at Bull Run; Walker received his majority early in
'62, and Pegram became captain on the reorganization.
But it was not until the great struggle in front of Richmond, in July of '62, that the battery came into marked
prominence. At Mechanicsville it held the post of
honor, and paid the price which the post of honor ever
exacts. Here first to the Army the young captain gave
proof of that stubborn courage and literal obedience to
orders which all men thereafter looked for in him. Exposed to a murderous fire of infantry, to the convergent
fire of five six-gun batteries, long after night came
down the thunder of his guns told that he was
tenaciously holding his ground. But there was surprise mingled with admiration when it became known
to the Army on the next day that of his six guns four
had been disabled before nightfall, that two of his officers had been badly wounded, more than half his
horses killed, and that of the ninety dashing cannoneers
who had on yesterday galloped into action more than
fifty lay killed and wounded on the field.

"The day after 'Mechanicsville' he equipped thoroughly the two guns which had not been disabled, and
again applied to Gen. Hill to have the advance. Everywhere during the Seven Days that plucky section and
its young captain found their place where the battle
raged hottest. Richmond, in her joy of triumph, a joy
chastened by the sorrow which victory ever brings, was
not unmindful of her youthful hero. The town rang
with his praises—praises closest to a soldier's heart—
from the lips of wounded men, who had seen him in the
dust and sweat of battle, and who spoke of him as only

brave men can speak of each other. His name was introduced into the play by one of the actors at the theater, and elicited the most tumultuous applause. The player declared that the boy captain fought at such close quarters because he was too near-sighted to see a dozen yards, and would never open fire until he saw the enemy. At this the bronzed and bearded veterans in the pit rose and cheered lustily. Meanwhile the young captain remained modestly at his camp, riding into the city but rarely to visit his immediate family, and blushing painfully when any one spoke to him of the attention his gallantry had excited. Especially annoying to him were the fulsome praises showered upon him by newspapers. His distress at these paragraphs was a great source of amusement to his comrades. 'Why, this is simply disgusting,' he would say; 'every man at the front will be laughing over it.' But the men at the front were never prone to laugh at good fighters, and gave even more exaggerated accounts of his achievements than did the florid paragraphs of the journals.

"A few days of rest, and his battery, newly equipped and recruited, was on the march to Cedar Mountain with Jackson's flying column. Here again his guns, pushed up within eighty *yards* of the enemy, were served with such rapidity and precision as won a nod of approval even from the great leader, always so chary of praise. About nightfall, when Gen. Jackson had determined to press the retreating enemy, Pegram's guns, supported by Field's Brigade, were advanced within close range of the spot where the enemy was supposed to have halted. In a few moments a heavy column was seen marching on the flank of the guns. Owing to the uncertain light it was impossible to tell whether it was a column of Federals or of our own men. The officers of the support differed in opinion regarding the matter, and time was precious. Pegram at once turned his battery over to his 1st lieutenant, saying: 'McGraw, I shall ride up close to these fellows; keep a sharp lookout, and if you see me wave my hat, open all the guns.' In a moment he was galloping towards the column now within a hundred yards, reined in his horse close to the silently-moving mass, turned, and waved his hat. Another moment and he rode at full speed into the line of guns, where old Stonewall sat on his sorrel watching the column. Pegram cried out in great glee: 'Pitch in, men; Gen. Jackson is looking at you!' The enemy were broken in a few minutes by his rapid fire, but speedily put three batteries into position and returned it. For 2 hours this single battery fought 18 guns of the enemy, and it was not until 10 o'clock that his heated and disabled Napoleons were silenced. His loss was proportionally, very nearly as great as at Mechanicsville; but he was determined to push on with Walker's Battalion to Manassas, where for the second time his guns did good service on that glorious field."

CHAPTER XVII

AUGUST 14, McClellan, with the main body of his army began his movement to Fortress Monroe, from which point his troops were to be transferred to the vicinity of Alexandria, for the purpose of moving out to the support of Pope. Burnside's Corps which had reached Fredericksburg began to move up the Rappahannock for the same purpose. Gen. Lee personally took command at Gordonsville on the 15th, to which point Jackson had returned on the 12th. On the 13th, Longstreet's command consisting of 19 brigades was ordered to Gordonsville by rail, and Hood with 2 brigades to Hanover Junction, R. H. Anderson's Division being ordered to proceed from Drewry's Bluff to Louisa Courthouse.* As soon as it was positively learned that Burnside had left Fredericksburg, Hood was ordered to join Longstreet. On the 18th, the Reserve Artillery, which had not taken part in Jackson's operations about Orange, was ordered to proceed by road to Gordonsville.† Leaving his camp about Richmond on the afternoon of the 19th, the same day Pendleton was directed to halt his command upon reaching the North Anna, behind which Ripley had been ordered to mass Smith's Division for the purpose of opposing the reported advance of a Federal column over the Fredericksburg Road. Tarrying here for a time, Pendleton was soon ordered to join Gen. Lee, the Reserve reaching Louisa Courthouse on the 27th. From this point its route was deflected to Rapidan Station. While Pendleton himself, by dint of hard riding, succeeded in joining Gen. Lee on the battlefield of Second Manassas, the Reserve Artillery, as seen, was lumbering along far to the rear at the rate of about 20 miles a day.

---

*Rebellion Records, Series I, Vol. XII, Part III, pp. 928, 929, 931.
†Ibid., p. 965.

On the 19th, Gen. Lee had published his order for the
advance of his army from Gordonsville to begin early
the following morning. Longstreet's command constituting the right, and Jackson's constituting the left
wing, were to cross the Rapidan at Raccoon and Somer-
ville Fords, respectively, moving in the direction of
Culpeper Courthouse, the latter followed by R. H.
Anderson's Division in reserve, with which Col. S. D.
Lee's newly-organized battalion of 6 batteries was to
move. This reserve battalion was composed as follows:

Bath Battery,	Capt. J. L. Eubank.
Portsmouth (Grimes') Battery,	Lieut. Thomas J. Oakham.
Bedford Battery,	Capt. T. C. Jordan.
Richmond Battery,	Capt. W. W. Parker.
Rhett's South Carolina Battery,	Lieut. Wm. Elliott.
Ashland Battery,	Capt. Pichegru Woolfolk, Jr.

The mass of Pope's troops was near the Rapidan,
opposite Orange Courthouse, where they had been confronting Jackson at Gordonsville. The commanding-
general becoming apprised on the 18th of Lee's plans
and numbers by means of a captured autograph communication of the latter, at once ordered his army to
fall back behind the Rappahannock, where he would be
nearer his base and more promptly reënforced by a part,
at least, of McClellan's army. By the night of the
19th the Federal Army lay behind the river, its left
opposite Kelly's Ford, and its right behind Hazel Run,
near Rappahannock Station. The following night the
Confederates had crossed the Rapidan, and Longstreet,
on the right, had gained contact with the Federal left
at Kelly's Ford. On the 21st, Jackson moved forward
from his bivouac at Stevensburg to the river, his front
extending from the railroad bridge to Beverly Ford.
At the latter point, Col. Rosser with two regiments of
cavalry crossed the river, dispersing the opposing
infantry and disabling one of Banks' batteries which
had been posted behind the ford. With a section of
Pelham's horse battery, Rosser's force remained on the
north side of the river until late in the day, supported

from the other bank by Taliaferro's 8 divisional batteries under Maj. L. M. Shumaker. When Stuart withdrew before King's Division and some of Sigel's troops, sent up by McDowell to retake the ford, an active artillery duel ensued during the remainder of the day between the opposing batteries, a cannonade without material results on either side.

The main point to be noticed in connection with the Artillery in this movement is that it was comparatively well organized in divisional masses, only a few batteries being assigned to brigades, and that it was kept well up to the front in the advance, with the exception of the Reserve. It would seem that Pendleton's remonstrance against the inadequate use of the Artillery on the Peninsula had had some effect, though of course the error which had been previously committed with respect to the neglect of the arm had been perceived and appreciated by Gen. Lee. Its organization was now, approximately, as follows:

RIGHT WING OR LONGSTREET'S CORPS

ANDERSON'S DIVISION

Lieut.-Col. Stephen D. Lee, Chief of Artillery

1. Bath Battery,	Capt. J. L. Eubank.
2. Portsmouth Battery,	Lieut. Thomas J. Oakham.
3. Bedford Battery,	Capt. T. C. Jordan.
4. Richmond Battery,	Capt. W. W. Parker.
5. Rhett's South Carolina Battery,	Lieut. William Elliott.
6. Ashland Battery,	Capt. Pichegru Woolfolk, Jr.

WILCOX'S DIVISION

1. Thomas Battery,	Capt. Edwin J. Anderson.*
2. Dixie Battery,	Capt. W. H. Chapman.†

HOOD'S DIVISION

Maj. B. W. Frobel, Chief of Artillery

1. Charleston (S. C.) German Battery,	Capt. W. R. Bachman.
2. Palmetto (S. C.) Battery,	Capt. Hugh R. Garden.
3. Rowan (N. C.) Battery,	Capt. James Reilly.

---

*Wilcox's Brigade.
†Featherston's Brigade.

KEMPER'S DIVISION

1. Macbeth (S. C.) Battery,   Capt. R. Boyce.*

CORPS RESERVE ARTILLERY (RIGHT WING)

Col. John B. Walton, Chief of Artillery

1. 1st Co. Washington Artillery,   Capt. C. W. Squires.
2. 2d Co. Washington Artillery,   Capt. J. B. Richardson.
3. 3d Co. Washington Artillery,   Capt. M. B. Miller.
4. 4th Co. Washington Artillery,   Capt. B. F. Eshleman.
5. Norfolk Battery,   Capt. Frank Huger.
6. Goochland (Leake) Battery,   Capt. Wm. H. Turner.
7. Donaldsonville (La.) Battery,   Capt. Victor Maurin.
8. Lynchburg Battery,   Capt. M. N. Moorman.
9. Loudoun Battery,   Capt. A. L. Rogers.
10. Fauquier Battery,   Capt. R. M. Stribling.

LEFT WING OR JACKSON'S CORPS

Col. Stapleton Crutchfield, Chief of Artillery

TALIAFERRO'S DIVISION

Maj. L. M. Shumaker, Chief of Artillery

1. 2d Baltimore Battery,   Capt. J. B. Brockenbrough.
2. Alleghany Battery,   Capt. Joseph Carpenter.
3. Hampden Richmond Battery,   Capt. Wm. H. Caskie.
4. Winchester Battery,   Capt. W. E. Cutshaw.
5. 1st Rockbridge Battery,   Capt. Wm. T. Poague.
6. Lee Battery,   Capt. Charles J. Raine.
7. 8th Star Battery,   Capt. W. H. Rice.
8. Danville Battery,   Capt. George W. Wooding.

A. P. HILL'S DIVISION

Lieut.-Col. R. Lindsay Walker, Chief of Artillery

1. Fredericksburg Battery,   Capt. Carter M. Braxton.
2. Richmond Battery,   Capt. W. G. Crenshaw.
3. Letcher Battery,   Capt. Greenlee Davidson.
4. Middlesex Battery,   Lieut. W. B. Hardy.
5. Branch (N. C.) Battery,   Lieut. John R. Potts.
6. Pee Dee (S. C.) Battery,   Capt. D. G. McIntosh.
7. Purcell Battery,   Capt. Wm. J. Pegram.

---

*Evans' Brigade.

EWELL'S DIVISION

Maj. A. R. Courtney, Chief of Artillery

1. Staunton Battery,	Lieut. A. W. Garber.
2. 4th Md. or Chesapeake Battery,	Capt. Wm. D. Brown.
3. Louisiana Guard Battery,	Capt. Louis E. D'Aquin.
4. 1st Maryland Battery,	Capt. Wm. F. Dement.
5. Bedford Battery,	Capt. John R. Johnson.
6. Henrico Courtney Battery,	Capt. James W. Latimer.

Thus with Lee's Army, numbering between 47,000 and 55,000 men, were 43 batteries, with a total of about 175 guns, or something over 3 guns per 1,000 of all arms.* With Longstreet's Corps were 22, and with Jackson's, 21 batteries. The total personnel did not exceed 2,500 men.

In addition to the light batteries of the Army, there were, however, with the cavalry, Pelham's and Chew's horse batteries. About this time the Washington (S. C.) Battery, Capt. James F. Hart, was converted into a horse battery, but it did not rejoin the Army until September 2.

In Longstreet's Corps, a large reserve force of 10 batteries is found collected under the immediate command of Col. Walton, an organization only approximating the corps artillery reserve of the following year, for 6 of these batteries were used at this time in a purely individual capacity.

On the morning of the 22d, Jackson, seeking to gain the enemy's right, left the position 'he had previously occupied, Longstreet having been ordered over thereto from Kelly's Ford, and moved towards the fords near Warrenton or Fauquier White Sulphur Springs, where he arrived during the afternoon, having crossed the Hazel River at Welford's Mill. Longstreet had, meanwhile, been engaging the enemy in an active artillery combat at Beverly Ford.

Although aware of the movement on his right, Pope held the mass of his army near Rappahannock Station

---

*For strength of Lee's army, see Ropes, p. 198; Allan, p. 199; *Four Years With General Lee*, Taylor, p. 60; *Southern Historical Papers*, Vol. VII, p. 181.

in order to hold the railroad and keep open the route for his reënforcements from Fredericksburg, both of which were threatened by Longstreet. During the various active movements that ensued, resulting after much vacillation, in Pope's occupying with his whole army a position between Sulphur Springs and Warrenton, the Artillery had been actively employed both by Longstreet at Beverly Ford and by Jackson against Sigel, in his flanking movement on the Federal right. On the 24th, Jackson's artillery had also been active along the river from Sulphur Springs to Waterloo, A. P. Hill's Division holding the Confederate side of the river. Practically all of the artillery of the two corps had been engaged.

It now became known that Pope had plans of his own, and that Lee had been foiled in his effort to cross the river. At this juncture it also became evident that Pope's 50,000 men would soon be increased to 130,000 or more, and though Lee's strength would soon exceed 70,000, immediate action on his part was necessary. Without waiting for his reënforcements, since the delay would in effect only contribute to the disparity in numbers between the two armies, Lee now decided to make one more effort to fall upon Pope's rear.

Accordingly, late on the 24th, Jackson, with 22,000 men, was ordered to cross the Rappahannock beyond Pope's right flank, and move by forced marches through Thoroughfare Gap until he struck the Orange and Alexandria Railroad in the Federal rear.

In order to make possible this movement, Lee now gave the most brilliant example of the use of artillery which had yet occurred in the war. The success of Jackson's movement depended absolutely upon its secrecy, and yet it was necessary for him to withdraw his guns from under the very eyes of the enemy. It was accomplished on the following day. Perceiving that the Federals had largely withdrawn from the lower fords along the Rappahannock, Longstreet, leaving but a small force in his old position, was ordered up to relieve Jackson, the latter's guns having maintained their fire until nightfall, making a brave display of force. Upon the arrival of Longstreet, his guns were quietly substituted for those of Jackson under the cover of night, continuing the fire with great activity at dawn.

Late on the 24th, Jackson's Corps had been assembled about Jeffersonton, where the troops were relieved of all baggage and trains. Nothing in the way of a train but the ambulance and ammunition wagons and a few beeves on the hoof was to accompany the light column and its artillery. Marching northwest to Amissville, and then north to Salem, with the artillery in the rear, Jackson covered 26 miles on the 25th. On the 26th, the column was under way at daybreak, and now turned eastward. Passing through Thoroughfare Gap in the Bull Run Mountain, it reached Gainesville about 3 P. M., from which point Jackson marched to Bristoe, Ewell's Division arriving there about sunset after a march of 25 miles. The presence of the Confederates being now discovered, Trimble's Brigade hastened on another 4 miles to capture Manassas Junction before reënforcements could arrive from Alexandria. This he gallantly did, capturing the Federal works with 2 light batteries complete and fully mounted. When Jackson arrived at Manassas Junction early the morning of the 27th, with Taliaferro's and Hill's divisions, he had with him the entire divisional artillery. Thus, in little more than 48 hours, Jackson's 21 batteries, with four-horse teams, had covered over 55 miles, no mean performance even with the most superior full teams of draught animals.

In the meantime, Longstreet by ostentatiously planting fresh batteries and keeping up a heavy fire of artillery in periodical cannonades, had succeded in deceiving Pope throughout the 25th and the morning of the 26th into believing that a crossing was to be attempted either at Sulphur Springs or Waterloo Bridge.* About noon of the latter day, however, leaving Ander-

*Rebellion Records, Series I, Vol. XII, Part II, p. 66.

son's Division at Sulphur Springs to observe the enemy,
Longstreet with about 25,000 men set out to follow
Jackson's route, bivouacking at Orleans that night and
reaching White Plains the next day, 24 miles west of
Thoroughfare Gap. Meantime, Pope, possessed of a
great desire to crush Jackson at Manassas, ordered all
his forces to that point on the 28th.

When Pope reached the battlefield on Manassas
plains which he had sketched out for himself, his
antagonist was not to be found, for Jackson lay hidden
in the woods within seven miles of the ruins of Manassas.
It was not until 5 P. M. that King's Division of Mc-
Dowell's Corps accidentally developed his presence
while marching from Gainesville to Centreville to join
the main Federal body in pursuance of Pope's orders.

Jackson's position lay about a mile north of the Warrenton pike, near Groveton. As soon as King's brigades began to stream by, utterly unconscious of the
former's presence, Jackson ordered Lawton's and
Trimble's brigades to the attack, and Wooding's and
Garber's batteries to trot forward and open fire upon
the center of the column opposite them. Gibbon sent
a regiment to drive off the guns, thinking perhaps he
had encountered a part of Stuart's Cavalry, with its
horse batteries, and also opened upon them with his own
two batteries, which, admirably served, soon compelled
the Confederate guns to limber up and shift their positions. To the support of Wooding and Garber, Jackson
had ordered up from his rear 20 more pieces which failed
to arrive, due to the thickness of the woods, though
two of Pelham's guns were brought forward. For
2½ hours the conflict raged with heavy loss to both sides,
the Federals, who had displayed great courage, finally
withdrawing at nightfall. Surprised while marching *en
route* by the fire of two batteries that were supported by
a large force of infantry, and again when ordered to drive
off a supposed small cavalry force, the Federal Infantry
as well as their two batteries, neither of which had been
in action before, sustained and inflicted serious losses

under circumstances which would have justified confusion among seasoned troops. They could not have been taken at a greater disadvantage, and while they lost 1,100 out of 2,800, among the 4,500 Confederates engaged, the loss was not less than 1,200. The rifled Federal guns had undoubtedly carried off the artillery honors.

On the morning of the 29th, Jackson realized, as he gazed upon the heavy masses forming on the hills opposite him, that the day was a critical one, for whether Longstreet had broken through Thoroughfare Gap or not, it would be many hours before he could reënforce the Second Corps on the battlefield of July 21, 1861.

Jackson's three divisions occupied a long, flat-topped ridge, standing about a mile north of the Warrenton-Centerville Road, and commanding the approaches from the south and east, was an unfinished railroad bed running some 500 yards below the crest. Before the right and the right center of the position, about $1\frac{3}{4}$ miles in length, lay green pastures, almost free of obstacles to the fire of the defenders for a distance of 1,300 yards, and sloping to a brook known as Young's Branch. The left center, and left, however, were shut in by a thicket near Groveton, from 400 to 600 yards in width, which crossed the cut, and reduced the field of fire at that point. Within the position behind the copses and folds in the land, there was ample cover for reserves. Behind the deep cuttings and high embankments of the railroad bed, the advanced line was strongly placed. The left, slightly refused, rested on a rocky spur near Bull Run, commanding Sudley Springs Ford, and the road to Aldie Gap. Between this eminence and the creek lay an open cornfield.

On the wooded ridge 500 yards to the left rear of the infantry line, 16 guns were posted and the 24 pieces of Poague's, Carpenter's, Dement's, Brockenbrough's, and Latimer's batteries were stationed in rear of the right center.

The left of the position was occupied by A. P. Hill's Division of 6 brigades in 3 lines; the center by Trimble's and Lawton's brigades of Ewell's Division, and the right by Jackson's old division of 4 brigades, now commanded by Starke, also in 3 lines. Early with 2 brigades and a battery, occupied a wooded knoll where the railroad bed crossed the highroad in the right rear of the main line, and Stuart protected the flanks, meantime endeavoring to gain touch with Longstreet whose approach was from the right rear. Thus Jackson had taken up a most defensible position with his 18,000 men, and placed every gun in position, for which there was room on the ragged crest. Behind the deep ditches and high parapets formed by the railroad bed were roughly 5 muskets per running yard of front, with a clear field of fire, except at one point, up to the limit of their effective range, the same being true with respect to the guns from which a plunging fire would have to be encountered by the attacking infantry.

Jackson's disposition of his artillery was a wise one, from which many advantages were to be expected. If the enemy's long range pieces elected to engage in a duel with the batteries on the ridge above and to the rear of his infantry, then the latter would be relieved of the fire of the opposing batteries, and, should the enemy decide to hammer at his infantry in the railroad cuts and behind the fills with his artillery, the supporting batteries would be free to play either upon the hostile guns or the attacking columns at will. Little effect with common shell could be had, at best, against the natural line of works, which Jackson had availed himself of for his infantry, and before the assaulting columns could gain the position, the fire of the enemy's guns would become masked. From every consideration, then, the Confederates seemed possessed of a position guaranteeing a fire superiority over the enemy. That such proved to be the case in the battle of Groveton is borne out by the repulse of overwhelming numbers. That Jackson and Crutchfield had employed much judgment in the disposition of their artillery is not to be denied, and in this engagement many of the advantages of modern indirect fire accrued to the defense, that is, the attacker, since he did not possess a greatly superior number of guns, was forced to neglect either the artillery or the infantry of his adversary by reason of their entire separation.   Again, Jackson gives us the first example of the kind to be found in the operations of Virginia. In the study of his battles too little attention has been paid such considerations, elements of his success, particularly on this occasion, which can not be overlooked. A general who makes good use of his artillery holds in his hand a strong trump card.

CHAPTER XVIII

SECOND MANASSAS

Shortly after 5 a. m. on the 30th, while the Confederates were still taking up their positions, the Federals began to move down the heights near the Henry House about 2 miles distant, in imposing masses, and about 7 o'clock, 4 divisions deployed in several lines at the foot of the hills, their skirmishers engaging the Confederate pickets, and 3 batteries came into action on a rise northeast of Groveton, opposite the Confederate center.

On the right and left of the Groveton wood, Jackson's two large groups of guns had a clean field of fire which they utilized with splendid effect, completely checking the attacking columns in their front, the enemy's infantry entering the wood, however, from which the Confederates, protected in a measure from the fire of Pope's batteries by the thickness of the cover, succeeded in driving them. The batteries of Poague, Carpenter, Dement, Brockenbrough, and Latimer, under Maj. Shumaker, were now thrown forward from the right to shell the retreating columns. These batteries were met by the fire of those of the enemy which had been shelling the woods, and a fierce duel ensued, lasting until perhaps 10:30 a. m., when Shumaker withdrew his batteries. The Federal guns were now moved more to their right to prepare the way for another attack on Hill's right. About noon the second assault was repulsed, although the Federals reached the Confederate position in such strength as to require the third line of Hill's Division to assist in clearing the wood, a section of Pegram's Battery moving out with the infantry to fire upon the retreating foe.

Meanwhile the divisions of Reno, Kearney, and Hooker had reached the field from Centreville, and about 1 p. m. they were ordered to renew the attack.

Kearney on the right was completely foiled by the fire of the left group of guns, but Hooker and Reno entering the woods, portions of their heavy columns actually crossed the railroad line and engaged in the most desperate hand-to-hand encounter with Field's and Thomas' brigades. Again reënforcements were sent forward from Hill's third line and, repelling the assault, pursued the enemy through the wood to the open ground beyond, where Pender's Brigade, encountering a destructive artillery fire, fell back to the thicket somewhat disorganized. Seeing Pender's retirement, Grover's Brigade of Hooker's Division, being in reserve, was ordered to deliver a counterstroke and performed the task with such splendid courage that, unsupported, it carried a considerable part of the Confederate line in the wood.

In the third attack, the Federal infantry column had been well supported by the fire of its guns, 2 of which, rifled pieces, had been moved well forward to the right, causing Braxton's Battery to be ordered to Hill's left to reply to them. Before the fourth assault was undertaken, the batteries of Crenshaw and Latham had also been moved out to the left to drive off the 2 Federal guns and secure oblique fire to their own right. They succeeded in silencing the 2 guns.

While the Federals had forced Hill back about 300 yards, they were themselves thrown into disorder and the arrival of Early's and Lawton's brigades now enabled Hill once more to regain his position and drive the enemy from the wood. He was ably assisted by Crenshaw's and Latham's batteries which delivered a destructive fire upon the enemy at a range of not over 450 yards, and Starke's Brigade captured the two 3-inch Federal rifles which had caused so much trouble.

It was now nearly 6 o'clock. The Federals had never been able to reach close quarters with the Confederates, either on the right or left of the Groveton wood over the approaches dominated by Crutchfield's artillery groups, although, at a cost of 4,000 men, they had four times reached the line in the wood where little artillery fire was encountered. The contrast is significant and clearly illustrates the fact that artillery efficiency is not to be measured by the losses it sustains nor by those which it inflicts. Indeed, it is very often the case that the greater the influence the guns exert upon the course of a battle, as at Groveton, the fewer the losses the detachments sustain, by reason of their ability to hold the enemy at ranges beyond the fire effect of the latter. Had the groups of guns at Groveton proved inadequate to check the attacking columns opposite them, and had those columns been able to advance to close quarters in spite of the fire of the opposing guns, then the artillery, having failed to accomplish the mission assigned it, would undoubtedly have suffered heavy losses. As it was, it suffered little.

Again, the effectiveness of artillery is not to be measured by the losses it inflicts. We often hear the sneering criticism that at such and such a battle but 1 or 2 per cent of the enemy's loss was due to the fire of the artillery. Any such test is entirely erroneous. Not only do the guns exert a tremendous moral effect in support of their infantry, and adverse to the enemy, but they do far more. They often actually preclude heavy damage from the enemy by preventing him from essaying an assault against the position the guns occupy. Then, again, by forcing the enemy to seek cover, they eliminate their antagonists to that extent, and though they are able to inflict little damage upon the enemy while he is under cover, they not only reduce his volume of fire, but render that which is delivered less effective. Let us hear no more of artillery efficiency as measured by the number of its victims.

Had the terrain permitted Jackson to post a large group of guns so as to command the approach to the Groveton wood, the Federal loss would have been much less than it was by reason of the fact that Pope's dense columns would never have come within the zone of effective musketry fire, since they would have been held at arm's length by the artillery. The weakest point of Jackson's line was clearly the one the approach to which was not commanded by his guns, yet at that point the attack being more successful than elsewhere, the heaviest losses were incurred by the enemy, only a small percentage of which were inflicted by the artillery.

Throughout the latter half of the day, the divisions of Longstreet's Corps, which had forced their way through Thoroughfare Gap, were arriving on Jackson's right, to oppose which the troops of Reynolds, McDowell and two of Porter's divisions had taken position. Longstreet, on his arrival, instead of prolonging Jackson's right, had inclined his line forward, thus forming with the former an obtuse angle.

While approaching his position in line, Gen. Hood, about 11 A. M., ordered forward his divisional batteries under Maj. Frobel to assist Jackson's right group of guns in holding Reynolds at bay. Commencing about 1 P. M., a duel with the enemy's batteries near Groveton House continued about 2½ hours in which the hostile guns were silenced and driven from the field. In this duel, Bachman's and Reilly's batteries, Garden's not being engaged because not armed with rifled pieces, expended about 100 rounds. The incident is mentioned because it clearly shows the change which had taken place in the tactical employment of artillery. Here we find a division commander, instead of keeping his battalion in the rear, ordering forward his artillery to cooperate with the guns of another commander, even before the position is reached. To accomplish his movement, it was necessary for Frobel to have the right of way, a thing quite unheard of for the artillery on the Peninsula. So we see that a marked advance is not only to be noted in Jackson's use of his artillery on the defensive, but that indications of better tactical employment while advancing to the attack are to be found in the battle of Groveton, which ended about 9 P. M., after Hood and Evans had overthrown King.

On the morning of the 30th, the Confederate line, about 4 miles long, was occupied by about 47,000 men, exclusive of 2,500 cavalry. Pope with 65,000 men and 28 batteries compactly massed under his own eye, might expect in the course of several hours a reënforcement of 42,000 men from Alexandria.

While the Federal commander was making his dispositions to renew the battle of the day before, a long range and ineffective cannonade was indulged in by the opposing artilleries. Although with the 28 Federal batteries there were not over 125 guns, practically all of them were rifled pieces and many were of heavy caliber. It is quite certain that the 43 Confederate batteries present, with a total of perhaps 175 guns, were outmatched in point of metal, for the best artillery material in Lee's Army was with the reserve which had not yet come up.

The Federal line of battle, when finally formed, was short and strong. From its right on Bull Run opposite Jackson's left, to its left, which rested just across the Warrenton pike, near Groveton, the distance was less than 3 miles. Deployed in the front line were 20,000 infantry, with 40,000 held in great compact masses to be hurled in columns whenever needed, a formation Napoleonic in the grandeur of its density.

Satisfied with his railroad line, Jackson clung to his old position, but a number of changes were effected in the posting of the guns. The left group of 16 guns remained as before, but 18 guns from the right center group were advanced by Col. Crutchfield to a position from which they could enfilade any columns that might attempt to assault the infantry line.* Still farther toward the turnpike and about half a mile west of Groveton, was stationed another group of 18 guns drawn from Longstreet's reserve and in command of Col. S. D. Lee. The ammunition chests of all the batteries had been replenished during the night.

---

*From the batteries of J. R. Johnson, Rice, Wooding, Poague, Carpenter, Brockenbrough, Latimer, and D'Aquin.

Col. Lee's Battalion, composed of the batteries of Eubank, Parker, Rhett, and Jordan, was skillfully posted on the high ground just west of the Douglas House, the guns pointing northeast, or at right angles to Jackson's line, overlooking and commanding the wide tract of undulating meadow stretching away for a mile or more in front of the Stonewall and Lawton's divisions. The entire open space in front of Jackson's line was now, therefore, exposed to a cross-fire from the 3 formidable groups, besides that from the batteries on the infantry line.

To the right of Jackson, Stuart's Hill was strongly occupied by Longstreet, and this wing of the Confederate Army, held always under cover, was gradually swung forward until it occupied a line almost perpendicular to the unfinished railroad.

With slight knowledge of Longstreet's position, it would seem, or at least with an utter failure to grasp the meaning of Porter's reports, Pope, satisfied that Jackson would abandon his position, determined to launch his superb columns once more against it. The weight which he apparently lacked the previous day he thought he had now secured. So, about noon, he sent forward a swarm of skirmishers along his whole front to clear the way for the 3 great lines in their rear.

The advance of the skirmishers did not provoke the fire of the guns, but when the compact lines came within range, the heavens rocked with the roar of the Confederate batteries. Meantime, Jackson's brigades, which had retired to the thickets behind their lines, a move that had misled Pope into believing the position was only weakly held, rushed down the hillside to reoccupy the improvised works of the railroad bed. The whole force of Pope's blow falling on Jackson's thinned line, the pressure was tremendous and reënforcements from Longstreet were called for.

By this time, the left of Pope's assaulting columns had come within the reëntrant angle which Longstreet's line formed with that of Jackson's, and Longstreet grasped the unusual opportunity presented to enfilade with his guns the left of the Federal reserves as they advanced. The rapidity with which the foremost lines of the Federals had reached Jackson's line, masked in large measure the guns on his right which were unable to fire upon the enemy without doing great damage to the Confederates. Crutchfield's and Lee's groups, therefore, turned their attention to the advancing reserves. Though half of their guns were short range pieces, even these proved effective on the nearest part of Porter's column, while the others poured a storm of iron over all parts of the field. Meanwhile, the Federal guns at the Dogan House and elsewhere behind their line devoted themselves principally to Jackson's front in an endeavor to prepare a way for the attacking infantry. But two batteries seem to have engaged Crutchfield and Lee, who had much the better position, and were considerably overshot by the enemy. No serious effort, whatever, was made to neutralize the artillery masses of the Confederates.

It was now that, instead of sending Jackson a reënforcement of infantry as called for, Longstreet ordered Bachman's and Reilly's batteries of Frobel's Battalion over from the hill in front of the Groveton House, where they had been engaged with the Federal guns in the Dogan House orchard, to the right front of S. D. Lee's group, from which advanced point they opened a raking fire with terrific effect into the left rear of Porter's dense column. These two batteries added all that was needed to put an end to the attack. Before the second battery, Reilly's, with its howitzer section gained its position, the enemy began to retire, and in less than 10 minutes after the effect of the guns began to be felt, Porter's troops gave up the contest and retired in confusion to the woods through which they had advanced. In vain now did Pope endeavor to stem the tide of disaster. A great mass of troops from the various commands, which had become mingled, was again gallantly urged forward, but this time their advance not being so

COLONEL JOHN THOMPSON BROWN
ACTING CHIEF OF ARTILLERY, SECOND CORPS
Killed at the Wilderness, 1864

rapid as before, Crutchfield's and Lee's guns were able to find the range before the Federals closed with Jackson's line. Thoroughly disorganized by the flanking fire of the artillery, the great Federal column was now driven back by a counter-charge of two of Jackson's brigades, and Pope's battle was lost.

Anticipating Lee's wishes, Longstreet, as soon as he saw Porter's defeat in the center, ordered his whole line forward at the charge, advancing his batteries along the turnpike with the infantry in an endeavor to take the Henry House plateau, on which the Federal regulars and the best troops, including a number of batteries, were making a desperate stand. This force, assisted by a flanking fire from his left upon Longstreet's advancing columns, checked the attack at nightfall, the Federal left crossing Bull Run after dark. The opportunity presented to Longstreet to capture this portion of the Federal Army, had he had a large and well-organized reserve artillery, was an unusual one. But this was not to be. That he used his available guns with exceptional skill is not to be denied.

From the battlefield of Second Manassas, Lee gleaned some 30 pieces of Federal ordnance, while the Confederates lost none.

Some idea of the intensity of the Confederate artillery fire in the battle of Second Manassas may be gained from the expenditures in ammunition of the 1st, 2d, and 3d batteries of Washington Artillery. Capt. Squires reported an expenditure of 400 rounds, Capt. Richardson of 178 rounds, and Capt. Miller of 356 rounds. By one section of the Dixie Battery, 297 rounds were fired; Stribling's Battery expending 354, and a section of Maurin's Battery 119. None of these batteries were engaged as continuously as were those under Crutchfield and Lee. The expenditures of the latter must have been enormous, certainly not less than 600 rounds per battery, or 150 per gun.* Let us compare this expenditure with that in other battles.

_____

*The expenditure of Waterman's Rhode Island Battery was 500 rounds, and of Hazlett's regular battery, 6 pieces, 1,000 rounds, *Rebellion Records,* Series I, Vol. XII, Part II, pp. 468, 469.

In the battle of Leipzig, 1813, the expenditure of the Austrian guns was 199 rounds per gun in the 3 days, or 66 per gun per day. The greatest expenditure in one day by a Prussian battery, 1866, was 180 rounds per gun, at Blumenau; by an Austrian battery, 217 per gun at Königgrätz.

In 1870, the Prussian batteries averaged at Vionville, 89 rounds per gun; 35 per cent of the batteries fired over 100 rounds per gun. At Gravellote-Saint Privat, the Prussian guns averaged 55 rounds; 16 per cent of the batteries firing over 100 rounds per gun; the French average being 90 rounds per gun, but no battery exhausted its normal ammunition supply. During the whole war the 15 batteries of the German Guard expended but 270 rounds per gun.

At Gettysburg, the Federals averaged 102 rounds per gun for the 3 days, or 34 rounds per day for each of the 320 guns engaged, the greatest individual battery expenditure reported being 1,380 rounds for the 3 days, or a daily average of 77 rounds per gun per day. The Confederate expenditure on this occasion was probably 100 rounds per gun or an average of 33 per day, the greatest expenditure for 1 battery being 882 rounds, or 73 rounds per gun per day.

At the Sha-ho, in 1904, the Artillery of the 34th Russian Division averaged 278 rounds per gun per day. At Liaoyang, the Artillery of the 1st and 3d Siberian Corps averaged 420 rounds per gun per day. At Tashichiao, Colonel Patchenko's Battery fired 522 rounds per gun, which was the greatest expenditure for a single battery ever reported for one day.

Now, if we confine ourselves to the days of muzzle-loading field pieces, it is seen that the expenditure at Second Manassas compares favorably with that of the greatest artillery conflicts of history, exceeding perhaps that at Gettysburg.

The Confederate Artillery losses in this battle were: killed, about 30; wounded, about 90. In Lee's Battalion there were but 6 wounded, a fact to be borne in mind by those who would rate the service of field artillery by the magnitude of its losses, for probably no one force exerted a greater influence upon the final result of the battle than did this group of 18 guns.

At the battle of Second Manassas, many decided advances in the tactical employment of the Confederate field artillery are to be noticed. It is true, the defensive attitude assumed by Jackson gave him the same advantage in point of time to dispose his guns as was enjoyed by McClellan in the various fights on the Peninsula. Yet, the grouping of his artillery was by no means accidental. It was disposed with a special mission in view and to each piece was assigned a definite sector of fire. Not only were 40 of his guns well massed, but others were posted along the infantry lines in positions from which they were free to move from point to point, as developments might require. The principal features and advantages derived from his artillery position have already been discussed. It has also been noticed that when Longstreet began to arrive, his batteries preceded many of his infantry brigades, instead of being choked off from the field by infantry columns unwilling to give them a right of way. The massing of Lee's Battalion in advance of Jackson's right flank was a masterly move, and showed clearly that the lesson of Malvern Hill had been well digested. And then, as if to demonstrate to the Army the tremendous influence of which even a handful of guns, well served, is capable of exerting, at the very crisis of Pope's powerful infantry attack Longstreet ordered 2 batteries into action with decisive effect, followed by a general rush to the front of the few remaining batteries capable of following up the repulsed attacking columns.

The grave defect in Lee's tactics, from an artillery point of view, was the absence of his reserve. Had Pendleton's battalions with their superior material, a part of which at least was equal to that of the enemy, been on hand to engage in Lee's counter stroke, the fruits of the victory would certainly have been greater.

The comparative ineffectiveness of the Federal Artillery was due to a number of causes. In the first place, the disadvantage of inexperience in the attack now rested upon it. There was no Hunt present to direct the massed fire of the batteries and consequently they frittered away their efforts as individuals. In the second place, Crutchfield and then Lee occupied vastly superior positions from which they invited the fire of the heavier hostile guns, in order to divert it from the infantry line. And, in the third place, the Federal Artillery was definitely assigned the mission of shaking Jackson's Infantry line, which it could not attempt, by reason of his dispositions, without utterly neglecting his artillery. Thus, not only did it fail to neutralize the latter, leaving it sufficient in itself as events proved to hold at bay the attacking columns in all but a single quarter, but roughly handled by the opposing guns more or less free from hostile artillery fire, and quite without the effective zone of musketry, the Federal Artillery was unable to accomplish the undivided task assigned it.

Groveton and Second Manassas were battles in which the rôle of the artillery was a supreme one. In vain do we find their true features disclosed in the numerous accounts of Lee's battles, which have been contributed to history. On the contrary, they have been masked in narratives in which the influence of the infantry position behind the railroad bed is presented as the most potent element of Lee's and Jackson's success. But, far above that accidental field work stood the guns of Stapleton Crutchfield and Stephen D. Lee, in imposing masses with ready thumbs upon the vents and hands upon the rammers. And never in the history of war have more superb or denser columns recoiled before the muzzles of an artillery.

CHAPTER XIX

AFTER the battle of Second Manassas, Gen. Lee decided that the time was a propitious one for the invasion of Maryland and therefore headed his columns towards Leesburg as soon as he was satisfied of the retreat of Pope to Washington, the movement beginning September 3.

On that day the Reserve Artillery arrived at Sudley, Pendleton having reported in person to Gen. Lee during the battle on August 29, after temporarily turning over his command to Lieut.-Col. Cutts on the 17th.

In the meantime, a considerable force of field artillery had been collected about Richmond and Col. T. S. Rhett assigned to the command of the permanent batteries as well as the former. Lieut. James Howard, Artillery Corps, with temporary rank of lieutenant-colonel, and Lieut.-Col. C. E. Lightfoot, Provisional Artillery, were assigned to duty under Col. Rhett to command the permanent works of the inner line and the field guns of the outer line, respectively.

In the defenses about Richmond at this time there was an artillery force of 89 officers and 1,693 men present, with an aggregate present and absent of 2,983, including the companies of heavy artillery. Near Petersburg, Capt. S. T. Wright also had about 120 men and 13 field pieces.*

Between the battle of Malvern Hill and the Maryland invasion, the field artillery passed through a distinct transition. The former affair had, as has been shown, directed the attention of many minds to the artillery problem. The faith of the Army in an arm of such latent ability, vouched for by the high character of

---

*Rebellion Records, Series I, Vol. II, Part II, p. 601.

its officers, was unimpaired. Every one recognized the
capabilities of the gunners and felt that a solution would
soon be effected. But how to accomplish the results
expected of them was a serious task for the gunners.
The battle of Second Manassas proved an object lesson
of the greatest value. In that battle the Artillery
rendered yeoman service, justifying the faith and the expectations of all. The tremendous effect of concentrated artillery fire had left no doubt as to the value
of masses of guns. The names of Crutchfield, S. D.
Lee, Lindsay Walker, Pegram, and the other gallant
artillerymen whose talents had been so ably displayed,
were on the lips of every soldier in the Army, and a
spirit of intense admiration for the Artillery sup-
planted the criticisms hitherto so rife. The "long arm"
had vindicated itself. Yet, many improvements were
possible and steps were immediately taken to raise the
standard of efficiency of the Artillery.

It was now generally perceived that more guns
should accompany the divisions, and that the old system
of isolating batteries by attaching them to brigades
simply crippled the power of concentrating them in
action. It was also realized that reserve artillery did
not mean a great mass of guns rumbling along in rear
of the army, but that its true purpose was its active
use under the direction of the commanding-general
whose wider grasp enabled him to throw the reserve artillery into action with the greatest effect upon the issue.

When Gen. Pendleton's reserve column reached
Leesburg, it had with it much of the best material in
the service, but many of the batteries with the divisions
were much depleted in personnel and horses, and the
material of others was of the most defective character.
In fact, the Artillery in general showed the effects of
the long marches and the severe fighting of the preceding month, the former not less wearing than the
latter. It was at once decided, therefore, to weed out
those batteries in the poorest condition, using the men

and effective animals drawn therefrom for the purpose of strengthening others. The horses were at this time particularly run down.*

The more depleted batteries, including Leake's Goochland, Stribling's Fauquier, Rogers' Loudoun, Fleet's Middlesex, Latham's Branch North Carolina, and Anderson's Thomas batteries, with all the animals of the artillery and train unfit for service, were ordered to be detained at Leesburg in command of Maj. Richardson, who was directed to proceed with them as soon as possible to the neighborhood of Winchester and establish there a remount depot and recruiting station for the Artillery.

In the effort to place the Artillery on a more effective footing, it was designed to attach one battalion to each of Longstreet's 5, and Jackson's 4 divisions, with an additional reserve battalion for each of these corps and a general reserve for the entire army. Each battalion, whether with the divisions or in the reserve, was to have its own field officer. A battalion assigned to a division fell under the command of the Division Chief of Artillery. The foregoing was the general plan of the reorganization, but it was not rigidly adhered to as shown by the assignments of the batteries and battalions in effect during the Maryland campaign.† At one time during the operations in Maryland, D. R. Jones' Division of Longstreet's Corps had with it but one battery and Walker's Division but two batteries. At Sharpsburg, Ewell's Division had with it but two batteries, having left four at Harper's Ferry. On the other hand, D. H. Hill not only had Maj. Pierson's Battalion with his division at Sharpsburg, but Maj. Jones' Battalion of the reserve was also assigned him. With Longstreet's Corps, there were also two reserve battalions, Walton's of four, and Lee's of six batteries, whereas no reserve battalion was assigned as an integral part of Jackson's Corps, Jones' Battalion being first

*See G. O. No. 102, A. N. V., September 4, 1862, *Rebellion Records,* Series I, Vol. XIX, Part II, p. 592, and G. O. No. ——, September 5, Ibid., p. 595.
†*Rebellion Records,* Series I, Vol. XIX, Part I, pp. 803-810. *Battles and Leaders,* Vol. II, pp. 600-603.

detached from the general reserve for the purpose, and later Brown's First Virginia Regiment. Roughly, the batteries and battalions were assigned as follows:

1ST CORPS OR RIGHT WING (Longstreet)

Col. Henry Coalter Cabell, Chief of Artillery

McLaws' Division

Maj. S. P. Hamilton, Chief of Artillery

1. Manly's North Carolina Battery,   Capt. Basil C. Manly.
2. Pulaski (Ga.) Battery,   Capt. John P. W. Read.
3. Richmond Fayette Battery,   Capt. Miles C. Macon.
4. 1st Co. Richmond Howitzers,   Capt. E. S. McCarthy.
5. Troup (Ga.) Battery,   Capt. H. H. Carlton.

R. H. Anderson's Division

Maj. J. S. Saunders, Chief of Artillery

1. Donaldsonville (La.) Battery,   Capt. Victor Maurin.
2. Huger's Norfolk Battery,   Capt. C. R. Phelps.
3. Grimes' Portsmouth Battery,   Lieut. Thompson.
4. Lynchburg Battery,   Capt. Marcellus N. Moorman.

D. R. Jones's Division

1. Fauquier Battery,   Capt. Stribling.*
2. Loudoun Battery,   Capt. Arthur L. Rogers.*
3. Wise Battery,   Capt. J. S. Brown.
4. Goochland Battery,   Capt. Leake.*

Walker's Division

1. Petersburg Battery,   Capt. James R. Branch.
2. Stafford Battery,   Capt. David A. French.

Hood's Division

Maj. B. W. Frobel, Chief of Artillery

1. Charleston German Battery,   Capt. W. K. Bachman.
2. Palmetto (S. C.) Battery,   Capt. H. R. Garden.
3. Rowan (N. C.) Battery,   Capt. James Reilly.
4. Macbeth (S. C.) Battery,   Capt. R. Boyce.

*Left at Leesburg.

1st Reserve Battalion

Col. John B. Walton

1. 1st Co. Washington Artillery,   Capt. C. W. Squires.
2. 2d Co. Washington Artillery,   Capt. J. B. Richardson.
3. 3d Co. Washington Artillery,   Capt. M. B. Miller.
4. 4th Co. Washington Artillery,   Capt. B. F. Eshleman.

2d Reserve Battalion

Col. Stephen D. Lee

1. Ashland Battery,   Capt. Pichegru Woolfolk, Jr.
2. Bedford Battery,   Capt. T. C. Jordan.
3. Brook's South Carolina Battery,   Lieut. William Elliott.
4. Bath Battery,   Capt. J. L. Eubank.
5. Madison (La.) Battery,   Capt. Geo. V. Moody.
6. Richmond Battery,   Capt. W. W. Parker.

2ND CORPS OR LEFT WING (Jackson)

Col. Stapleton Crutchfield, Chief of Artillery

Ewell's Division

Maj. A. R. Courtney, Chief of Artillery

1. Bedford Virginia Battery,   Capt. Jno. R. Johnson.
2. Louisiana Guard Battery,   Capt. Louis E. D'Aquin.
3. 1st Maryland Battery,   Capt. Wm. F. Dement.†
4. 4th Md. or Chesapeake Battery,   Capt. Wm. D. Brown.†
5. Courtney or Henrico Battery,   Capt. J. W. Latimer.†
6. Staunton Battery,   Lieut. A. W. Garber.†
7. Charlottesville Battery,   Capt. J. McD. Carrington.*

A. P. Hill's Light Division

Lieut.-Col. R. Lindsay Walker, Chief of Artillery

1. Richmond Battery,   Capt. Wm. G. Crenshaw.
2. Fredericksburg Battery,   Capt. Carter M. Braxton.
3. Letcher Richmond Battery,   Capt. Greenlee Davidson.*
4. Purcell Richmond Battery,   Capt. Wm. J. Pegram.
5. Pee Dee (S. C.) Battery,   Capt. D. G. McIntosh.
6. Middlesex Battery,   Capt. Fleet.‡
7. Branch (N. C.) Battery,   Capt. A. C. Latham.‡

---

*Left in Richmond in August.
†Left at Harper's Ferry, and not at Antietam.
‡Left at Leesburg.

J. R. JONES' DIVISION

Maj. L. M. Shumaker, Chief of Artillery

1. 2d Md. or Baltimore Battery,   Capt. J. B. Brockenbrough.
2. Alleghany Battery,   Capt. Jos. Carpenter.
3. Danville Battery,   Capt. George W. Wooding.
4. Richmond Hampden Battery,   Capt. William H. Caskie.
5. Lee Battery,   Capt. Charles J. Raine.
6. 1st Rockbridge Battery,   Capt. Wm. T. Poague.

D. H. HILL'S DIVISION

Maj. S. F. Pierson, Chief of Artillery

1. Alabama Battery,   Capt. R. A. Hardaway.
2. Jeff Davis Alabama Battery.   Capt. J. W. Bondurant.
3. Peninsula Battery,   Capt. Wm. B. Jones.
4. King William Battery,   Capt. Thomas H. Carter.

GENERAL RESERVE ARTILLERY

W. N. Pendleton, Chief of Artillery

1ST REGIMENT VIRGINIA ARTILLERY

Col. John Thompson Brown

1. Powhatan Battery,   Capt. Willis J. Dance.
2. 2d Co. Richmond Howitzers,   Capt. D. Watson.
3. 3d Co. Richmond Howitzers,   Capt. Benj. H. Smith, Jr.
4. Salem Battery,   Capt. A. Hupp.
5. Williamsburg Battery,   Capt. John A. Coke.

CUTTS' BATTALION

Lieut.-Col. A. S. Cutts

1. "D" Battery, Sumter Battalion, Capt. James A. Blackshear.
2. "C" Battery, Sumter Battalion, Capt. John Lane.
3. "A" Battery, Sumter Battalion, Capt. H. M. Ross.
4. "B" Battery, Sumter Battalion, Capt. G. M. Patterson.
5. Lloyd's North Carolina Battery, Capt. W. P. Lloyd.

JONES' BATTALION

Maj. Hilary P. Jones

1. Morris Louisa Battery,   Capt. R. C. M. Page.
2. Richmond Orange Battery,   Capt. Jefferson Peyton.
3. Goochland Battery,   Capt. W. H. Turner.
4. Long Island Battery,   Capt. A. Wimbish.

NELSON'S BATTALION

Maj. William Nelson

1. Amherst Battery,	Capt. T. J. Kirkpatrick.
2. 2d Fluvanna Battery,	Capt. John J. Ancell.
3. 1st Fluvanna Battery,	Capt. Charles T. Huckstep.
4. Richmond Battery,	Capt. Marmaduke Johnson.
5. Milledge's Georgia Battery,	Capt. John Milledge.

MISCELLANEOUS RESERVE BATTERIES

1. Winchester Battery,	Capt. W. E. Cutshaw.
2. Dixie Battery,	Capt. W. H. Chapman.
3. Magruder Battery,	Capt. T. J. Page, Jr.
4. 8th Star Battery,	Capt. W. H. Rice.
5. Thomas Battery,	Capt. E. J. Anderson.*

CAVALRY CORPS (Stuart's Horse Artillery)

1. Chew's Battery,	Capt. Robert Preston Chew.
2. Pelham's Battery,	Capt. John Pelham.
3. Hart's Battery,	Capt. J. F. Hart.

At the battle of Sharpsburg but two battalions, Cutts' and Nelson's of three batteries each, remained in the general reserve with Pendleton along the river, and many of the batteries with the Army when it left Leesburg soon disappeared, as we shall see.

Though not distributed exactly as contemplated, there appear to have been 29 batteries assigned to the 1st Corps, grouped in 6 battalions, 26 batteries accompanying the Corps in the Maryland operations; and to the 2d Corps 25 batteries, grouped in 4 battalions, 22 batteries crossing the Potomac. In the Reserve we find 4 battalions with a total of 19 batteries and 5 batteries unassigned. There were then on the rolls of the Army some 78 batteries, of which number 71 engaged in the Maryland operations. The total personnel of these 71 batteries approximated but 4,000 men, for numbers of them were so weak as to be either disbanded or consolidated with others at an early date.

In the report of Gen. Pendleton, dated September 24, 1862, it is stated that to each of Longstreet's five battalions was attached a battalion of artillery with a 6th

*Left at Leesburg.

battalion as the corps reserve, with a total of 112 pieces,
viz.: 45 rifles, 13 Napoleons, and 54 common smooth-
bore guns, and that to each of the 4 divisions of Jackson's Corps was also attached a battalion of artillery
with a 5th battalion as the corps reserve, with a total
of 123 pieces, viz.: 52 rifles, 18 Napoleons, and 53 common smooth-bore guns. This statement does not include the batteries of E. J. Anderson, Blackshear, J. S.
Brown, Chapman, Coke, Fleet, John R. Johnson,
Leake, Lloyd, Nelson, T. J. Page, Jr., Rogers, Thompson, and Wimbish, which were disbanded under a general order of October 4, 1862; nor account for those of
Cutshaw and Rice, which were consolidated with
Carpenter's and Wooding's batteries on September 26;
nor for Boyce's, Moorman's, and Woolfolk's batteries.
But, as the material, men, and animals of the disbanded
batteries were distributed among the remaining ones,
it would seem that with Lee's army in Maryland there
were 225 guns, in addition to 12 with the three horse batteries and 36 in the Reserve, or a grand total of about
300 guns. McClellan estimated the number at 400, a
figure not so absurd as Gen. Early and others have considered it.

In order that the character of the armament of Lee's
artillery at this time may be seen, the following table
is inserted:

NAME OF BATTERY	20-pounder Parrotts	10-pounder Parrotts	3-inch rifles	24-pounder howitzers	12-pounder howitzers	Napoleons	Whitworths	Blakelys	6-lb. S. B. guns	Total
Lewis		2	2							4
Grandy		2			2				2	6
Maurin		2	1						3	6
Huger		1	1						2	4
Manly			1		2				3	6
Carlton		2			1				2	5
McCarthy		2							2	4
Read		1			1				2	4

Name of Battery	20-pounder Parrotts	10-pounder Parrotts	3-inch rifles	24-pounder howitzers	12-pounder howitzers	Napoleons	Whitworths	Blakelys	6-lb. S. B. guns	Total
Dearing		1			1				2	4
Macon		2			1				4	6
Stribling				2		4				6
Bachman						4				4
Garden					1	1			2	4
Reilly		2	2	2						6
Branch		1	2		3					6
French		3			3					6
Squires		1	2							3
Miller						2				2
Richardson					2	2				4
Eshleman					2				2	4
Jordan			2		1				1	4
Rhett	2	2								4
Moody			2	2						4
Parker			2		2					4
Eubank			1		1				1	4
Bondurant			2		2					4
R. C. M. Page			2		1				3	6
Peyton (Fry)			1		1				3	5
Hardaway			2					1		3
Carter		1			2				2	5
Braxton			2						4	6
Latham						2			2	4
McIntosh		1	1		1	1				4
Davidson			1			2			1	5
Crenshaw					1	1			2	4
M. Johnson			2		2					4
Pegram		2				2				4
Brockenbrough			1		1			2		4
Raine			3		1					4
Caskie		1							3	4
Lusk		1	1						2	4
Carpenter			2			2				4
Wooding		2	1			1				4
Brown		2	1							3
Balthis									2	2
Dement									4	4
Carrington			2		2				2	6
Latimer			2			2				4
D'Aquin		1	2							3
Poague	2	2								4
Smith		2			2					4
Dance			1		2				1	4
Watson		2			1					*3
Hupp					2				2	4
Brooke					1	1			2	4

*Watson's Battery also had one Hotchkiss rifle.

From the foregoing table it will be seen that absolutely no uniformity of armament obtained in the divisional batteries, either as to the character of the material or the number of pieces. The following table shows the armament of some of the reserve batteries, there being but 12 rifled pieces with Pendleton.

NAME OF BATTERY	20-pounder Parrotts	10-pounder Parrotts	3-inch rifles	Hotchkiss rifle	James rifle	Whitworth rifle	12-pounder howitzers	Napoleons	6-lb. S. B. guns	Total
Lane	2	3					1			6
Ross								2	1	3
Blackshear								3	3	6
Kirkpatrick								2	4	6
Massie									6	6
Milledge		1	3	1	1					6

It is impossible exactly to determine the strength of the Army of Northern Virginia at this time, but the most conservative estimate does not place the maximum strength of the infantry at more than 30,000 men. Taking this figure and 300 as the number of guns with the Army, it will be seen that the proportion had reached 10 guns per 1,000 infantry. Deducting the guns of the Reserve, those of the Horse Artillery, and those left at Harper's Ferry, and the proportion actually with the divisions at Sharpsburg appears to have been about 9 per 1,000, the largest yet found. The assignment of Walton's and Lee's battalions to Longstreet, and Brown's Regiment to Jackson, as corps reserves, foreshadowed the artillery reorganization of 1863, and again we find an analogy in the development of the artillery in the Civil War and in the Prussian campaigns of 1866 and 1870-71.

Hohenlohe, summarizing the revolution in the tactical employment of field artillery which Prussian experience brought about, states that in 1866 great un-

willingness was shown to employ much artillery to prepare the action, but that in 1870, intentionally from the
first, as many guns as possible were brought into play.
He then shows that even at the moment when the fight
was at its height, a strong reserve of all arms was held
out in 1866, a practice which kept at least half of the
great mass of reserve artillery of the 1st Army from firing a shot at Königgrätz, when the fire of every gun
was needed, whereas in 1870 such a practice was so opposed to the tactical ideas of the time that even the
name "Reserve Artillery" was abolished, and replaced
with that of "Corps Artillery."   Then again, in 1866,
we find the Prussian reserve marching as near the tail
of the column as possible, and on some occasions days
in rear of the Army, just as in the case of the Confederate reserve in the Cedar Mountain-Second Manassas campaign.   Whereas, in 1870, the Prussians even
sent their reserve guns, then called corps artillery,
ahead, as in the case of the Guard and the 3d Corps at
Saint-Privat, and the 5th, 11th, and 12th corps at
Sedan.   As a parallel to this we find the reserve battalions of Walton, S. D. Lee, and Brown, moving into
Maryland with the most advanced columns.   In
Prussia, two wars were necessary to bring about such
developments, simply because of the brevity of the
first, lasting as it did but seven weeks, whereas in
America the tactics of the artillery had to be developed
in a single period of continuous campaigning.   The
Prussians naturally derived a great advantage from the
interim between their activities, which afforded them
a breathing spell during which they found opportunity
for serious reflection upon, and digestion of, their recent
experiences.

By the afternoon of September 7, the mass of Gen.
Lee's army had reached Frederick, Maryland, Gen.
Pendleton reporting with the Reserve Artillery on the
morning of the 8th.

In advancing into Maryland, Gen. Lee, whose army
was greatly depleted by straggling and lack of shoes

for his infantry, took into consideration the character of
his old opponent, McClellan. His principal cause of
anxiety was not so much the smallness of his army (for
in the ranks were those only who had best stood the
strain of two campaigns) as it was the difficulty of securing ammunition, especially for the artillery. Without
an ordnance officer of Alexander's ability, it is difficult
to see how the invasion of Maryland in 1862 would
have been possible. The brevity of the campaign, however, coupled with almost superhuman efforts on the
part of the ordnance officers, relieved the situation.

When the Army reached Frederick, two developments affected its proposed movements. In the first
place, Halleck, instead of following McClellan's advice and ordering the garrison of 12,000 men at
Harper's Ferry to fall back, directed it to remain there.
In the second place, the people of the North forced Mc-
Clellan to move out from Washington at once, to drive
Lee from Maryland, whether he would or no. It therefore became necessary for the latter to dispose of the
force at Harper's Ferry while holding off McClellan,
or to return with his whole army to Virginia in the
event his new line of communication up the Valley was
not cleared of the enemy. Not impressed with the
necessity of abandoning Maryland, Gen. Lee on the
9th ordered Jackson to seize Harper's Ferry, and held
D. H. Hill with a small force at South Mountain, while
Longstreet moved to Boonsboro.

Harper's Ferry was to be invested by three columns,
the first under Jackson himself from the south, the second under J. G. Walker from the east, and the third
under McLaws from the north. Leaving Frederick on
the morning of the 10th, Jackson moved westward and
crossed the Potomac at Williamsport on the 11th.
After driving in a small portion of the enemy from
Martinsburg, he reached Halltown in view of Bolivar
Heights, strongly held by the garrison of Harper's
Ferry, on the 13th. Meanwhile, Walker reached
Loudoun Heights on the east early that day, and find-

ing them unoccupied, succeeded in placing five pieces of
artillery in position before noon the next day. McLaws,
driving a small hostile force into Harper's Ferry, succeeded in occupying Maryland Heights on the north
before the night of the 13th, and the next morning cut
a road to the crest, over which Maj. Hamilton, Divisional Chief of Artillery, dragged two guns from Read's
and 2 from Carlton's batteries, into position before 2
P. M. the 14th.

Bolivar Heights, lying below and to the south and
west of Maryland Heights and Loudoun Heights, respectively, was now commanded by the guns of Mc-
Laws and Walker, so that when a Federal battery
opened upon Walker at 1 P. M. the 14th, the four pieces
on Loudoun Heights silenced it within two hours. The
elevation to the guns of Maryland Heights was so great
that McLaws was free to join in the cannonade without
fear of injury from the Federal guns.

When Jackson on the night of the 13th learned that
McLaws and Walker were both in position, he moved
forward from Halltown. On the morning of the 14th,
he ordered A. P. Hill to advance on the Confederate
right along the west bank of the Shenandoah, directing
him to turn the enemy's flank and get into Harper's
Ferry in his rear, if possible. Lawton, with Ewell's
Division, moved along the Charleston turnpike which
passed over Bolivar Heights about the center of the
Federal position, and J. R. Jones moved against the
enemy's right near the river.

Jones soon seized a position for Poague's and Carpenter's batteries near the river and commanding the
enemy's right, on which the guns of McLaws were
already playing, and during the night Lieut.-Col. R.
Lindsay Walker, Chief of Artillery, A. P. Hill's Division, placed Pegram's, McIntosh's, Davidson's, Braxton's, and Crenshaw's batteries in position on an eminence commanding the Federal left. While Hill and
Jones were thus taking up their positions, Lawton advanced during the night along the pike and formed his

line in front of the Federals on Bolivar Heights. He was supported by batteries posted by Col. Crutchfield on School House Hill. Guns from the batteries of Brown, Dement, Garber, and Latimer, ten pieces in all, were then taken by Crutchfield across the Shenandoah at Kelly's Ford and moved down stream to a position opposite the left of the enemy's line of entrenchments, to which a road for the guns had to be cut. This position, although commanded by Bolivar Heights, yet secured a fire into the rear of a work on the enemy's left, where there was an embrasure battery of four pieces, just opposite A. P. Hill and forming the keystone of the position.

For several hours after dark on the 14th, while Walker and Crutchfield were placing their batteries, the Confederate guns on Maryland and Loudoun Heights engaged in a duel with the Federal Artillery on Bolivar Heights, presenting a scene of surpassing grandeur, but striking terror into the hearts of the besieged.

At dawn on the 15th, the attack was ordered to begin and was opened by the fire of Col. Walker's group of guns, soon joined by those of Crutchfield on the east side of the Shenandoah, the batteries on School House Hill, those near the Potomac, and the guns on Maryland and Loudoun Heights. The gunners were almost immediately driven from the Federal work, commanded by the ten pieces which Crutchfield had so skillfully placed across the river.

After about an hour of concentration upon the enemy's position, his artillery and musketry fire were almost subdued by the great circle of guns, whereupon orders were issued to carry the Federal position by storm. But again the battery in front of Hill's Division was gallantly manned and reopened its fire only to be silenced by Crutchfield's group, after another hour of firing. Meanwhile, Pegram and Crenshaw moved their batteries up to within 400 yards of the Federal works and poured a rapid enfilading fire into them.*

*It was not Carpenter's Battery as stated by Allan, but Crenshaw's. See Walker's Report.

As the infantry approached the Federal position, about
8 A. M., a white flag was displayed, and as soon as the
artillery could be caused to cease firing the surrender
was effected, the Confederates taking 11,500 prisoners,
13,000 stand of arms, 49 field pieces, and 24 mountain
howitzers.

The losses in the Confederate Infantry at Harper's
Ferry were not over 100, mostly wounded. The Artillery loss probably did not exceed 10 men, yet
Harper's Ferry vividly illustrates the power of artillery.
An assault on Bolivar Heights by infantry without the
support of a large number of guns would have been
as costly as it would have been doubtful of success. And
this Jackson knew.

From a tactical standpoint, Jackson's movements
were splendidly conceived and superbly executed. He
employed his artillery, almost every effective piece being brought to bear on the enemy's position, in a way
above criticism. True, the opportunity presented for
its use was a rare one, yet the fact remains that he
grasped it and saved his infantry almost to a man, and
those that were lost were not sacrificed in an assault until the hostile guns were practically silenced. Seldom
has a general been fortunate enough to secure so
thorough an artillery preparation.

The work of Crutchfield, of Lindsay Walker, and of
the other artillery officers was brilliant, and again
Pegram displayed that dauntless spirit which soon made
his name a by-word in the Army.

We look in vain for a parallel to Harper's Ferry in
the Civil War, and involuntarily turn to Sedan. The
great artillery battle of the Franco-German War was
on a grander scale, of course, than that at Harper's
Ferry, there being engaged in the terrible "circle of
fire" five great artillery groups with a total of 540
guns, whereas Jackson had fewer than 75 in action.
Yet, the *mise en scène* of Sedan was not as awe inspiring in its grandeur as that at Harper's Ferry. In fact,
no battlefield could be more sublime in its altitudes than
the latter.

As soon as possible after the surrender of Harper's Ferry, Jackson prepared to join Gen. Lee, leaving A. P. Hill's Division to take charge of the captured property.

Arriving on the 16th, the Chief of Ordnance at once collected the 73 captured guns, sending them to Winchester along with a large supply of ammunition unsuited to the field pieces. With the exception of canister, there was little field artillery ammunition captured by the Confederates at Harper's Ferry.

While Jackson had been engaged at Harper's Ferry, the 1st and 9th corps of McClellan's army, with 18 batteries, had appeared before D. H. Hill at South Mountain. After a desperate fight, Hill, reënforced by four of Longstreet's brigades, succeeded in checking the advance of the enemy, until the Reserve Artillery and the ordnance trains at Boonsboro could move off to a position of safety.

When the Reserve Artillery under Gen. Pendleton, consisting on the 14th of the battalions of S. D. Lee, Brown, and Nelson—Cutts having been sent to the support of D. H. Hill*—retraced its steps to Boonsboro from Hagerstown, it was first ordered to be placed in position along the Beaver Creek Heights, which was done before nightfall. But when it became apparent that Hill's position had been overlapped and that a retirement was necessary, Gen. Pendleton was ordered to send Lee's Battalion to Centreville to report to Longstreet and take the rest of his command by the shortest route across the Potomac at Williamsport and guard the fords of the river.

Leaving Beaver Creek about midnight, Pendleton's command with Alexander's reserve ordnance train reached the intersection of the Sharpsburg, Boonsboro, Hagerstown and Williamsport roads about daybreak the following morning, at which point information was received that a large cavalry column of the enemy was near at hand. Immediate steps were taken to repel an

---

*See *Rebellion Records*, Series I, Vol. XIX, Part II, p. 547.

attack and to protect the trains by organizing the stragglers and teamsters at hand. The hostile force consisted of Gregg's Brigade of 3 regiments of cavalry
under Col. Davis, which had escaped from Harper's
Ferry on the 14th. Although narrowly missing Pendleton's column it later met Longstreet's reserve ordnance
train and burned 45 wagons of precious ammunition.

Upon reaching the river the defense of the Williamsport ford and the adjacent lower one was assigned Col.
Brown's Battalion, Gen. Pendleton continuing with
Nelson's Battalion and Alexander's train to Shepherdstown. By 10 a. m. on the 16th, the passage at that point
was also well guarded.

Meanwhile the demands upon the Chief of Artillery
from Sharpsburg, the point upon which Gen. Lee had
determined to concentrate, for long-range field pieces
were becoming most pressing, so that when Jackson's
column arrived, Col. Crutchfield was directed to return
to Harper's Ferry and bring up all the heavy captured
rifles he could find. Upon his return, however, he discovered that Col. Alexander had already directed most
of the captured material to be sent to Winchester. Before leaving Harper's Ferry, Crutchfield had found it
necessary to leave the batteries of Brown, Dement,
Latimer, and Garber, for sheer lack of horses. For the
same reason, Col. Walker was forced to leave Davidson's Battery behind. Impressing a sufficient number
of draught animals for the first three of his batteries
above named, securing two 3-inch captured rifles for Dement, and filling the caissons with a fresh supply of Federal ammunition, Crutchfield now proceeded to Sharpsburg, but arrived too late to take part in the battle of the
17th. Meanwhile, Brown's Battalion had been relieved
from duty at the Williamsport fords and moved forward as the reserve of Jackson's Corps, one battery of
which, Watson's, being the only one engaged in the
battle of Sharpsburg. Nelson's Battalion at this time
consisted of the batteries of Kirkpatrick, Milledge,

Ancell, Marmaduke Johnson, and Huckstep, the armament of which was very light, and therefore they were not called upon.*

The surrender of Harper's Ferry had come in the nick of time. By a rapid night march of 17 miles Jackson arrived at Sharpsburg on the 16th, Walker the same day, and McLaws at sunrise on the 17th, and A. P. Hill, leaving a brigade at Harper's Ferry, arrived during the battle. Thus the Army was concentrated at Sharpsburg before the close of the 17th.

When Longstreet and D. H. Hill had fallen back upon Sharpsburg, the Federal Army passing through the various gaps followed upon their heels. The greater part of the 16th was spent by McClellan in putting his troops in position along the ridge east of the Antietam, a creek flowing along the Confederate front and on the west side of which Longstreet and D. H. Hill were in position.

The Confederate position stretched across the angle formed by the Potomac and the Antietam, the latter a deep stream of more than 60 feet in width, overshadowed by a tangle of trees, that filled the bottom from which the ground on both sides ascends to the ridges. Just beyond the one on the west runs the Hagerstown pike, which is about a mile distant from the stream. On the reverse slope of the western ridge, falling as it does to the Potomac, lay the small village of Sharpsburg, behind the center of the Confederate line, which followed the main crest just east of the Hagerstown pike. A mile north of the village and on the pike Lee's left center rested near the Dunkard church, behind which lay a tract of trees known as the west wood, 500 yards in front of which stood a smaller wood known as the east wood. Extending southward from Sharpsburg the line rested its right on a wooded-spur overlooking the Antietam where it turns westward to the Potomac.

---

*On October 4, 1862, Ancell's and Huckstep's batteries were consolidated and became Massie's Battery.

From the main position just across the Hagerstown pike, open slopes, broken by long ravines, fell eastward to the bottom, affording the Confederates an admirable field of fire to the stream from 1,000 to 2,500 yards distant. Many lanes crossed the Confederate front, the sunken ones, together with the numerous low stone walls near the village, forming natural entrenchments of great strength for the defenders.

In the west wood, not only was there an entire absence of undergrowth, but the ground was intersected with waist-high outcroppings of rock which afforded excellent protection from hostile fire. But this portion of the line was the weak point, for the enemy was able to approach it closely through the east wood, and also threaten the flank under cover of a larger thicket which spread across the pike some distance to the north. Behind and between these screened approaches from the Antietam lay several small farms with orchards and stone fences, among which an attacking force, if checked, might rally, and near the Dunkard church were also a number of cottages and barns which offered cover.

The only ford across the Antietam was commanded by the bluff on the extreme right, yet a number of stone bridges remained intact. That nearest the Potomac, over which the road to Harper's Ferry passed, was defended by rifle pits and enfiladed by batteries. The next, known as the Burnside Bridge, just east of Sharpsburg, was well commanded by the western ridge, and the one opposite the Confederate center could be raked throughout its length. But one more to the north at Pry's Mill was entirely screened from the Confederates' view and fire, and was left unguarded, laying as it did a mile and a half east of the west wood and behind the east and Poffenberger woods.

While the position was an exceptionally strong one with the pike, an excellent lateral communication for the most part under cover, and numerous other intersecting roads, it possessed the grave disadvantage of being paralleled by the ridge east of the Antietam, along which, though slightly commanded by the hostile position, McClellan had ample space to deploy his 275 pieces of artillery. The superiority of his ordnance in weight and range far overbalanced the Confederate advantage in elevation. The range from ridge to ridge in no place exceeded 2,000 yards, but at many points approached that limit. The Federal guns were therefore able to deliver upon the hostile batteries a damaging fire to which little effective reply could be made. Not only was McClellan able to engage the Confederate 10-pounder rifles and 6-pounder guns with his 20-pounder Parrotts, but a greater discrepancy had to be contended with by the latter, for their projectiles and fuses were of very inferior quality, whereas those of the enemy were of the best. Not alone, then, will a comparison between the guns themselves suffice, for inferior ammunition reduced still further the comparative efficiency of the lighter ordnance. It was his ready grasp of the situation that led Gen. Lee to make such pressing demands upon Pendleton for all the heavy rifled pieces the latter could possibly forward from Harper's Ferry and Shepherdstown on the 16th and 17th.

As his troops arrived, Gen. Lee assigned Jackson to the left of the position with his 5,500 men and the 16 guns he had brought up from Harper's Ferry, and later Hood was placed in his rear. Next, on Jackson's right, came D. H. Hill with 5,000 men and 26 guns. Longstreet with 8,000 men and 50 guns held the center and right, the Washington Artillery commanding the bridge in his front and Eubank's Battery the Burnside Bridge with Richardson's on a hill slightly to its rear. Walker's Division of 3,500 men, and Branch's and French's batteries with 12 guns, was held as a reserve in rear of Toombs' Brigade on the extreme right. Munford's two regiments of cavalry, with Chew's Battery, were stationed on the extreme right to hold the bridge at the Iron Works and keep open the line of communications with Harper's Ferry, while Stuart with Fitzhugh Lee's Brigade of cavalry and Pelham's four guns was stationed behind the extreme left. Thus on the line from Nicodemus Run to the Potomac, a distance of three miles, were about 20,000 infantry, 2,500 cavalry, and about 2,000 artillerymen with 108 guns, Pendleton holding the fords of the river with 1,000 men, including a small infantry escort, and 26 guns. Urgent orders had been dispatched, however, for A. P. Hill to come up with his 13,000 men and 60 guns.

At 2 P. M. on the 16th, Hooker was ordered to cross the Antietam at Pry's Mill and attack the Confederate left. The movement being discovered, Hood was ordered into the front line, having already placed a number of his guns on a rise in the open ground east of the Hagerstown pike. A spirited combat now ensued between Hood and Meade, lasting until dark, resulting in the former regaining the east wood and driving Meade therefrom after he had once taken it. The artillery on both sides was active, Poague's Battery rendering valiant support to Garden's, Bachman's, and Reilly's batteries, of Frobel's Battalion, Hood's Division, all of which were much punished. In this affair, the howitzer section of Rhett's Battery, Lee's Battalion, was also engaged. Meanwhile, the rifled sections of Rhett's and Parker's batteries, and one rifled piece of Jordan's Battery, of Lee's Battalion, had been engaged in firing upon the Federal Infantry massing opposite the center, suffering some loss from the heavier guns of the enemy. Earlier in the day, Squires' Battery of rifles, Walton's Battalion, posted near the center, indulged in an artillery duel of about an hour's duration with the enemy. Before night, however, both Walton and Lee withdrew their battalions behind the cover of the ridge forming the infantry position.

On the morning of the 17th, S. D. Lee established a large group of guns in rear of Longstreet's center, to support Walton's batteries, all of his guns being necessarily much exposed to the Federal artillery fire. Another large group of guns was established by D. H. Hill not far in rear of his center near the Clipp, Roulette, and Mumma houses. Though Hill's Infantry had been much reduced at South Mountain, he was well supported by artillery, having Jones' reserve battalion of 14 guns, his divisional batteries, or those of Carter, Bondurant, and Hardaway, with their 12 pieces, under Maj. Pierson, Cutts' reserve battalion consisting of Ross's, Patterson's, Blackshear's, and Lane's batteries, with their 24 pieces, and Lloyd's Battery of 4 guns. Of the 16 guns of Jones' and Ewell's divisions of Jackson's Corps present, all except those of Poague's Battery were attached to Stuart, and placed by him under Pelham on the extreme left, Crutchfield not having arrived with Brown's, Dement's, Latimer's, and Garber's batteries from Harper's Ferry.

McClellan, on the morning of the 17th, had available 87,164 men and 275 guns. Upon gaining contact with the Confederates, Gen. Hunt, Chief of Artillery, at once selected an excellent position for 10 batteries of his reserve. In his report he states: "They overlooked the enemy and swept most of the ground between them and our troops. They were well served, especially the guns of Benjamin's Battery. Their field of fire was extensive, and they were usefully employed all day, and so constantly that the supply of ammunition for the 20-pounders ran short." It should here be noted that in Lee's entire army there were but six 20-pounder field pieces.

All during the successive and more or less isolated attacks of Hooker, Mansfield, and Sedgwick on Lee's left, of French and Richardson on his center, and of Burnside on his right, Hunt's great masses of guns played upon the Confederate batteries and their infantry lines, adding the tremendous weight of their metal to that of the corps and division batteries, with the several assaulting columns. As to the effect of Hunt's Reserve Artillery, we may judge from the report of D. H. Hill, who, as we have seen, controlled the largest group of Confederate guns. He wrote: "Positions were selected for as many of these guns as could be used, but all the ground in my front was commanded by the long range artillery of the Yankees, on the other side of the Antietam, which concentrated their fire upon every gun that opened and soon disabled it." And Col. S. D. Lee, the batteries of whose reserve battalion were distributed along the center and left center, afterwards declared that "Sharpsburg was Artillery Hell." The latter statement is no doubt correct, but Hill's is somewhat exaggerated, for the artillery of his portion of the line undoubtedly rendered most effective service, in spite of Hunt's batteries, the fire of which they disregarded when necessary for them to play upon the advancing columns of the enemy.

Jones' Division was all on the left of the pike, drawn up in two lines, facing northward, the first extending from the road to the Nicodemus house, the other in the northern edge of the west wood. Near the turnpike, one of Poague's rifles and two of Raine's howitzers were posted in the front line, while to the left rear Pelham was in position with a number of batteries. On the east of the pike, and in prolongation of Jones' line, was Lawton's Division.

At 3 A. M. on the 17th, Hooker renewed his attack, Doubleday on the right, Ricketts on the left, and Meade in reserve close behind. As this splendid force of 10 brigades and 10 batteries advanced to the attack, Hunt's guns 3,000 yards to the east opened a heavy enfilade fire upon the Confederate left, but disregarding both this and the fire of the batteries in their front, Poague, Raine, and the three batteries of Woolfolk, Parker, and Rhett, which Col. Lee had ordered into position near the Dunkard church, opened a continuous fire upon the infantry of the enemy with splendid effect. But as the Federal Infantry advanced, with Campbell's Battery in the front, Jones' first line was forced back upon the wood and its leader was carried wounded from the field. Poague and Raine after firing a few shots now retired their guns to a position in rear of the west wood, from which they continued to fire.* To the east

* These guns were not abandoned as stated by Henderson. See Poague's Report.

of the road, Lawton's Division, with the three batteries
of Lee's Battalion firing over the infantry from the rear,
first checked Meade and then drove him back upon six
batteries massed on his right, whereupon a section of
Jordan's Battery under Capt. J. S. Taylor was sent
forward by Col. Lee with Lawton's line, but was soon
driven back by the opposing batteries.

About this time the Confederate skirmishers, creeping through the corn in front of the west wood, shot
down the gunners and many horses of Campbell's Battery, all but taking the guns, and Starke, who had succeeded Jones, led his line forward once more. Meanwhile, the fire from Pelham's, Poague's, Raine's, and
Col. Lee's guns near the church, had been most effective,
though the right group suffered severely from Hunt's
fire as well as from that of two of Hooker's batteries.
Col. Grigsby, who in turn succeeded Starke, now held
the original position of his division, but Lawton, having
forced back Meade, was now himself being driven, for
with splendidly-served batteries the Federals were again
pushing forward, only to be checked by the arrival of
Hood's Division, with Frobel's Battalion of divisional
artillery. Capt. Bachman, galloping out into the cornfield with a section of Napoleons, opened fire upon the
enemy at a range of 150 yards. But in a few minutes
Hooker's skirmishers, creeping up to within 50 yards
of the guns, drove them from the field with the loss of
a number of men and many horses. Meanwhile the
rifled section of the battery had gone into action on the
turnpike, Reilly's Battery supporting the infantry from
a position further in rear. Garden's or the third battery
of the battalion had been left in position near Longstreet's center, with Walton's Battalion.

To Hood's support, D. H. Hill now sent over Ripley's, Colquitt's, and Garland's brigades, which in
column in the order named and on Hood's right struck
the left of the Federal attack and assisted in driving the
enemy a second time back upon their guns. Meanwhile, Woolfolk's, Parker's, and Rhett's batteries, much

damaged and with ammunition exhausted, the first leaving a piece on the field, had been ordered to the rear to refit, and Moody's Battery sent into position in their place. But as Hood's line advanced, Moody's guns were masked. Without hesitation the gallant officer with a section of his battery dashed forward 300 yards into a ploughed field and from a position in advance of the infantry for 15 minutes delivered a galling fire upon the enemy. Lieut. Gorey, an officer of another battery, who, seeing Capt. Moody's guns advancing to a post of such danger, had begged to be allowed to accompany them, was shot through the head and killed while sighting for the final shot.

It was now 7:30 A. M. and Mansfield's Corps was rapidly approaching to the support of Hooker's shattered troops which had rallied about their artillery. On Hood's left, J. G. Walker's two brigades and G. T. Anderson's Brigade had arrived from the extreme right, and Early had taken position in the west wood, where the remnants of Jones' Division remained. Pelham, joined by Poague, meanwhile had moved 13 pieces to a position just in rear and to the immediate left of Jones' old line, from which he was able to sweep the open ground from the Nicodemus house to the Dunkard church. Thus with ready perception he had grasped the key-point of Jackson's whole line, and yet placed his guns where they were entirely free from Hunt's fire, which relentlessly continued to play upon the Confederate left. Whatever may be said of McClellan's disjointed attacks in this quarter, Hunt at least did his part in the matter of artillery support. But in Pelham he found an equal in the aggressive handling of artillery, for no one movement on either side bore a greater influence upon the final issue of the battle than did the advancement of Pelham's group during the interim between Hooker's and Mansfield's attacks. This was a move on the chess board, though perhaps by a pawn, which baffled the most powerful pieces of the enemy. It was one of those master strokes by a subordinate of highly-developed initiative, which has so often been found to play a major part in the tactical success of the superior.

It is perhaps incorrect to speak of an interim between the first two attacks on Jackson, for Mansfield's overlapped Hooker's, his massed divisions pressing forward in time to check Hood's advance, and forcing his division back with fearful loss through the thirty-acre cornfield, east of the pike, to the church. Ripley and Colquitt were also being driven back to the same point from the east wood, to which they had advanced in following up Ricketts, by Greene's Division and Knapp's Battery. At this time Hood and Lawton held the southern part of the west wood, Ripley's and Colquitt's brigades retiring from the line towards D. H. Hill's position along the "bloody lane." But, while the Federals had gained all the ground north of the church and east of the pike, Jackson's left, by means of Pelham's guns, had held fast. No troops, however brave, could cross the space which Pelham's group so perfectly commanded. The Confederate line, when the lull succeeding Mansfield's repulse came, ran northward from the Dunkard church, almost parallel to the pike, while the Federal line near Miller's house faced south, its center in the east wood, and its left near the church, facing west. So far, less than 8,000 Confederates with perhaps 35 guns actually engaged, had, though suffering terribly themselves, foiled both Hooker's and Mansfield's corps, aggregating not less than 20,000 men, and 60 or more guns present on the field.

The lull about 9 A. M. was of short duration, for Sumner's columns were fast approaching from the north, and Porter was preparing to throw a heavy force, accompanied by his horse batteries, and supported by his corps artillery as well as Hunt's guns, across the Boonsboro Bridge opposite the Confederate center. Meanwhile Gen. Lee was sending his last reserves then on the field, McLaws and R. H. Anderson's divisions, to the front line, the former to Jackson's right at the Dunkard church, and the latter to the support of D. H. Hill. Before following up Sumner's or the third attack, let us turn to the center.

Soon after Col. Lee withdrew the three batteries of his battalion, and Jordan's section, from their positions near the church, he was ordered by D. H. Hill to mass his battalion along the ridge between the church and Sharpsburg, just west of the pike. From this position he was able to support Hill by firing over his infantry upon the extreme left of the Federal attack, which, overlapping Jackson, fell upon Hill's left. But in this position the batteries were so severely punished by Hunt that upon the arrival of McLaws they were ordered about a mile to the rear to replenish their ammunition and make such repairs as were possible.

After the retirement of the five batteries of Lee's own battalion, viz., Woolfolk's, Moody's, Jordan's, Parker's, and Rhett's, which had been heavily engaged in supporting Jackson, D. H. Hill had in position behind him Cutts' reserve battalion of 5 batteries with 26 pieces in addition to his divisional battalion of 4 batteries with 16 guns under Maj. Pierson. Further to the right, and behind Longstreet's center, was Walton's Battalion with 16 pieces, the 12 guns of Eubank's, Branch's, and French's batteries, the last two having been left by J. G. Walker's Division, being still opposite the Burnside Bridge. Bachman's Battery had also been ordered to the rear to refit. Save for a few companies of skirmishers, not a Federal soldier had yet crossed the Antietam south of the Dunkard church, and they had been driven to cover by Squires' Battery, which then withdrew to cover behind the crest with the other batteries of Walton's Battalion, allowing the enemy to expend many rounds of ammunition in a one-sided duel.

Sumner, who had gained contact with Jackson's line, now threw three divisions, Sedgwick's leading, and all in the closest order, against the west wood and the Roulette house. As the head of the column emerged from the east wood, moving across the cornfield beyond the turnpike, Greene, of Mansfield's Corps, advanced from his position near the church. Early, with a handful of Jones' Division, still holding the west wood, now moved rapidly forward to meet the attack almost solely opposed by Pelham's guns, and striking Greene's left flank drove him back. At this moment McLaws advanced in line through the west wood with the church on his right and struck Sedgwick in flank, and with Early's assistance Sumner's leading division was quickly driven off towards the north, losing nearly 2,000 men in a few minutes.

In vain did Sumner's guns, massed with those of the corps which had preceded him on the slope north of the cornfield, hurl canister at McLaws' and Early's lines. As Col. Cabell brought up McLaws' divisional battalion of artillery, the batteries, plying whip and spur, dashed to the front, unlimbering and firing as they advanced. Read's Battery, which went into action in the open on the right of the wood, alone lost 14 officers and men and 16 horses in as many minutes, and Carlton's Battery further to the left and in front of Ransom's Brigade was all but cut to pieces by the opposing guns.

Meanwhile Pelham's group on the extreme left continued its fire with great energy in an effort to beat down the storm of shot, shell, and canister from the Federal Artillery, but while it sought in vain to silence the great group of guns much damage was done them and at least a part of their fire diverted from McLaws and Early. Now again the fleeing mass of Federals rallied upon the artillery position, as Hooker and Mansfield had done before, a position which Stuart had vainly attempted to turn all through the forenoon. During the successive combats it had proved the source of many evils to the Confederates, and never once had the guns of the enemy been driven therefrom, though Pelham, greatly outmatched in the number of pieces as well as the weight of his metal, had with unsurpassed courage and skill done all of which his men and material were capable.

On the right of the west wood, as Early's men forced
Greene back upon the east wood, and were about to
capture Knapp's Battery, which had so harassed them,
"A" Battery, 4th United States Artillery, under Lieut.
Thomas, galloped into action beside Knapp, and together they gave a superb exhibition of what light
batteries are capable of doing even in the face of
point blank musketry fire.   In position near the southwest corner of the east wood, on the Smoketown road,
almost surrounded by Aiken's North Carolina Regiment, they were saved only by the timely arrival of
Smith's Division of Franklin's Corps, the latter now
coming upon the field and forming a line between the
church and the east wood, sheltered by a rise in the
ground.   At this juncture, the Confederates having
been checked by Franklin's fresh divisions, the fighting
was reduced to an active artillery duel, at ranges from
600 to 1,500 yards, and the attention of Cabell's and
Pelham's batteries were principally devoted to the most
advanced Federal group near the Miller house, composed of Cowan's, Frank's and Cothran's batteries, to
the support of which Hancock had been sent.   At least
15 Federal batteries were in position to the right front
of Pelham.   While the infantry of neither side was able
to assume the aggressive, the Confederates were well
satisfied, since they had repossessed themselves of and
continued to hold the west wood, under cover of which
their lines had reformed before 10:30 A. M.

At last Jackson's trials were over and opposite him lay
three shattered corps and a fourth or Franklin's with all
its ardor gone.   With less than 19,400 men and 40 guns
engaged on his part of the line, he had held at bay at
least 30,500 infantry and 25 superb batteries with not
less than 100 guns, all of which had been handsomely
supported by Hunt's powerful mass of long-range
rifles.   In their assaults, extending over a period of five
hours, the Federals had lost 7,000 officers and men,
while the Confederate losses on the left up to 10:30 A. M.
were 5,754, or 29 per cent of those engaged.

When Sumner's Corps came upon the field about 9:30 A. M., French's Division overlapped Jackson and fell upon D. H. Hill with great fury, soon joined by two brigades of Franklin's and Richardson's divisions. The main attack fell upon that part of the line from a point just southeast of the church past the Roulette and Piper houses.

At a point about one-third of the way from the church to Sharpsburg, a sunken lane, running from the east side of the turnpike, zigzagged into the Boonsboro road halfway between the village and the Antietam. This erratic route, now know as the "bloody lane" by reason of the slaughter which occurred therein during Hill's defense, at first descending in an easterly direction, soon meets a hollow where the lane to the Clipp house branches to the northeast. From thence the main lane runs southeast, ascending abruptly to the Boonsboro road. North of the sunken lane, and between it and the east wood were the Clipp, Roulette, and Mumma houses in the order named from the south, the last being the "burning building" so constantly referred to in the reports. Within the salient formed by the "bloody lane" is a plateau on which stood the Piper house. In rear of this plateau, or flat-topped hill, the land gently dips to the west, rising again to a ridge of greater elevation just west of the Hagerstown pike, which lies in the depression. It was from this ridge that Lee's Battalion, after firing for some time upon French's left, had been forced to withdraw about 10 A. M. by Hunt's guns, and it was in the depression running along its front to the south as far as the village that Jones, Cutts, and Walton, had held their artillery battalions under cover.

Although French assaulted Hill's position with great vigor, he was able to make little permanent headway, in spite of numerous efforts, but when Richardson came to his assistance the Confederates were forced back out of the "bloody lane" after a desperate defense, through the fields and the orchard in front of the Piper house.

But at the latter point the Federal advance was checked by a terrific fire from Cutts' guns now with Col. Lee on the ridge beyond the pike. But on the left of Richardson's line the Federals now gained the rise of ground on Hill's right and also drove the Confederates defending it towards the Piper house, exposing the men holding the sunken lane to a destructive enfilade fire. Cutts' and Jones' reserve battalions and Hill's divisional batteries under Maj. Pierson, utterly disregarding the tremendous shower of shot and shell which Hunt poured upon them, now massed across the pike and sought to repel the advancing enemy; but as the foremost batteries opened fire they were silenced and swept from the field. Realizing the weakness of Hill's line, Longstreet ordered Miller's Battery of the Washington Artillery to the support of Hill, which promptly went into action on the ridge behind the line, but withdrew to cover after losing a number of men. As the enemy again advanced, Capt. Miller, dashing forward across the pike with the remaining section of his battery, two Napoleons, went into action and for half an hour delivered an effective fire upon the enemy. Again, he moved forward, almost to the Piper house, ordering a sergeant to bring up a fresh caisson when his limbers were emptied. Joined by another piece, Miller's three guns, supported by a handful of infantry which had rallied about them, now delivered a rapid fire with canister. But the gunners falling rapidly, Longstreet, who was watching the battery, ordered his own staff to man the guns, and these gallant officers, firing with the greatest coolness and rapidity, succeeded in checking the enemy. Miller with ammunition exhausted was at this juncture relieved by Boyce's South Carolina Battery. Exposed to both a direct and reverse fire from Pleasonton's horse batteries now on the Boonsboro pike, and those in front of Porter across the Antietam, Boyce's men suffered heavily. While galloping into action, a caisson exploded, but, unlimbering within a few yards of the Federal line, the gallant battery drove it back with a furious discharge of canister, firing 70 rounds in a few minutes. This battery lost 19 men and 15 horses. Nothing was ever more gallant than its conduct.

The Federals retiring to the ridge from which they had advanced, now brought up Robertson's horse and Graham's light batteries to drive off Boyce, but Hill had repossessed himself by 1 P. M. of the Piper house and, aided by every battery which could be brought into action, held French beyond the sunken lane and Richardson on the crest beyond the orchard. Thus, with 7,000 men and about 50 guns in action, Hill had repelled a force of not less than 10,000 Federals.

About this time Col. Lee was forced to order all of the batteries in action behind Hill to the rear to refit, but not until relieved by Capt. Moorman in command of Maj. Saunders' Battalion of four batteries of R. H. Anderson's Division.

While this change was being effected four regular batteries of the enemy pushed across the Boonsboro bridge and came into action on either side of the road. Squires' and Garden's batteries on the south side of the road at once uncovered and several times broke the advancing Federal infantry line with their canister, but the enemy renewed his attacks again and again.

In the meantime, about 3 P. M., Squires' Battery was relieved by 12 pieces of Col. Lee's Battalion, all that could be refitted after the wreck of the morning, which, returning to the field, were posted about Sharpsburg. Moody's Battery now moved to the right, two pieces of Parker's and two of Jordan's Battery were placed at the left, and Rhett's two remaining guns went into action on the ridge just north of the village. These batteries as well as those they had relieved were exposed to a heavy fire of infantry and artillery, the skirmishers of the enemy approaching to within 150 yards of them, after having been driven back five or six times by Moody's and Squires' batteries. Finally, Garnett's Brigade, with Moody's Battery firing canister while advancing with the infantry, drove the enemy from the ridge just northeast of the village which they had taken, and the other batteries which had been joined by Carter's were now moved to a more advanced position south of the Boonsboro pike, which they held until forced to fall back by Burnside's success on their right.

Though ordered to attack at 9 A. M., it was not until 1 P. M. that Burnside made a vigorous effort to force the bridge in his front. Upon the crossing, Eubank's Battery kept up a plunging fire along with Richardson's further to the rear, but the latter, having expended all its ammunition and having one of its two Napoleons dismounted by Benjamin's Battery across the stream, withdrew temporarily. Meanwhile, Eshleman was plying with case and canister the Federals who were attempting to cross the ford below the bridge. But, in spite of the desperate resistance of the four brigades guarding the bridge, Burnside with the aid of Tidball's horse battery drove the Confederate skirmishers from his front and forced his way over. Pushing rapidly over the ridge towards Sharpsburg, he was almost unopposed, except by Maj. Frobel's batteries of Hood's Division, which were now returning to the field. Throwing Brown's Battery of D. R. Jones' Division well forward, Frobel also sent one of Reilly's sections and Garden's Battery of his own battalion into action at a range of not over 100 yards from the enemy, and thus checked the advance, though he lost most of his horses and many of his men in so doing. In a few minutes, all but three pieces were disabled, and their ammunition was exhausted. Running the disabled pieces to cover by hand, the gallant gunners were now ordered to retire them as the Federal Infantry rapidly occupied and then passed the position the batteries had abandoned. As the swarm of skirmishers almost overtook the guns, shooting down the cannoneers and horses, Lieut. Ramsay with the 2d section of Reilly's Battery arrived on the scene from the rear, and boldly going into action in a field on the right of the road from the bridge, enfiladed the enemy's line with canister, hurling its ex-

treme left back in confusion. To oppose the Federals
in this quarter, there being no available infantry, every
battery which could be spared from other sections of
the field was ordered to the right. First Carter, galloping along the east side of the village, then Poague, came
to the support of Ramsay. At this instant occurred
one of those incidents which make war grand. As a
section of the Rockbridge Battery, which had been detached from Pelham on Jackson's left, with lathered
horses and battle-stained men dashed past Gen. Lee on
its way to the point of threatened rout, Robert E. Lee,
Jr., the youngest son of the great Commander-in-
Chief, and a private in the battery, raising himself to an
erect posture, saluted with military precision his noble
father. Where in all the history of war is such another
incident to be found? Where such material for the
brush of a Messonier? The kith of Bonaparte bore the
baton, but the kin of Lee fought at the muzzle with
hands upon the rammer staff.

Truly one might say that Sharpsburg was a day of
glory for the Confederate Artillery. Without Pelham's guns, to deny the approach, never could Jackson
have withstood the shock of those dense masses still
ominously banked against his left. Without the gallant
Miller and Boyce to check the onrushing columns of
Richardson, and Col. Lee's guns to hold the enemy at
bay, D. H. Hill had been swept from the field. And
now, when the thin grey lines had been brushed aside
like so much chaff by Burnside's dense and ever-increasing force, naught but the shattered remnants of his batteries saved Lee from utter rout. Like bees to honey,
the batteries from left and center now swarmed to the
post of danger. Miller, Eshleman, Richardson, Squires,
Eubank, Garden, Reilly, Bachman, Brown, and Carter,
regardless of the hail of iron poured upon them by Von
Kleiser's, Taft's, Weed's, Durell's, Clark's, Simmons',
Benjamin's, Muhlenberg's, Cook's, McMullen's, and
other batteries across the Antietam, and free from mo-
lestation, heeded only the task assigned them. Not a one

but gladly undertook it, willing to sacrifice men, guns, and self, if only the surging wave of blue could be momentarily checked, for A. P. Hill was now at 3:30 P. M. arriving with his veteran light division from Harper's Ferry, and Lindsay Walker with four batteries was near at hand.

Hill's Division had marched 17 miles in 8 hours. His arrival was in the nick of time, for the Confederate batteries were now either totally disabled, or practically without ammunition, having for some time in the most exposed positions been doing the work of infantry while the superbly served Federal batteries played upon them at will. The village of Sharpsburg was all but taken, with all that that meant to Lee. Toombs alone, with a handful of men in support of the batteries, was formed in the path of the enemy. Dashing through the fields, Braxton's, Pegram's, McIntosh's, and Crenshaw's batteries, the first commanded by Lieut. Marye, heralded the approach of Hill's three brigades under Gregg, Branch, and Archer, and going into action within a few yards of the Federal flank, at once became involved in a desperate struggle for existence. In fact, McIntosh was soon forced to abandon his pieces. On the right of McIntosh and Crenshaw, whose positions were to the right of Toombs' rallied line, Pegram had also been pouring a continuous fire of canister into the enemy's lines, and further still to the right was Braxton.

Gathering their strength, Toombs' and Archer's brigades now swept forward from the road, striking the Federal left in flank, recapturing McIntosh's guns, and driving Rodman back upon the massed guns in front of the bridge. This left Wilcox's Division mainly on the north side of a ravine separating it from the bridge. Quickly perceiving his opportunity Col. Walker ordered Pegram with the only one of his pieces for which ammunition was left, and Braxton's Battery, to an elevation just north of the Snively house from which they poured a terrific enfilade fire down Wilcox's line at a range of about 500 yards.

To the left and in advance of Crenshaw, Carter's and the Donaldsonville Battery under Lieut. Elliott now went into action, Carter, Elliott, Crenshaw, Pegram, and Braxton, almost unaided by the musketry of the infantry, literally driving Wilcox from the field with their fire delivered on his front and both flanks. From their elevated position Pegram and Braxton continued their fire with splendid effect upon the Federals near the bridge until nightfall closed the engagement, the precision of their practice having attracted the attention of friend and foe.

The Confederates made no attempt to follow up the success which had attended the complete overthrow of Burnside, and as darkness enveloped the battlefield, worn out and exhausted by eight days of continuous marching and fighting, dropped to the ground where they stood to seek repose in sleep. But, even more fatigued than their men, the division commanders now sought Gen. Lee to urge, without exception, his withdrawal during the night. Unmoved by the universal opinion, and relying upon his confidence in McClellan's lack of heart for a resumption of the struggle, the great leader, possessing that supreme moral courage which so few possess, even though lions when aroused, merely ordered his generals to collect their remnants, and strengthen the lines for a possible conflict on the morrow.

The morning of the 18th, Lee turned his attention to the offensive plan which Jackson had attempted to execute the preceding day, to turn the extreme Federal right, which Stuart and Pelham had failed to do, reporting the task impossible.

Nothing can so well describe the situation on the morning of the 18th as the account of Col. S. D. Lee, whose gallantry and heroic efforts the day before had more than once saved the Confederate Army from defeat. Sending this officer to make a reconnaissance of the Federal right with Jackson, who had supported the views of Stuart and Pelham, Gen. Lee patiently awaited their report, continuing to urge Gen. Pendleton to send forward all the rifled pieces and stragglers he could collect.

Of his reconnaissance, Col. Lee wrote: "During the morning a courier from headquarters came to my battalion of artillery with a message that the commander-in-chief wished to see me. I followed the courier, and on meeting Gen. Lee, he said: 'Col. Lee, I wish you to go with this courier to Gen. Jackson, and say that I sent you to report to him.' I replied, 'General, shall I take my batteries with me?' He said: 'No, just say that I told you to report to him, and he will tell you what he wants.' I soon reached Gen. Jackson. He was dismounted with but few persons around him. He said to me: 'Col. Lee, I wish you to take a ride with me,' and we rode to the left of our lines with but one courier, I think. We soon reached a considerable hill and dismounted. Gen. Jackson then said, 'Let us go up this hill, and be careful not to expose yourself, for the Federal sharpshooters are not far off.' The hill bore evidence of the fierce fight the day before.* A battery of artillery had been on it, and there were wrecked caissons, broken wheels, dead bodies, and dead horses around. Gen. Jackson said: 'Colonel, I wish you to take your glasses and carefully examine the Federal line of battle.' I did so, and saw a remarkably strong line of battle, with more troops than I knew Gen. Lee had. After locating the different batteries, unlimbered and ready for action, and noting the strong skirmish line in front of the dense masses of infantry, I said to him: 'General, that is a very strong position, and there is a large force there.' He said: 'Yes, I wish you to take 50 pieces of artillery and crush that force, which is the Federal right. Can you do it?' I can scarcely describe my feelings as I again took my glasses, and made an even more careful examination. I at once saw such an attempt must fail. More than 50 guns were unlimbered and ready for action, strongly supported by dense lines

---

*This hill as suggested by Henderson was probably the one held by Pelham on the 17th.

of infantry and strong skirmish lines, advantageously posted. The ground was unfavorable for the location of artillery on the Confederate side, for, to be effective, the guns would have to move up close to the Federal lines, and that, too, under fire of both infantry and artillery. I could not bring myself to say all that I felt and knew. I said: 'Yes, General. Where will I get the 50 guns?' He said: 'How many have you?' I replied: 'About 12 out of the 30 I carried into action the day before.' (My losses had been very great in men, horses, and carriages.) He said: 'I can furnish you some, and Gen. Lee says he can furnish some.' I replied: 'Shall I go for the guns?' 'No, not yet,' he replied. 'Col. Lee, can you crush the Federal right with 50 guns?' I said: 'General, I can try. I can do it if any one can.' He said: 'That is not what I asked you, sir. If I give you 50 guns, can you crush the Federal right?' I evaded the question again and again, but he pressed it home. Finally I said: 'General, you seem to be more intent upon my giving you my technical opinion as an artillery officer, than upon my going after the guns and making an attempt.' 'Yes, sir,' he replied, 'and I want your positive opinion, yes, or no.' I felt that a great crisis was upon me, and I could not evade it. I again took my glasses and made another examination. I waited a good while, with Jackson watching me intently. I said: 'General, it can not be done with 50 guns and the troops you have near here.' In an instant he said: 'Let us ride back, Colonel.' I felt that I had positively shown a lack of nerve, and with considerable emotion begged that I might be allowed to make the attempt, saying: 'General, you forced me to say what I did unwillingly. If you give the 50 guns to any other artillery officer I am ruined for life. I promise you I will fight the guns to the last extremity if you will only let me command them. Jackson was quiet, seemed sorry for me and said: 'It is all right, Colonel. Everybody knows you are a brave officer, and would fight the guns well,' or words to that effect. We soon reached

the spot from which we started. He said: 'Colonel, go
to Gen. Lee, and tell him what has occurred since you
reported to me. Describe our ride to the hill, your examination of the Federal position, and my conversation
about your crushing the Federal right with 50 guns,
and my forcing you to give your opinion.'

"With feelings such as I never had before, nor ever
expect to have again, I returned to Gen. Lee, and gave
a detailed account of my visit to Gen. Jackson, closing
with the account of my being forced to give my opinion
as to the possibility of success. I saw a shade come
over Gen. Lee's face, and he said: 'Colonel, go and join
your command.' For many years, I never fully understood my mission that day, or why I was sent to Gen.
Jackson. When Jackson's report was published of the
battle, I saw that he stated that on the afternoon of the
17th, Gen. Lee had ordered him to move to the left with
a view of turning the Federal right, but that he found
the enemy's numerous artillery so judiciously posted in
their front, and so near the river, as to render such an
attempt too hazardous to undertake. I afterwards saw
Gen. J. E. B. Stuart's report, in which he says that it
was determined, the enemy not attacking, to turn the
enemy's right on the 18th. It appears Gen. Lee ordered
Gen. Jackson on the evening of the 17th to turn the
enemy's right, and Jackson said that it could not be
done. It also appears from Stuart's report and from
the incident I relate, that Gen. Lee reiterated the
order on the 18th, and told Jackson to take 50 guns
and crush the Federal right. Jackson having reported
against such an attempt on the 17th, no doubt said that
if an artillerist, in whom Gen. Lee had confidence,
would say the Federal right could be crushed with 50
guns, he would make the attempt."

The incident recounted by Col. Lee is a dramatic one.
The temptation offered the brave artilleryman to allow his professional duty to be overborne by the desire to retain the approval of Jackson, the soldier who
had never flinched from even the seemingly impossible,

was a great one. Just as he wrote, Col. Lee could not have known during the battle that Jackson's views coincided with his own. On the contrary, it was most natural for him to believe that Jackson regarded him as unwilling at heart to essay the proposed task.

This whole affair again illustrates those tactical views of Jackson's which we have had occasion to note at White Oak Swamp and Cedar Mountain. He realized the futility of frontal attacks against massed batteries without a proper artillery preparation, and to secure such he knew was quite impossible at Sharpsburg on the 17th and 18th. He knew that even had the Confederate batteries been fresh and full-manned, instead of badly wrecked as they were, another Malvern Hill stared him in the face. Yet, no doubt sensible of the criticism to which he had been subjected for his delay at White Oak Swamp while seeking to subdue the fire of the hostile guns, in order not to sacrifice his infantry, even though confirmed in his view of the situation by Stuart and Pelham, the latter an artilleryman of unquestioned intrepidity, Jackson threw the burden of the decision upon the commander-in-chief himself, through the medium of the latter's technical adviser, Col. Lee. In this his action was well considered, and the delicate manner in which he convinced Gen. Lee of the error in which he was about to fall beautifully illustrates Jackson's loyalty to his chief.

But another feature is to be noted, and that is the submission by Gen. Lee and Gen. Jackson of purely technical questions concerning the guns to skilled artillerymen. In this matter the change for the better is most noticeable. Never once, as far as can be ascertained, had the infantry assaults of the Peninsula been held in abeyance pending an artillery reconnaissance. In every instance until now the columns had been furiously hurled against all but impregnable positions without the slightest deference being paid to the professional opinion of artillerymen; nor were their views even sought. But now we first find Jackson consulting Pelham, and though but confirmed by the latter in his views, naïvely suggesting to his commander-in-chief that he, too, avail himself of an expert technical opinion. An artilleryman, and one in whose loyalty, as well as in whose ability and courage, the highest confidence is reposed by him, is sent to make the reconnaissance, and the ultimate decision withheld pending his finding. No longer is the advice of the "old war horse" alone sought on artillery matters, as at Malvern Hill. In vain did Longstreet urge the frontal attack on the 17th as the proper counter-stroke. The certain fate of such a move was painted in lurid colors. The flashes of a hundred guns running together streaked the opposite hillside with a line of red, through which no infantry might hope to pass. Malvern Hill had not been lost in vain, and Gen. Lee turned towards his enemy's flank, waiting, so patiently listening, for some news of Jackson's success. But the Federal move which baffled Pelham was the massing in a single group of 30 heavy rifled pieces on a well-prepared position, about one mile north of the west wood, and 900 yards from the river, at a point where the Hagerstown pike ascends to a commanding ridge. Opposed to this great battery, so skillfully placed, the damaged guns of Pelham would have been almost as useless as old Brown Bess.

When Gen. Lee received from the lips of one of his ablest artillerymen a confirmation of Jackson's report, his troops still lay in line of battle. Not a halo of smoke had hovered above the guns, not a rifle-shot had broken the awful stillness of the morning. With bated breath and tense with anxiety, the two armies lay watching each other so silent it almost seemed the life blood had ebbed from their veins. The stricken hundreds which held the foremost lines were scarce less motionless than those who survived. And what a contrast this the night hour in which Lee set his columns in motion for Virginia bore to that when but recently, with bands playing and mid cheers from 40,000 throats, the sons of the South crossed to the land of their foe. Now, as the dejected, battle-rent regiments, some reduced to mere platoons, waded out into the Potomac, with faces turned southward, even the splashing of feet in the water jarred upon the overwrought nerves of the men. The Army of Northern Virginia was experiencing a new sensation, for though its resolve was never higher, its back was towards the enemy.

We find those who speak of Sharpsburg or Antietam as a drawn battle. So it was in every tactical sense of the word. Strategically, however, the Maryland campaign had ended in defeat and the great battle of September 17 was the culmination. Lee had crossed the Potomac with the intention of carrying the war into the enemy's country. He had scarce crossed before he was fighting for existence, with one foot of his army at all times on the other side of the dividing line. Now he was returning to the southern shore, even thankful that the avenue of retreat lay open. During the night of the 18th, the Army of Northern Virginia, with all its trains and artillery, had recrossed the Potomac at Boteler's Ford. As the rear wagons containing the wounded, and the splintered remains of the last battery to leave its position, approached the ford, Gen. Lee, still at the post of greatest danger near the north shore, with a great sigh and as if to relieve his soul of pain, expressed his thanks to God. No words can so well fix in history the failure of the First Maryland Invasion as that fervent prayer of the Confederate leader with all that it meant. In connection with Gen. Lee's withdrawal from Sharpsburg, one instinctively recalls Moses, the deliverance of the Israelites and of the Confederates both being percarious from a military point of view.

No serious attempt was made by McClellan to press the Confederates until the next day, Fitz Lee's cavalry having held off Pleasanton until the crossing was effected. Meanwhile, Gen. Pendleton, with Nelson's reserve battalion of artillery crowning the heights opposite the ford with its guns, had been collecting other batteries as they crossed and placing them in position to repel the enemy, momentarily expected to appear. Soon 44 guns were thus secured. Capt. Maurin with three rifled pieces was placed to the right, about 250 yards from the river, and Lieut. Maddox with one piece on his left. Upstream then came Milledge with four rifles and a howitzer, and Chapman with one rifle and one Napoleon. On the brow of the cliff overlooking the ford so as to rake it and its approaches, Capt. Marmaduke Johnson, with two 6-pounders and two howitzers, was placed. Above the road leading through the ravine from the ford, Capt. Kirkpatrick with two 6-pounders and two 12-pounder howitzers occupied the brow of the cliff from which position he was able to cross fire with Johnson, and next to him Capt. Huckstep took position with his four 6-pounders. To the left of Huskstep was Braxton's Battery, and further along Capt. Barnwell, of Pendleton's staff, placed a 12-pounder Whitworth and two 10-pounder Parrotts under Capt. Hardaway; two of the Washington Artillery batteries were also posted on the brink of the ravine by Col. Long of Gen. Lee's staff, while eleven pieces were held in reserve for an emergency.

About 8 A. M. on the 19th, Pleasanton appeared at the ford with a large force of cavalry, and Gibson's, Tidball's and Robertson's horse batteries with their eighteen pieces opened on the Confederates. An artillery duel had continued for about two hours when the Federal 5th Corps arrived. The Confederate infantry support of about 600 men left with Gen. Pendleton now replied to the enemy while the guns economized their ammunition as much as possible. About noon the Federal Infantry took cover behind a canal bank on the north side of the river, from which their sharpshooters greatly harassed the Confederate gunners. The situation of the isolated batteries was now critical and though much criticism of Gen. Pendleton has resulted from his failure to hold the ford, it is not suggested by Alexander and others how it should have been done. Pendleton had on the 18th sent Ancell's Battery to Shepherd's Ford, four miles above Boteler's, and on the 19th, he had been forced to dispatch 200 men of his infantry to its support, sending an equal number to the ford below him, opposite which the enemy had appeared with a number of guns and commenced to shell the small cavalry force stationed on the south shore. Lee was not ignorant of the precarious task which had been assigned his Chief of Artillery, for on the 19th he had instructed him by letter to fall back that evening if the pressure of the enemy became too great, adding that a few guns only need be left with the cavalry, which had been ordered to relieve him.* Col. Munford, with his cavalry and Chew's horse battery, had promised to be on hand by night. So any suggestion that Pendleton deserted his post is an improper one.

During the afternoon the battery commanders began to report their ammunition exhausted, but such only as were able to withdraw their guns unseen by the enemy were allowed to retire. Shortly after nightfall, while some of the batteries were moving off, the infantry remaining near the ford broke badly and fled down the road from the river, a large body of skirmishers having rushed across the stream and routed them. Capt. Maurin was now compelled to spike his 10-pounder Parrott, Capt. Milledge and Johnson each a 12-pounder howitzer, and Capt. Huskstep one of his 6-pounders, all of which were abandoned.† In the retirement the Confederate batteries lost 7 men and 26 horses.

While the batteries were moving off from the river as best they could in the night, Gen. Pendleton sought in vain to induce Gen. Pryor, but two miles inland, to return and cover the position he had occupied, but Hood, the division commander, not being found, he continued his search for Gen. Lee, who ordered Jackson to take

---

*Memoirs of W. N. Pendleton, p. 225.
†The piece lost by Milledge was one of the two brass howitzers belonging to the Cadet Battery of the Virginia Military Institute, cast by order of President Taylor, in 1855, and presented to the Corps of Cadets. The mate of the lost piece is now the evening gun of the Institute, and has been used as such since 1866.

COLONEL STEPHEN DILL LEE
(Transferred from the Artillery and afterwards Lieutenant-General
Army of the West)

the necessary steps to hold the enemy in check. The next morning Jackson sent A. P. Hill's Division towards the river, he and Pendleton accompanying it. As Hill moved up at an early hour in two lines, he found a force of about 3,500 men of Porter's Corps along the Charles Town road. Under cover of a tremendous fire of artillery from the north shore, the Federals maintained a stubborn resistance along the crest of the ravine. But soon Porter ordered Sykes to recross, and, during the attempt to execute the movement, Hill's brigades made a superb charge, driving the remaining regiment into the river, this single command suffering a loss of 282 men out of 800 present.

Hill had not a single gun in action. His divisional battalion under Col. Walker was no doubt blocked on the narrow roads leading south when his orders were received to drive Porter back, and there was no time to wait for them. But his assault on the Federal position in the face of numerous well-served guns cost him a loss of 261 men of his sorely-depleted brigades. The affair indicates that Hill's Infantry, at any rate, had lost none of that fierce *élan* for which the Light Division had ever been famous.

The Federals now desisted from further attempts to overtake Lee's army, McClellan's attention being wholly devoted to Stuart's threat against his rear, the latter having crossed the Potomac near Williamsport.

The actual losses of the Confederate Artillery in material in the campaign had been slight, although the batteries were veritable wrecks, over half of their horses having succumbed either on the road or in battle. Walton's Battalion had abandoned but one caisson before withdrawing from Sharpsburg, and that had been destroyed. At Crampton Gap, Capt. Carlton, of Cabell's Battalion, had lost a 12-pounder howitzer, Read and Lloyd of the same command having lost elsewhere one 3-inch rifle, and one 6-pounder with two caissons, respectively. In Col. Lee's Battalion, the loss was comparatively great, Jordan having lost a howitzer caisson, Rhett a howitzer limber, Parker the rear chests of a howitzer caisson, Moody a forge, Woolfolk a 12-pounder howitzer and limber, and Moorman two 10-pounder Parrotts with part of a caisson. In addition to the foregoing were the losses at the ford by Maurin, Milledge, Johnson, and Huckstep, viz., the four pieces, already enumerated.*

In personnel, Col. Lee's Battalion alone had lost 2 officers and 8 men killed, and 2 officers and 75 men wounded, an aggregate loss of 85, not less than 25 per cent, an enormous percentage for artillery. Col. Walton's Battalion had lost 4 men killed, and 3 officers and 27 men wounded; Jones' Battery of Pierson's Battalion, D. H. Hill's Division, had suffered a loss of 26 men, or fully 50 per cent of its strength. Maj. Frobel's Battalion of Hood's Division sustained a loss of about 23 men. In the division reports of casualties the Artillery losses are in many cases not separately enumerated, but a conservative estimate, based on those reported, fixes the Artillery losses at not less than 300 officers and men.† Among the former were Capt. J. S. Taylor, of Col. Lee's staff, and Lieuts. Dabney and Pringle of Carter's and Garden's batteries, respectively, all of whom fell mortally wounded while performing their duty with great gallantry.

But, as has been remarked before, artillery losses do not spell artillery efficiency and service rendered. In fact, there is little relation between them. Had the Confederate batteries been able to beat down the fire of the powerful Federal guns, especially those of Hunt, they would have saved the infantry hundreds of men. As it was, they were unable to do this, and, in repelling the infantry columns of the enemy, were exposed to more serious losses than if they had for the most part merely engaged in an artillery duel. Surveying the battlefield on the 16th, such men as Cols. Lee and Walton, Majs. Cutts, Jones, Pierson, and Frobel, had all realized at a glance what was before them. They

---

*For above see *Rebellion Records*, Series I, Vol. XIX, Part I, p. 844, and Pendleton's and Barnwell's reports, Ibid., pp. 834, 837.
†See Guild's report, Longstreet's return, Ewell's return, Vol. XIX, Part I, pp. 810, 843, and 974, respectively, also individual reports of Walker, Walton, Lee, Frobel, and others.

saw at once that the work of the gunners was to be a task of self-sacrifice. If they were to render the infantry that service of which they were alone capable, the artillery of the enemy must be in large measure ignored by them, for in a duel with the superior ordnance of McClellan, their guns would be completely out-matched. With firm resolve, they therefore, determined to devote their energies to the attacking infantry, heed-less of the exposure to the hostile artillery. Trans-mitted to the men and officers of their commands, such was the spirit which animated the Confederate Artillery in this great battle which Col. Lee afterwards character-ized as "Artillery Hell." How well the gunners carried out their resolve has been shown. In every quarter of the battlefield they saved the day for Gen. Lee. With Hill in the center, the Artillery at one critical instant alone remained in action to check the enemy and save that portion of the line from rout. Later Burnside's advance was stayed by the Artillery unsupported ex-cept by Toombs' shattered brigade, utterly incapable of further effective resistance, and dashing upon the field the batteries of Walker's Battalion, coming to the re-lief of those already in action, had hurled Rodman, then Wilcox, back from Sharpsburg. Their share in saving Lee's right is well attested by the insignificant losses which the infantry of A. P. Hill's Division suffered in coöperating with them, and again by the Federal re-ports which repeatedly refer to the Confederate bat-teries as the cause of the withdrawal of Burnside's di-visions.

In the battle of Sharpsburg necessity developed a mobility among the light batteries which was surpris-ing. A study of the reports shows that the same battery was engaged in widely-separated positions, in spite of enormous losses and deficiencies in horses. We have seen how Carter moved from point to point under a tremendous fire, as occasion required. And again, how Poague, after incurring severe losses in the morning on the extreme left with Jackson and Pelham, reappeared in action in the afternoon at the threatened point on the extreme right. These rapid changes of position were typical of many of the batteries engaged, for the groups which were originally established were essentially unstable by reason of the superiority of the enemy's artillery fire, which forced them to dissolve whenever they opened. It was necessary, therefore, for batteries to be constantly shifted about and detached from their own battalions and groups in order to close with the attacking infantry. Dispersed, these batteries were able to assist in repelling the enemy with their canister, drawing upon themselves only a portion of the hostile artillery fire when they went into action. Massed, they were overwhelmed by the concentrated fire of superior guns. We therefore find the usual order of things reversed, due to the undisputed fire of Hunt's masses. At Sharpsburg, the Confederate batteries were more effective individually than grouped, because they were forced to devote their energies to the hostile infantry wherever it threatened and because by dispersing they so divided the attention of Hunt that much of the concentrated effect of his guns was lost. Upon whatever point the great Federal masses of guns shifted their sheaves of fire, from some other quarter a Confederate battery sprung into action relieved for a time at least of the merciless hail of iron soon sure to be directed upon it. But meanwhile these isolated batteries had individually inflicted terrific losses upon the attacking infantry.

Sharpsburg, at which the Federals hurled their masses upon the Confederate positions, was in no way similar to Malvern Hill. In the latter battle the artillery superiority rested with the defenders whose guns completely prevented the artillery preparation for the infantry attack by sweeping the hostile batteries from the field. At Sharpsburg, on the contrary, the attack retained its artillery superiority throughout, and yet, though the effect of the artillery preparation was tremendous, the infantry was unable to press home. From a tactical standpoint, this anomaly is solely explainable (since the courage of the Federal Infantry was superb) by the unsparing support which the infantry of the defense received from its batteries, the guns of which invariably reopened when the hostile guns were masked by the assaulting columns. This was made possible only by the Confederate batteries moving into the closest proximity with the enemy; and, being willing and able to do that, their ordnance, comparatively inferior in point of range, was almost as effective upon infantry masses with case and canister as the superior material of the enemy would have been in their hands. In fact 6-pounders and light howitzers were even more effective with canister at ranges from 150 to 300 yards, than the heavier rifled pieces with shell would have been. All these matters are worthy of much consideration. It is such factors that enter into the problems presented by many battles.

We have seen that the number of guns borne on Lee's muster rolls at this time aggregated about 300, giving a proportion on paper of between 9 and 10 pieces per 1,000 men of the infantry. But no such proportion was to be found on the battlefield of Sharpsburg. A number of batteries were still on the road from Harper's Ferry with Crutchfield when the battle closed; others remained at Harper's Ferry; some had been left at Richmond, or sent to Winchester. In addition to these, the batteries of Col. Brown's regiment and Maj. Nelson's battalion of the reserve took no part in the action. Yet these two commands were being employed for a purpose closely connected with the maneuvers of the Army, and should not be excluded for that reason. Actively employed, then, whether actually engaged or not, were not less than 200 guns, which, considered in connection with an infantry force of 30,000 men on the field of battle, gave a proportion of between 6 and 7 pieces of artillery per 1,000 men of the other arms, still an unusually large proportion, to which the repulse of McClellan's superior force was in great measure due.

As to the expenditures of the various batteries at Sharpsburg, we have no record. The recordation of such matters was a refinement little known or appreciated by the gunners of 1862. They were more concerned with a multitude of other matters which demanded their attention than with statistics for future study, and most of the gallant battery commanders who fought their guns at Sharpsburg were as unable immediately after the battle as the survivors are to-day to state with any degree of accuracy whether they expended 200, 300, or 500 rounds on the 17th of September. But every circumstance points to an immense expenditure on the part of some of the batteries engaged, and it is not extravagant to believe it equaled, if it did not exceed, the average of Second Manassas.

With the final episode of the first invasion of the North, the Confederate Artillery already, since Second Manassas, highly regarded, sprang into a position of preëminence among its sister arms.* The distinguished reputation which the artillery branch of the Confederate service had acquired, rested not upon its comparative. efficiency with the same branch of the Federal Army, for all recognized the superiority of the latter, in organization, drill, discipline, material, and equipment. It was but the direct result of the personal character of its officers and men, who, except in courage, were overweighed in all that made for the force of their blows. In other branches of the Confederate service there were few names among the subordinate officers as well known as those of Stephen D. Lee, Stapleton Crutchfield, John B. Walton, and Lindsay Walker, and those of gentle Tom Carter, bold Preston Chew, stern Poague, youthful Willie Pegram, and dashing John Pelham had become by-words in every Southern household. Few armies have ever boasted such a brilliant galaxy of gunners, combining as they did the unflinching resolve of maturer manhood with the bravery of youth, as was to be found towards the close of 1862 in Lee's field artillery.

---

*In a letter from Gen. T. T. Munford, himself a cavalryman, to the author, he declares the artillery to have been the most distinguished branch of the Confederate service.

CHAPTER XX

AFTER his retreat from the Potomac Gen. Lee rested his army between Winchester and Bunker Hill, a section still rich in food supplies, while the Cavalry watched the enemy. At last his worn men were given a chance to recuperate their strength, and in the vast rolling meadows of the Valley, with grasses still green and sweet, the weary animals of the Artillery found rest and invigorating food.

The base of supplies of the Army was now Staunton, more than 100 miles distant, but passing back and forth over the metalled highway of the Valley, the wagon trains were kept busy bringing ammunition, food, and clothing, until the Army was again placed on a footing of preparedness for further campaigning. But horses and wagons were particularly scarce, in spite of all that Maj. Richardson and the other artillery officers sent to Winchester from Leesburg had been able to do. As late as October 20, the Chief of Ordnance alone reported a deficit of 55 wagons with their teams for Longstreet's reserve ordnance train, and 41 for that of Jackson's Corps, and in nearly every report and communication of the battalion and battery commanders at this time, the scarcity of horses for their batteries is mentioned. Just after the Maryland campaign the general condition of the field artillery in point of personnel, material, horses, and equipment, was distressing.

On September 22, Col. Crutchfield reported every battery of Maj. Pierson's Battalion, D. H. Hill's Division, as unfit for duty, and ordered them to Martinsburg to refit, and to rest and reshoe the horses. In Jackson's old division the condition of Maj. Shumaker's Battalion, composed of Poague's, Carpenter's, Cutshaw's, Caskie's, Rice's, Wooding's, Brockenbrough's, and

Raine's batteries, was even worse. For the 28 guns of these eight batteries, not less than 128 horses were necessary to make them really serviceable, and 204 were needed to properly mount the batteries. Some of these batteries had actually less than 20 animals available for duty, and their harness was particularly defective, others being equipped with 12-pounder howitzers drawn by 6-pounder limbers.

Of Maj. Courtney's Battalion, Ewell's Division, few of the batteries had been present at Sharpsburg. Crutchfield reported three batteries in excellent order, having been refitted by him at Harper's Ferry, two others in fair condition but needing better guns, and two disabled. The last two were also sent to Martinsburg to refit, and for them alone 30 horses were needed.

In A. P. Hill's Division, such of Maj. Lindsay Walker's batteries as had been refitted at Harper's Ferry were in fair condition, in spite of their service at Sharpsburg.

The condition of the artillery of Longstreet's Corps was undoubtedly worse than in Crutchfield's battalions, for nearly all the batteries of Cols. Lee, Walton, and Cabell, and of Majs. Jones, Cutts, Frobel, and Saunders, had been exposed to a terrific punishment at the hands of Hunt. In fact a number of the batteries were individually reported totally disabled, as was Cabell's entire battalion.

In point of personnel, the extent of the depletion of the batteries in general may be estimated from the return of the strength of Lee's and Walton's battalions on September 22, at which time the ten batteries included in the report mustered 39 officers and 632 men present for duty, an average battery strength of but 64 men. Yet, the minimum strength of a battery was prescribed by law to be 80 men.

Within one week, however, the return of stragglers and absentees brought the strength of Walton's Battalion up to 281 officers and men present for duty, with an aggregate present and absent of 355, or a battery average of nearly 90 men. In Lee's Battalion, 433 officers and men were reported present for duty, with an aggregate present and absent of 561, or a battery average of 93 men. At the same time, the personnel of about 20 reserve batteries was reported as 55 officers and 716 men present, with an aggregate of 1,027 present and absent, which shows an average battery strength of but 50 men.

The 7 batteries of Courtney's Battalion, Ewell's Division, reported an average strength at this time of but 49 men present, but of 72 present and absent.

Such conditions demanded an immediate remedy, and steps were at once taken to place the Artillery on a better footing.

As early as the 26th the batteries of Carpenter and Cutshaw, under command of the former, were consolidated, and Wooding was given command of Rice's Battery consolidated with his own; four guns were allowed each battery, and any that remained were ordered to be turned over to the reserve. Capt. Cutshaw had been badly wounded and Rice had resigned. But further than this Gen. Lee had not cared to go without express authority from the Secretary of War, upon whom he called, September 28, for instructions to reorganize and reconstruct all the unserviceable batteries and to dispose of surplus officers according to their merits.* Gen. Lee's communication to the Secretary of War was at once referred to the President, the latter's attention being called in the endorsement to the fact that Congress had refused to authorize the consolidation of companies, even objecting to the disbanding of them, and that in consolidating batteries it was difficult to select the best officers to remain in the service. But the President wisely declared legislation on this point by Congress unnecessary and sanctioned Gen. Lee's action.

To bring the animals of the Army up to a state of efficiency Gen. Lee now, in a general order, which is a model of its kind, established definite and rigid regu-

---

*See *Rebellion Records*. Series I, Vol. XIX, Part II, pp. 629 and 632, S. O. No. 201, September 26, 1862, and letter of Lee to Randolph, September 28, 1862.

lations for their use and care. Inasmuch as it shows both the importance which the deficiency of horses had assumed, as well as the methods pursued in the Artillery for husbanding the strength of the indispensable companion of the gunner, the order is given in full.*

"HEADQUARTERS, ARMY OF NORTHERN VIRGINIA,
"October 1, 1862.

"ORDERS—No. 115.

"II. The general commanding desires to impress upon all officers in charge of horses of the army the urgent necessity of energetic and unwearied care of their animals, and of preventing their neglect and abuse. Officers in charge of wagon trains will be held to a rigid accountability for permitting their teams to be overdriven, misused, or neglected. Division quartermasters and commissaries will report all instances of the kind in trains under their charge.

"III. Artillery horses especially must be kept in good condition. To this end the Chief of Artillery will personally supervise all the reserve, and see that all instances of neglect are corrected, by penalty when deserved, and by suitable provisions when the evil has resulted from necessity. He will cause every practical arrangement to be made for supplying the horses of his command with sufficient and suitable food, sparing no effort or reasonable expense.

"IV. Division commanders are reminded of their responsibility for the condition of their artillery, and especially of its horses. On the march, they will see that the halting places are selected for their batteries where water and food can be obtained. They will charge their Chiefs of Artillery to secure, by rigid personal attention, adequate supplies of forage from the quartermasters to whom that duty is committed. They will see that, when in the vicinity of the enemy, every possible opportunity is improved for resting, watering, and feeding their horses. When the army is quiet, division artillery will be diligently cared for by division commanders and their Chiefs of Artillery. Their batteries must be kept under control, and not allowed to scatter at will. If scarcity of forage renders impracticable a full supply for the horses retained with divisions, and it becomes necessary to send batteries elsewhere for sufficient food, they must go together with proper officers to supply and supervise them, and report statedly to their division commander, or they must be sent to the reserve camp to be there supplied, and report immediately to the general Chief of Artillery.

---

*Rebellion Records, Series I, Vol. XIX, Part II, p. 642.

"V. Horses worn down, past recovery, will be turned in to the chief quartermaster, who will send them off immediately, under proper regulations, to good pasturage, where they must be attended to and cared for under the supervision of responsible agents.

"VI. Battery horses will in no instance be ridden, except while in use by the usually mounted non-commissioned officers of the company, and by them only on duty. Their use, except with the battery, and then in battery service, is strictly prohibited, and Chiefs of Artillery will arrest and bring to trial all violating this order.

"By order of Gen. R. E. Lee.

R. H. CHILTON,
Assistant Adjutant-General."

The foregoing order not only gives us an insight into the abuses of the past, but also into the system adopted for the care and preservation of the animals during subsequent campaigns. In all green armies, the abuse of horses is a constant source of annoyance to the authorities, and one not familiar with the mounted service can scarcely realize how very greatly their neglect cripples the efficiency of the troops. The Confederate Army was fortunate in this respect, inasmuch as the teamsters and drivers were generally quite accustomed to the handling of horses. In the South nearly every soldier, whether in the infantry, cavalry, or artillery, had been a horseman from early youth, and they only needed to be directed and controlled in order to get the best results from their teams and mounts. Then, too, the Southern horse was generally of a better breeding and hardier stock than the heavier animals of the North, and Northwest, in which draft blood preponderated. Especially was this true in Virginia, where many blooded sires were owned by the gentry. Hardly a farmer in the State but owned a number of superior horses. The great sport of the people, since early colonial days had been fox-hunting, and therefore the original supply of horses was drawn from those trained in cross-country runs, and inured to the hardships of field and forest. Such animals were peculiarly fitted for military usage when properly fed and cared for, and largely accounted for the effectiveness of the mounted men of Lee's army before the animals were exhausted by the strain of continuous campaigning.

For the trains a large supply of mules was available, animals especially adapted to the rough work exacted of them, and requiring far less forage and attention than horses. Yet the supply was not unlimited, and became scarcer and scarcer as the war progressed and successes enabled the enemy to take from the Confederacy the great breeding grounds of Louisiana, Mississippi, Alabama, Tennessee, Kentucky, and Missouri.

So far the field artillery had been little troubled with the disease known as "sore tongue and soft hoof," which was ravaging the horses of McClellan's Cavalry, and which early in November had attacked Stuart's mounts to such an extent that the Commander-in-Chief in a letter to the latter took occasion to refer to the matter in a spirit of particular concern.*

As early as November 14 the necessity of purchasing horses in Texas for Stuart's Cavalry had impressed the Secretary of War, and before the 20th, Maj. Hart had been directed to secure 1,000 in that quarter. These small animals were of course unsuited for artillery draught purposes, but their purchase tended to relieve the situation in Virginia by leaving the heavier horses for the light batteries.

On October 2, obedient to the instructions of the Commander-in-Chief, Gen. Pendleton made an extensive report on the condition of the Field Artillery. Declaring the number of light batteries too large, some he stated to be inadequately officered, and some, though well commanded and entitled to the highest respect for the honorable service they had rendered, so reduced in personnel and horses as to preclude the possibility of restoring them to efficiency by reason of the expense and enormous number of horses such a step would entail. He proposed that the fairest possible standard be adopted to determine which batteries should be dis-

---

*Rebellion Records, Series I, Vol. XIX, Part II, p. 703.

banded, their officers relieved from duty, and their men, horses, and equipment distributed among those batteries retained in service. The proposed test to be applied consisted of: First, services rendered; second, the efficiency of the officers; and third, the existing conditions and prospects of the battery as a whole. In summing up his recommendations in this respect, he wrote:

"1st. Laudable service undoubtedly entitles a company to honorable continuance, provided it be not forbidden under one or both of the other conditions.

"2d. Officers thoroughly efficient have a prior claim. Good service for a season, under special circumstances, may have been rendered where some essential requisites for maintaining a battery through protracted difficulties are lacking. To pass upon such characteristics is delicate, yet, under existing responsibilities, essential.

"3d. Where the two preceding conditions concur, it is probably best to invigorate a battery to the utmost practicable; but if either fails, in case of a company much reduced below the service standard, it would seem right to merge it in some others."*

In pursuance of such views, the Chief of Artillery then recommended that the four companies of the Washington Artillery of Louisiana be consolidated into two 6-gun batteries, for the reason that, in spite of their gallant and meritorious service and the generally high character of the officers, there seemed little prospect of recruiting them up to the minimum strength allowed with volunteers and conscripts from other States. Already, before entering Maryland, it had been necessary to attach to Walton's Battalion while at Leesburg, 32 Virginians, 5 from Leake's Battery, and 27 from Anderson's, and these men were urgently needed for the batteries of their own State. Without these there remained but 212 men present and 227 present and absent for the four Louisiana batteries, or an average strength at best of but 57 men. Under the existing battalion organization of four 4-gun batteries, with a forge and a battery wagon, and three escort wagons for each battery, 310 horses were required, in addition to those

---

*Rebellion Records, Series I, Vol. XIX, Part II, p. 647.

for battalion headquarters, whereas if consolidated, 210 horses would suffice, and the two resulting batteries with a strong personnel and 12 guns would be more effective than 16 pieces distributed among four weak batteries.

The ten batteries of Col. Brown's reserve command, or the First Virginia Regiment, were recommended to be consolidated into six batteries by disbanding Wyatt's, Young's, Ritter's, and Coke's batteries, the first three of which were on duty in Richmond. It was urged that 1st Lieuts. Thurmond, Pendleton, and Robertson, of Wyatt's, Coke's, and Ritter's batteries, respectively, should be by all means retained in the Artillery, as also 2d Lieut. S. H. Hawes, of Coke's.

In Jones' reserve battalion, it was proposed to consolidate the four batteries into two, by disbanding Wimbish's, and Turner's batteries for inefficiency. In this battalion, Capt. Peyton of the Orange Battery was recommended to be dropped for continued absence and unfitness for command, 1st Lieut. Fry to be promoted to succeed him. Certain other promotions and dismissals among the officers were recommended.

Lieut.-Col. Cutts' Battalion of four batteries was proposed to be consolidated into three, by relieving the officers of Capt. James A. Blackshear's Georgia battery and distributing 22 of his men to Ross's, 29 to Lane's, and 42 to Patterson's batteries, of the Sumter Battalion, thus raising the personnel of each to 150 men present for duty. The Sumter Battalion was one of the strongest in personnel in the Army at this time.

Nelson's reserve battalion, of four batteries, it was also thought, should be reduced to three by disbanding Ancell's Fluvanna Battery, and by dropping Capt. C. T. Huckstep, retaining 1st Lieut. John L. Massie, an admirable officer, and promoting him captain in Huckstep's place, while 1st Lieut. B. F. Ancell was recommended to be assigned to duty with the resulting battery. Many other changes in the officers of the battalion were recommended.

Thompson's Battery, or Grimes' of Portsmouth, was also reported below the standard, and it was proposed to consolidate it with the other two batteries, Moorman's and Huger's, of Saunders' Battalion, R. H. Anderson's Division.

In every case the battalion commanders were to select for the batteries retained the best material, horses, and equipment of the disbanded units, turning in any surplus that might remain.

In the case of other batteries to be disbanded, the recommendations were as follows:

For unfitness for their duties all the officers of Lloyd's Battery, of Cutts' Battalion, were to be relieved and of his 85 men, 55 to be assigned to Manley's Battery of Moore's Battalion, McLaws' Division, and 28 to Reilly's Battery, Frobel's Battalion, Hood's Division, these batteries being all from North Carolina.

Chapman's Dixie Battery, mustering but 32 men present for duty, was to be disbanded and its men and horses assigned to Pegram's Battery of Walker's Battalion, A. P. Hill's Division.

The Wise County Battery, or Brown's, having but 48 men on the rolls, and its gallant captain having been seriously wounded, was to be disbanded and its men and horses transferred to Col. Lee's Battalion. The record of this battery was especially fine. It had served with distinction in every battle from Bull Run to date, and lost two commanders, Capts. Alburtis and Brown.

The Hanover Battery, or G. W. Nelson's, with but 60 men, was also to be disbanded, 20 of the men going to Kirkpatrick's Amherst Battery of Nelson's reserve battalion, and 40 to Woolfolk's Ashland Battery of Lee's Battalion. Capt. George Washington Nelson, though highly regarded as a fighter by his superiors, was thought to be better fitted for duty as a cavalry aide than as a battery commander.

With 52 men and 50 horses on its rolls, J. R. Johnson's Battery, of Bedford County, but recently organized, instead of being given the 48 horses called for by its captain, was to be disbanded and its men equally distributed to Dearing's and Stribling's batteries.

Rogers' Loudoun Battery, though having rendered good service, was to be disbanded since its captain was absent, its lieutenants indifferent, and its prospects poor. Its 45 men were also to be transferred to Stribling's Fauquier Battery.

The Thomas Artillery, or Anderson's Battery, an organization with a splendid record, had become so reduced in efficiency that it had not been allowed to accompany the Army into Maryland. The 29 men still on duty with this battery, and the 27 to be returned to it by the Washington Artillery Battalion, with its 22 remaining horses, and two senior lieutenants, were to be assigned to Caskie's Hampden Battery.

Capt. Leake's Battery, its service having been principally on the South Carolina coast, bearing but 48 men and 58 horses on its rolls, all in poor condition, was to be consolidated with Carter's King William Battery.

The Magruder, or T. J. Page's Battery, was to be disbanded, its 45 men and 25 horses being assigned to Col. Lee's Battalion. Capt. Page himself was recommended for duty on Col. Lee's staff, and Lieut. Magruder for retention in the service.

Though eulogized by Gen. A. P. Hill and his Chief of Artillery for the service it had rendered in several actions, Fleet's Middlesex Battery was to be broken up, 46 of its men having been assigned to Woolfolk's, Ancell's and Marmaduke Johnson's batteries at Leesburg. For insubordination, and misconduct, its officers were still under arrest and awaiting trial by court-martial. The payrolls, descriptive lists, horses and material had all been greatly neglected, and 50 of its men reported sick when but four were actually unfit for service. It had no sergeants and no roll existed when the men were transferred.

Stribling's and Bondurant's batteries required much work to place them in serviceable condition.

The changes thus proposed and already effected by the Chief of Artillery involved a reduction of the Artillery by 19 batteries. The entire number borne on the rolls of the Army of Northern Virginia had been 73, so that under the proposed reorganization but 54 batteries were contemplated in addition to the horse artillery.

When the unusually hard service which Lee's artillery had experienced, the general unpreparedness of the Confederate government for the arming and equipping of such a large number of batteries, the peculiar requirements of the arm and the utter lack of training on the part of all its men and many of its officers are taken into consideration, one is not surprised at the recommendations of the Chief of Artillery. On the contrary, the condition of the Artillery at this time in many respects is surprising and argues well for those who had charge of its organization and equipment, and especially for the officers who had led the batteries in battle. The fact that so few officers had proved unsuitable to the artillery service, a service most exacting in its many requirements, is a high tribute to the character of the Southern soldier. But as has been pointed out before, the men of the South were peculiarly adapted to mounted service in the field, and the Army of Northern Virginia was exceptionally favored by circumstances in having a large number of officers available who by no means were mere untrained volunteers. In addition to numbers of efficient artillerymen of the Old Army, such as Magruder, Alexander, Lee, and Pelham, were a great many who had received superior instruction in gunnery at the Virginia Military Institute, under Gilham and Jackson, such as Crutchfield, Walker, Carter, Carpenter, Cutshaw, Chew, Truehart, Latimer, and many others. With a backbone of officers of this character, the efficiency of the Field Artillery was readily to be accounted for. It was perhaps more favored than any other branch of the service in the quality of its officers, with respect to the junior as well as the senior grades. Among the lieutenants of the Field Artillery were to be found many trained and able officers who could not have been induced to transfer even with advanced rank from the service of the guns, which held for them a peculiar fascination. For this reason, men like "Jimmie" Thomson, the Carpenters, Milton Rouse, Huger, and Breathed, were found for years serving as mere subalterns in the Artillery.

The recommendations of Gen. Pendleton were almost immediately adopted, the only departure from them being with respect to the reduction of the Washington Artillery Battalion in deference to Col. Walton's objections, who represented that the circumstances attending the organization of his battalion, and its acceptance into the service of the Confederate States in its original form were peculiar. Unwilling to violate any arrangement or agreement which might have been made in the past, Gen. Lee decided to retain the battalion intact, except that the weakest section of Miller's Battery was directed to turn in its guns to the Ordnance Department. *Special Orders No. 209, A. N. V., October 4, 1862,* in which the proposed changes were made effective, were then forwarded to the Secretary of War and, his attention being called to the fact that the measure was imperatively necessary, his approval was requested. The reduction of Walton's Battalion to three batteries was urged if it could be done without breach of faith, and the meritorious officers relieved from duty recommended to be retained in their present grades, and, if necessary, commissioned in the Provisional Army as ordnance or artillery officers.

To insure the speedy and proper reorganization of the Artillery as ordered the Chief of Artillery was authorized and directed to associate with himself in the work Cols. J. Thompson Brown and Stephen D. Lee.

On October 8, the Secretary of War advised Gen. Lee that his action, though supported by the Adjutant-General, was in his own opinion without authority of law, but that in view of the imperative necessity therefor, he had induced the President to recommend legislation to supply the defect, meanwhile withholding his own decision. The question, a purely political one, fortunately resulted in no embarrassments to Gen. Lee, who was firmly supported by the President and the Adjutant-General. But one may rest assured the reorganization met with serious objections, and produced many heart-burnings, on the part of those most affected, namely, the inefficient officers who were thereby relieved from duty. Upon some of the officers whose commands were disbanded necessary hardships were of course entailed, and such was the case with Capt. John R. Johnson.*

The tri-monthly return of October 10 shows an encouraging increase in the number of men with the batteries. On that date, for Lee's and Walton's battalions, together containing 10 batteries, the personnel is given as 35 officers, 738 men present for duty, with an aggregate present and absent of 1,107 men. The average effective battery strength was, therefore, over 70 men, and on paper about 110.† But Col. Brown's six batteries mustered at this time only 13 officers and 311 men, or an average strength of but 51 men present, the same on paper being nearly 90 men. In the Reserve Artillery, that is in Cutts', Jones', and Nelson's battalions, composed of 8 batteries, a total of 54 officers and 858 men was reported present with an aggregate of 1,027 present and absent. The average effective strength of the reserve batteries was therefore about 107 men. A considerable increase in the number of Brown's effectives, that is 8 officers and about 100 men, appears in the return of November 10.

Before the middle of October and before the consolidation of the batteries and the turning in of the surplus guns, some 40 in number, had been effected, the activity of the enemy became noticeable and in the midst of his work Gen. Pendleton was ordered to pre-

---

*Rebellion Records, Series I, Vol. XIX, Part II, p. 662. See Gen. Lee's letter to Gen. Early on the subject of Capt. Johnson.
†Ibid., p. 660.

pare to move at a moment's notice since it was not designed to give battle about Winchester. But fortunately a further respite ensued and the work of reorganization and equipment continued.

The fine ordnance captured at Harper's Ferry proved a great bone of contention among the battery commanders. Enough requests for McClellan's 73 field pieces were received to have made the issue of double the number necessary in order to fill all the demands. The material of the Artillery was quite deficient, and was a cause of much anxiety to all concerned. As late as December 5, Gen. Lee wrote the Secretary of War, that during the past campaigns he had been much handicapped by the superiority of the Federal artillery over his own, a fact which he attributed in part to the greater experience of the enemy's gunners but principally to the better quality of their ammunition and ordnance. Though these advantages were being rapidly diminished by the increasing efficiency of his artillery personnel and the substitution of heavier guns for the light pieces with which his batteries were originally armed, yet the disparity was still keenly felt. The ammunition, he stated, was being more carefully prepared, and captured ordnance had been made full use of, but long-range pieces were urgently needed. If sufficient metal could not otherwise be secured for their manufacture, he recommended that the Chief of Ordnance melt up the old bronze 6-pounders, and if necessary a part of the 12-pounder howitzers for the purpose of recasting 12-pounder Napoleons. The best material for field service in his opinion were 12-pounder Napoleons, 10-pounder Parrotts, and the improved 3-inch rifles. Batteries armed with such pieces would, he declared, greatly simplify the question of ammunition supply by reducing the number of calibers in use, and the weight of metal to be transported. For special service, he requested to be supplied with additional 20- and 30-pounder Parrotts, closing his communication with an urgent recommendation that the subject of field artillery material receive the immediate consideration of the War Department, and the remark that "the contest between our 6-pounder smooth-bores and the 12-pounder Napoleons of the enemy is very unequal, and, in addition, is discouraging to our artillerists."*

This communication was at once referred to Col. Gorgas, Chief of Ordnance, who returned a circular of his department showing that J. R. Anderson & Co., of the Richmond Tredegar Works, had already been given directions to work night and day to turn out material such as Gen. Lee desired, and that Col. Baldwin, Chief of Ordnance, A. N. V., had been requested to turn in all the discarded pieces both at Staunton and with the Army to be recast. This circular, dated November 13, 1862, was as follows:

"Until further order, no artillery will be made except the following caliber:

"Bronze—Light 12-pounder Napoleon guns; caliber, 4.62.

"Iron—For field battery of maneuver, 10-pounder Parrotts, banded; caliber, 2.9. For field battery of reserve, 20-pounder Parrotts on 12-pounder carriages; caliber, 3.67. For siege guns, 30-pounder Parrotts on 18-pounder siege carriages; caliber, 4.2."†

These guns were to be forwarded to the Army as rapidly as completed, and, as we shall see, a few of the heavier ones were received during the first days of December.

Early in October a court of inquiry was appointed to investigate the circumstances connected with the disorderly withdrawal of the two infantry regiments of Lawton's command, which had been left as a support for the Reserve Artillery at Shepherdstown. But in the records no suggestion of misconduct on the part of the artillery officers is to be found, a significant fact for those who insinuate lack of persistence on the part of Gen. Pendleton and his subordinate commanders. If at any time during the months of September and

---

*Rebellion Records, Series I, Vol. XXI, pp. 1046-7. Letter of Gen. Lee to Secretary of War. Also see Ibid., p. 1048, Lee to Gorgas.
†Ibid.

October the Chief of Artillery appeared to be lacking
in energy, despite the results he actually accomplished
in the matter of collecting material, horses, and stragglers, in addition to his routine duties during the campaign, and in looking up woolen mills and arranging for
the manufacture of clothing and equipment, subsequent
thereto, along with the labor of personally directing the
reorganization of the Artillery, it is only necessary to
state that every communication of Gen. Lee bears the
imprint of his undiminished confidence in Gen. Pendleton, whose unfortunate physical condition was nevertheless well known to the Commander-in-Chief. While
on the Peninsula, he had contracted a severe case of
malaria, which would have justly entitled him to a leave
of absence from field duty while recuperating. The
anxiety, exposure, and loss of rest during the days and
nights, especially from the 14th to the 20th of September had brought on him a return of his debilitating
malady. But despite much actual suffering and frequent enforced prostration, the old officer refused to relinquish his labors and kept bravely at his post.

That Gen. Pendleton did not possess the vigor of
youth and the initiative which goes with it is undoubtedly true, and there were no doubt those in the service
who would have brought to the office he filled superior
qualities in many respects. Pendleton certainly did not
possess the forceful character of Gen. Hunt, the Federal Chief of Artillery, but he did possess a conservative and mature judgment which Gen. Lee evidently
highly valued. Although but 53 years of age at this
time, Gen. Pendleton was aged beyond his years, and
an old man in the Army of Northern Virginia where the
greatest were so young. Jackson, the Hills, Hood, Mc-
Laws, and even Longstreet, were many years his juniors,
and in his association with his Chief of Artillery, a man
of the most intellectual temperament and Christian
character, Gen. Lee, himself senior in point of age to
most of his officers, must have found much agreeable
relief from the cares and harassments of his awful responsibility.

Then there was another factor entering into Pendleton's retention in a position of so great importance and for which, in the opinion of many a man of greater professional aptitude, and more forceful traits of character, mental and physical, might have seemed better suited. Pendleton was the senior in age of all others in his arm of the service, senior even to Walton. Besides, he was a graduate of West Point, which fact added to the priority of his claim. Should he have been relieved from active command, as he might well have been by reason of his physical condition, a serious question as to his successor would at once have arisen and a host of aspirants would have entered into the jealous turmoil incident to the necessity of such a selection. The retention of Pendleton as Chief of Artillery by Gen. Lee is but another evidence of the latter's sagacity, for he realized that he was still free to assign those duties requiring the vigorous qualities of youth to Pendleton's lieutenants whenever circumstances seemed to demand it, and yet retain the many admirable qualities, especially as an administrator, possessed by the senior.

There were covert insinuations made during the war that Gen. Pendleton was lacking in courage, and similar suggestions have recurred since its close. Instead of combating such a belief on the part of those who gave credence to it, Gen. Alexander has strengthened the voice of the scandal-mongers by never failing to take a slap at his own chief. It is not intended here to assert that Gen. Alexander ever declared Pendleton to have lacked courage, but he does expressly charge him in his book with inactivity both in the Peninsula and in the Maryland campaign in such words as to leave a loop-hole for those maliciously inclined. He, of all others, must have known that Gen. Pendleton was not a coward. The Army gossip was well known to him, and it was his duty to express himself in unequivocal terms, if not to defend his former commander. The writer has made it his duty to discuss the matter of Gen. Pendleton's bearing with many of the latter's former subordinates, and no evidence of the truth of the scandalous charges has been found. On the contrary, Capt. William T. Poague, a man of the most dauntless courage and of the highest Christian character, declare that on a number of occasions when exposure was necessary he witnessed the bearing of Gen. Pendleton under fire, and that he was as calm, self-possessed, and apparently as courageous, as any man could well be. Capt. William Gordon McCabe, as intrepid an officer as was to be found in the Army of Northern Virginia, and possessing those qualities which made him the adjutant and fit companion of Pegram, also denies from personal observation that Gen. Pendleton was lacking in courage.

That Pendleton possessed ample courage is a fact exceptionally well established by Lee's regard for him. Gen. Lee did not gather about him, in offices of high trust, men with weak hearts, but that Pendleton was not given to unnecessarily exposing himself and that he was not a man with the reckless bravery of youth is no doubt true. So much by way of defense of an able and courageous officer.

While the Artillery had been resting and recruiting in camp near White Post, its reorganization was completed, the guns captured at Harper's Ferry equitably distributed among the batteries, including the two 20-pounder Parrotts, and in addition two Whitworth rifles, the latter brought up from Richmond. These important pieces were credited with a range of five miles.

The batteries were now formed into organized battalions as fully as possible. The battalions previously formed really possessed little organization as tactical units, but were merely collections or groups of battery units possessing practically no tactical cohesion. The divisional batteries fell under the control of a senior officer simply in his capacity of chief of artillery, and his functions were administrative rather than tactical.

On November 7, the returns of the Army showed the following assignment of the Artillery:

With the First Corps, in command of which Longstreet had been retained with the rank of lieutenant-general, were 30,319 infantry, and about 1,620 artillery, with 112 guns, of which 54 were light smooth-bore pieces.

In the Second, or Lieut.-Gen. Jackson's Corps, were 30,054 infantry and about 1,740 artillery, with 123 guns, of which 53 were also light smooth-bore pieces.

The Reserve Artillery, consisting of Brown's, Cutts', and Nelson's battalions of 12 batteries, 16 rifled, and 20 smooth-bore pieces, mustered at this time an aggregate personnel of 900.

The horse batteries were with the cavalry division of 7,176 men.

The aggregate of Lee's Army November 17 was, therefore, 71,809 men and 291 guns.

Within the next two weeks, however, a considerable change in the Artillery occurred, for the returns of November 20 show a different organization, as follows:

In the First Corps were 5 divisions under McLaws, R. H. Anderson, Pickett, Hood, and Walker, with 2 reserve battalions of artillery of 6 and 4 batteries, respectively, and a personnel of 623 men.

The divisional artillery of the First Corps was assigned as follows: McLaws' Division, Cabell's Battalion, 4 batteries, 18 guns; Anderson's Division, 4 batteries, unorganized, 18 guns; Pickett's Division, 3 batteries, unorganized, 14 guns; Walker's Division, no artillery. Thus in the First Corps with 28,453 infantry, we find 24 batteries with a total personnel of about 1,463 men, and 99 guns, or a proportion of a little over 3 guns per 1,000 men of the infantry.

In the Second Corps were 4 divisions under Ewell, D. H. Hill, A. P. Hill, and Taliaferro, respectively, with Latimer's Battalion of 6 batteries and 26 guns assigned to Ewell; Jones' Battalion of 5 batteries and 22 guns to D. H. Hill, Walker's Battalion of 7 batteries and 28 guns to A. P. Hill; Brockenbrough's Battalion of 5 batteries and 22 guns to Taliaferro.* With the

---

*The battery assignments will be given later.

30,312 infantry of the Corps, there were then 23 batteries with a total personnel of 1,380 and 98 guns, or about the same proportion of guns to infantry as in the First Corps.

The Reserve Artillery consisted of Brown's Battalion with 6 batteries, Cutts' with 3 batteries, and Nelson's with 3 batteries, with a total personnel of 718 men and 36 guns.

With the entire Army of 38 brigades of infantry, aggregating 58,765 men, we therefore find 59 batteries with 233 guns, or a general proportion of about 4 guns per 1,000 infantry.

Two additional batteries of horse artillery had now been raised, to the commands of which Capts. M. W. Henry and M. N. Moorman were assigned.* Pelham had meanwhile been promoted, taking command of the battalion of 5 horse batteries, the old Stuart Horse Artillery falling to his former lieutenant, Capt. James Breathed, than whom no more gallant gunner ever pulled a lanyard. With Pelham's 5 batteries, viz., Chew's, Breathed's, Hart's, Moorman's, and Henry's, were 22 pieces, a number of them imported Blakelys. To the 8,846 men of Stuart's Cavalry, the horse artillery with a personnel of about 300 men, bore a proportion of about $2\frac{1}{2}$ guns per 1,000.

With the Army of Northern Virginia, November 20, 1862, composed of 58,765 infantry, and 8,846 cavalry, there were 63 batteries with a total personnel of 3,861, and 252 guns, in by far the highest state of efficiency, except as to horses and clothing for the men, yet attained by Lee's artillery.

Forage being all but exhausted around Winchester late in October, Gen. Pendleton, who had completed the work of reorganization, was sent by Gen. Lee to explore the routes over the Blue Ridge Mountains and ascertain the capacity of Fauquier and Loudoun counties to the east for maintaining the Army.

*Henry's Battery was formed by dividing Pelham's original battery. Henry was soon promoted major and succeeded in command of this battery by McGregor. Moorman's Battery was simply converted from a light to a horse battery.

Now let us go back and follow the operations of the cavalry, in which the horse artillery had of course been engaged.

Only two days of rest were allowed Stuart's command after his return from Chambersburg, for on the 16th of October two Federal columns had advanced, one under Humphreys from Shepherdstown to Smithfield, composed of 6,000 infantry, 500 cavalry and a horse battery, and the other under Hancock from Harper's Ferry to Charles Town, consisting of 1½ divisions of infantry, 4 regiments of cavalry, and 4 pieces of artillery. The purpose of the Federal reconnaissance was to develop, if possible, during Stuart's supposed absence, the whereabouts of Lee's army.

Humphreys' force was skillfully opposed by Stuart in person with Fitz Lee's Brigade, reënforced at Kearneysville near Shepherdstown by Winder's Brigade of infantry, where only a most determined attack on the part of the Federals succeeded in forcing the Confederates back. On the following day Stuart was joined by Hampton's Brigade, and after reaching Leetown, from which point Humphreys reconnoitered towards Smithfield, the Federal column retraced its steps.

Hancock's column had, meanwhile, been opposed by Col. Munford with several regiments of cavalry, one piece of Chew's horse battery, and three pieces of the 3d Company of Richmond Howitzers under Capt. B. H. Smith, Jr. The most stubborn resistance on Munford's part failed to prevent Hancock from occupying Charles Town where he remained until noon on the 17th, when he returned to Harper's Ferry. In the report of his operations, Col. Munford made special mention of the gallantry of Capt. Smith, who lost a foot and was captured in Charles Town as his last piece was retiring from the field. He also commended Lieut. J. W. Carter, of Chew's Battery, who although wounded early in the day returned to his gun as soon as his wound was dressed.

Having ascertained by means of this reconnaissance that the Confederate Army was still in the Valley, McClellan crossed the Potomac at Harper's Ferry with two divisions of the 9th Corps and Pleasonton's Cavalry and pushed back the hostile pickets east of the mountains as far as Snicker's gap. While Gen. Lee was preparing to meet the Federal advance, Stuart with Fitz Lee's Brigade, and Breathed's and Henry's horse batteries with 6 guns under Maj. Pelham, crossed over the mountains into Loudoun County, bivouacking near Bloomfield on the night of the 30th. So depleted was the cavalry by the disease known as "greased heel" among the horses, that the brigade numbered less than 1,000 men. After driving a small force of the enemy's cavalry from Mountville on Goose Creek, Stuart pursued to Aldie, where he met the head of Bayard's Cavalry Brigade coming from Washington, which he defeated in a sharp encounter, driving it to the cover of its artillery well posted on a line of hills east of the village. Pelham's batteries had not been able to keep up with Stuart, but soon arrived and, dashing into position, engaged the Federal guns. Bayard was soon forced out of his position, and during the night, after a vain effort to make a stand, fell back to Chantilly.

While these movements were in progress, D. H. Hill's Division of Jackson's Corps had been dispatched by Gen. Lee to the vicinity of Paris and Upperville, via Ashby's Gap, and on November 1 Stuart disposed his troops to cover its front. Learning that Pleasonton was advancing upon Philemont, he moved through Union to meet him. Pleasonton drove in Stuart's advanced guard, but declined to attack his main column. On the 2d of November, Pleasonton's cavalry brigade with Pendleton's horse battery was reënforced by a brigade of Doubleday's infantry division and a New Hampshire battery, thus giving the Federals the preponderance of artillery in the proportion of 12 to 6 pieces, a circumstance which gave Stuart much concern.

The successful resistance he had been able to oppose to the enemy was in large measure due to the skillful handling of his guns upon which he constantly depended. Maj. McClellan, Stuart's Chief-of-Staff, writes: "Two spirits more congenial than Stuart and Pelham never met on the field of battle. Stuart's fondness for the use of artillery was almost excessive; Pelham's skill in its management amounted to genius. Stuart and Pelham imparted to the horse artillery an independence of action and celerity of movement which characterized it to the end of the war, and which was nowhere equalled or imitated, except in the same arm of the Federal service. The achievements of the batteries attached to both the Federal and Confederate cavalry are worthy of a separate record, and of the careful attention of military men."*

Such were the views of the Confederate cavalrymen regarding their horse batteries and gunners and when expressed by the Chief-of-Staff himself they bear particular weight.

Just what Chew was to Jackson and Ashby, Pelham was to Stuart. "It is doubtful," says Gen. Munford in a letter to the author, "if either could have accomplished what they did without these remarkable artillerymen."

Notwithstanding Pleasonton's superior force, Stuart offered him resistance near Fleetwood on November 2. About 8 A. M. the Federals began to deploy both their infantry and cavalry and some 6 or 8 pieces of artillery in his front, and Stuart, dismounting his troopers, took position behind the stone fences which were very numerous in that section, affording both sides excellent cover. "Having to watch all the avenues leading to my rear, my effective force for fighting was very much diminished, but the Stuart Horse Artillery, under the incomparable Pelham, supported by the cavalry sharpshooters, made a gallant and obstinate resistance, maintaining their ground for the greater part of the day, both suffering heavily, one of our caissons exploding from the enemy's shot."†

---

*The Campaigns of Stuart's Cavalry, McClellan, p. 173.
†Stuart's Report.

It was during this engagement that Pelham performed a feat of arms second only to that which he was
soon destined to accomplish at Fredericksburg. Conducting a howitzer some distance in advance of his
cavalry supports to a hill, and concealing the piece, he
opened fire upon a body of the enemy's cavalry in the
valley beneath him, putting it to flight, and then pursuing the panic-stricken men actually captured their
standard, a number of their arms, equipments, horses,
and some prisoners as well, without the loss of a single
gunner or horse of his own battery.

But, in spite of Pelham's prowess, the enemy returned and enveloped the Confederate position which
compelled Stuart's withdrawal to Seaton's Hill, about
a mile in rear, where the Federals were held at bay until
dark. Repeatedly assailing this position, Pleasonton
was each time repulsed by the fire of Pelham's guns,
the latter sighting the pieces himself. And such was
the accuracy of Pelham's aim that on one occasion he
struck down a color bearer with a single shot at a range
of 800 yards.

During the night Stuart withdrew his command to
Upperville, where he proposed to offer further resistance on the 3d. Pleasonton was again reënforced, this
time by Averell's Cavalry Brigade and Tidball's Horse
Battery, whereas the only reënforcements acquired by
Stuart was Hardaway's Battery, with a Whitworth gun
from D. H. Hill's Division, which had moved back
through the gap toward Front Royal.

About 9 A. M. Pleasonton attacked Stuart, who resisted him as upon the preceding day until late in the
afternoon, when the Confederates withdrew. As the
Federals approached Paris and Ashby's Gap, Hardaway's Whitworth opened upon them at long range, one
of its shells killing Gen. George D. Bayard, of the Federal Cavalry. This same gun, under the same officer,
was later stationed on the extreme right near the Yerby
house at Fredericksburg, and all through the battle
greatly annoyed Burnside's troops on the plain below.

Meanwhile, the fact had been discovered that McClellan's whole army was advancing southward, and on October 27, Longstreet's Corps had been set in motion to confront it, while Jackson remained about Millwood keeping D. H. Hill opposite Ashby's Gap. The Reserve Artillery was ordered to follow Longstreet at a convenient distance and to encamp upon its arrival at Culpeper. The reserve ammunition train under Col. Alexander accompanied Pendleton. Moving on the 1st of November, and marching *via* Nineveh, Front Royal, Chester Gap, Gaines' Cross-Roads, and Sperryville, the column reached camp at Culpeper on November 4. On the 6th, Col. S. D. Lee, who had acquired a distinguished reputation as an artillerist, and to whose advice at Sharpsburg the Commander-in-Chief had himself deferred, was relieved from the command of his battalion of artillery and ordered to Richmond, receiving there his promotion as a brigadier-general of infantry, and assigned to duty at Vicksburg, Miss. The following day, Lieut.-Col. E. P. Alexander, Chief of Ordnance, A. N. V., was placed in command of Col. Lee's Battalion, but retained immediate charge of the reserve ordnance train, until relieved of ordnance duty and permanently transferred to the Artillery on December 4. On that date, Lieut-Col. Briscoe G. Baldwin, a graduate of the Virginia Military Institute, who had served since the beginning of the war as assistant ordnance officer, was promoted Chief of Ordnance, A. N. V., vice Alexander relieved. Until the surrender at Appomattox, Col. Baldwin fulfilled his responsible office with great success.*

The transfer of Alexander in reality entailed only a slight promotion, but in effect it was more than the mere advancement incident thereto. His abilities as an organizer, and his reputation as a youthful officer with exceptionally mature judgment, as one possessing unusual professional learning, coupled with wide experience in many branches of the service, and as a man

---

Rebellion Records, Series I, Vol. XXI, p. 1046.

of great initiative, and yet not too bold, was well known
to the Army. The apparent desire on the part of Gen.
Lee was to secure to himself an artilleryman as good as,
if not better than, the one whom justice required him to
relieve, for the reward given Col. Lee by promoting
him was a well-deserved one.

Upon the occupation of Upperville by Pleasonton,
Stuart had divided his force, sending Col. Douglas with
three of his regiments to Piedmont, as a rear-guard for
his trains, and moving his remaining two regiments back
to Ashby's Gap, where he joined Hardaway's detachment supported by a small infantry force left with him
by D. H. Hill. Pleasonton, though showing little disposition to advance upon the Gap, had sent Averell's
Brigade after Stuart's trains, forcing the latter to dispatch Rosser with his two remaining regiments to the
support of Douglas, while he repaired to Millwood for
instructions from Jackson. Stuart was directed to remain in the Valley, so as to be on McClellan's flank,
instead of following Longstreet.

Rosser joined Douglas on the evening of the 3d of
November at Markham's, to which point the latter had
retired, leaving Averell in possession of Piedmont. The
following morning Rosser offered the Federals battle.
The engagements which ensued resulted in the Confederates withdrawing after a stiff fight during which
reënforcements for Averell were sent up by Pleasonton.
As an artillery affair, the action at Markham's is notable on account of the superb gallantry of Henry's
horse battery. Averell reported that he actually
captured 300 of Rosser's men, and two of Henry's guns,
but was forced to relinquish them, which accords with
an unwritten tradition among the Confederate Cavalry
that on this occasion two of Henry's guns, one of which
was the Napoleon with which Pelham distinguished
himself at Fredericksburg, were most gallantly handled.
These pieces were manned by the famous "French Detachment," which, though surrounded by the Federal
cavalry, and attacked at the same time both in front

and rear, kept their guns in action while the gunners sang the Marseillaise Hymn, being finally relieved by a charge of one of Rosser's regiments. Though the incident is not officially recorded, the story, resting entirely upon tradition, but circumstantially corroborated by Averell's statement, is a pretty one and should be preserved. At any rate we know that Henry's Battery played an important part in the affair.

Rosser now retired to Barbee's Cross Roads, where he was joined by Stuart and Hampton's Brigade on the night of the 4th, and here Stuart determined to make a stand. Occupying the crest of the hill immediately north of the town with his artillery and sharpshooters, he held his main body at the Cross Roads. The enemy attacked at 9 A. M. and a brisk artillery duel ensued, lasting some hours. But Stuart, having been informed that the enemy had reached Warrenton, concluded that the attack upon him was but a feint, and at once withdrew along the Flint Hill and Orleans roads, the enemy not pursuing.

On November 7, Pleasonton attacked Stuart at Amissville, where he claimed to have captured two guns. Gen. Stuart, however, makes no mention of this loss. Moreover, in his report of the battle near Middleburg, on June 19, 1863, he distinctly declares that the Blakely gun, which he was compelled to abandon on that field, was the first which the horse artillery had lost during the war.

Pleasonton, following up Stuart on the 8th and 9th of November, came in contact with Longstreet's Corps at Corbin's Cross Roads on the 10th. Meanwhile, on the 7th, Burnside had relieved McClellan and soon the Federay Army was set in motion towards Fredericksburg, only to find itself again confronted by its vigilant adversary. W. H. F. Lee's Cavalry Brigade guarded the lower Rappahannock, while Hampton and Fitz Lee picketed the river above.

In all Stuart's operations up to this point, and in the reconnaissances that preceded the battle of Fredericks-

burg, in which the command was almost constantly engaged, either in fighting or marching, the Artillery took
an important part. Again Stuart pays his tribute to
Pelham. "The Stuart Horse Artillery comes in for a
full share of this praise, and its gallant commander,
Maj. John Pelham, exhibited a skill and courage which
I have never seen surpassed. On this occasion (Corbin's
Cross Roads, November 10, 1862), I was more than
ever struck with that extraordinary coolness and
mastery of the situation, which more eminently characterized this youthful officer than any other artillerist
who has attracted my attention. His *coup d'oeil* was
accurate and comprehensive, his choice of ground made
with the eye of military genius, and his dispositions always such in retiring as to render it impossible for the
enemy to press us without being severely punished for
his temerity." These are words which any soldier might
be proud to have used in connection with his name, and
when we consider that they occur in the report of a
cavalry commander, they should be all the more dear
to the artilleryman. In the same breath Stuart had to
say of the cavalry the following: "In all these operations, I deem it my duty to bear testimony to the gallant
and patient endurance of the cavalry, fighting every
day most unequal conflicts, and successfully opposing
for an extraordinary period the onward march of Mc-
Clellan." It should be observed that he does not
mention by name a single officer in his corps for especial
commendation, except the "incomparable Pelham."
This fact gives us some insight into the value he placed
upon the latter's services.

The camp selected for the Reserve Artillery at Culpeper, was an excellent one about a mile from the town,
where clear streams furnished water, and kept the meadows fresh late into the winter, and where woods sheltered
the animals from the bleak north winds. A brief though
welcome rest was here secured for the men and animals.

About this time the field batteries were inspected, and
in order to show the thoroughness of the system of in-

spection, the following abstract from Gen. Lee's comments on the report of Col. Edwin. J. Harvie, Inspector-General, A. N. V., concerning Frobel's Battalion, of Hood's Division, is quoted: "Capt. Reilly's Battery is spoken of as being in very fine condition, showing intelligence and highly-commendable pride in officers and men, that care having been bestowed upon horses, guns, etc., which secures true efficiency, and gives evidence that a due regard for the interests of the service and a proper attention on the part of officers will keep artillery horses in good order and guns and equipment serviceable.

"Captain Bachman's German Artillery is reported, with exception of 6 horses greatly reduced, as in fair condition; leather equipment, however hard and stiff, requiring Capt. Reilly's system to soften and supple them, the use of Neat's foot-oil, which he obtains from cattle-feet thrown aside at commissary pens.

"Capt. Garden's Palmetto Light Artillery reported as inferior to Capt. Bachman's, the horses showing neglect, axles of pieces and harness requiring grease. This battery, however, is reported as improving under your orders."*

Such sidelights as these are very interesting to the artilleryman. They present a familiar view of great value as well, and it would seem that the orders on the subject of the horses were being closely followed up. But while the equipment of the batteries was being carefully preserved, the necessities of the men were very pressing. Maj. John J. Garnett, appointed Inspector of Ordnance and Artillery of Longstreet's Corps, November 14, 1862, reported on that date 95 of Col. Alexander's 360, and 64 of Col. Walton's 225 men, barefooted.† Yet, on the 19th, these battalions and the Reserve, the men of which were in an equally deplorable condition, were ordered to break camp and march over muddy, half-frozen roads towards Fredericksburg, special injunctions against straggling be-

---

*Rebellion Records, Series I, Vol. XIX, Part II, p. 719.
†Ibid., Vol. XIX, Part II, p. 721, and Vol. LI, Part II, p. 645.

ing announced, and the gunners were directed to dismount and assist the horses by hand in all difficult places.*

Meanwhile, in the absence of Col. Walton, Col. Alexander had been acting Chief of Artillery, Longstreet's Corps, Col. Walton not returning from sick leave until December 8. Capt. Eshleman commanded the Washington Artillery Battalion in his absence.

After a rough march, extending over five days, the Reserve Artillery arrived in camp near Fredericksburg on November 23. Winter had set in unusually early and with great severity. Provisions were scarce, and often there were short nations even for headquarters. But the men, though barefooted and without heavy clothing, were in excellent spirits and bore their privations with cheerful fortitude, and they made every effort by building shelters to save their horses. It was a noble but pathetic sacrifice on the part of these men, with half-frozen feet, to plod about the hillsides and thickets cutting brush in order that the teams might rest and be protected from the bitter night winds. Similar performances are rarely recorded even in the history of war.

*Ibid., Vol. LI, Part II, pp. 649, 650.

CHAPTER XXI

On November 7, the six Federal corps comprising the Army of the Potomac, which lay between the Bull Run Mountains and the Blue Ridge, contained 125,000 officers and men present for duty, with 320 field pieces.* Accompanying the order of this date superseding McClellan with Burnside, were urgent suggestions that something be done by the latter. Organizing his army into three Grand Divisions under Sumner, Franklin, and Hooker, the new Federal commander promptly issued his orders, and Sumner moved towards Fredericksburg on the 15th, reaching Falmouth just opposite the town two days later. The remainder of Burnside's army took up the march on the 16th, concentrating in rear of Sumner on the 19th.

The batteries of Lee's army were at this time assigned as follows:

1ST CORPS (Longstreet)

Col. J. B. Walton, Chief of Artillery

R. H. ANDERSON'S DIVISION

1. Donaldsonville Battery,   Capt. Victor Maurin.
2. Norfolk Blues Battery,   Capt. C. R. Grandy.
3. Norfolk Battery,   Capt. Frank Huger.
4. Pittsylvania Battery,   Capt. John W. Lewis.

McLAWS' DIVISION

Col. H. C. Cabell, Chief of Artillery

1. Manly's North Carolina Battery,   Capt. B. C. Manly.
2. Pulaski (Ga.) Battery,   Capt. J. P. W. Read.
3. 1st Co. Richmond Howitzers.   Capt. E. S. McCarthy.
4. Troup (Ga.) Battery,   Capt. H. H. Carlton.

---

*The strength of Lee's army at this time we have seen was 71,809 men with 275 guns, the latter soon reduced to 255.

PICKETT'S DIVISION

Capt. James Dearing, Chief of Artillery

1. Lynchburg Battery,   Capt. James Dearing.
2. Richmond Fayette Battery,   Capt. Miles C. Macon.
3. Fauquier Battery,   Capt. R. M. Stribling.

HOOD'S DIVISION

Maj. B. W. Frobel, Chief of Artillery

1. Charleston German Battery,   Capt. W. K. Bachman.
2. Palmetto (S. C.) Battery,   Capt. H. R. Garden.
3. Rowan (N. C.) Battery,   Capt. James Reilly.

RANSOM'S DIVISION

1. Petersburg Battery,   Capt. J. R. Branch.
2. Stafford Battery,   Capt. R. L. Cooper.

CORPS RESERVE

1ST RESERVE BATTALION

Col. J. B. Walton

1. 1st Co. Washington Artillery,   Capt. C. W. Squires.
2. 2d Co. Washington Artillery,   Capt. J. B. Richardson.
3. 3d Co. Washington Artillery,   Capt. M. B. Miller.
4. 4th Co. Washington Artillery,   Capt. B. F. Eshleman.

2D RESERVE BATTALION

Lieut.-Col. E. Porter Alexander

1. Bedford Battery,   Capt. Tyler C. Jordan.
2. Bath Battery,   Capt. J. L. Eubank.
3. Madison (La.) Battery,   Capt. George V. Moody.
4. Richmond Battery,   Capt. William W. Parker.
5. Brooks (S. C.) Battery,   Capt. A. B. Rhett.
6. Ashland Battery,   Capt. P. Woolfolk, Jr.

2D CORPS (Jackson)

Col. Stapleton Crutchfield, Chief of Artillery

EWELL'S DIVISION

Maj. A. R. Courtney, Chief of Artillery

1. Charlottesville Battery,   Capt. James McD. Carrington.
2. 4th Md. or Chesapeake Battery, Capt. Wm. D. Brown.
3. Henrico or Courtney Battery,   Capt. J. W. Latimer.
4. 1st Maryland Battery,   Capt. Wm. F. Dement.
5. Louisiana Guard Battery,   Capt. Louis E. D'Aquin.
6. Staunton Battery,   Capt. W. L. Balthis.

D. H. HILL'S DIVISION

Maj. Hilary P. Jones, Chief of Artillery

1. Hardaway's Alabama Battery,   Capt. R. A. Hardaway.
2. Jeff Davis Alabama Battery,   Capt. J. W. Bondurant.
3. King William Battery,   Capt. Thomas H. Carter.
4. Morris Louisa Battery,   Capt. R. C. M. Page.
5. Richmond Orange Battery,   Capt. C. W. Fry.

A. P. HILL'S DIVISION

Lieut.-Col. R. L. Walker, Chief of Artillery

1. Branch (N. C.) Battery,   Capt. A. C. Latham.
2. Richmond Battery,   Capt. Wm. G. Crenshaw.
3. Fredericksburg Battery,   Capt. Carter M. Braxton.
4. Richmond Battery,   Capt. Marmaduke Johnson.
5. Richmond Letcher Battery,   Capt. Greenlee Davidson.
6. Pee Dee (S. C.) Battery,   Capt. D. G. McIntosh.
7. Richmond Purcell Battery,   Capt. Wm. J. Pegram.

TALIAFERRO'S DIVISION

Capt. J. B. Brockenbrough, Chief of Artillery

1. Alleghany Battery,   Capt. Joseph Carpenter.
2. Danville Battery,   Capt. George W. Wooding.
3. Richmond Hampden Battery,   Capt. W. H. Caskie.
4. Lee Battery,   Capt. Charles J. Raine.
5. 2d Rockbridge Battery,   Capt. J. A. M. Lusk.

2D CORPS RESERVE BATTALION

1ST RESERVE BATTALION

Col. J. Thompson Brown

1. Warrenton Battery,   Capt. James V. Brooke.
2. Powhatan Battery,   Capt. Willis J. Dance.
3. 2d Co. Richmond Howitzers,   Capt. David Watson.
4. 3d Co. Richmond Howitzers,   Capt. Benj. H. Smith.
5. 1st Rockbridge Battery,   Capt. William T. Poague.
6. Salem Battery,   Capt. A. Hupp.

ARMY RESERVE ARTILLERY

Brig.-Gen. William Nelson Pendleton

1ST RESERVE BATTALION

Lieut.-Col. A. S. Cutts

1. "A" Battery, Sumter (Ga.) Batt.,   Capt. H. M. Ross.
2. "B" Battery, Sumter (Ga.) Batt.,   Capt. George M. Patterson.
3. "C" Battery, Sumter (Ga.) Batt.,   Capt. John Lane.

2D RESERVE BATTALION

Maj. William Nelson

1. Amherst Battery,   Capt. Thomas J. Kirkpatrick.
2. Fluvanna Battery,   Capt. John L. Massie.
3. Georgia Regular Battery,   Capt. John Milledge, Jr.

MISCELLANEOUS BATTERIES

1. Ellis' Georgia Battery,   Lieut. W. F. Anderson.
2. Hanover Battery,   Capt. George W. Nelson.

From the foregoing schedule of assignments, it is seen that during the Fredericksburg campaign not less than 63 batteries, exclusive of the five horse batteries, were with Lee's army.

On December 20, the six batteries of Brown's Battalion, which was early taken from the General Reserve and assigned as the corps reserve of Jackson's Corps, mustered 20 officers and 434 men present, and reported an aggregate of 684 present and absent. The average effective battery strength was therefore about 75, and on paper 114. Walton's and Alexander's battalions, with a total of 10 batteries, mustered 41 officers and 629 men present and reported an aggregate present and absent of 966. The effective battery strength was therefore 67, and on paper 96. The eight batteries of the General Reserve reported an effective strength of 42 officers and 683 men, which gives an average effective battery strength of about 90 men, and on paper there appeared an average strength of 120.

Taking the average effective battery strength throughout the Army at 3 officers and 70 men, there must have been in the Army of Northern Virginia an effective artillery personnel of about 200 officers and 4,500 men, while on paper the strength of the Field Artillery was not far from 7,000 officers and men. But for all practical purposes a minimum of 4,500 should be deducted from the figures given for Lee's Infantry, which generally included the Artillery personnel.

Had Burnside upon reaching Falmouth on the 17th immediately crossed the river and taken possession of the hills along the southern bank of the Rappahannock, as he might have done, Gen. Lee would have been compelled to take up a defensive position nearer Richmond. That the possibility of having to fight nearer Richmond was considered by Lee as late as the 23d is shown by the fact that Maj. Moore's Third North Carolina Artillery Battalion which had reported to Pendleton for duty, and which he had ordered on the 22d to rejoin G. W. Smith's command at Richmond, was on the former date directed to occupy a strong position on the south side of the North Anna, and commanding the important railroad bridge between Fredericksburg and Richmond.* Moore reached Richmond before receiving the modification of his orders, but at once retraced his steps, occupying the designated position on the 28th.

Instead of seizing the southern bank, however, Burnside simply occupied the Stafford Heights, or the hills on the north side of the river overlooking the plain of

---

*The horses of this battalion were in poor condition, and Maj. Moore was directed to do all in his power to make them more serviceable.

Fredericksburg, crowning them with his heavy guns
under protection of which he began the construction
of bridges for his crossing.   The narrowness of the
Rappahannock, its winding course, and deep bed presented opportunities to accomplish this work practically
unopposed by the Confederates, unless they should elect
to sacrifice their men and guns to the overwhelming fire
of Burnside's batteries.

There were only three Confederate cavalry regiments
under Col. Ball guarding the river at Fredericksburg
when Burnside commenced his movement in that
direction, but on the 15th Gen. Lee ordered a regiment
of infantry and Lewis' Battery from near Richmond
to reinforce this small force.   Reaching Fredericksburg
on the 17th, just before Sumner's advance guard arrived at Falmouth, a spirited duel occurred between
Lewis' Battery and a rifled battery under Capt. Petitt,
the latter having decidedly the best of it as his adversary
had but four very inferior guns.

Upon reaching Falmouth, Sumner had favored an
immediate crossing, but Burnside would not consent
thereto, and for three weeks delayed while the Confederates each day rendered his ultimate move less probable
of success.   "Opportunity in war is like a woman," Napoleon said.   "If you fail to meet her to-day, you need
not expect her to meet you to-morrow."   Burnside's
golden opportunity, offended by his neglect to keep the
tryst, had eluded him forever.

On the 20th, his whole army was near Fredericksburg.
Longstreet on the day before reached the town, *via*
Raccoon and Morton's fords, and rapidly disposed two
of his divisions with their artillery on the hills to the
west and southwest of the place.   On the 21st, Sumner
summoned the town to surrender before 5 P. M., under
penalty of being bombarded the next day.   Of this Gen.
Lee wrote: "The weather had been tempestuous for
two days, and a storm was raging at the time of the sum-
mons.   It was impossible to prevent the threat to shell
the city, as it was completely exposed to the batteries

on the Stafford hills, which were beyond our reach. The city authorities were informed that while our forces would not use the place for military purposes, its occupation by the enemy would be resisted, and directions were given for the removal of the women and children as rapidly as possible. The threatened bombardment did not take place; but in view of the imminence of the collision between the two armies, the inhabitants were advised to leave the city, and almost the entire population, without a murmur, abandoned their homes. History presents no instance of a people exhibiting a purer and more unselfish patriotism, or a higher spirit of fortitude and courage, than was evidenced by the citizens of Fredericksburg. They cheerfully incurred great hardships and privations, and surrendered their homes and property to destruction, rather than yield them into the hands of the enemies of their country."*

Although the weather was most inclement, the thermometer being near zero, almost the whole population removed and found the best shelters they could, cheerfully giving up their homes to the battlefield. The neighboring country homes and churches were filled, some times with dozens of families, to whom rations were issued by the commissaries, and many women and children encamped in the forest in brush and blanket shelters, where the sight of their cheerfully borne sufferings nerved many a heart for the coming struggle. Though the Federals did not shell the town after certain representations were made by the Mayor, it was inferred from the negotiations that the bombardment would simply be postponed, and this understanding was responsible, Gen. Alexander tells us, for the construction of many of the earthworks which contributed to the repulse of Burnside's assaults on Marye's Hill.†

By November 22, Longstreet's other two divisions, with Lane's Battery, had arrived and the First Corps extended its line along the southern heights, overlooking the town, from Banks' Ford on the west to Hamilton's Crossing on the east.

*Rebellion Records, Series I, Vol. XXL, p. 551, Lee's Report.
†Gen. E. P. Alexander's Southern Historical Papers, Vol. X, p. 383.

Lee and Jackson had both originally opposed resisting Burnside's advance at this point, by reason of the fact that in case he was defeated the Stafford Heights, which he would undoubtedly hold with a strong rear guard, afforded him too free an escape, whereas if he were overthrown at such a point as the North Anna, with lengthened communications, his retreat would be far more difficult.* But Burnside's procrastination enabled Lee to so strengthen the Rappahannock position that he deemed it wise to avail himself of it for defense in preference to the weaker one on the North Anna, in spite of the foregoing objections and Jackson's reiterated protests. The developments had simply committed the Confederates to the line along which they had gradually by circumstances been led. The Federals had placed themselves behind a broad river, and it is an established fact that rivers influence military operations mainly in that they delay the movements of the attacker, and during the passage afford the defender an opportunity of engaging the attacking troops in detail. Gen. Lee knew this and could not bring himself to relinquish what he perceived to be a real, present advantage for those advantages which might develop later on, provided war with its uncertainties played him no tricks. He also saw that in failing to seize the southern bank of the river, Burnside had placed it in his power to occupy it in force, the time allowed him further enhancing his advantage by enabling the development of communications which only served to increase the mobility of the defense.

Lee's principal fear, and also Jackson's, was that, in view of the difficulty of the attack on a well-defended river line, which is rarely attempted, Burnside would refrain from making an effort to force the Confederate position, and resort to a turning movement. But Lee in dealing with the Federals always minimized the probability of their acting upon the soundest strategical principles. He had learned by experience that they

*Military Memoirs of a Confederate, Alexander, p. 287.

were prone to disregard the rules of war, and was ever willing to take advantage of their neglects. Thus he had divided his army before Pope, and again in the Maryland campaign, where he also fought the battle of Sharpsburg with his back against the Potomac, and with but one avenue of retreat, and that one behind an exposed flank, and later he indulged in a most risky division of force at Chancellorsville. Lee's strategy was based upon his own moral supremacy over his adversaries. In declining to be bound by established principle, he simply availed himself of that supremacy, increasing it by success, instead of neglecting an element which made it possible for him to disregard the dictates of the most approved general principles. With an army possessing great cohesion, in addition to the utmost mobility of its parts, a change in tactics in the face of the enemy is possible, although the whole has been seemingly committed to the original plan of attack. But Lee knew full well from experience that the ever present bungling of his opponents, even when in the execution of a prearranged plan, would render unsuccessful any extemporaneous maneuvers on their part, however brilliantly conceived. At any rate, he felt that tactical surprises, if attempted, would be more apt to present him with opportunities than to take him unawares. We should not attempt to solve Lee's strategy by cut and dried formulæ. The controlling factor in his problems was the character of his adversary, and of that factor he never lost sight. Pitted against a Napoleon and a Moltke, Lee would never have fought the battles of Second Manassas, Sharpsburg, Fredericksburg, and Chancellorsville.

Finding the Confederates determined to contest his crossing at Fredericksburg, the Federal commander endeavored to effect one at Skinker's Neck, about 15 miles below the town, but the premature appearance of a number of gunboats near Port Republic and other movements in that direction disclosed his design, and D. H. Hill's and Early's divisions were ordered up from Orange Courthouse to oppose the projected crossing. When Burnside endeavored to push across on the 5th, he found it impossible, Hill's and Stuart's artillery having driven off his gunboats. In this work Pelham's horse batteries and Milledge's and a section of Poague's Battery, were most effective, in spite of Gen. D. H. Hill's sarcasm directed at the gunners. These batteries were provided with very poor ammunition, and the flight of the heavy projectiles were, therefore, most erratic. As they tumbled short, or burst in air, or failed to burst altogether, the remarks of "Old Raw-Hide" were extremely biting.*

When Burnside's balloonists reported Jackson's divisions massed behind the guns, he abandoned his project in this quarter and determined to effect his crossing at Fredericksburg. His plan was now to cross at the town, also to push a force around Lee's right at Hamilton's crossing, thus interposing between the main Confederate force and that at Skinker's. Something had to be done, and he could no longer delay in making his effort.

On December 10, Burnside finally issued his orders for an attack. In his report he said: "I concluded that the enemy would be more surprised at a crossing, at or near Fredericksburg, where we were making no preparations, than by crossing at Skinker's Neck, and I determined to make the attempt at the former place. It was decided to throw four or five pontoon bridges across the river, two at a point near the Lacy house, one near the steamboat landing at the lower part of the town, one about a mile below, and if there were pontoons sufficient, two at the latter point."†

The pontoon trains were to arrive at their designated positions by 3 A. M. December 11, and at daylight the construction of the bridges commenced. It was estimated that these bridges, from 400 to 440 feet long, with the thermometer at 24 degrees above zero, would

---

*Gen. D. H. Hill, a man of much dry wit and very outspoken, an able officer whose opportunities were unequal to his abilities, had received the name of "Raw-Hide" by reason of his having shod numbers of his men with moccasins.
†*Rebellion Records*, Series I, Vol. XXL, p. 87.

be completed in between two and three hours, the working parties being screened from the Confederate fire by the town. On the Stafford hills above the plain 179 Federal guns were placed in position during the night to cover the proposed crossing, and to keep down any hostile musketry fire from the opposite bank. Where two bridges were thrown, one was to be reserved for the batteries.

Among the Federal guns which crowned the Stafford Heights, from Falmouth to Pollock's Mill, a distance of some 3½ miles, were six 20-pounder Parrotts, and seven 4.5-inch siege guns so placed as to be able to sweep the town of Fredericksburg and the plain, and to bring to bear a formidable fire upon the most distant heights occupied by the Confederates.

The Federal commander had not reckoned upon the all but impregnable character of Lee's position. It might have been turned, as pointed out by Jackson, by way of the upper fords, but a frontal attack was destined to fail. The Rappahannock, navigable to Fredericksburg, is there about 140 yards wide. The Stafford Heights along the north side have an elevation of about 150 feet, and completely command the plain below and across the river. On the southern side is Taylor's Hill close to the river and 1½ miles upstream and across from Falmouth. From Taylor's Hill an irregular ridge extends southeastward, which leaves between it and the river a plain gradually spreading out to a width of a mile at Fredericksburg, and increasing below the town. This plain, with an elevation of about 30 feet above the river, is intersected by Hazel Run just below, Deep Run about half a mile, and the Massaponax River some four miles beyond the town, all flowing through deep, ravine-like banks from the highland across the plain to the river. Lengthwise, and near the middle from end to end, the flats were intersected by a broad, unpaved, worn-out stage road, which descending into the plain from Taylor's Hill passed through the town, and bifurcated just short of the Massaponax, its

branches leading to Port Republic and Richmond
respectively. This hollowed-out roadway was bordered
by ditches and low cedar hedges which afforded excellent
cover for infantry. Not far from the base of the foot-
hills southeast of the town, and almost parallel to the
stage road, ran the Richmond and Fredericksburg Railroad, with an embankment about 3 feet high, almost
parallel to the stage road until it reached Hamilton's
Crossing, at which point it turned southward towards
Richmond.

The northern end of the ridge or that portion consisting of Taylor's, Stanbury's, and Marye's Hills,
was for the most part open, though much cut up by the
headwaters of Hazel Run. The center and southern
portions, consisting of Lee's Hill, the Howison house
ridge, and Prospect Hill, were covered with a dense
wood, which nowhere extended into the plain, except
between Deep Run and Hamilton's crossing where the
swampy sources of a small stream were covered with
brush and timber to a point midway between the railroad and the stage route. Low in front, with an elevation above the plain of between 40 and 50 feet, with
many indentures sloping towards the river, the ridge
gradually rises to a crest, lower in elevation than that
of the Stafford Heights, and then falls towards the
south and the Massaponax. About one mile from the
northern limit of the plain, and directly east of Stansbury's and Marye's hills, was the main part of Fredericksburg, a town of about 4,500 inhabitants, extending halfway back to the base of the ridge from the
southern bank of the river. On the north edge of the
town was a mill, to which two branches of a canal flowed,
one from the river at the base of Taylor's Hill, and one
from the river immediately opposite Falmouth. Leaving the western branch of the canal at a point just in
front of Stansbury's Hill, a race or ditch ran almost
parallel to the river and behind the town into Hazel
Run. This ditch lay in a depression, the south bank
of which also afforded cover for troops. Leaving the

COLONEL WILLIAM NELSON
ACTING CHIEF OF ARTILLERY, SECOND CORPS

center of the town in a direction perpendicular to the river, the Plank Road to Orange Courthouse, crossing the mill race, passed over Marye's Hill. The Telegraph road, leaving the town just below the former, continued parallel with it until it reached the foot of Marye's Hill, when it followed the base around to its right for half a mile to Hazel Run, which it crossed, then ascended Lee's Hill, whence it took a southeasterly course toward Richmond. At the circular base of Marye's Hill, this road, hollowed out by long use, was bounded by stone fenses.

The Confederate position was well taken along the ridge to the south and west of Fredericksburg, that is from Taylor's Hill to the Massaponax. Realizing the inequality of the contest which he would be called upon to wage when activities were resumed, Lewis on the extreme left had, on the night of the 23d, taken up a position on the plateau to the right of and below the summit of Taylor's Hill and had begun to construct gun-pits and epaulments for his guns. Meantime, Grandy's Battery of Anderson's Division had also arrived, coming up from Richmond, and prepared a position in like manner on Lewis' right. On the 17th, Gen. Lee, learning of Sumner's movement, had ordered Longstreet with McLaws' and Ranson's divisions, with Cabell's Battalion of the former, and Branch's and Cooper's batteries of the latter, to Fredericksburg, and Lane's Battery of the General Reserve with its two 20-pounder Parrotts, was sent forward with them. Lane at once intrenched on the heights overlooking the bend of the river above Falmouth, retaining his position on the extreme Confederate left. Overruling Col. Cabell's advice to occupy Taylor's Hill with his artillery, McLaws placed his batteries on the crest of the hill between the Telegraph road and Howison's barn. In this position Read, with one 10-pounder Parrott, one 12-pounder howitzer, and one 3-inch rifle; Manly with three 6-pounders, one 3-inch rifle and two 12-pounder howitzers; Carlton with two 10-pounder Parrotts; and

McCarthy with two 3-inch rifles, at once intrenched, while the less effective pieces of their batteries were held under cover only to be used against attacking infantry. Cooper's and Branch's batteries of Ransom's Division joined Cabell's batteries, the former with three 10-pounder Parrotts also intrenching.

On the 19th, the remaining divisions of Longstreet's Corps were ordered up, the Reserve Artillery and the ordnance train following. At the same time Jackson was directed to proceed to Orange Courthouse with all dispatch. Leaving his old camp on the 19th, he set out from Winchester on the 22d. He passed through Strasburg on the 25th, and Madison Courthouse on the 26th, and reached his appointed rendezvous, without a straggler, the following day, having marched 120 miles over execrable roads in eight days, two of which were devoted to rest.

On the 29th, Lieut. W. F. Anderson in command of Ellis' Georgia Battery arrived from Richmond with two "Long Toms,"* or 30-pounder Parrotts, sent forward by Col. Gorgas, and pits were constructed for them near the Howison house group under Col. Cabell, and his assistant, Maj. S. P. Hamilton.

In the meantime the two remaining batteries of Anderson's Division, Maurin's and Huger's, came up and intrenched immediately north of the Plank Road, and Moorman's, Macon's, and Stribling's batteries of Pickett's Division, joined Cabell's group on the ridge behind McLaws' Division, all except one 10-pounder Parrott of Macon's and a similar piece of Moorman's being well retired. Frobel's Battalion of Hood's Division, consisting of Reilly's, Bachman's, and Garden's batteries, intrenched along the northern part of the ridge, running from Deep Run to Hamilton's Crossing, the guns commanding the valley of the stream.

Of Walton's reserve battalion which occupied Marye's Hill from the Telegraph to the Plank Road, two 3-inch

---

*"Long Tom" was the name given the big 30-pounder Parrott captured at First Manassas. The name was also used by the Boers in 1899 to designate their big guns.

rifles and one 10-pounder Parrott of Squire's 1st Company, two 12-pounder Napoleons of Miller's 3d Company, and two 12-pounder howitzers and two 12-pounder Napoleons of Eshleman's 4th Company, or nine pieces in all, were placed in individual pits and epaulments on the military crest. Richardson's 2d Company was on detached duty with Pickett's Division. Further to the left and beyond Maurin and Huger, Alexander's reserve battalion occupied the Stansbury Hill, Rhett's Battery, however, being established south of the Plank Road; two rifles of Parker's Battery occupied pits in front of the Stansbury house, while his two howitzers were concealed behind the buildings for use against the infantry columns of the enemy. The batteries of Jordan, Woolfolk, and Moody were also held behind the rear crest of the plateau, from which position they could move into pits on the forward crest, or be sent to the most threatened points as needed. The sixth battery of the battalion, or Eubank's, joined Cabell's group behind McLaws, as did the General Reserve. The batteries under Alexander and Walton and those of R. H. Anderson's Division thus commanded the entire plain from Hazel Run northward to the westward bend of the river, as well as the opposite bank, at a range of 1½ miles, while Cabell's group of nearly 50 pieces could sweep the flats from Fredericksburg southward, crossing fire with Frobel's guns beyond Deep Run. The distribution of the artillery was excellent in every respect, and illustrates the correct method of guarding a line of river by a series of strong artillery groups so placed as to be able to concentrate their fire on the various approaches to the position to be held. Furthermore, the tactics employed were far superior to those at Antietam, for at Fredericksburg the inferior artillery was not ruthlessly exposed, but held entirely under cover until it could be effectively brought into action, thus concealing as well as protecting the lighter pieces from the superior fire of the enemy while the heavier guns, necessarily placed in position, were intrenched. The whole plan was most skillfully conceived.

Its main features were as follows: the long range pieces, protected by intrenchments, would engage in the preliminary action, conserving their ammunition and refraining from any waste in a useless duel with the superior artillery of the enemy. These guns were to inflict as much damage as possible, however, on the enemy while crossing the river and forming for attack, and to take advantage of all exposures on his part in whatever quarter of the field. In so doing they would necessarily disclose their positions. It was not expected that they could subdue to any great extent the hostile artillery fire. When the infantry columns of the enemy with their light batteries advanced to the assault and came within range of the lighter pieces, they would move into hitherto undisclosed positions, and open with the maximum effect, assisting in the overthrow of the attacking columns, before they were silenced by the guns of the enemy. So soon as the fire of the enemy's batteries of position were shifted to the fresh batteries, the heavier Confederate guns would be free again to play upon the hostile groups, shaking their fire, or to assist in the repulse of the infantry, as circumstances dictated to be best.

By reason of the character of the terrain, Gen. Lee had wisely determined only to resist the enemy after he had effected his crossing, and as the southern hills were commanded by the opposite heights, it became necessary to construct earthworks for his artillery. The work of locating the Confederate batteries had been assigned to Gen. Pendleton, who with the skillful aid of Cols. Cabell and Alexander and Capt. S. R. Johnson, of the Engineers, after making a most comprehensive reconnaissance, prepared the general plan of defense. In this work the services of Col. Alexander were of course invaluable. Both an engineer and an artilleryman of experience, he had constantly before him the necessities of communication, necessarily fore-most in the mind of one so familiar with the duty of ammunition supply. The Confederate dispositions were hence most judicious.

Until Lee's army was concentrated at Fredericksburg, the burden of the defense had fallen upon the Artillery. While Burnside's men were working like beavers planting their heavy batteries, Pendleton and his artillery officers had also been busily at work. The Confederate batteries, such as they were, were carefully classified and marked so that every staff officer might readily find them. So placed that the maximum field of fire might be secured to the guns, the best possible lateral communications were prepared by the engineers. In the preparation of the position, the services of the infantry as well as of the gunners were utilized to the utmost, and gangs of negroes were brought up to assist in the work of intrenching.

The weather was extremely severe during all this work. Lack of tools and frozen ground made the work slow, and when Burnside finally attacked, individual pits for about 40 guns had been dug, but these were without shelter for ammunition or infantry supports. Along the Telegraph road at the base of Marye's Hill a ditch had been dug on the lower side of the road and the dirt thrown forward and banked against the stone fence which bounded it. A work was constructed near the mouth of the Massaponax, in which Capt. Ross's Battery of the Reserve was placed to stop any gunboat which might pass Pelham's guns further down the river. Little artificial cover could be provided for the infantry, in view of the labor that intrenching entailed under the existing conditions. In this execrable weather the only shelter for the men, a few still without shoes, and most of them totally unprovided with adequate clothing, consisted of "lean-to's" constructed by throwing tarpaulins and blankets over poles, or fashioned with brushwood, leaves, and mud. But fire-wood was plentiful and in some way the men managed to keep the blood coursing through their veins. Provisions were none too bountiful. Beef on the hoof, cornmeal, and black-eyed peas comprised the great bulk of the commissary issues, coffee and hog meat being rare treats even for the general officers and their staffs.

On the morning of the 11th, Longstreet's Corps held the ridge in rear of Fredericksburg, with Anderson's, McLaws', Ransom's, Hood's, and Pickett's divisions, aggregating 33,400 infantry, and about 1,500 artillery-men, with about 100 guns.* Of Jackson's Corps, A. P. Hill's Division of 11,533 infantry, and about 450 artillerymen, with 7 batteries, was near Yearly's house, five miles south of Fredericksburg; Taliaferro's Division of 4,690 infantry, and about 325 artillerymen with 22 guns, was at Guiney Station, nine miles south of Fredericksburg; Early's Division of 7,340 infantry, and 380 artillerymen, with 26 guns, was at Skinker's Neck, 12 miles down the river; and D. H. Hill's Division of 8,627 infantry and 325 artillerymen, with 22 guns, was at Port Royal, 18 miles below the town.

Pendleton with the Reserve Artillery, less Brown's Battalion, now assigned as reserve of the Second Corps, with 752 officers and men, and about 20 guns, was in rear of Longstreet's line.

Of the cavalry division under Stuart, aggregating 9,146 present for duty, Hampton's Brigade was immediately on the left of Longstreet along the river and watching Banks' and United States fords; Fitz Lee's Brigade was with Longstreet; W. H. F. Lee's Brigade was along the river near Port Royal, and Rosser's Brigade was in rear near the Wilderness Tavern, watching the left flank and upper fords.

Including the staffs and the five horse batteries the grand total, present for duty, December 10, was 78,513 and about 250 guns, the largest concentrated army Gen. Lee had yet handled.

*The return of the 1st Corps for December 10 shows a total of 34,944 officers and men present for duty. See *Rebellion Records*, Series I, Vol. XXI, p. 1057. Of this number there were 37 officers and 586 men in Walton's and Alexander's reserve batteries, and there were 14 divisional batteries besides, with a total of not less than 50 officers and 840 men present for duty. Deducting the artillery personnel of about 1,500 officers and men from the total present for duty we have about 33,400 as the strength of Longstreet's Infantry.

Opposed to him was an army of 118,952 men and 324 guns, with reënforcements aggregating 27,724 men near at hand and actually *en route,* and in addition a force about Washington of 51,970 with 284 guns of position and 120 field pieces. For the advance upon Richmond and the defense of Washington, the Federals had, therefore, 198,546 men present for duty and about 900 guns. If Burnside should defeat Lee, Richmond would be lost. But if Lee defeated Burnside and captured his entire army, the most serious part of his work would not have begun.

Burnside's attempt to cross the river in his front had been expected for some days, notice of which was to be given the Confederates by the firing of two guns of Cabell's group. At 2 A. M. on the 11th, the pickets reported that pontoon trains could be heard in motion, and at 4:30 A. M. the Federal working parties had commenced to throw their bridges. About 5 A. M. the signal guns were fired and the Confederate brigades and batteries at once moved into their appointed positions, the latter having been held behind the crest of the ridge, so as not to disclose their whereabouts until they actually opened fire.

Gen. Lee had committed the task of resisting the crossing to Barksdale's Mississippi Brigade supported by a regiment or two from Anderson's Division. At Deep Run, the Confederate skirmishers having little or no shelter from the hostile guns, were capable of but little resistance, and before noon the Federals had completed two bridges at that point. At the town Barksdale's men, under cover of the houses, were more successful, repeatedly driving off the working parties until at last, about 11 A. M., the engineers abandoned the task. Burnside now ordered every gun in range to fire 50 rounds into the town. About 100 pieces responded with terrific effect upon the buildings, many of which were either completely demolished, or set on fire, but none of the Confederates were injured. The bombardment was simply one of those useless expenditures of ammunition resorted to for lack of more effective measures. The heavy fog of the morning had now almost disappeared, and the panoramic view from the Confederate position was superb. Gen. Alexander thus describes it: "The city, except its steeples, was still veiled in mist, which had settled in the Valley. Above it and in it incessantly showed the round white clouds of bursting shells, and out of its midst there soon rose three or four columns of dense black smoke from houses set on fire by the explosives. The atmosphere was so perfectly calm and still that the smoke rose vertically in great pillars for several hundred feet before spreading outward in black sheets. The opposite bank of the river, for two miles to the right and left, was crowned at frequent intervals with blazing batteries, canopied in clouds of white smoke.

"Beyond these, the dark blue masses of over 100,000 infantry, in compact columns, and numberless parks of white-topped wagons and ambulances massed in orderly ranks, all awaited the completion of the bridges. The earth shook with the thunder of the guns, and high above all, a thousand feet in air, hung two immense balloons. The scene gave impressive ideas of the disciplined power of a great army, and of the vast resources of the nation which had sent it forth."

But the grand cannonade failed to drive Barksdale's men from their posts of vantage, and again they opened fire upon the returning bridge builders. At last, at the suggestion of Gen. Hunt, still Chief of Artillery, Army of the Potomac, volunteers crossed the completed bridges under cover of the artillery fire, and approaching the town occupied the Confederate sharpshooters sufficiently to enable the bridges opposite the town to be completed, the attempt being resumed about 4:30 P. M. During the continuance of Barksdale's street fighting, which lasted until after dark, the Confederate batteries had for the most part remained silent by reason of the fog, which hid the crossings from view during the morning, making good practice impossible. The

orders against wasting ammunition in useless cannonades were most stringent. This was left to the enemy
who fired intermittently throughout the day upon the
Confederate position, inflicting only slight damage
upon the men and guns by reason of the works which
sheltered them.

Late in the day, observing a small column of hostile
infantry approach the upper pontoon bridge, Lewis'
Battery opened fire and drove the enemy behind the
Lacy house, and shortly afterwards it again fired upon
some cavalry and artillery which made its appearance
across the river, but the action of this battery was not
unnecessarily prolonged. Maurin's Battery near the
Plank Road also fired a few shots towards evening.

About 7 P. M., the Federals having occupied Fredericksburg, Col. Walton was directed to make his preparations to rake the streets of the town at the first signal
of their advance, and Ransom, who had posted his two
batteries, Branch's and Cooper's, on the Telegraph
Road, was ordered to do the same, also being directed
to secure tools from Gen. McLaws and connect the
small gun pits in his front with rifle-trenches.* Not a
gun was fired by Alexander's, Walton's, Cabell's, and
Frobel's groups during the day, though they had all
received orders during the early morning to do what
they could to impede the construction of the bridges.

Thus passed away Thursday, the 11th, on which day
Burnside only succeeded in throwing his six bridges, his
artillery utterly failing to uncover the Confederate batteries. Lee now ordered A. P. Hill and Taliaferro to
come up from the rear and relieve Hood and Pickett,
who were to close on the center and hold the ground
between Deep and Hazel runs. During the night, with
the thermometer 26 degrees above zero, Hill and Taliaferro completed their preparations, and, breaking camp
before daybreak, arrived at their designated positions
about noon on the 12th. Col. Crutchfield, who had preceded the movement of these divisions and reconnoitered

---

Rebellion Records, Series I, Vol. LI, Part II, pp. 661, 662.

the position assigned them, directed Col. Walker to select positions for his guns along the ridge from Hamilton's Crossing to Deep Run. As soon as they arrived, Col. Walker placed McIntosh's and Pegram's batteries with sections from Crenshaw's, Latham's, and M. Johnson's batteries, the latter commanded by Lieuts. Clutter, Potts, and Ellett, respectively, or a total of 14 guns, on the height immediately above the railroad on the extreme right of the ridge known as Prospect Hill.

Braxton's Battery in command of Lieut. Marye with 5, and Davidson's with 4 guns were sent to the left of the line, where they were mingled with those of Talia-ferro's Division. The 21 guns assigned to the left were placed in position as follows: just at Bernard's cabins and to their left 9 guns, consisting of 6 rifles, 2 Na-poleons, and one 6-pounder of the batteries of Raine, Caskie, and Braxton, all under the immediate charge of Capt. Davidson, and about 200 yards in front of these, to their right and across the railroad, 6 rifles, 3 Na-poleons, and three 6-pounders from the batteries of Carpenter, Wooding, and Braxton, all under the im-mediate command of Capt. J. B. Brockenbrough. Hood's three batteries meanwhile moved from their po-sition on the northern salient ridge south of Deep Run to one at the base of the hills north of the run and im-mediately across from Franklin's bridge.*

During the 12th, Sumner at the town and Franklin at the Deep Run bridges took over their grand divi-sions, which, when in line, extended from the center of the town towards Deep Run about parallel to the river and between it and the Richmond road. No attempt was made by the Federals on the Confederate position, nor did Gen. Lee make any serious opposition to the crossing, though the long-range guns were again ordered to inflict as much damage as they could upon the enemy.† Rhett's and Parker's batteries from their

---

*Henderson is mistaken as to the number of guns with the Light and Taliaferro's divisions. He shows a disposition of 47 guns; there were but 35. He counted Brockenbrough's group twice. See Crutchfield's Report, *Rebellion Records*, Series I, Vol. XXI, p. 636. Henderson merely copied the error of Allan. Alexander also copied the error.
†*Rebellion Records*, Series I, Vol. LI, Part II, p. 661.

positions near the Plank Road and the Stansbury house, respectively, fired upon the town, enfilading the main streets, but always drawing upon themselves a storm from the opposite bank. During the day one of Col. Cabell's batteries, discovering a light battery in position along the enemy's line, drove it beyond Deep Run, where it joined a number of others, all too far removed from the Confederate position to be harmful. Lewis' Battery on the extreme left of Longstreet's line was also engaged about 3 P. M., firing upon an infantry brigade, and later upon a cavalry column, which made their appearance at the ford opposite his position, and Maurin's Battery dropped a few 10-pounder shells among some skirmishers near the town, and occasionally fired upon the masses across the river.

About 2 P. M., the fog having lifted sufficiently to enable Col. Walton's gunners to see as far as the river, his batteries fired upon a column of the enemy below the town for a few minutes until it dispersed and sought cover behind the inequalities of the ground. Hundreds of rounds of ammunition were wasted by the enemy in a one-sided cannonade during the 12th. That night the various artillery commanders were informed that the enemy was expected to attack Longstreet's right and Jackson's front in the morning. Jackson was now ordered to Fredericksburg with Early's and D. H. Hill's divisions, both of which with their artillery arrived at Hamilton's Crossing about dawn on the 13th, Hill having marched 18 and Early 12 miles during the night. Upon arriving, Capt. Latimer, Acting Chief of Artillery, Early's Division, reported to Col. Crutchfield and was ordered to hold his six batteries under cover in rear. Behind D. H. Hill's Division on the extreme right, Capt. Carter, Acting Chief of Artillery, also held his five divisional batteries in readiness to relieve those under Col. Walker on Prospect Hill, and Col. Brown's Corps Reserve was kept under cover in the rear. Across the railroad from Prospect Hill were two of Stuart's cavalry brigades, and Maj. Pelham with sev-

eral horse batteries, and Milledge's and Lane's batteries of the General Reserve, the latter with two 20-
pounder Parrotts. In all, Pelham had 18 guns. An
imported Whitworth rifle of large caliber and great
range was posted on the wooded heights northeast of the
Yerby house in charge of Capt. Hardaway.

During the night Ross's Battery returned from its
position below the Massaponax, and was assigned to
Maj. S. P. Hamilton's group of Cabell's guns on the
hill behind McLaws. A section of 6-pounders from this
battery with Patterson's Battery of Cutts' Battalion
was dispatched to Hood's front in charge of Maj. T. J.
Page, Jr. Capts. Barnwell and G. W. Nelson were
now placed in charge of the two 30-pounder Parrotts
of Ellis' Battery on Lee's Hill. With Kirkpatrick's
and Massie's batteries, Maj. Nelson was then directed
by Gen. Pendleton to take up a position near the Telegraph Road, in rear of and commanding the plateau of
Marye's Hill, so that it could be swept if carried by the
enemy. Rhett's Battery was similarly stationed near
the Plank Road.

Burnside's belated plan was now to seize Prospect
Hill with Franklin's Corps, and Marye's Hill as well
as the heights occupied by Cabell's and Hamilton's batteries with Sumner's Corps. Franklin was to move
around to the right of Hamilton's Crossing and sweep
along the avenues of communication, which the Confederates had prepared in rear of their position, from
Prospect Hill to the Telegraph Road, thus connecting
with Sumner. The plan, if successful, would not only
cause the Confederates to evacuate their strong lines in
the woods along the base of the hills and behind the railroad embankment, but would prevent the withdrawal of
the artillery groups under Walker, Carter, Latimer,
Davidson, and Brockenbrough, in position along the
forward crest of the ridge. Hooker was to hold four divisions in support of Sumner and to send two to Franklin.

Burnside had detected the weakest point in the Confederate line, which was in A. P. Hill's front about op-

posite the middle of the ridge from Hamilton's Crossing to Deep Run. Although Jackson held a line of but
2,600 yards with 30,000 men or about 11 men to the
yard, his formation was very deep and not dense in the
front line held by A. P. Hill. Just to the left of Walker's
batteries, posted in a trench within the edge of the
woods, was Archer's Brigade of Hill's Division with its
left resting on a coppice extending well forward into
the flats. Beyond the coppice, but nearer the railroad
embankment, lay Lane's Brigade of the same division
with its right about 600 yards from Archer's left. In
the gap behind the coppice was an open field 200 yards
in breadth. About 500 yards in rear of the gap, along
the military road constructed by the Artillery as a
lateral communication, lay Gregg's Brigade. On
Lane's left rear was Pender's Brigade, in front of which
was Capt. Davidson's group of 9 guns, the 12 pieces
under Brockenbrough being in front of and across the
embankment from Lane. Field's Brigade supported
Walker's group on the extreme right and Thomas' Brigade was held in rear of Pender's right and Lane's left.
Across Deep Run was Hood's Division, with Frobel's
artillery group. Jackson's disposition had been made
before Early and D. H. Hill came up and they with
Taliaferro were left in the third line farther back even
than Gregg, a change under fire being deemed hazardous. His position was very similar to that occupied by
him at Second Manassas. In his front was the railroad embankment, in his rear were the wooded heights,
upon his flanks were the massed batteries under the general supervision of Crutchfield, and opposite his center
was the wood projecting beyond the embankment, forming the same defect from which he was again to suffer.
Maj. Von Borcke, a Prussian officer of Stuart's staff,
had on the 12th seen the danger lurking in the gap and
had suggested that the thicket should be levelled, but it
was considered too miry to be passable and no steps were
taken to correct the evil. Col. Crutchfield, who saw
that a space of 800 to 1,000 yards of Jackson's front

was undefended by direct artillery fire, examined the wood most carefully with a view to establishing howitzer batteries behind it, which by canister fire might keep it clear, but found it impracticable to do so in the time left him before the action, but he instructed Capts. Brockenbrough and Davidson to reserve their fire until the enemy's infantry had approached to within close range. By the fire of their advanced pieces he hoped that the approach to the wood would be commanded. Col. Walker's group could only cross-fire with them by firing very obliquely to the left.

Early in the morning, Meade's Division moved down stream about 700 yards beyond the ravine near the Smithfield house, and turning sharply to the right crossed the Richmond road. While Meade was forming his division in column of brigades opposite the coppice which projected from the dip in the ridge held by A. P. Hill, under cover of a rise in the ground between the road and the embankment, his supporting batteries opened a desultory fire upon the Confederate position as if feeling its strength, but no reply was elicited.

Maj. Pelham commanding Stuart's horse batteries, and the light batteries assigned to Jackson's extreme right, had moved his guns forward with the dismounted cavalry, which occupied a line extending from the southern base of Prospect Hill towards the river on the north side of the Massaponax. With the unerring eye of genius, he now seized the opportunity which the exposed flank of Meade's column presented him. Galloping forward with two 12-pounder Napoleons of Henry's Battery, along the road leading from Hamilton's Crossing to the Richmond Road, and concealing his movements by using the cover of the ditches and hedges, he gained a tangled ravine just beyond a marshy stream less than 400 yards from Meade's flank, from which point he opened a rapid fire upon the astonished Federals. Meade's leading brigade at once began to waver and seek cover, threatening to throw the whole division

in confusion, while four Pennsylvania batteries, called to
the left by Meade, and soon joined by two others, together sought to overthrow Pelham. One of his pieces
was soon disabled, but rapid changes of position enabled
him to defy the opposing batteries for nearly an hour,
though well in advance of Jackson's line and unsupported except by several small troops of dismounted
cavalry. Pelham finally retired in obedience to Stuart's
peremptory order, but not until his limbers had been
emptied, nor until he had delayed the advance of 4,500
Federals and caused Franklin to dispatch Doubleday's
entire division to guard Meade's flank, a task which absorbed its efforts during the remainder of the day. He
had also caused the explosion of one of the enemy's
caissons.

Upon his withdrawal, Pelham took up a position with
all the batteries under his command across the railroad
from Hamilton's Crossing, from which he was able to
cross-fire to some extent in front of Hill's center with
the guns of Brockenbrough's group advanced beyond
the railroad.

Gens. Lee and Jackson were present together on the
extreme Confederate right, and were eye-witnesses of
the contest between Pelham's Napoleon and the Federal batteries.

Franklin had now advanced several batteries to the
Richmond Road, which, together with the batteries on
Stafford Heights, for half an hour subjected the wooded
ridge occupied by Hill to a heavy cannonade, the effect
of which was generally slight, except upon Walker's
batteries. The position of these batteries, though obscured from the view of the enemy, were more in the
open than the infantry, but Walker's guns remained
silent, as did the infantry, reserving their fire for
Meade's column at closer range. About 11 A. M., the
Federal advance was resumed under cover of a great
number of guns, and when the first line came within
800 yards of Jackson's center the silent woods awoke.
First Walker, then Davidson, then Brockenbrough,

pushed their guns from the covert, and as Jackson's 35 guns, aided by those of Pelham to the right, which were promptly advanced, opened fire, the Federal leader realized the insufficiency of his artillery preparation. "From front and flank came the scathing fire; the skirmishers were quickly driven in and on the closed ranks behind burst the full fury of the storm. Dismayed and decimated by this fierce and unexpected onslaught, Meade's brigades broke in disorder and fell back to the Richmond Road."*

Upon Meade's troops the effect of Pegram's and McIntosh's fire from Walker's group was especially destructive, but the troops on their left were not so promptly checked. Gibbon's Division had come under the fire of Brockenbrough's and Davidson's guns, which succeeded in at once driving off the skirmishers with canister, but in doing so they disclosed their positions and drew upon themselves the concentrated fire of a number of field batteries which caused them much loss. Again and again the skirmishers advanced into the woods, and finally working around to the right, began firing upon the batteries. While serving as gunners, Capts. Brockenbrough and Wooding were both shot. The axles of two rifled field pieces in Wooding's and Caskie's batteries breaking from the recoil, and the ammunition of Raine's Battery proving so defective that none of the shells burst, it became necessary about 10:30 A. M. for Brockenbrough to retire from his advanced position, and for Col. Crutchfield to order Capt. Latimer, Early's Acting Chief of Artillery, who was holding his divisional batteries in reserve, to take the rifled section of his own, and the three rifles of Brown's Chesapeake Battery, under Lieut. Plater, to the left to replace the five pieces disabled or withdrawn.

For the next hour and a half an artillery duel, in which over 400 guns took part, raged over the whole field, and in some way the Confederate batteries managed to hold their own with the powerful ordnance of

---

*Henderson, p. 388.

the Federals. The fire of Crutchfield's three groups and Pelham's guns had almost alone hurled Meade and Gibbon back, so completely sweeping the open ground in Walker's front that the attack in that quarter was not renewed. Meantime Col. Crutchfield had also directed D'Aquin's Battery, and the Staunton Battery under Lieut. Garber, both of Latimer's Battalion, to join Maj. Pelham, to whom, about noon during the lull succeeding Meade's repulse, he also sent Graham's 10-pounder Parrott section of Poague's Battery, the rifled section of the 3d Howitzer's under Lieut. Utz, and a short while later, Watson's 2d Howitzers with two 10-pounder Parrotts and a brass rifle, and one 3-inch rifle of Dance's Battery, all of Col. Brown's Corps Reserve then being held in readiness behind Hamilton's Crossing. When these pieces reached Pelham, Gen. Stuart ordered Col. Rosser to take one of Watson's rifles under Lieut. Pleasants, and Dance's piece, and move out to the point from which Pelham had fired upon the enemy during the morning, but little good was now accomplished since the enemy's flank was well protected, and the horses and gunners suffered greatly before the pieces were retired.

Nothing had been accomplished by Reynolds' attack, except that Gibbon on Meade's right had succeeded, with great loss, in driving Brockenbrough's twelve pieces back across the railroad, the artillery on Jackson's left meanwhile having been reënforced by Latimer's fresh guns. The Confederate line, as a whole, remained unshaken, and its artillery, which had borne the brunt of the contest, with a few exceptions, had suffered slight loss, that having been more than made good by ordering into position a number of the batteries which had been held in reserve. Truly Second Manassas was being repeated.

Before Reynolds' attack on Jackson's line had come to a standstill, Burnside about 11 A. M. had ordered Sumner to make a diversion against Lee's left in favor of Franklin. Unfortunately for Sumner the strongest point of the Confederate position, Marye's Hill, was designated as his point of attack, and added to the impregnable character of the position was the necessity of his crossing the mill race between the heights and the town before the assaulting columns could deploy. Having crossed the obstacle, however, a rise in the ground enabled the Federals to deploy under cover. From this inequality of the ground the land, open and somewhat broken, gently rose to the Telegraph Road, at the base of Marye's Hill. Towards the left of the attacking column, the Hazel Run ravine, which separated Marye's Hill from Lee's Hill, or Cabell's position, ran out into the plain. Along the depression ran the unfinished roadbed of the Fredericksburg and Orange Railroad, which branched off from the main line, passing southward through the flats, just below the town. Between the old railroad bed, and the Plank Road lay the ground over which Burnside directed Sumner to advance.

At the base of the hill and in the wide roadbed of the Telegraph Road, sunken about four feet and artificially prepared by throwing dirt forward over the stone wall which bounded it, Gen. Cobb of McLaws' Division, with three regiments of infantry, was in position. From the point where the Telegraph Road struck the base of Marye's Hill and turned southward, the Confederate line was prolonged northward to the Plank Road by a shallow trench, in which the 24th North Carolina lay. All along the line the infantry could move under cover. To the rear and well above them, occupying a front of about 400 yards, were the nine gun-pits of Walton's Battalion, supported by Cooke's Brigade of Ransom's Division 200 yards in rear, and the remaining regiments of the same division 400 yards further back with Moseley's Battery of 6 guns. Walton's guns, 2 rifles of Maurin's and 3 pieces of Moody's Battery now north of the Plank Road, bore directly upon the approaches to Marye's Hill, and Cabell's and Hamilton's groups on Lee's Hill were able to cross fire in its front with Alexander's and R. H. Anderson's batteries on the Stansbury Hill, but only at a point well forward.

Sumner's troops had been formed in the town early in the morning, French's Division of the 2d Corps in the lead. When Longstreet detected signs of their advance, he directed Alexander "to throw a hundred shells down the streets of the city, and towards the (pontoon) bridges," and this fire had hardly begun when French moved forward about noon, Parker's, Rhett's, Moody's, and Maurin's batteries continuing their fire all the while. The instant French cleared the town, Walton's guns opened with great precision, the effect of their fire being so destructive that Longstreet himself sent him a note in which his congratulations were included, urging him by all means to keep his batteries well supplied with ammunition.* Cabell's heavier guns, including the two 30-pounder Parrotts under Capts. Barnwell and Nelson, also opened with effect until French succeeded in crossing the mill race about 300 yards from the town and so sought shelter behind the rise 400 yards from the base of Marye's Hill. Sturgis' Division, meanwhile, had been directed to support French's on the left. Thrown forward, Ferrero's Brigade and Dickenson's Battery were immediately brought under the fire of Cabell's guns on Lee's Hill, which completely commanded the ravine and the unfinished railroad bed by means of which the enemy was seeking to reach the right rear of Marye's Hill. The conformation of the ground was such that Walton's guns were unable to sweep down this ravine. Dickenson was almost immediately killed, and his battery disabled and withdrawn. Ferrero was checked by Cabell's fire and held under cover of a depression in the ravine from which his men engaged in a heavy musketry fire, principally upon the batteries on Lee's Hill. The various brigades and divisions which during the day endeavored to advance by way of the ravine all met the same fate. It was simply impassable for infantry.

---

*Rebellion Records, Series I, Vol. LI, p. 662.

During French's deployment, Arnold's regular battery went into action on the edge of the town and opened upon Marye's Hill, and the great mass of guns on Stafford Heights, which had been shelling the Confederate position generally, now concentrated their fire on Walton's batteries, the gunners of which behind their earthworks devoted their energies solely to the infantry columns of French, who had, after deploying, sent forward three regiments of skirmishers. As the line cleared the cover behind which the Federals had deployed, Cobb's Infantry from behind the stone wall rose and opened a rapid musketry fire upon it at a range of less than 500 yards, and Walton now began to hurl canister at the enemy until the skirmish line disappeared behind a low terrace about 250 yards from the Confederate Infantry, seizing some of the small houses on the Telegraph Road to the right. The remainder of Kimball's Brigade now reached Col. Mason's three regiments, but as Andrews' and Palmer's brigades left their cover they were swept from the field in great confusion by the fire of Walton's and Alexander's guns, a few only reaching Kimball's line, the great majority returning to their former position. After eleven separate efforts on the part of the Federals to reach the hill, a lull of about 20 minutes occurred while Hancock was preparing to attack. French, Sturgis, and Griffin had all been repulsed with great loss, and the Confederates were little shaken by the tremendous cannonade of the Federal batteries, although they had lost both their 30-pounder Parrotts by explosion, one bursting at the 39th and the other at the 54th round, after most effective use. Near the left one of these big guns under Capt. Nelson, Gens. Lee, Longstreet, and Pendleton had watched the awe-inspiring conflict, the Chief of Artillery himself frequently directing the fire of the big piece. Longstreet and Pendleton were both standing within 10 feet of it when it burst. A smaller Parrott was immediately substituted, and orders sent to Capt. Lane to bring the big

Whitworth to Lee's Hill from its position below the Massaponax in front of the Yerby house, but it did not arrive until after dark.

Before Hancock commenced his attack, Longstreet, desiring to drive Kimball's men from behind their cover, directed Capt. O. Latrobe of his staff to take a 10-pounder Parrott of Maurin's Donaldsonville Battery from out its pit, and, moving it forward to the left, enfilade the enemy's line. The attempt meant almost certain destruction, as two Federal batteries had been concentrating their fire throughout the morning on Maurin's gun-pits, having almost silenced his pieces after he had fired about 200 rounds. The suggestion was no sooner made than acted upon, however, but a staff officer alone was not to do the work, for Lieut. Landry directed his gunners to move the pieces forward by hand to the designated position. Before the first three shots were fired, five gunners were down, including the corporal, and as the piece was loaded for the fourth time, it was struck by a shell which destroyed a wheel. But the three shots directed by Landry and Latrobe were not wasted, for not only did the shells burst in the very midst of the crouching Federals, but the daring deed, seen by hundreds of the Confederate soldiers, inspired them in a way that nothing but such heroic actions on the field of battle can do. The names of Lieut. Landry, of Corporal Morel, of Cannoneers Dernon Leblanc, Francis Perez, Claudius Linossier, Adolph Grilke, and Francis Babin, are worthy of the best traditions of their ancestors who fought with the great Napoleon.

Just as Hancock's advance commenced, Ransom sent Cooke's Brigade to the crest of Marye's Hill, one regiment going down to the sunken road to reënforce the Georgia regiments, Cobb having been killed by a sharpshooter.

Hancock's superb division now pressed forward in column of brigades with intervals of 200 paces, Cook leading, then Meagher, with Caldwell in rear. Issuing from the town under a terrific artillery fire, they formed along the canal, and then charged up the slope towards the sunken road. On past French's isolated skirmishers dashed Hancock's men. As they advanced up the slopes towards the Confederate position, the supporting batteries from the Stafford Heights were caused to cease firing upon Marye's Hill for fear of throwing shells among their own infantry. It was now about 1 P. M., and as the Federal batteries became masked the smooth-bore or lighter Confederate pieces uncovered and went into action, adding their fire to that of the heavier guns, without fear of the hostile artillery. The Confederate canister swept great gaps from end to end through the Federal column, while the shells bursting among the charging lines hurled small groups of men into the air. As they swept on to within 100 paces of the hill, Walton's guns also poured canister among them, and the musketry fire both from the sunken road and the crest of Marye's Hill redoubled in intensity. Under this murderous maelstrom of iron and lead, the Federal Infantry was at last checked, and, falling like leaves, retired to the cover which marked French's farthest advance, but not until a number of the bravest men had actually approached to within 25 yards of the sunken road, only to be shot down or taken prisoners. Meagher's Brigade kept on to the town. Of the 5,006 men led forward by Hancock, 2,013 remained dead or wounded upon the field. In the sunken road and on the crest were less than 2,000 infantry. In the charge of 400 yards they could not have averaged more than two shots apiece. From this fact, we are able to appreciate what must have been the deadly effect of the Confederate guns. In several of the Federal accounts of the battle, it is stated that one-fifth of the casualties suffered by Burnside were from the fire of artillery. This estimate covers the losses on the whole field, so that in the charge of Hancock's Division on Marye's Hill, it is fair to assume that not less than half of the losses were due to the artillery, a remarkable record. This belief is borne out by the fact that the killed were found in great numbers behind cover impenetrable to the musket balls.

So soon as the Federal batteries were unmasked by the withdrawal of Hancock's troops, the short-range Confederate guns again sought cover from their fire. A lull now ensued, and only the field batteries near the town continued to fire upon Marye's Hill, Cabell and Hamilton concentrating their guns upon these.

Hancock, also, had been severely repulsed, but Howard was moving out of the town with his division to renew the assault. Meantime the four Confederate regiments in the sunken road were reënforced by four more while the infantry force on the forward crest was also increased by Ransom, and additional reserves brought up under cover of the ridge. Behind the stone wall the Confederates now stood in four ranks.

Howard's Division charged forward as gallantly as had Hancock's, and with the same result. Again the assaulting columns masked the supporting batteries, and again did the lighter pieces of the Confederates, more effective even than the rifled guns at short range, uncover, and pour canister and shell into the dense blue masses. Here and there the Federals sought the available shelter, but most of those who escaped unwounded retired upon the town. Fearing a counter attack, Gen. Couch ordered Hazard's regular battery into action near the edge of the town at a point about which the defeated infantry might rally.

It was now 3 P. M. and four of the five divisions under Sumner's command had been dashed to pieces against Marye's Hill, and two under Franklin against Prospect Hill. In neither quarter were the Confederates shaken, but Burnside ordered the attack to be renewed all along the line.

Meanwhile, Poague had alone been engaging Reynolds' batteries with his 20-pounder section, which Col. Crutchfield had ordered Col. Brown to send up to Walker. The exact range of the Confederate batteries having been obtained by the enemy, the lighter pieces were withdrawn again to cover. While bringing up the howitzer section of Dance's Battery, Lieut.-Col. Coleman of the Corps Reserve Battalion was severely wounded, and Lieut. J. B. McCorkle of Poague's Battery was killed. Severe losses were being sustained from the accurate fire of the Federal batteries. It should be mentioned here that Poague's Battery had, upon receiving orders late the night before to rejoin its corps, marched 16 miles in the night over the most difficult half-frozen roads, in four hours, a fact which seems all but incredible.

About the time French was assaulting Marye's Hill, on the Confederate left, Reynolds was reforming under the cover of his batteries to make another assault on Jackson's position. Meade's Pennsylvanians were rallying, Gibbon was constantly strengthening his line, and the flank was well protected by Doubleday, who was still, however, fully occupied by Stuart's dismounted men and Pelham's guns. When Meade and Gibbon were at last ready to renew their efforts, Hancock had just about begun his assault on Marye's Hill.

Reynolds had posted 21 guns on the right of Gibbon, and 30 on the left of Meade, both groups near the Richmond Road, those on the Stafford Heights forming a second tier. Preceded by clouds of skirmishers, and under cover of a tremendous artillery fire, Meade and Gibbon advanced in columns of brigades, the whole covering a front of about a thousand yards. As they rushed forward, Crutchfield's guns opened as before, but with less effect than formerly, by reason of the overwhelming and accurate fire of the batteries of the enemy concentrated on his positions, hitherto disclosed. Even Pelham's group of guns was receiving full attention from the enemy. Those portions of the Federal line opposite Lane and Archer, which came under the direct fire of Crutchfield's guns, were soon checked, however, but the center reached and entered the tongue of woods extending into the plain, thus at once threatening Archer's left and Lane's right flank. As the Federals swept onward through the wood they brushed aside the regiment which Archer had sent into the thicket, and, forcing back Lane's and Archer's exposed flanks, took a number of prisoners. So rapid was their advance that Gregg's line 500 yards in rear was reached almost before he was aware of the enemy's approach, and mistaking the charging columns for a Confederate command retreating, he was struck down in front of his brigade, while endeavoring to stay its fire. A desperate struggle now ensued between Gregg's men and the Federals, a part of the former having been thrown into confusion by the suddenness of the attack. But Jackson, having detected the victorious advance of the enemy, had sent for Early's and Taliaferro's divisions, which soon hastened up and, threatening to surround Sinclair's Brigade in the lead, drove it back in confusion through the gap into which it had penetrated, involving Magenton's supporting brigade in the disorderly withdrawal. Hoke's Brigade of Early's Division meantime drove off the Federals who had carried the trenches on Archer's left, and the whole of Meade's Division was again in retreat. Early pursued the routed enemy beyond the railroad, but as Birney's troops of Hooker's Corps advanced to Meade's assistance, he fell back and took position behind the embankment.

While Meade was forcing his way through the center, Gibbon was engaged in an assault upon A. P. Hill's left center, held by Lane. Bringing Hill's, Thompson's, and other batteries into action against Davidson's and Latimer's guns in front of the Bernard cabins, Gibbon's Division advanced in three lines, the first two being hurled back by Lane's musketry and the left group of guns. The third line under Root, however, was not to be checked, and sweeping over Lane's trenches drove his men back into the woods at the point of the bayonet. But, just as Early and Taliaferro arrived and drove back Sinclair's leading brigade of Meade's Division, thus uncovering Root's left flank, Thomas' Brigade of A. P. Hill's Division, which had been held in reserve behind Pender on the left of Hill's line, came up and struck Root's exposed right. After a stubborn struggle, Root's Brigade retired in confusion to the stage road, from which it had advanced.

On the right of Reynolds the batteries of Smith's Corps had kept up a heavy cannonade upon the guns of Latimer and Davidson, and Frobel's group with Hood north of Deep Run, but it was not until about 3 P. M., after Gibbon and Meade had both been repulsed, that a serious effort was made by Brooks' Division of Smith's Corps to seize the line of the railroad in its front. On the south side of the run was Pender's Brigade, of A. P. Hill's Division, with skirmishers behind the embankment, and on the north side was Law's Brigade of Hood's Division. Moving under cover of the Deep Run ravine, the Federals came upon the flank of Pender's advanced line and drove it from the railroad, but while waiting for reënforcements, two regiments of Law's Brigade and one of Pender's charged, driving them back with severe loss to the Richmond Road and reoccupying the line of embankment.

Such was the situation of the Confederate right when Sickles' Division of the 3d Corps came up to the support of Reynolds and made a counter-attack impracticable on the part of Jackson. Doubleday's Division, on Reynolds' left, had been completely neutralized by Stuart's constant threat, and the fire of Pelham's guns. Franklin's efforts had thus come to a standstill by 2:30 P. M. Indeed, he was not only defeated, but had probably been saved the loss of his field batteries by the timely arrival of Sickles.

When about 3 P. M. Burnside's order came to Franklin to renew his attack, the latter took upon himself the responsibility of remaining quiet, his failure to obey the orders he received leading to his subsequent removal from command. The sole activity on his part for the rest of the day was a heavy artillery fire from his batteries, causing considerable loss to Crutchfield's men.

About 3:30 P. M., it became necessary to relieve Pegram's and McIntosh's batteries, both having exhausted their ammunition and suffered severe losses. The fresh batteries of the corps reserve were then brought forward to take the place of the batteries withdrawn, and Hupp's Battery was sent beyond the railroad later in the day, to drive off the sharpshooters of the enemy, which had for some time annoyed the gunners. Col. Brown's six batteries lost during the remainder of the day no less than 10 killed and 26 wounded.

At 1:30 P. M., Hooker had been ordered to cross the river and attack Marye's Hill, but with a knowledge of what had befallen French, Hancock, and Howard, and that Franklin's efforts on the left had again been unsuccessful, he urged that the attempt to drive Lee from his strong position be abandoned, at least for the day. But Burnside was relentless.

The Confederates employed the lull during Hooker's preparations to reënforce the force in the sunken road by still another regiment, and to bring up some of the reserves to the infantry position along the crest. Meanwhile the caissons were rapidly being refilled from the reserve ammunition train, and the Artillery was generally taking a long breath except the batteries on Lee's Hill, which continued to fire on the Federal masses near the town and in the Hazel Run ravine.

With eleven regiments in the sunken road, and six on the forward crest, all fully resupplied with ammunition, Marye's Hill was now even more securely held than during the previous attacks upon it. The fresh assault was preceded by the heaviest artillery preparation the Federals had yet attempted. Among the field batteries Randall's and Hazard's were especially active and effective.

When the artillery fire was at its height, Hooker launched Humphreys' Division along the Telegraph Road, with Sykes' to the right *en échelon*. As these troops advanced, Griffin's Division moved forward

from near the railroad depot and joined Humphreys'
left.   Their advance to the line occupied by the men of
the commands which had preceded them was quite successful and rapid, for they were all but free from the
fire of artillery.   Just after the attack commenced Col.
Walton's Battalion had exhausted its ammunition and
the refilled caissons had as yet failed to return from the
ammunition train in rear, necessitating the substitution
in the pits of other pieces.   Col. Alexander had held
Woolfolk's and Jordan's batteries under cover of the
ridge during the day and now, quickly ordering forward the four pieces of the former and two guns of the
latter, he undertook to relieve Col. Walton's batteries
in the face of a heavy fire, losing many horses and men
in so doing.   Moody was also directed to transfer three of
his pieces from his own pits to the left to those formerly
occupied by Capt. Miller's guns.   In making the change
a piece was capsized which added to the delay in opening fire with the guns which did not begin their work
until the enemy was within 300 yards of the position.
When Alexander's nine guns opened upon the advancing infantry which had reached the cover behind
which the men of the preceding commands were lying,
Humphreys' leading brigade dropped to the ground
and commenced to fire wildly.   Walton's guns were
now seen galloping to the rear and the rumor sped down
the Federal line that the hill was being evacuated, which
enabled Humphreys to get his men to their feet.   Placing himself, mounted, with great gallantry at their
head, he induced them to make a final effort to cross
the 200 yards of intervening ground, being received by
a whirlwind of musketry fire from behind the stone
wall, and canister from Alexander's guns, which now
opened from above.   But when the brigade came within
80 yards of the Confederate Infantry, it broke and fled
to the rear.   Tyler's, or his second brigade was now
coming up, and Humphreys, after having the Federal
batteries directed to cease firing, again essayed to lead
his men to the Confederate position, with a view of

carrying it with the bayonet. After they had mingled for a time with those seeking cover in their path, as in the case of Allabach's Brigade, Humphreys was also able to lead Tyler's men forward, but all in vain. The shriveling fire of the Confederates simply swept them from the field. Over 1,000 men of the division commanded by the noble Humphreys lay killed and wounded upon the ground.

Added to the fire of the guns on Marye's Hill, was that of Parker's Battery, which Alexander had posted near the Stansbury house. The fire of this battery was so oblique that many of the Federal officers mistook it for the fire of their own guns from the rear.

Griffin's Division, exposed to the fire of Cabell's and Hamilton's guns, had been checked on the left of Humphreys, and Hooker, seeing their failure, had recalled Sykes. Although several fresh brigades pressed forward to Griffin's most advanced line before dark, when night fell the Federals had been hopelessly defeated, and the shattered troops under cover of Sykes' Division, which was sent forward about 11 p. m. to relieve them, withdrew to the town or were reformed along the canal bank and from thence retired from the field.

The Confederate fire ceased only when the flashes of the Federal guns no longer gave targets, but no one in Lee's army conceived that the battle was over, for only four of the nine Confederate divisions had been engaged. Nor had Burnside himself abandoned the idea of driving the Confederates from their positions, proposing during the night to form the Ninth Corps in column of regiments and lead it in person against Marye's Hill at dawn. During the night he issued the necessary orders for the renewal of the attack, but subsequent to the issuance of these orders, he was dissuaded by certain of his officers from making another effort. This was very fortunate for the Ninth Corps, for a copy of the order directing it to assault at dawn had come into the possession of the Confederates. With full knowledge of the plan of attack, and the point to be assaulted, Longstreet had strengthened his intrench-ments and the force holding them, and had caused most careful arrangements to be made during the night for reënforcing the front line, and supplying the men en-gaged with water and ammunition. Every gun which could be spared from other parts of the line was brought up by the Chief of Artillery, and placed in a covered position, from which it would bear directly upon the ground over which the dense Federal column was to at-tack, and a long line of reserve caissons was placed im-mediately behind the ridge from the filled chests of which a plentiful supply of ammunition could be quickly drawn for the already well provided batteries. Not a serviceable piece was left in reserve, except those the gun detachments of which were so depleted and ex-hausted as to render them unfit for further exertions, such being the case with Maurin's Battery, which was relieved by Moody's 24-pounder howitzer section, and a rifled piece of Jordan's Battery. The 12-pounder howitzer section of Moody's and the 6-pounder section of Woolfolk's batteries had also to be relieved.

Maj. Nelson's battalion of 6-pounder batteries was so disposed as to be able completely to sweep the ascent to Lee's Hill, and Walton's Battalion, much damaged, was held immediately in rear of Marye's Hill.

During the night, Capt. Parker discovered a position from which the canal bank in his front could be en-filaded, and the Federals thus prevented from forming under cover as before. Col. Alexander immediately ordered Moody to take his 12-pounder section which had been relieved, filling up his detachments from Woolfolk's Battery, and construct pits for his guns in this position.

Fearing lest Burnside might renew the attack under cover of darkness, Gen. Pendleton with the assistance of his staff prepared a number of incendiary shells, with which the buildings along the Telegraph Road in front of the Confederate position might be set on fire, thus illuminating the field, but as events turned out these shells were not used.

On the right, Jackson had brought up to his front line every battery in his corps capable of going into action. Capts. Carter and Latimer, Acting Chiefs of Artillery, of D. M. Hill's and Early's (Ewell's) divisions, respectively, had the day before fully engaged all their batteries towards the close of the day, and the corps reserve had also been entirely engaged in order to relieve Walker's batteries. The latter, meantime, had found time to rest and refit.

In the Confederate ranks the utmost confidence of administering a more crushing repulse than had been previously administered to the Federals was entertained, and the men, especially the gunners, the effect of whose fire was more noticeable than that of the infantry, awaited the enemy's attack with keen impatience. Never in the history of war, perhaps, was an army on the defense more willing to be attacked by overwhelming numbers. The Confederates were even anxious less Burnside might fail to hurl his masses upon them, the plan of the latter having been fully disclosed to the troops in order to expedite the necessary preparations which had to be made during the night. Not only were those upon whom the assault was expected to be made pleased to occupy the post of greatest danger, but the men in less threatened quarters were disappointed that the brunt of the fighting was not to fall upon them. In their zest for the fray, there was even something savage, though not inhuman. It was simply the desire of strong men to strike hard when the time came. So when the day at last broke, the Confederates eagerly looked and listened for signs of Burnside's advance. The long hours passed away in silence until about 10 o'clock, when the fog lifted and a vicious sharpshooting broke out from Sykes' regulars in front of Marye's Hill. A desultory cannonade from Stafford Heights also commenced.

Seeing Sykes' men lying down in the swale, and, in the language of Burnside, "holding the first ridge," Capt. Moody, from the advantageous position in which he had placed his 12-pounders, opened upon them from their right. The Federals were amazed, and, after a few shots from Moody's guns, those who were unable to find fresh shelter broke and fled to the town, pursued by the fire of the guns on Marye's Hill. This ended for the day the annoying sharpshooting from the "first ridge."

The day wore on without any serious effort being made by the Federals, whose batteries across the river all but ceased firing on Marye's Hill, by reason of a number of premature explosions of their shells having caused losses among their infantry in advance of the town. Relieved of the fire of these batteries as well as of that of the sharpshooters, the Confederate gunners were free to work in their pits and continued to fire throughout the day upon any masses which appeared in or about the town.

During the night of the 14th, the earthworks and lines were still further strengthened by the Confederates, abattis being prepared and arrangements of all kinds for defense being more fully completed. A large supply of ammunition arriving from Richmond, the ordnance trains moved up closer to the Confederate position, and even more batteries were now ready to resume activities. But again, on the 15th, the Federals remained inactive, while the Confederates worked openly at their defenses, and that night in the midst of a heavy storm, the noise of the wind preventing his movements from being heard by his enemy, Gen. Burnside withdrew his tremendous army from the plain, crossing the Rappahannock with all the troops and guns between 7 P. M. the 15th and 7 A. M. the 16th. The feat was a superb one, and, as Gen. Alexander states, its successful accomplishment reflected upon the vigilance of the Confederates. The real opportunity for the use of Pendleton's incendiary shells was lost.

Had Burnside's movement been detected, the river crossing lit up by the flames of nearby buildings would have presented a rare spectacle to the Confederates. A few shells from the longer range pieces, the Whitworth and Poague's 20-pounder Parrotts, for instance, would most certainly have thrown the Federal columns into confusion, or forced them to forego the crossing and remain in the plain. Had they persisted in the attempt to cross the river a second Borodino would have ensued, for sending only a part of his infantry forward to the town, with perhaps a dozen short-range batteries, Gen. Lee would have been able to throw Burnside's army into a veritable panic. Meanwhile, the bulk of his army with the longer range batteries could have held the position against a possible reverse, the guns neutralizing to some extent the batteries on Stafford Heights. But those batteries would in all probability have been unable to fire upon Lee's pursuing columns, all but mingled with the enemy, and it is quite improbable that in the circumstances Burnside's troops would have remained sufficiently in hand to deliver an effective counter-stroke. Night, the noise and confusion incident to the storm, the turbulence of the river, the uncertainty of the number of the enemy upon their heels, and the inevitable losses which even the few Confederates would have been able to inflict upon the struggling masses at the bridges and the crowded approaches thereto, are all elements which would have contributed to a direful disaster to the Federal Army. It is indeed a grave question whether, when once the withdrawal had begun, Burnside could have held a rear guard in position. But assuming that he could have held off the Confederates, he would have at least suffered tremendous losses at the bridges and the almost certain loss of his rear guard, or been forced to forego the withdrawal. There would have then remained for him the alternative of renewing the effort to cross the river a succeeding night, or the task of cutting his way out of the plain through Lee's position.

A subsequent attempt to recross the river would have
been anticipated by Lee, whose preparations to prevent the withdrawal would have been complete, and
there is every reason to believe that other assaults on
the Confederate position would have been more disastrous than those already made.   Indeed, Burnside's
Army, conscious of the *cul-de-sac* in which it had been
placed, would have been in much the same plight as that
of the French Army at Sedan.   Desperation, unattended
by discipline and confidence, would have taken the
place of the fine *morale* which inspired the Federals in
their first attacks, and while, no doubt, they would have
defended themselves with the stubbornness of the wild
animal driven to bay, the army would have been utterly
lacking in cohesion and that collective will-power which
makes successful effort possible.   Surely it cannot be
argued that in such circumstances Burnside could have
secured that coöperation which under the most favorable conditions he had failed to attain.

   The inertia of the Confederates is difficult to explain.
The escape, for escape it was in every sense of the
word, of Burnside was but the realization of the fear
which had led both Lee and Jackson originally to oppose the defensive position of Fredericksburg.   True,
Jackson had urged a counter-stroke in the form of a
night attack on the 13th, his proposition being over-
ruled as too hazardous.   Gen. Lee's views on this point
were no doubt well considered and correct, for the conditions on that night were by no means similar to those
obtaining two nights later.   The very essentials of the
Confederate ability to destroy Burnside's army lay in
the latter's attempt at recrossing the river, no thought
of which was entertained by the Federals when Jackson proposed to attack them.   But Gen. Lee had every
reason to believe that Burnside would make another
great effort to drive him from his position, the very
order for the attack being in his hands.   There was
every indication that the Federal effort was but post-

poned, and he believed that his task of destroying the enemy would be all the more simple after the latter had received another crushing repulse.

Yet, while Gen. Lee's tactical attitude may be reasonably explained, the question arises, why was he not informed of the move in the game which would, if known to him, have required aggressive action? The same answer has to be made to this question that has been made to many others—imperfect provision for securing information. In this instance no one in particular was at fault. The men were exhausted by cold, hunger, and long sustained effort. For hours they had remained under the greatest tension of expectancy, and at last when it became apparent to all that the enemy would not assault in the blinding storm, the nervous relaxation was overpowering. Not only did the outposts, videttes, and contact patrols naturally seek shelter from the elements, thereby blinding the army as a whole, but Burnside took every precaution to see that they should remain in their blind security and assurance that no offensive move would be made by him. Thus coupled with the negative efforts of Lee's outposts, were the positive efforts of the enemy to keep them in darkness.

To the cavalry especially no blame whatever should attach in connection with Burnside's withdrawal. The peculiar situation of the two armies was such as to preclude its presence except on the flanks, and in its proper sphere of action Stuart's brigades had more than done their duty. Particularly was this true as regards Lee's right flank, where Stuart and Pelham both rendered splendid service. Recognizing that a large cavalry force assigned to the duty of guarding a flank should not remain passive and merely wait until it suited the enemy's turning columns to move against it and drive it back, Stuart had adopted the adage that "prevention is better than cure" and had hung on the enemy's flank, thereby meeting him more than half way. He clearly saw that by pushing forward into contact with the enemy's flank, any enveloping movement on the latter's part would be abandoned, unless in force, or in any circumstances the enemy's infantry masses could be delayed sufficiently long to enable Gen. Lee to make the necessary dispositions to meet them. Stuart's tactics at Fredericksburg might well have contained a lesson for Kuropatkin's cavalry at Mukden, where great masses of troopers remained inert on a line with, or in rear of, the flank they were supposed to protect, waiting for the Japanese to arrive before even the mere intelligence of their coming was transmitted.*

Pelham has for all time illustrated the power of guns in the hands of a dashing and energetic horse artillery-man, associated with a bold cavalry leader. Almost un-aided and with a single piece he entirely neutralized Doubleday's whole infantry division throughout the critical hours of the battle after first breaking the shock of Meade's column already moving to the assault. Hanging upon the exposed flank of the enemy, appearing and reappearing when and where least expected, like a gnat in the eye of a great beast, he was never driven from the field, but, retiring to a more secure position from which at any time he was free to return to the immediate flank of his opponent, he brought more and heavier guns into action. Thus when his original liberty of action was denied him, he did not remain idle, but constantly maintained his threat as a cavalryman, while rendering yeoman service as a light artilleryman.† And so, it may be remarked, the study of Fredericksburg is fruitful of many positive lessons in the tactics of the mounted arm, both for its troopers and its gunners.

As to the tactical employment of the artillery in general, little need be said, for the narrative of events has already disclosed lessons which the most casual reader could not fail to detect. As an example of the manner in which an inferior artillery should be employed,

---

*Cavalry in the Russo-Japanese War, Count Gustav Wrangel.
†Horse artillery is cavalry in one sense of the word.

Fredericksburg has few superiors. The expectations which prompted the disposition of the Confederate guns were more than realized. Refusing to sacrifice his artillery in a duel against great odds, Lee simply held the bulk of it under cover until the superior guns of the enemy were masked, whereupon it went into action with the utmost liberty and effect. Generally speaking, only his heavier ordnance was pitted against the artillery of the enemy, and that was protected by intrenchments which Sharpsburg had taught to be necessary. Thus the numerical superiority of the enemy's guns was in a measure offset by art.

Fredericksburg was in a much higher degree than either Second Manassas or Sharpsburg an artillery affair. The Federal Army was overthrown by the guns of Lee's army. The fact that Burnside was vastly superior to Lee in point of artillery is the best evidence of the service the Confederate gunners rendered. One-half of Lee's infantry, or five out of nine infantry divisions were engaged, while the batteries which crowned the heights above them were in almost continuous action. When Pendleton, Alexander, Brown, Cabell, Walker, Pelham, Hamilton, Nelson, Jones, Carter, and Latimer contemplated the extent to which they had warded off the blow directed at the gallant infantry, they must have experienced a feeling of supreme satisfaction in the knowledge that they had done their duty. No higher ambition can come to the gunner than to merit the full confidence of his sister arm. It should be his one desire, as it is his duty, to relieve the infantry of so much of the shock of battle, as he can divert to himself, even if he succumb under the blow. By such unselfish conduct alone can he win the esteem and the confidence of the whole army and instill in the breasts of his comrades in arms that affectionate regard for the artillery which Lee's gunners had won for their arm before the close of 1862. No spirit of caste jealousy now existed between the gunners and the infantry of the Army of Northern Virginia. No feeling on the part of either that they had left aught undone which they well might have done made them resentful of the other's prowess and attainments. Only a feeling of mutual respect existed between them, and willingly the infantry pressed to the roadside to help forward their batteries. For each there was an allotted task and confidence in the other's ability to perform the work assigned it was mutual. The *esprit de corps* of many of the batteries was superb. They were but clans with tartans distinct, their chieftains known to all, and as some gallant gunner at the head of his battery galloped to the front, the infantrymen by the wayside, or in the trenches, vied with each other in springing to their feet to wave a generous salute of recognition. In the advancing rush and rumble of the guns, there was an inspiring note for the foot soldier, and in the knowledge that no sacrifice in their support would be too great for the infantry, there was encouragement to the gunners to make that sacrifice unnecessary. The *entente cordiale* existing between the sister arms was the natural consequence of services rendered. It could never have arisen from mere theoretical potency. What soldier of Jackson's army could suppress his admiration for Pelham and his men, who under the very eyes of the whole corps had with dauntless courage assailed, unaided, a Federal division? What soldier of Longstreet's Corps whose heart failed to respond to the emotions which such deeds as those of Landry and of Parker are wont to generate?

Verily the plain of Fredericksburg was an amphitheatre upon which the Confederate Artillery won the proud acclaims of a martial race, the leaders of which, whether friend or foe, have echoed their applause through the pages of history. Gens. Lee, Longstreet, Jackson, A. P. Hill, McLaws, in fact all the Confederate commanders, in their reports of the battle of Fredericksburg, speak again and again of the "rapid," "destructive," "well-directed," "demoralizing," "murderous," "accurate," "efficacious" fire and "extraordinary" effect of their guns at all points, and of the "unflinching" courage, "unshaken steadiness," "animation and spirit" with which they were "admirably served," and repeatedly mention with high commendation individual commanders and batteries.

The tribute paid the Confederate Artillery by the Federal commanders is even more emphatic as to the important and preëminent part it played in the repulse of Burnside's Army. Their reports—from those of Gens. Burnside, Franklin, Sumner, Hooker, French, Hancock, Howard, Couch, Meade, Reynolds, Birney, and Doubleday, to those of officers commanding brigades, regiments, companies, and especially batteries,— characterize the fire of the opposing artillery as murderous, deadly, terrific, destructive, continuous, severe, galling, vigorous, furious, heavy, enfilading, cross, and concentrated. In some instances special reference is made to the effect of individual batteries or guns, which unless exceptionally well served would have made no particular individual impression.

But of all the encomiums bestowed by the commanders of high or low degree, the most prized by the soldiery of the Army was that epithet, dearer than life itself to a soldier, which Lee himself applied to a gunner when he wrote in his report of the heroic exploit of "the gallant Pelham." Was it mere opportunity, was it fate, or was it genius which enabled this youth to act such an heroic part upon the stage of immortality? Glorious indeed was that feat which wrested from a great commander such mention of a subaltern's name in a brief account of so great a battle.*

Of the battery expenditures in the battle of Fredericksburg there is, as in the case of Sharpsburg, no record.

The losses of the Artillery as itemized, and only in part separated from those of the infantry, aggregate about 50 killed and 250 wounded. The entire loss probably exceeded 400, or about 10 per cent of the personnel engaged. This figure is relatively enormous, as

---

*Gen. Lee's report of the whole battle of Fredericksburg covers less than two pages in the Official Records.

compared with the losses of the Confederate Army, which were 608 killed and 4,116 wounded. Col. Walker's Battalion alone lost 11 killed and 88 wounded, including a disproportionate number of officers, while Brown's Battalion lost 10 killed and 26 wounded. The batteries of Taliaferro's Division, under Brockenbrough, lost 2 killed and 28 wounded, while Pelham's casualties were 3 killed and 22 wounded, and Latimer's 4 killed and 21 wounded.

On the left the artillery was less exposed to the musketry fire of the infantry and the losses of Alexander's, Cabell's, and Hamilton's batteries, principally by reason of the pits which protected the detachments, were less than those sustained by Jackson's gunners, although they were more constantly engaged.

The heaviest individual losses were those of Poague's Battery, in which the casualties were 6 killed and 10 wounded of a personnel of 60 men; and Carpenter's, in which the losses were 1 killed and 25 wounded out of 65 men.

While the Confederates lost no guns and captured none, the loss of the batteries in horses was especially heavy. Long exposure to the elements in the severe weather which had prevailed added a heavy toll to the number killed in action.

CHAPTER XXII

THE battle of Fredericksburg was over, but Burnside's army rested securely under the protection of its
batteries beyond the river, the Confederates still holding with their pickets the line formerly occupied by
them. The troops, meanwhile, were withdrawn and immediately commenced the construction of cabins, huts,
and every form of shelter both for the men and horses,
but all remained near at hand in rear of their positions
in line. Walton's three batteries and a number of others
were at first left in position on outpost duty, but most
of these were withdrawn to the rear on the 18th. The
signal for the various batteries, brigades, and divisions
to hasten back to the lines was to be given by Anderson's batteries on the left, if danger threatened in that
quarter, and by one of Hood's or Pickett's batteries if
on the right, in either case repeated by Cabell. On the
morning of the 19th undue activity on the part of the
enemy, his bridges still being intact, caused the alarm
to be given, and immediately the troops moved forward
to repel an attack, but the alarm proved to be a false
one and the Confederates returned to their unfinished
camps.

As soon as actual hostilities ceased, many citizens of
Fredericksburg returned to their homes and all orders
to destroy the enemy's bridges were countermanded, for
fear of drawing the fire of the hostile batteries upon the
town. The suffering of the people had been great
enough, many returning to find their dwellings in ashes
and their effects destroyed or removed. So great were
the hardships imposed upon the residents of Fredericksburg that Gen. Longstreet invited his troops in a general order of the 18th to contribute to a fund for their

relief. The response from the soldiery was immediate. The officers and men of the Washington Artillery Battalion had previously collected a purse of $1,391 for the relief of the Charlestonians, whose more-pressing wants, however, having been adequately supplied, they now unanimously voted to divert the fund to the aid of the destitute people of Fredericksburg. Thus we see that these generous Louisianians not only contributed their blood and valour to the defense of Virginia, but gave of their wealth for the alleviation of her people's suffering as well.

On the 24th, by reason of the scarcity of forage, it became necessary to disperse the batteries of the Army. Lane's Battery of the General Reserve, Rhett's of Alexander's Corps Reserve, Lewis' of Anderson's, Read's of McLaws', Stribling's of Pickett's, Reilly's of Hood's, and French's of Ransom's divisions, were retained near the positions they had occupied along the front of Longstreet's Corps. In Jackson's Corps, Poague's Battery of the Corps Reserve, Hardaway's of D. H. Hill's, Carpenter's of Taliaferro's, and Brown's of Early's divisions, were also retained. The remaining batteries of the 1st Corps were sent under the command of Col. Walton, Chief of Artillery, to the vicinity of Childsburg, about midway between the Mattapony and the North Anna rivers, Col. Crutchfield conducting those batteries of the 2d Corps which had been relieved to a point about five miles from Bowling Green. The General Reserve Artillery and Alexander's Battalion were ordered to be placed in cantonments by the Chief of Artillery along the North Anna, as he might see fit, and Gen. Pendleton was charged with the supervision and administration of the entire arm, and with the rigid enforcement of the regulations for the care of the animals, lest many of the batteries should have to be disbanded in the spring for lack of horses.* The sections to which the Artillery was thus assigned for winter quarters possessed particularly good

*Rebellion Records, Series I, Vol. XXI, p. 1109.

grass lands and it was hoped that a sufficient supply of forage would be found to carry the horses through the winter.

Longstreet with the divisions of Hood and Pickett and their respective divisional artillery battalions under Majs. Henry and Dearing, after the inactivity of Burnside was assured, was ordered February 18 to the district south of Petersburg, where the ravages of war had not yet been seriously felt. Jackson's Corps, with McLaws' and Anderson's divisions of the 1st Corps, remained along the Rappahannock guarding the line from United States Ford above Fredericksburg to Port Royal, 25 miles below.

Late in January, the Federals, by extending along the north of the river, seemed to threaten renewed activities, and Jackson's men were kept busy preparing to meet the enemy wherever he might attempt a crossing. Meanwhile, Gen. Lee was urging forward the work on the Napoleons and the Whitworth gun carriages, which he had called upon the Ordnance Bureau to make for use along his front.*

The strength of the Field Artillery of the Army on the last day of 1862 shows an increase in spite of the inroads of the Fredericksburg campaign. The General Reserve consisted of 5 batteries, 30 pieces, and 437 horses, with a personnel of 30 officers and 549 men present for duty, and an aggregate present and absent of 778. In the 1st Corps were 19 batteries, 83 pieces, and 405 horses, 70 officers and 1,576 men present for duty, with an aggregate present and absent of 2,311, and in the 2d Corps there were 31 batteries, with 125 guns, and about 700 horses, 99 officers and 2,365 men present for duty, and a paper strength of 3,966.

The Field Artillery then consisted of some 65 batteries, 240 guns, 1,550 horses, 199 officers, and 4,490 men present for duty. The average battery in the field, therefore, was composed about as follows: 3 officers, 81 men, 4 guns, and 30 horses, with a paper strength of about 130 officers and men.†

---

*Rebellion Records, Series I. Vol. XXI, p. 1109.
†Rebellion Records, Series I, Vol. XXI, p. 1082.

Considering the vast improvement which had already been made in its material and the measures in process of completion for its better armament, the increase both in the experience and the numbers of its personnel, the condition of the Artillery was relatively good in all respects, except as to the horses and the horse equipment, the deficiency in these two items being a serious menace to the general efficiency of the arm at all times.

The returns for January 1863 show no depletion in artillery personnel, so there could have been few deserters.

Early in January, Gen. Pendleton assigned Capt. G. W. Nelson, and 1st Lieut. E. P. Dandridge, both unattached, to batteries, the first to duty as Inspector of the Artillery of the First Corps and the General Reserve, and the latter to the same duty in the Second Corps. They were ordered to enter immediately upon the work of inspection, and were particularly directed to report upon the following points:

"1st. Condition of horses, guns, harness, ammunition, and wagons.

"2d. The strength of each battery in officers, enlisted men, horses, and equipments.

"3d. The supply of forage, its source, and prospect in future.

"4th. The position of camp, its advantages or evils.

"5th. The attention to, or violation of, rights of citizens, etc.

"6th. They will also report absences and their occasion; they will attend to all matters of importance to the service in each case, as, for instance, what hospital arrangements are made; they will regularly record the result of their observations and inquiries, and make punctual and exact reports of the same. When horses are presented for condemnation, they will carefully examine them and pass upon their condition, reporting at the same time the apparent causes thereof. It is very desirable that these inspections should be made promptly, and to this end great diligence will be needed."*

The foregoing plan of inspection gives one an excellent idea of the measures adopted to bring up the batteries to a more efficient footing. The inspections were industriously carried out as ordered, and Pendle-

*Rebellion Records, Series I, Vol. XXV, Part II, p. 613.

ton exerted himself to the utmost to see that every effort was made to correct or to counteract defects as they developed. In addition to this work he had, after collaborating with Cols. Crutchfield and Alexander, whose judgments he most respected of all his officers, prepared a comprehensive plan for the reorganization of the Artillery, and on February 11, submitted it in writing to the Commander-in-Chief.* In this plan it was contemplated that the Artillery should be completely organized into battalions, a thing which had only partially been effected. We have frequently spoken of a group of batteries assigned to a division as a divisional battalion when in fact it was not. The plan also included the promotion of many officers in order to furnish the requisite field officers for the proposed battalions. Promotion on a large scale at once involved a serious question. The more southern states were acutely jealous of Virginia in the matter of commissions, and, cognizant of this spirit on their part, Gen. Lee had ever sought to minimize the evil effects resulting therefrom by limiting Virginia to a number of field officers in proportion to the number of troops she furnished. Even then, the Old Dominion possessed a preponderance of the higher officers. But no man could say that Virginians unduly profited from favoritism. In fact, good men were frequently kept from well-deserved promotion in deference to this rule of policy.

Pendleton's recommendations comprise a brief history of the artillery arm up to the time they were made. Between the lines one familiar with the politics of the Army may read much. From a perusal of these lines of the Chief of Artillery, replete with suggestions, one gains a most comprehensive idea of conditions as they were, and, in order that nothing may be lost from the meaning of Pendleton's words, they are here given as he wrote them:

"The objections to the brigade batteries and division groups now existing are obvious. Burdened as are brigade and division commanders, they can scarcely extend to batteries thus assigned

---

*Rebellion Records, Series I, Vol. XXV, Part II, p. 614.

that minute supervision which they require, and the supply officers, whose chief care lies with considerable bodies of infantry, cannot devote to one or more batteries the time and attention they imperatively need. This is injuriously experienced in time of pressure. The existing arrangement moreover affords insufficient scope for field officers of artillery. Batteries, besides, permanently attached in this way, can scarcely be assigned elsewhere, whatever the emergency, without producing some difficulty, almost as if a vested right were violated. But, most injuriously of all, this system hinders unity and concentration in battle.

"Toward remedying these evils, it is respectfully proposed that in each corps the artillery be arranged into battalions, to consist for the most part of four batteries each, a particular battalion ordinarily to attend to a certain division, and to report to, and receive orders from, its commander, though liable to be divided, detached, etc., as to the commanding general or corps commanders may seem best; past associations to be so consulted in the constitution of these batteries as that each shall, as far as practicable, contain batteries that have served together, and with the division which the battalion is still ordinarily to attend. These battalions ought to have, it is believed, two field officers each, a surgeon, an ordnance officer, and a bonded officer for supplies, if not both quartermaster and commissary. Such battalions, with the officers proposed to command them, are presented to view in the accompanying schedule.

"It will be noticed that two batteries are proposed to be transferred from the Second Corps to the First, in order to equalize them as nearly as may be. One of these, Thompson's, the Louisiana Guard Artillery, heretofore attached to Gen. Early's Division, is in the schedule put into the Battalion P, to operate with Gen. Pickett's Division. The other, Latham's, a North Carolina Battery, heretofore attached to Gen. A. P. Hill's Division, is placed in the Battalion H to operate with Gen. Hood's Division.

"In the Second Corps, Dement's Battery, now attached to Gen. Early's Division, is proposed to be placed in the Battalion T to operate with Gen. Trimble's Division, because Lieut.-Col. R. S. Andrews, proposed to command that battalion, expressly requests it, that being his original battery. In this corps, also, five batteries are proposed to constitute the battalion to operate with Gen. A. P. Hill's Division, because that is a large division, and because it has hitherto been attended by a strong artillery force.

"Four batteries remaining in the Second Corps, after thus constituting battalions to attend the several divisions, are combined in a new reserve battalion, corresponding in that corps with the Washington Artillery, First Corps.

"It will be seen that this plan involves the least possible disturbance to existing relations, while it equalizes force and provides a

more effective organization.   Existing reserve battalions are
proposed to remain as they are.

"Batteries, it is recommended, should be rendered homogeneous
in armament as soon as practicable by interchange of guns with
other batteries.   All the batteries of each corps to be supervised
by and report to the Chief of Artillery for the corps, as representing the Lieutenant-General commanding, and the whole in both
corps to be superintended by and report to the general Chief of
Artillery, as representing for this arm the General commanding.

"For convenience, a certain alphabetical designation is suggested for the battalions, the initials of the division commanders
at the present time being adopted, rather than the usual letters in
order, because the latter might seem like a numerical designation
to assign some precedence of one battalion over another.

"Attention is asked to a few words respecting the officers
proposed.

"*First Corps: Battalion A:* Maj. J. J. Garnett, who is well
known to Gen. Longstreet, and highly appreciated by him as an
efficient officer.   His merit and services no doubt entitle him to
the command and grade of Lieutenant-Colonel proposed for him.*

"Maj. Charles Richardson, with Gen. Anderson, may well be
retained as the Second Field Officer of that battalion.   These
officers are both from Virginia.

"*Battalion M:* Col. Cabell, of Virginia, and Maj. Hamilton, of
Georgia, who have long directed the artillery attached to Gen.
McLaws' Division, should probably have command of this battalion.

"*Battalion P:* Maj. Dearing, well known to and approved by
Gens. Longstreet and Pickett, and recently promoted to command
the artillery attached to Pickett's Division, can well command this
battalion.   He is from Virginia.

"Capt. Read, of Georgia, now commanding a battery in Gen.
McLaws' Division, has been heretofore recommended several times,
I believe, for promotion as a gallant, intelligent, and meritorious
officer, and may be usefully and justly made Major, to coöperate
with Maj. Dearing in his battalion.

"*Battalion H:* Maj. Kemper, so justly appreciated for his
gallantry and for long and efficient service, may well be given
command of this battalion, with the rank of Lieutenant-Colonel.
He is from Virginia.

"Maj. Thomas Jefferson Page, Jr., heretofore associated for a
season with Maj. Kemper, and at another time with Gen. Hood,
might serve well as the Second Field Officer in this battalion.

"*Washington Artillery Battalion:* Col. Walton, of course, remains as long as he wishes in command of this.   He is known to
be from Louisiana.

---

*Maj. Garnett had previously served on Longstreet's staff, having rendered
valuable services in the Artillery on the Peninsula.

"*Alexander's Battalion:* Lieut.-Col. Alexander, of Georgia, is really entitled to the full rank of Colonel at the head of this battalion. We have no more accomplished officer. His commission should date from his original assignment to the command.

"Maj. J. R. C. Lewis, for some time attached to the battalion as its Second Field Officer, should probably retain the position. He is from Virginia.

"It is respectfully suggested that the officer to act as Chief of Artillery to the Corps might be most efficient in that capacity if relieved from the burden of a special command.

"*Second Corps: Battalion R:* Maj. T. H. Carter, some time since promoted to command the artillery of Gen. D. H. Hill's Division, was even then recommended for the rank of Lieutenant-Colonel, as fully earned by his distinguished services, and eminent merit, and may well be made Lieutenant-Colonel and given command of this battalion. He is from Virginia.

"Capt. C. M. Braxton, now commanding a battery in Gen. A. P. Hill's Division, has been recommended for promotion. He also has fully earned it by efficient service and would, no doubt, be highly approved by Lieut.-Col. Walker and by Gen. Hill as the Second Field Officer in this battalion. He is from Virginia.

"*Battalion L:* Lieut.-Col. R. L. Walker, of Virginia, so justly distinguished for long and gallant service, has been recommended for the full rank of Colonel. He might justly receive it and have command of this battalion.

"Capt. W. J. Pegram, now commanding a battery in Gen. A. P. Hill's Division, has been recommended for promotion. He has also fully earned it by efficient service, and would no doubt be highly approved by Lieut.-Col. Walker and by Gen. Hill as the Second Field Officer in this battalion. He is from Virginia.

"*Battalion T:* Maj. R. S. Andrews, so severely wounded at Cedar Mountain, but now nearly recovered and on duty in Richmond, desires and richly deserves the rank of Lieutenant-Colonel and the command of this battalion. We have no more brilliant and thoroughly meritorious artillery officer. His recommendations are ample, nor can a doubt remain as to the propriety of his having this promotion and command. He is from Maryland.

"Capt. J. W. Latimer, now commanding a battery in Gen. Early's Division, is highly recommended by Col. Crutchfield, and earnestly desired by Maj. Andrews to be promoted and associated with him as the Second Field Officer in this battalion. He is from Virginia.

"*Battalion E:* Maj. H. P. Jones, now in command of the artillery of Gen. Trimble's Division, under special request from Gen. W. B. Taliaferro, when in command of that division, has been recommended for promotion, and might worthily be made

COLONEL THOMAS HILL CARTER
ACTING CHIEF OF ARTILLERY, SECOND CORPS

Lieutenant-Colonel and have command of this battalion. In addition to much gallant service he is a very judicious and faithful officer. He is from Virginia.

"Capt. J. Gibbs Barnwell, of South Carolina, is well entitled to promotion, and would make an excellent field officer in this battalion. He has mainly served as an ordnance officer with the General Reserve Artillery, but in repeated instances has taken command in action and admirably performed his part. He is a capital artillerist, and in general merit has perhaps no superior.

"*Battalion N, Reserve:* Capt. Hardaway, now commanding a battery in the division lately under Gen. D. H. Hill, at present under Gen. Rodes, is a fine officer entitled to promotion, and some time since recommended for it; indeed, his initials were, to the end he might be commissioned as Major, asked of the undersigned by the War Department. His merit and his services entitled him to this rank, and it is believed he would well command this battalion. He is from Alabama.

"Capt. Brockenbrough, of Virginia, now suffering from a painful wound received at Fredericksburg, has been recommended for promotion. He has well served since the beginning of the war, and would do well as the Second Field Officer in this battalion.

"*Brown's Battalion:* Col. J. T. Brown, of Virginia, for months past in command of this battalion, should of course retain it.

"Capt. Poague, of Virginia, now commanding a battery in this battalion, is a superior officer, whose services have been scarcely surpassed. He has been recommended for promotion, and should justly receive it. He might well be made a Major in this battalion.

"*General Reserve: Cutts' Battalion:* Lieut.-Col. Cutts, an efficient officer, should retain command.

"Capt. Lane, commanding a battery in this battalion, a trained officer, gallant, and efficient, has been recommended for, and deserves promotion. During a long furlough of Lieut.-Col. Cutts, he has commanded the battalion, and would make for it a good Major. The companies are large, the batteries have each six guns, and a second field officer would secure its greater efficiency. Capt. Lane is from Oregon, though accredited to Georgia.

"*Nelson's Battalion:* Maj. William Nelson, long in command of this battalion, is as gallant and efficient an officer as we have in his grade. He has served from the beginning of the war as Captain and Major, has exhibited courage of the highest order and fidelity undeviating, and well deserves the rank of Lieutenant-Colonel. He is from Virginia.

"Maj. A. L. Rogers, also of Virginia, might usefully serve as the Second Field Officer in this battalion. Its batteries are all of six guns.

"The recommendations for promotion are believed to be in strict accordance with the merits of the officers and the wishes of Gens. Longstreet and Jackson, and of other commanders best qualified to judge.

"The proportion between the number of field officers of artillery thus proposed belonging to Virginia and those from other States is very nearly coincident with that between the number of batteries from Virginia and those from other States. Of the whole number of batteries, 35 are from Virginia and 24 from other States. This would give of the 28 field officers proposed, about 17 from Virginia and 11 from other States. Of those actually recommended 18 are from Virginia and 10 from other States.

"Should this organization be mainly approved and ordered, ordnance officers, surgeons, and supply officers can be applied for by the several battalion commanders.

"Toward accomplishing an efficient adjustment of the whole in time for the probable opening of the spring campaign, it is important that an adequate supply of suitable guns be furnished as soon as possible by the Ordnance Department. Nearly all the bronze short-range guns of the Second Corps were several weeks ago sent to Richmond to be recast into Napoleons. None have been sent from the First Corps, nor from the General Reserve, because Col. Gorgas advised against it, on the ground that the Department had as much metal as it could cast for a number of weeks.

"Four battery battalions might be armed with good rifles and Napoleons in nearly equal proportions, two batteries to have rifles altogether, and two to have Napoleons altogether. Larger battalions to have perhaps a corresponding proportion, or more Napoleons. Batteries in reserve to have heaviest metal. It is hoped that, much as a number of battery horses will probably be reduced in strength by the occasional scarcity of food incident to the difficulty of transporting it, in spite of all efforts, a sufficiency will be at hand for the batteries proposed when the campaign opens. Some 400, sent for to Georgia in the fall by the undersigned, have, under advisement with the Quartermaster's Department in Richmond, been stopped on the border of North Carolina, for the sake of being easily foraged. Other droves the Quartermaster's Department will, it is hoped, have collected, so that such animals as are unserviceable with the batteries may be replaced by others comparatively fresh and strong."

The proposals of Pendleton contemplated that in the First Corps there should be 4 divisional battalions and 2 corps reserve battalions, with a total of 26 batteries and 112 guns; and in the Second Corps 27 batteries with

116 guns, organized into 6 battalions as in the First Corps. The General Reserve was to consist of 2 battalions, of 3 batteries each, with a total of 36 pieces. Thus in the entire Army there were to be 14 artillery battalions, each with 2 field officers and a staff, and a total of 264 guns, exclusive of those of the Horse Artillery.

Four days after the receipt of Gen. Pendleton's recommendations, the Commander-in-Chief promulgated the proposed organization of the Artillery, withholding, however, the appointment of the additional field officers pending an investigation of their individual merits. On March 2, Gen. Lee forwarded his recommendations to the President with such revisions in Pendleton's as seemed proper to him for one reason or another, the appointments being soon made, and finally announced in *Special Orders No. 106, A. N. V., April 16, 1863.** The Field Artillery organization was now as follows:

1st CORPS

Col. John B. Walton, Chief of Artillery

CABELL'S BATTALION

Col. Henry Coalter Cabell
Maj. S. P. Hamilton

1. Troup (Ga.) Battery,	Capt. Henry H. Carlton.
2. Pulaski (Ga.) Battery,	Capt. John C. Fraser.
3. 1st Co. Richmond Howitzers,	Capt. E. S. McCarthy.
4. "A" Battery, 1st N. C. Reg't,	Capt. B. C. Manly.

GARNETT'S BATTALION

Lieut.-Col. John J. Garnett
Maj. Charles Richardson

1. Norfolk Light Artillery Blues,	Capt. Chas. R. Grandy.
2. Pittsylvania Battery,	Capt. John W. Lewis.
3. Donaldsonville (La.) Battery,	Capt. Victor Maurin.
4. Norfolk (Huger's) Battery,	Capt. Jos. D. Moore.

Rebellion Records, Series I, Vol. XXV, Part II, pp. 651, 728.

DEARING'S BATTALION

Maj. James Dearing
Maj. J. P. W. Read

1. Fauquier Battery,	Capt. R. M. Stribling.
2. Richmond Hampden Battery,	Capt. Wm. H. Caskie.
8. Richmond Fayette Battery,	Capt. Miles C. Macon.
4. Lynchburg Battery,	Capt. Joseph G. Blount.

HENRY'S BATTALION

Maj. M. W. Henry

1. Charleston German Battery,	Capt. W. K. Bachman.
2. Palmetto (S. C.) Battery,	Capt. Hugh R. Garden.
8. Rowan (N. C.) Battery,	Capt. James Reilly.
4. Branch (N. C.) Battery,	Capt. Alexander C. Latham.

CORPS RESERVE

ALEXANDER'S BATTALION

Col. E. Porter Alexander
Maj. Frank Huger

1. Bath Battery,	Capt. J. L. Eubank.
2. Bedford Battery,	Capt. Tyler C. Jordan.
8. Madison (La.) Battery,	Capt. Geo. V. Moody.
4. Richmond Battery,	Capt. Wm. W. Parker.
5. Brooks (S. C.) Battery,	Capt. A. B. Rhett.
6. Ashland Battery,	Capt. Pichegru Woolfolk, Jr.

WASHINGTON ARTILLERY BATTALION

Col. John B. Walton

1. 1st Co. Washington Artillery,	Capt. C. W. Squires.
2. 2d Co. Washington Artillery,	Capt. John B. Richardson.
8. 3d Co. Washington Artillery,	Capt. M. B. Miller.
4. 4th Co. Washington Artillery,	Capt. Benj. F. Eshleman.

2D CORPS

Col. Stapleton Crutchfield, Chief of Artillery

WALKER'S BATTALION

Col. Reuben Lindsay Walker
Maj. William J. Pegram

1. Pee Dee (S. C.) Battery,	Capt. E. B. Brunson.
2. Richmond Battery,	Capt. Wm. G. Crenshaw.
8. Richmond Letcher Battery,	Capt. Greenlee Davidson.
4. Richmond Purcell Battery,	Capt. Jos. McGraw.
5. Fredericksburg Battery,	Capt. E. A. Marye.

CARTER'S BATTALION

Lieut.-Col. Thomas H. Carter
Maj. Carter M. Braxton

1. Jeff Davis Alabama Battery,   Capt. Wm. J. Reese.
2. King William Battery,   Capt. W. P. Carter.
3. Richmond Orange Battery,   Capt. C. W. Fry.
4. Morris Louisa Battery,   Capt. R. C. M. Page.

ANDREWS' BATTALION*

Lieut.-Col. R. Snowden Andrews
Maj. Joseph W. Latimer

1. 4th Md. or Chesapeake Battery, Capt. Wm. D. Brown.
2. Alleghany Battery,   Capt. Jos. Carpenter.
3. 1st Maryland Battery,   Capt. Wm. F. Dement.
4. Lee Battery,   Capt. Chas. J. Raine.

JONES' BATTALION

Lieut.-Col. Hilary P. Jones
Maj. J. B. Brockenbrough

1. Charlottesville Battery,   Capt. James McD. Carrington.
2. Staunton Battery,   Lieut. Alexander H. Fultz.
3. Richmond Courtney Battery,   Capt. W. A. Tanner.
4. Louisiana Guard Battery,   Capt. C. Thompson.

CORPS RESERVE

BROWN'S BATTALION

Col. John Thompson Brown
Maj. R. A. Hardaway

1. Warrenton Battery,   Capt. James V. Brooke.
2. Powhatan Battery,   Capt. Willis J. Dance.
3. 1st Rockbridge Battery,   Capt. Archibald Graham.
4. Salem Battery,   Capt. A. Hupp.
5. 3d Co. Richmond Howitzers,   Capt. Benj. H. Smith, Jr.
6. 2d Co. Richmond Howitzers,   Capt. David Watson.

McINTOSH'S BATTALION

Maj. D. G. McIntosh
Maj. Wm. T. Poague

1. Alabama Hardaway Battery,   Capt. William P. Hurt.
2. Richmond Battery,   Capt. Marmaduke Johnson.
3. 2d Rockbridge Battery,   Capt. John A. M. Lusk.
4. Danville Battery,   Capt. Geo. W. Wooding.

*For final assignment of Thompson's, Brown's, and Caskie's batteries, see *Rebellion Records*, Series I, Vol. XXV, Part II, p. 667, Special Order No. ——, March 14, 1863.

GENERAL RESERVE

Brig.-Gen. William Nelson Pendleton

CUTTS' BATTALION

Lieut.-Col. Allen S. Cutts
Maj. John Lane

1. Battery "A", Sumter (Ga.) Batt.,   Capt. H. M. Ross.
2. Battery "B", Sumter (Ga.) Batt.,   Capt. Geo. M. Patterson.
3. Battery "C", Sumter (Ga.) Batt.,   Capt. John T. Wingfield.

NELSON'S BATTALION

Lieut.-Col. William Nelson
Maj. Thomas Jefferson Page, Jr.

1. Amherst Battery,   Capt. Thomas J. Kirkpatrick.
2. Fluvanna Battery,   Capt. John L. Massie.
3. Georgia Battery,   Capt. John Milledge, Jr.

HORSE ARTILLERY

Maj. R. F. Beckham

1. Chew's Battery,   Capt. R. Preston Chew.
2. Stuart Horse Artillery,   Capt. James Breathed.
3. Lynchburg Beauregards,   Capt. Marcellus N. Moorman.
4. 2d Stuart Horse Artillery,   Capt. Wm. N. McGregor.
5. Washington (S. C.) Battery, Capt. James F. Hart.

Thus we see that the only changes in Pendleton's plan were the substitution of Maj. M. W. Henry as a battalion commander for Maj. Del. Kemper, and Maj. D. G. McIntosh for Maj. R. A. Hardaway, the latter, however, being given his majority, while neither Capt. Squires nor Capt. Barnwell was promoted. Longstreet desired to wait until Col. Walton's return in the case of the former, Walton being on recruiting duty in Louisiana. Majs. J. R. C. Lewis and A. L. Rogers were also omitted in the new organization. The former transferred to another arm of the service, and was succeeded by Capt. Frank Huger, the only West Pointer still commanding a battery.*

*See letter of Pendleton to Lee, *Rebellion Records,* Series I, Vol. XXV, Part II, pp. 628-9.

The law approved January 22, 1862, authorized field officers for the Artillery in the proportion of a colonel for every 40, a lieutenant-colonel for every 24, and a major for every 16 guns. Based upon 264 guns, the Army was entitled to 6 colonels, 11 lieutenant-colonels, and 16 majors. The organization as completed included 6 colonels, 7 lieutenant-colonels, and 16 majors.* But three vacancies existed, therefore, among the field officers.

The departure from Pendleton's recommendations for promotion in the Second Corps were due almost entirely to Col. Crutchfield, who warmly advocated the promotion of either Brockenbrough or Chew in preference to Maj. Jones and Capt. Barnwell, and in his opposition to the advancement of the latter officers he was supported by Jackson.†

Col. Crutchfield particularly urged the promotion of McIntosh, which he finally secured, yet Jones was also promoted. The placing of Hardaway in command of a battalion was also opposed by Crutchfield. "He is an excellent artillerist, a good shot, and very fond of the scientific parts of the service," said Crutchfield, "but not good at managing men, hard on his own horses, and not at all apt to require the captains of batteries under him to take good care of their horses. He is rather indifferent to what he regards as the drudgery of the service, and while the qualifications he does possess will render him a very valuable field officer of artillery, it will not be in the sphere of the constant commandant of a battalion."

The foregoing remarks are quoted because they give us some idea of the qualities which were considered requisite on the part of a battalion commander. More than mere brilliancy seems to have been required.

The correspondence between Lee and Jackson respecting the appointment of artillery officers in the Second Corps is quite interesting, the latter's attitude

---

*Including Lieut.-Col. L. M. Coleman, of Brown's Battalion, invalided from wounds received at Fredericksburg.
†*Rebellion Records*, Series I, Vol. XXV, Part II, p. 633-4.

being characteristic. He insisted upon the privilege of exercising control over promotions in his corps. "I have had much trouble resulting from incompetent officers having been assigned to duty with me, regardless of my wishes," he wrote. "Those who assigned them have never taken the responsibility of incurring the odium which results from such incompetency."* This was strong language to address to the Commander-in-Chief.

When Gen. Lee forwarded his recommendations for promotion in the Artillery to the President, he took occason to state that "No class of officers in the Army has learned faster or served better than the Artillery."†

Before the end of February, Longstreet, having been informed by Col. Crutchfield that Jackson had asked for Col. Alexander to be made brigadier-general of infantry, vice Lawton, wrote Gen. Lee inquiring if Maj. Pelham could be spared by Stuart to fill Alexander's place, suggesting Pelham's promotion, and Maj. Terrell's appointment to succeed him in command of the Horse Artillery. But nothing came of the matter, probably by reason of Alexander's unwillingness to relinquish his commission as colonel in the Artillery for one as a brigadier-general of infantry. His present duties were far more important and attractive to one of his tastes than those incident to the office of a brigadier. At any rate he was not transferred, though his promotion was requested by Gen. Lee.‡

On February 20, Lieut. Dandridge returned his report covering the inspection of 29 batteries of the Second Corps.§ The items of the report comprise an accurate and complete record of the condition of Jackson's artillery, which may be regarded as typical of the arm. The harness and ammunition was generally reported as good and most of the horses, of which there was an average number of about 55 to a battery, were

---

* *Rebellion Records,* Series I, Vol. XXV, Part II, pp. 644-5-6.
† Ibid., p. 651.
‡ *Rebellion Records,* Series I, Vol. XXV, Part II, p. 645.
§ Ibid., pp. 634, 638.

found in a serviceable condition, very few instances of neglect having been detected. Most of the batteries possessed several two- or four-horse wagons for purposes of foraging, having to haul their hay and grain varying distances, some as far as 60 miles over execrable roads, until provision was made to transport forage by rail to the artillery camps. Until these arrangements were completed, corn was principally secured in Essex County, and from Hanover Courthouse. Some forage was found about Guiney Depot, Hamilton's Crossing, Milford, and in King William County.

Most of the batteries mustered a personnel of about 100 officers and men, and some as high as 140, but few less than 90. The number of absentees exclusive of the sick was not excessive, though there were exceptions. Carter's Battery reported 2 officers and 133 men present for duty, 1 officer and 6 men detached, 4 absent with leave and 71 deserters. The last figure must have been for the whole period of the war. Sickness was prevalent, many of the batteries having as many as 20 men on the sick list, and few less than 8. Latham's Battery with 4 officers and 114 men present, 1 man on furlough, 1 absent without leave, and 9 on detached duty, reported 39 sick, while Pegram's Battery with 3 officers and 108 men present, 1 officer on leave, 1 man on detached duty, and 3 absent without leave, reported 55 men absent sick. But it must be remembered that frequently men not sufficiently well clad, or who did not possess shoes good enough to permit of their exposure to the cold and mud of winter, were carried on the rolls as sick. At any rate, the poor clothing with which the men were provided would account for many minor cases of sickness during this exceptionally severe winter.

The condition of the men with respect to clothing was perhaps no better or no worse than in the Army in general. Nothing gives a better understanding of the wants in this respect than the following anecdote concerning the Chief of Artillery himself. Late in Decem-

ber, Gen. Pendleton was found one afternoon by Maj.
Page of his staff busily engaged with needle and thread.

"What are you doing, General?" he asked.

"Mending my trousers. The only thing I could find
for a patch was this old piece of collar," replied the
Chief.

"Well, it's a great waste of time, for nobody will
ever be able to tell one end of your shirt from the other,"
rejoined the Major.

Knowing that the Chief of Artillery was forced to
rob his shirt for the benefit of his breeches, we are led
to wonder how the private gunner managed to hide his
nakedness!

Fortunately for the poor soldiers, timber was plentiful with which to erect crude but comfortable cabins.
For an insight into the life they led during the cold
winter of 1862-63, surrounded on all sides by poverty
and distress, the reader would do well to peruse those
vivid pages which so well and so touchly record the
minutiæ of a private soldier's life in the Army of Northern Virginia.* The story is a pathetic one, told in a
vein of ineffable sweetness in spite of the ghastly features which the recollections must have conjured up before the writer. It is a classic of its kind, and serves to
show that the lowering clouds of war could not keep at
least a few beams of sunlit happiness from sifting
through the chinks in the huts and hearts of the Confederate gunners during that long and trying winter.

January, February, and March, 1863, were months
of ceaseless activity on the part of the artillery officers,
of whom great diligence was required to provide the
necessary forage which had to be located, collected and
brought in from the back country. Then, too, the work
of overhauling harness and equipments, refitting the material, and culling out and turning in the inferior
ordnance to be replaced by the new Napoleons, kept
them busy. Some were dispatched to other parts of the

---

*Soldier Life, A. N. V., written by Carlton McCarthy, a private soldier in the
2nd Co. Richmond Howitzers.

South to look for horses, others to collect stores and supplies of all kinds. Col. Cutts even visited Georgia and Florida where he reported a large supply of provisions and thousands of beef cattle to be available for the Army.* Cutts had been absent on furlough since the return of the Army from Maryland.

Maj. John Page, Chief Quartermaster, Artillery Corps, was forced before the 1st of February to scour the country between Richmond and Gordonsville along the Virginia Central Railroad, and the rich James River Valley, for the necessary hay and grain for the batteries, the supply in Caroline County having all but been exhausted.†

Constant efforts were now being made not only to expedite the delivery of the new guns being manufactured by the Bureau of Ordnance, but to complete the quota of horses for every battery in the Army. Late in March statements of the various battalion commanders showed that in addition to those already furnished, at least 1,200 horses were needed for the battalions, exclusive of 170 for the General Reserve.‡ The Chief of Artillery, in his report to the Inspector of Transportation, stated three causes for the unusual deficiency in spite of the extraordinary efforts which had been made to maintain the draught animals in a state of efficiency. First, there were the losses in action, incident to the battles of the late fall and early winter; second, the breaking down and sickness of many animals due to the labor of hauling forage, the insufficiency of feed, and the rigours of the winter season; and third, the additional demand by reason of the substitution of heavier ordnance for the discarded 6-pounders, the former requiring 6-horse teams.

By April 1 the weather had so moderated that the deficiency of forage was partly counteracted by turning the horses into the meadows where the droves might browse and rest, the shoes of the horses being removed.

---

*A sufficient supply for two years, Ibid., p. 738.
†*Rebellion Records,* Series I, Vol. XXV, Part II, p. 599.
‡Ibid., p. 695.

The condition of the horses of the Army, and the deficiency in their number, was a source of grave concern to Gen. Lee. On April 16, in a letter to the President, in which he expressed the opinion that the aggressive should be resumed by May 1, he declared that his only anxiety arose from the immobility of the Army, owing to the condition of the horses and the scarcity of forage and provisions.* And again, on April 25, he wrote Gen. Pendleton that the destruction of horses in the Army had been so great he feared it would be impossible to supply all wants.

In an effort to economize horses the Chief of Artillery had ordered the field transportation in each battalion for staff purposes to be reduced to one 4-horse and one 2-horse wagon. The former was to suffice for the mess outfit, desks, papers, and tents of the field and staff, while the other was set apart for the surgeon and his medical supplies. The batteries were limited to one wagon per section for men and foraging purposes. The allowance for the batteries was considered inadequate by Col. Crutchfield, who asserted that three wagons to a battery were absolutely necessary, that being a reduction of one-fourth the number previously allowed. It was necessary, he claimed, to have an ordnance wagon in which spare harness, stores, and mess equipment could be transported, in addition to two forage wagons, one carrying the horse feed, while the other remained free to forage. The escort wagon in use in the Artillery had a capacity of 6 barrels of corn, that was 168 rations of 10 pounds each, or only two days' rations of corn for the battery complete. With but one forage wagon, the battery could not secure its provender until after it had reached camp and unloaded the wagon, the team having been on the march all day, whereas with an extra wagon, forage could be collected on the march, the teams saved extra work, and the battery horses regularly fed. Col. Crutchfield's views were adopted and the field transportation allowance of the Artillery fixed at three per

*Ibid., p. 725.

battery. Thus for a battalion of 4 batteries, the train consisted of fourteen 4-horse wagons. The Artillery train of the entire army, exclusive of ammunition columns, consisted of not less than 250 wagons and 1,000 horses, a saving of at least half of that number having been effected by Pendleton's rigid measures. Orders were also promulgated providing that no part of a battery or train should remain on a road when disabled, the officer in charge being required promptly to remove the carriages from the roadway. Batteries and trains were also prohibited from stopping in the line of march to water, or from attempting to regain their place in column when once having lost it for any reason.* The packs of dismounted gunners were to be carried by the men, and the baggage of field officers was limited to 65, and that of battery officers to 50 pounds. But one wall tent was allowed battalion headquarters, and one tent fly to the officers of each battery.†

The officers and men of the batteries with Jackson, were the most actively engaged of all during the winter. Of the work in which they were ceaselessly engaged, Maj. A. S. Pendleton of Jackson's staff, son of the Chief of Artillery, wrote on April 26:

"The greatest destruction and change in the appearance of the country is from the long lines of trenches and the redoubts which crown every hillside from ten miles above Fredericksburg to twenty miles below. The world has never seen such a fortified position. The famous lines of Torres Vedras could not compare with them. As I go to Moss Neck (Jackson's headquarters) I follow the lines, and 'have a ride in the trenches.' These are 5 feet wide and 2½ deep, having the earth thrown forward towards the enemy, making a bank still higher. They follow the contour of the ground and hug the bases of the hills as they wind to and from the river, thus giving natural flanking arrangements; and from the tops of the hills frown the redoubts for sunken batteries and barbette batteries, *ad libitum,* far exceeding the number of our guns; while occasionally, where the trenches take straight across the flats, a redoubt stands out defiantly in the open plain to receive our howitzers. . . . "

*G. O. No. 26, Second Corps, April 13, 1863, Ibid., p. 719.
†G. O. No. 58, A. N. V., April 20, 1863, Ibid., p. 739.

Before spring arrived much had been done under Pendleton's administration to place the batteries on a more effective footing. The losses among the officers had been especially large, and the comparatively few unsuited to command who remained were ruthlessly culled out, making way for the more efficient. In this respect the Field Artillery was especially favored. The peculiar character of the service of the guns is such that no officer may hide his inefficiency beneath the cloak of collectivism. At every turn even the junior officer of a battery is called upon to exercise positive command and to lead, not follow. Thus in the Field Artillery the laggard, the incompetent, is soon discovered.

One great incident of the winter should not be ignored inasmuch as Gen. Pendleton, Chief of Artillery, was not only constantly engaged in it, but actually led the movement. Religious interest and services had been kept up among the artillery commands from the beginning of the war under Gen. Pendleton's direction and guidance. Under the influence of Lee, Jackson, and Pendleton, the spirit of religion spread broadcast through the Army during the period of winter quarters from the battle of Fredericksburg to the spring campaign of 1863. Log chapels everywhere sprang up along Jackson's lines, and in them the men of all arms gathered together during the long winter evenings to hear the word of God. To systematize the religious work providing every portion of the field army with devout, faithful chaplains, was a task to which Jackson and Pendleton both addressed themselves with fervor, But the number of chaplains proving inadequate to meet all demands, the men themselves not infrequently preached to their fellows. The spirit of revival swept on and on through the ranks until few, however callous, held aloof from the meetings where so much of peaceful promise was to be found, and over all there seemed to spread a spirit of sanctity which did much to lighten the burdens of the soldiery, and inspire them to a faithful discharge of their duties. Christ walked abroad in the camps, and whispered many a word of consolation, of cheer, of forgiveness for their sins, to those lonely desolate men, who, in spite of cold, of hunger, of doubt, of loss of loved ones, and separation from everything dear to their lives, clung to their posts through that awful winter. "Courage, despair not," the sweet and hopeful voice whispered in their ears, and each dawn found the Confederate sentinel watching upon the post of consecrated duty.

He who fails to accord great weight to the religious influence projected into the Confederate cantonments along the Rappahannock while Jackson confronted the Federal host, fails utterly to understand why, when the men of the Northern Army, bountifully supplied with all that a wealthy nation could furnish, were deserting at a rate of 200 a day, the half-starved, half-naked, unpaid Confederates stuck to their tattered colors.* He fails to understand that it was that divine faith in themselves and in their cause, instilled by their leaders into their hearts along with a trust in God, and the promise of that "peace which passeth all understanding" which kept the soldiers of the Confederacy in the ranks, and made it possible for the frosted colors to be once more unfurled to lead them on to fresh victories. To such factors in war, the ordinary strategist, tactician, military historian, accords little consideration. He is too prone to deal merely with words of command and numbers. In disregarding the tears of repentance which wet the cheek of the Army of Northern Virginia in the winter of 1863, he but neglects the very cause of the steeling of its heart to all the sacrifices, all the sufferings, all the privations it was called upon to endure. "In war men are nothing; it is the man who is everything. The general is the head, the whole of an army. It was not the Roman Army that conquered Gaul, but Cæsar; it was not the Carthaginian Army that made Rome tremble in

---

*Hooker stated before the Committee on the Conduct of the War that when he relieved Burnside desertions were at the rate of 200 a day in the Army of the Potomac, and that the returns showed 2,922 commissioned officers and 81,964 enlisted men absent, the majority from causes unknown.

her gates, but Hannibal; it was not the French Army
that carried the war to the Weser and the Inn, but Tu-
renne; and it was not the Prussian Army which, for
seven years defended Prussia against the three greatest
powers of Europe, but Frederick the Great." So spoke
Napoleon, and many military writers tell us that an
army is but the reflex of its commander. The leader of
the Army of Northern Virginia in the winter of 1863
was Christ. Its moral stamina was, in the highest sense
of the word, God-given.*

As spring began to approach there were signs of renewed activity in both armies. As early as the 9th of
February, Fitz Lee's Cavalry Brigade had broken
camp in Caroline County, and leaving its winter quarters
moved to Culpeper Courthouse, where, on the 12th, it
relieved Hampton's Brigade from the duty of picket-
ing the upper Rappahannock. Crossing the river on
the 24th, at Kelly's Ford, Fitz Lee reconnoitered towards Falmouth, encountering the enemy's cavalry at
Hartwood church and actually driving it back into the
camps of the 5th Federal Corps. On the 26th, he returned to his new camp after taking 150 prisoners and
providing his men with a number of horses, much equipment, forage, etc. This exploit provoked the Federals
and Brig.-Gen. Averell, with his cavalry brigade, was
ordered on the 18th of March to cross the river at one of
the upper fords and to "attack and rout or destroy"
Fitz Lee's Brigade reported to be in the vicinity of Culpeper Courthouse. After detaching a force of 900 men
to look after the Confederate patrols north of the river,
Averell with 2,100 men and a horse battery reached
Kelly's Ford on the morning of the 17th. Lee's pickets
guarding the ford were driven off, and then Averell set
about crossing his command. The river was high and
swift, and the caissons and guns were entirely sub-

---

*The reader is invited to consult *Soldier Life, A. N. V.*, McCarthy; *Four
Years Under Marse Robert*, Stiles; *A Cannoneer Under Stonewall Jackson*, Moore;
Three Years in the Confederate Horse Artillery, Neese; *A Soldier's Recollections*,
McKim; and in marked contrast with these is *Recollections of a Private Soldier
of the Army of the Potomac*, Wilkeson.

merged, the artillery ammunition being carried across
in the nose-bags of the troopers. By 10 A. M. he was
ready to advance.

In the meantime, Fitz Lee at his camp near Culpeper
Courthouse had learned that the ford had been forced,
and immediately set his command in motion, meeting
Averell's column within half a mile of the ford. The
Federal line extended from the river near Wheatley's
Ford to the Brooks house, with sharpshooters posted
behind a stone fence running along the front and the
mounted reserves drawn up in the fields and woods in
rear on both sides of the road branching off from
Wheatley's to Kelly's Ford. Along his front, Averell
had deployed two regiments armed with carbines, and
supported by two sections of his horse battery. Fitz
Lee's leading regiment charged down the stone fence in
columns of fours, the men emptying their pistols as they
galloped along and driving off the defenders.

Gen. Stuart and Maj. Pelham had been attending the
session of a court-martial in Culpeper Courthouse as
witnesses and, expecting to return to Fredericksburg
on the 17th, borrowed horses and joined Lee's Brigade
when they learned of the impending cavalry fight. Being present by mere accident, Stuart declined to exercise command, but Pelham could not remain inactive on
the battlefield, and, seeing Lee's 3d Virginia Regiment
preparing for the charge described, rushed to its head
to assist Col. Owen in leading it. With the shout of
victory upon his lips, and while waving his hat aloft, he
was struck in the head by a piece of shell just as the
column passed by the Wheatley house. A single Confederate trooper reined up to carry the all but lifeless
body from the field across his pommel. Thus was the
body of the "gallant and incomparable" Pelham saved
from the enemy.

The leading Confederate regiments were met near the
Wheatley house by a part of the Federal reserves and
checked after a sanguinary mounted combat, the result
of which in view of Averell's superior force was to com-

pel Lee, for reasons of prudence, to retire to a strong position where he could employ his artillery with effect.
Withdrawing to the road from Brandy Station to
Kelly's Ford, he now formed a line across it near Carter's Run with an open field about 600 yards wide in his
front. On a hill north of the road, Capt. James
Breathed's Battery of four guns, formerly commanded
by Pelham, took up its position. Soon the enemy made
his appearance and opened fire with three pieces of
Lieut. Brown's section at long range. After awaiting
Averell's attack for some time, Fitz Lee, growing im-
patient, ordered a charge, and, routing the enemy, all
but captured his guns, the troopers driving the gunners
from their pieces in spite of their double-shotted canister
and spherical case.

Maj. McClellan states that Pelham was dead when
his body was removed by the trooper. John Esten
Cooke states that he lingered until after midnight, at
which time Stuart, grieved beyond all measure, telegraphed the family of Pelham in Alabama:

"The noble, the chivalric, the gallant Pelham is no more. He
was killed in action yesterday. His remains will be sent to you
to-day. How much he was beloved, appreciated and admired, let
the tears of agony we have shed, and the gloom of mourning
throughout my command, bear witness. His loss is irreparable."*

The young artilleryman's body was sent to Richmond
and there laid in state in the Capitol of Virginia at the
feet of Houdon's statue of the Arch Rebel, Washington.† Cooke tells us that "some tender hand deposited
an evergreen wreath, entwined with white flowers, upon
the case that contained all that was mortal of the fallen
hero." Soon his family conveyed the youthful soldier's
remains to his home in the far South, Virginia, the field
of his undying fame, surrendering them to Alabama, the
land of his birth.

"The Major-General commanding," wrote Stuart in
a general order, "approaches with reluctance the painful

*Pelham, "the Gallant," in *Wearing of the Gray*, by John Esten Cooke, p. 127;
The Campaigns of Stuart's Cavalry, McClellan, p. 211.
†See Col. William F. Gordon's famous poem, *Secessia*.

duty of announcing to the division its irreparable loss in the death of Maj. John Pelham, commanding the Horse Artillery. He fell mortally wounded in the battle of Kellysville, March 17, with the battle cry on his lips, and the light of victory beaming from his eye.

"To you, his comrades, it is needless to dwell upon what you have so often witnessed—his prowess in action, already proverbial. You well know how, though young in years, a mere stripling in appearance, remarkable for his genuine modesty of deportment, he yet disclosed on the battlefield the conduct of a veteran, and displayed in his handsome person the most imperturbable coolness in danger.

"His eye had glanced over every battlefield of this army, from the First Manassas to the moment of his death, and he was, with a single exception, a brilliant actor in all.

"The memory of the gallant Pelham, his many virtues, his noble nature and purity of character, is enshrined as a sacred legacy in the hearts of all who knew him.

"His record has been bright and spotless, his career brilliant and successful.

"He fell—the noblest of sacrifices—on the altar of his country, to whose glorious service he had dedicated his life from the beginning of the war."

The written records of the American conflict fail to disclose another such tribute from so great a commander as Stuart. The evergreen wreath placed upon his bier has long since shriveled and died—these words can never fade from the pages of history. Pelham is now a tradition of the Southland, nay more, of the American people. His fame is the heritage of a united country and an inspiration for all time to the soldier of whatever race. Of his death, the poetic Cooke wrote:

"Thus passed away a noble, lofty soul; thus ended a career brief it is true, but among the most arduous, glorious, and splendid of war. Young, but immortal—a boy in years, but heir to undying fame—he was called away from the scene of his triumphs and glory to a brighter world, where neither wars nor rumours of wars can come, and wounds and pain and suffering are unknown; where

> "Malice domestic, foreign levy, nothing
> Can touch him further!"

It would be vain indeed for the author to attempt to trace the record of Pelham's 24 years of life when already it has been done in the beautiful words of one of his comrades. In order that not even language may detract from his due, the following extract from John Esten Cooke's sketch is inserted:

"A son of the great State of Alabama, and descended from an old and honorable family there, he had the courage of his race and clime. He chose arms as his profession, and entered West Point, where he graduated just as the war commenced; lost no time in offering his services to the South, and received the appointment of First Lieutenant in the Confederate States Army. Proceeding to Harper's Ferry, when Gen. Johnston was in command there, he was assigned to duty as drill officer of Artillery, and in the battle of Manassas commanded a battery, which he fought with that daring courage which afterwards rendered him so famous. He speedily attracted the attention of the higher generals of the Army, and Gen. J. E. B. Stuart entrusted him with the organization of the battalion of Horse Artillery, which he subsequently commanded in nearly every battle of the war upon Virginia's soil. Here I knew him first.

"From the moment when he took command of that famous corps, a new system of artillery fighting seemed to be inaugurated. The rapidity, the rush, the impetus of the cavalry were grafted upon its more deliberate brother. Not once, but repeatedly, has the Horse Artillery of Pelham given chase at full speed to a flying enemy; and far in advance of all infantry support, unlimbered and hurled its thunders on the foe. It was ever at the point where the line was weakest; and however headlong the charge of the cavalry, the whirling guns were beside it, all ready for their part. 'Trot, march!' had yielded to 'gallop!' with the battalion; it was rushed into position, and put into action with a rush; and in and out among the guns where the bolts fell thickest was the brave young artillerist, cool and self-possessed, but, as one of his officers said the other day, 'as gay as a schoolboy at a frolic.' He loved his profession for its own sake; and often spoke to the officers above alluded to of the 'jolly good fights' he would have in the present campaign; but I anticipate my subject.

"Once associated with the command of Stuart, he secured the warm regard and unlimited confidence of that general, who employed his services upon every occasion. Thenceforth their fortunes seemed united, like their hearts, and the young man became known as one of the most desperate fighters of the whole army. He was rightly regarded by Jackson, and others, as possessed of a very extraordinary genius for artillery; and when any movement of unusual importance was designed, Pelham was assigned to the Artillery to be employed.

"His career was a brief one, but 'how glorious'! Let us glance at it.

"When the Southern forces fell back from Manassas in 1861, his batteries had their part in covering the movement and guarding the forks of the Rappahannock. During the campaign of the Peninsula, his Blakely was as a sentinel on post near the enemy; and at the battle of Williamsburg his courage and skill transformed raw militia into veterans. In the Seven Days' battles around Richmond, he won fadeless laurels. With one Napoleon, he engaged three heavy batteries, and fought them with a pertinacity which made the calm face of Jackson glow; and the pressure of that heroic hand, warm and eloquent of unspoken admiration. Soon afterwards, at the White House, he engaged a gunboat, and driving it away, after a brief but hot encounter, proved how fanciful were the terrors of these 'monsters'.*

"His greatest achievements were to come, however, and he hastened to record them on the enduring tablets of history. From the moment when his artillery advanced from the Rappahannock, to the time when it returned thither, to the day of Fredericksburg, the path of the young leader was deluged with the blood of battle. At Manassas he rushed his guns into the very columns of the enemy almost; fighting their sharpshooters with canister, amid a hurricane of balls. At Sharpsburg he had command of nearly all the artillery on our left, and directed it with the hand of a master. When the Army crossed back into Virginia, he was posted at Shepherdstown and guarded the ford with an obstinate valour, which was spoken in the regular and increasing reverberation of his deep-mouthed Napoleons, as they roared on, hour after hour, driving back the enemy.

"Of the day which succeeded that exciting period, many persons will long hold the memory. It was in an honest old country-house, whither the tide of war bore him for a time, that the noble nature of the young soldier shone forth in all its charms. There, in the old hall on the banks of the Opequon, surrounded by warm hearts who reminded him perhaps of his own beloved ones in Alabama; there in the tranquil days of autumn, in that beautiful country, he seemed to pass some of his happiest hours. All were charmed with his kind temper and his sunny disposition; with his refine-

*This was later done by Confederate batteries along the Rappahannock, and by Forrest's batteries in Tennessee.

ment, his courtesy, his high breeding, and simplicity. Modest to a fault, almost blushing like a girl at times, and wholly unassuming in his entire deportment, he became a favorite with all around him, and secured that regard of good men and women which is the proof of high traits and fine instincts in its possessor. In the beautiful autumn forests, by the stream with its great sycamores, and under the tall oaks of the lawn, he thus wandered for a time,— an exile from his own land of Alabama, but loved, admired, and cherished by warm hearts in this. When he left the haunts of 'the Bower' I think he regretted it, but work called him.

"The fiat had gone forth from Washington that another 'On to Richmond' should be attempted; and where the vultures of war hovered, there was the post of duty for the Horse Artillery. The Cavalry crossed the Blue Ridge, and met the advancing column at Aldie, and Pelham was again in his element. Thenceforward, until the banks of the Rappahannock were reached by the Cavalry, the batteries of the Horse Artillery disputed every step of ground. The direction of the Artillery was left, with unhesitating confidence, by Stuart to the young officer; and those who witnessed, during that arduous movement, the masterly handling of his guns, can tell how his confidence was justified. It was the eye of the great soldier, the hand of the born artillerist, which was evident in his work, during those days of struggle. He fell back neither too soon nor too late, and only limbered up his guns to unlimber again in the first position which he reached. Thus fighting every inch of the way from Aldie, round by Paris, and Markham's, he reached the Rappahannock and posted his artillery at the fords, where he stood and bade the enemy defiance. That page in the history of the war is scarcely known; but those who were present know the obstinacy of the contest, and the nerve and skill which were displayed by the young officer.

"That may be unknown, but the work done by Pelham on the great day of Fredericksburg is a part of history now. All know how stubbornly he stood on that day—what laurels encircled his young brow when night at last came. This was the climax of his fame—the event with which his name will be inseparably connected. With one Napoleon gun, he opened the battle on the right, and instantly drew upon himself the fire, at close range, of three or four batteries in front, and a heavy enfilading fire from thirty-pound Parrotts across the river. But this moved him little. That Napoleon gun was the same which he had used at the battle of Cold Harbor—it was taken from the enemy at Seven Pines,—and, in the hands of the young officer, it had won a fame which must not be tarnished by defeat! Its grim voice must roar, however great the odds; its reverberating defiance must roll over the plain, until the bronze war-dog was silenced. So it roared on steadily with Pelham beside it, blowing up the caissons, and continuing to tear up the enemy's ranks. Gen. Lee was watching it from the hill above, and exclaimed, with eyes filled with admiration, 'It is glorious to see such courage in one so young!' It was glorious indeed to see that one gun, placed in an important position, hold its ground with a firmness so unflinching. Nor, until his last round of ammunition was shot away, did Pelham retire; and then only after a peremptory order sent to him. He afterwards took command of the entire artillery on the right, and fought it until night with a skill and courage which were admirable. He advanced his guns steadily, and at nightfall was thundering on the flank of the retreating enemy, who no longer replied. No answering roar came back from those batteries he had fought with his Napoleon so long; he had triumphed. That triumph was complete, and placed forever upon record when the great commander-in-chief, whom he loved and admired so ardently, gave him the name in his report, of 'the gallant Pelham.'

"Supreme tribute to his courage—immortalizing him in history! To be the sole name mentioned beneath the rank of Major-General in all that host of heroes—and mentioned as 'the gallant Pelham'!"

"Thenceforward there was little for him to desire. He had never cared for rank, only longed for glory, and now his name was deathless. It is true that he sometimes said, with modest and noble pride, that he thought it somewhat hard to be considered too young for promotion, when they gave him great commands at Sharpsburg and Fredericksburg,—and called on him when the hardest work was to be done. But, he never desired a mere title he had not won, and did his soldier's duty thoroughly, trusting to time. So noble and important, however, had been his recent services that promotion was a matter of course. The President said, 'I do not need to see any papers about Maj. Pelham,' and had appointed him a Lieutenant-Colonel; and it only awaited the formal confirmation of the Senate, when he fell on the Rappahannock. His fall was a public calamity to the nation, but none to him. It was fit that such a spirit should lay down its great work before the hard life of the world had dimmed the polish of the good knight's spotless shield. He wanted no promotion at the hands of men. He had won, if not worn, the highest honors of the great soldier; and having finished his task, the gentle spirit took its flight, promoted by the tender hand of death to other honors in a brighter world."*

Such was the character, such were the military services of Maj. John Pelham, who in two years had thrice won the personal thanks of Jackson, and individual mention by the Commander-in-Chief, these two

---

*Pelham, "the Gallant," in *Wearing of the Gray*, Cooke.
Every child should read Cooke's Surry of Eagle's Nest, Mohun, Fairfax, etc.

being among the best and the bravest men, and certainly the greatest soldiers, in the Army of Northern Virginia. Well might Jackson have said to Stuart on the bloody field of Fredericksburg, "Have you another Pelham, General? If so, I wish you would give him to me!"

Pelham has been likened to both Murat and Marceau. Had he merely embodied the characteristics of such soldiers so extensive a mention of his name had not been made. He was far more than a skilled and dashing soldier. He was not only the pattern of his arm, injecting into the service of the guns an *élan* and spirit of self-sacrifice remarked by all, but he is to-day the Galahad, *sans peur et sans reproche,* of all artillerymen. Modern formulæ have by no means rendered impossible the deeds of another Pelham, nor is the effectiveness of field artillery yet determined by the rank of the gunner who lays the piece.

Pelham's brilliant career was but a phase of the Confederate artillery service. In the final analysis of his deeds, it was not so much what he actually did as what his name stood for among his comrades and his associates. The influence of such a spirit as his is far reaching. It is easy to place limits upon his actual accomplishments in a tactical sense—it is impossible to define the extent of his moral ascendency.

Yet, it must not be thought that the Field Artillery of Lee's army boasted no other figures of exceptional individualism. Indeed, there were many in whom may be noted those strong traits of character which typified the arm. Crutchfield, Walker, Alexander, Carter, Pegram, Chew, Caskie, McIntosh, Haskell, Breathed, McGraw, McCabe, Cutshaw, Thomson, Latimer, Carpenter, Poague, and many others were the very embodiment of all that was skillful, courageous, gallant, each possessing a peculiar individualism developed to the highest degree. From the sentiments and character of these men were developed the *élan* and the *morale* which gave to their arm that distinctive mien so characteristic of the

Field Artillery. In their make-up there was decidedly something of the Cavalier; their features were unhidden by the helmet of uniformity. No cuirass concealed their familiar figures; their hearts were encased only by that heroic resolve which, though powerless to shield from the dangers of mortal conflict, kept their souls unsullied, enabling them to breach the works of fame and transcend the ordinary limits of military glory.